ON FOR SIC

A PASSIO   CILIANS

A PASSION FOR SICILIANS

The World Around Danilo Dolci

JERRE MANGIONE

With a New Conclusion by the Author

Foreword by Alfred McClung Lee

Transaction Books
New Brunswick (U.S.A.) and Oxford (U.K.)

New material this Transaction edition copyright© 1985 by Jerre Mangione. Original edition copyright© 1968 by Jerre Mangione. Foreword copyright© 1972 by Alfred McClung Lee.

Library of Congress Catalog Number: 85-8500

ISBN: 0-88738-606-7 (paper)

Printed in the United States of America

Library of Congress Cataloging in Publication Data

Mangione, Jerre Gerlando, 1909-
     A passion for Sicilians.

     Reprint. Originally published: The world around
Danilo Dolci. New York : Harper & Row, 1972, c1968.
     1. Sicily—Social conditions.   2.   Dolci, Danilo.
I.   Title.
HN488.S5M34   1985   306'.0945'8   85-8500
ISBN 0-88738-606-7 (pbk.)

This book was first published in 1968 by William Morrow & Co., Inc. A Harper Colophon edition was published in 1972 under the title *The World Around Danilo Dolci*.

To Franco Alasia and to the memory of
    Michele Mandiello for reasons
    described in this book;

And to my brother Frank and my sisters
    Susan and Rita for reasons that need
    no description.

Acknowledgments

I am deeply indebted to Danilo Dolci for the time and thought he so generously gave to my project; for permission to quote from his published and unpublished writings, and for allowing me free access to the files and records of the Centro Studi e Iniziative.

I also received essential information from members of Danilo Dolci's staff, particularly from Franco Alasia; from the Danilo Dolci Trust of London; and from Tullio Vinay of Riesi and Pietro Panascia of Palermo, two Waldensian pastors whose dedicated efforts among the Sicilian poor merit more attention than I have given them.

A host of men and women of good will, whose names occur in these pages, contributed to the genesis of this work. I would also like to thank Kay Boyle, Kenneth Burke, Lisa Aversa Richette, Cipriana Scelba, and Robert E. Spiller for their help and encouragement. I am grateful to the Fulbright Program for the award which made my Sicilian researches possible, and to those two idyllic havens for writers, Yaddo and the MacDowell Colony, where large sections of the manuscript were written.

My thanks also go to Barry Slepian, of the University of Pennsylvania, for valuable editorial advice, and to Morris Garnsey, of the University of Colorado, for permission to use his letter to me about Danilo Dolci.

Finally, I am happy to acknowledge the aid and comfort I received from my wife, Patricia, whose constructive attitude toward my labors helped to banish obstructive demons.

Contents

TYRRHENIAN SEA

Sferracavallo
Isola delle Femmine
Mondello
Tomaso Natale
Monte Pellegrino
PALERMO

Gulf of
Castellammare
Terrasini
Cinisi
Carini
Montelepre
Solunto
Bagheria
Trappeto
Monreale
Scopello
Balestrate
Partinico
Borgetto
Piana dei Greci

TRAPANI
Erice
Castellammare
Jato R.
St. Giuseppe Jato
Portella
della Ginestra

Levanzo
Favignana
Segesta
Alcamo
St. Cipirello

S
Roccamena

Termini Imerese

Sciara

Salemi
Poggioreale
Corleone
I

Santa Ninfa
Gibellina
MARSALA
Salaparuta
Partanna
Montevago
Santa Margarita di Belice

C

Castelvetrano
Mazara del Vallo
Sambuca
Selinunte
Belice R.
Carboi Dam
Menfi

Sciacca

Montallegro

Siculiana
AGRIGENTO
Realmonte
Porto Empedocle

Palma di Montech

MEDITERRANEAN SEA

N

0   10   20
Scale of Miles

Foreword
to the Colophon Edition

"Ducks! There are ducks!"

The old peasant stopped Danilo Dolci on the road and shouted excitedly. For a moment, the renowned social reformer was puzzled; then the peasant added:

"Everything has changed so much with the new lake that even the ducks have noticed! They never stopped here before, but now they come down onto the water!"

The damming of the Jato river had made the difference—for ducks as well as for people. Dolci had long struggled to stimulate western Sicilians to force their government to complete that project. Now his joy at the blessings of irrigation in that unnecessarily arid area was surpassed only by his joy at what had happened to that peasant and to hundreds of other peasants and fishermen. As Dolci puts it, "Frow now on no one will be able to make this man believe that the face of the earth, his part of it, can't be changed for the better."

Thus in 1971 Dolci's world-famous program reached another high. In his own modest words: "Perhaps this is the first year, in our part of the world, that everyone is happy when it rains." Such success, however, has a great deal more than local importance: His social laboratory has worldwide significance. Through it, he offers practical and tested patterns for change to all who are dogged by poverty, misery, and violence. But even at a point of success, Dolci insists on convincing his associates and those who would emulate them that they cannot rest:

"There are moments when things go well and one feels encouraged. There are difficult moments and one feels overwhelmed. But it's senseless to speak of optimism or pessimism. The only important thing is to know that if one works well in a potato field, the potatoes will grow. If one works well among men, they will grow. That's reality. The rest is smoke. It's important to know that words don't move mountains. Work, exacting work, moves mountains."

The use of the Jato dam to irrigate 28,000 acres of western Sicily, with the cultivators controlling the distribution of the water, culminates one of the persistent efforts so well described by Jerre Mangione in this book. Once more, as in so many other projects, Dolci succeeded in spite of local racketeers and mafiosi, political apathy and venality, ecclesiastical distrust and stupidity, and ingrained peasant suspicion, ignorance, and conservatism. Gradually, he has led Sicilians to question their old saying, "He who plays alone always wins." He helps them to understand, on the contrary, that "men are weak as long as they are isolated. The people who had no power before now are the new power."

Others have tried to portray Dolci's seminal demonstrations of how "gli ultimi" (the last) can organize, grow, and change their lot. Others have written sentimentally and melodramatically about the people in Sicily's "triangle of poverty." But only Mangione sees Dolci, his associates, and his environment as they are, with the clear eye of a careful, yet brilliant reporter.

In his own articles and books, Dolci presents documentary materials, replete with vivid quotations from all sorts of participants. But Dolci, preoccupied as he is with sociological investigation and with discovering strategies for social change, does not reveal in his writings an integrated conception of the many-sided Dolci in the midst of his activities. He does not sketch a comprehensive play-by-play account of how he and his collaborators and opponents operate.

Mangione does what Dolci does not do: He gives us the sense of experiencing Dolci and a great many other real people in the midst of their difficult and sometimes creative lives. He recognizes their weaknesses, bitternesses, and also their strengths, their dignity. He records their conversations. He pictures and characterizes them. And he writes it all with the charm and grace of a novelist, a creator of fascinating literature.

Mangione, as an American-born literary artist of immediate Sicilian background, takes us intimately into the lives of his own family's people as they depart from their primordial ways to join the modern world. He has an inimate grasp of Sicilian and Italian idioms and thoughtways and can relate them to a broad human context. While retaining his objectivity, he uses his family and his ethnic ties to portray accurately their reactions to proddings by a dedicated and skillful reformer.

In consequence, a well-informed Italian, Cipriana Scelba, head of the Fulbright commission in Rome, writes about this book: Mangione's "depiction of life and people in Sicily has such a great immediacy that I could readily recover the direct feeling and impressions I had when I myself visited some of the places." He enables "the reader to form an opinion about the situations . . . without appearing to influence his judgment in any given direction." The American writer, Kay Boyle, amplifies this: "I have read it with the greatest interest, for it is an absorbing document, to say the least. I have long wanted to know all the answers to the many questions concerning Dolci's temperament as well as his work. Jerre Mangione provides these answers with grace, modesty, and beautifully balanced judgment."

Mangione's only close competitors in the portrayal of western Sicilian life are Dolci himself and, in an older generation, the famous folklorist and physician, Giuseppe Pitrè. Dolci, in his books, demonstrates his endless interest in listening to all manner of men by recording what they say, something Pitrè had done several generations earlier. There the parallelisms end. Dolci listens to people to help them reform their lives and their environment. Pitrè, in his many books on popular Sicilian traditions and rituals, was principally a recorder. Mangione, on the other hand, provides the setting and a full-length portrait of a unique social reformer so that we can come to our own conclusions about him and about the people with whom he works, as well as about the exportability of his procedures.

The uniqueness of a Gandhi, a Martin Luther King, Jr., or a Dolci confuses both popular critics and systematic students of social science. Many find it easy to point to what they take to be shortcomings. Mangione carefully records all manner of objections to how Dolci lives, works, agitates, treats his colleagues, gets financing and other backing, finds social leverages with which to work towards his goals. As I read many of Mangione's frank and colorful passages, I was often reminded of the poor physician-reformer in Henrik Ibsen's "An Enemy of the People" whose attempts to serve his fellow townspeople met with some preliminary successes but were finally crowned by his alienation from all.

The principled dedication of Dolci does tire some followers, does stimulate carping criticism, and does make for sectarian opposition. When anyone tries to change any social situation, all who have vested interests in the old—and that is often everyone—feel more or less anxiety and pain. Those with power try to mobilize against the change.

Dolci, as an actual reformer, is much more complex than Ibsen's simplified caricature. As with Gandhi and King, he does not illustrate a category; he is no recognizable type. Mangione makes this abundantly clear: Dolci is a unique human work of art, an intellectual who is a man of action and who functions as a facilitator of social change. As F. Mario Rotondaro notes in his review of this book: "Somehow, in Sicily, in South America, in much of Asia, individual initiative must be reclaimed, a refusal to bow to that which has been inevitable for centuries must be developed in the minds of the people. Whether or not Dolci is more St. Francis of Assisi or P. T. Barnum, he has undeniably done much to bring forth this spirit of rebirth in the land and people he loves."

Dolci characterizes his own efforts as "a work of education, one of discovery. We try to educate people to change their ways, to act on their own, to feel free, to stop being fatalistic." No wonder that his work is often compared with that of the great Chicano trade-unionist, Cesar Chavez of grape-picking fame, even though their methods differ.

Above all, Dolci knows human society, has tested human possibilities, and has searched his own strengths and weaknesses. He constantly finds ways to renew his following and to give fresh thrust to his nonviolent revolutionary drives, his aggressive and loving struggles. From my own acquaintance with Dolci and with social agitation, I must agree with Mangione when he says: "I have never known a more resourceful man." And Mangione, as the Los Angeles *Times* reviewer of this book pointed out, does not make Dolci "emerge as a saint but as a complex, paradoxical and often infuriating man with a passionate dedication."

In addition to the completion of the Jato dam, what other developments in this book have taken new turns? The trial of Matarella (now dead) versus Dolci and Alasia coninues to be stalled in the Roman courts. Lorenzo Barbera, who was Dolci's chief lieutenant, has now established a Center of his own in Partanna concerned with the problems of the Belice valley and with the building of the Belice dam. Dolci's Borgo at Trappeto attracts seminars and other study groups from many countries as well as training programs for local community leaders and cultural events. Fruit, vegetable, and wine cooperatives thrive and expand. Arts and crafts based upon local traditions are being resurrected and made more saleable.

The work of Dolci and his associates in the towns devastated by the disastrous 1968 Sicilian earthquake inspired his most ambitious current project in that area. It is the construction of a new educational center at Partinico. Many of the antiquated schools of the district were destroyed by the earthquake, and Dolci took it as an opportunity to create a new kind of school for children from four to fourteen. For this, he has had the help of funds received from the highly prestigious Sonning Award of the University of Copenhagen "for his contribution to European civilization." He has also received funds from national Dolci committees in many countries including the United States. With these conribuions, Dolci has bought the land, has had quite original plans drawn, and is getting ready to construct an experimental school. He wants this school to become an agency for the reform of elementary education throughout Sicily. The school will emphasize individual discovery and creativity, working with and through groups, coordinated planning, and community participation.

In addition to the Sonning Award, recent honors that have come to Dolci include an honorary degree in pedagogy from the University of Berne (Switzerland), the Socrates Award of Stock-

holm, and the Italian Prato Award. He has often been promi-
nently nominated for the Nobel Peace Award (not long ago by
the American Friends Service Committee), and it is hoped that
this will shortly come to him. In announcing the 1971 Nobel
Peace Award, the *New York Times* reported Dolci to be one of
two runners-up. Meanwhile, he has been welcomed at many of
the most important universities and colleges of the world as a
guest lecturer and seminar conductor.

Dolci's books and his appearances before educational groups
have joined with other influences that are producing more and
more university courses dealing with nonviolent aggression. Professor Paul Wehr of Haverford College's Center for Nonviolent
Conflict Resolution estimates that by the academic year 1971-72
more than one hundred colleges and universities, including learning centers as diverse as Harvard and Notre Dame, were offering
such courses. Dolci's activities and his Center for Study and Action
at Partinico have contributed significantly to this development.

As a final point I should like to emphize the manner in
which Mangione himself participates in *The World Around
Danilo Dolci*. As one of its reviewers (George P. Elliott) notes,
Mangione "has not intruded himself egotistically, trying to up-
stage Dolci. On the contrary, he has put himself in out of a kind
of modesty." Robert E. Spiller, another specialist in literature,
develops this point further: "Although this is a book about Dolci
and his mission, it is also a book about Mangione and fits into the
main line of his best work—the characteristically intimate and
delicately felt autobiography. It is not only the world around
Dolci, but the world around Mangione which gives you Dolci as
though you (the reader) were also involved in the same world."

Throughout the book I certainly found myself participating
in its many scenes through identifying myself with Mangione.
Without using tape-recorder, he has captured the thought and
flavor of a wide range of people as individuals in a most convincing and satisfying manner. Writing in *Book World*, the late
Gavin Maxwell, himself an expert on Sicily, dwells on this aspect
of Mangione's presentation: "What contributes perhaps more
than anything else to the book's rare flavor is the curious intimacy
of the writing, its uncensored appraisal of named personalities

(including Dolci himself), as though one were reading with the author's permission a very private diary that is usually kept under lock and key."

Now that many of my fellow social scientists are turning back again to the virtures of partcipant observation as the best way to learn about behavior in society, they and their students would do well to take this and other of Mangione's charming, perceptive, and vivid books as models of what participant observation can be. Those who first meet Sicilians through this author's *Mount Allegro, Reunion in Society,* and *The World Around Danilo Dolci* will have had a moving human experience never to be forgotten.

ALFRED McCLUNG LEE

A Proem to
Danilo Dolci

Centro Studi e Iniziative   7 January 1965
Partinico
(Palermo) Italia

Dear Jerre:

You will be welcome whenever you arrive. When you know the exact time, please advise me.

My collaborators and I eagerly look forward to your six-month stay with us. Your Fulbright research should prove most useful. Also it will be good to have you here as an observer and friendly critic of this difficult project, and to have you participating in a way that is commensurate with all that is human and wise within you. We shall be together a great deal, carrying out the work of the Center. You will be particularly helpful in our relationships with our English-speaking friends—Americans, Englishmen, Swedes, Norwegians, East Indians.

As for your living quarters, do not worry. Franco Alasia has already found a solution that should interest you: a clean and simple house with three rooms (including a bathroom with water!) in a simple neighborhood not far from the Center. (None of us lives at the Center; we are scattered all over Partinico so as to avoid giving the impression that we are a monastic order.) The rent will be 15,000 lire a month. Each of the three rooms is on a different floor; the room on the top floor extends into a terrace from which you can get a view of the sea. We think that you and Patricia will be comfortable there.

So come as soon as you can. But before you arrive, let me say that I hope you don't have any exaggerated notions about our work here. I don't want you to become disillusioned. We go forward (and sometimes backwards) step by step with considerable difficulty. As you real-

1

ize, however, this is something to expect in any enterprise that is worthwhile.

With warmest regards to you and Patricia.

Yours,
Danilo

A newspaper photograph of three men, handcuffed and chained to one another, gave me my first glimpse of Danilo Dolci. The photograph, taken in a Palermo courtroom, centered on a round, serene face with a large forehead. The rimless spectacles, as much as the bemused line of the lips, suggested an intellectual of sorts. A schoolteacher was my first guess, but the lack of a necktie and the white shirt buttoned to the neck also suggested a priest who had got into trouble. The grouping of the three men in the photograph recalled a gory print that hung over my childhood bed: there, too, the emphasis was on the center figure, the crucified Christ flanked by two anonymous men also on the cross.

As with the print, the photograph of the men chained together seemed to belong to a bygone era when the punishment was often greater than the crime. Dolci and the two men were neither murderers nor madmen, as one might have surmised. Their crime, according to the Public Prosecutor, was that they "had organized and led the willful trespass of a public property, to wit a road, by a large number of day laborers and subsequently obstructed the police in their lawful duty of restoring order." The press, disdaining the legal vocabulary, gave their crime a simple name that became part of the vernacular: "a strike in reverse," the first of its kind.

The strike involved about 150 unemployed workers, armed with spades, hatchets, and pickaxes, who on a February morning in 1956 began working on a dirt road outside of Partinico that was badly in need of repair. Besides clearing the road of loose stones and deep ruts, they hoped to draw attention to their desperate need for jobs by engaging in what they regarded as their constitutionally guaranteed right to work.

"At the beginning of the winter the situation was tense," Dolci told the court. "The number of robberies kept increasing; even our next-door neighbor went out to steal. A man was accused of murdering his brother for three thousand lire. The people came to

2

us for help, but there were too many of them for us to handle. We sent several telegrams to the authorities but nothing happened. What could we do? We were being pressed by the people to find some solution, some remedy . . ."

"They were repeatedly called upon to desist from this road work and to disperse," the chief of police charged. "It then became necessary to warn the demonstrators to cease their illegal action and this was effected by three blasts on the trumpet, as indicated in the Police Regulations. But their leaders, headed by Danilo Dolci, persisted in continuing their work, and the following words were uttered against the policemen present: *'Whoever goes against us workers is a murderer.'* These words were taken up by the demonstrators as a battle cry with the evident intention of insulting the police."

"According to the spirit of the Constitution, to deny a man his right to work is the same as murdering him," Dolci said to the court. "When the police were ordered to arrest me, I sat on the ground, as Gandhi would have done. They lifted me bodily and four or five of them carried me face downwards by my feet and wrists. When they realized that they might break a bone by carrying me this way, they turned me over with my face up and carried me in that position . . ."

The presiding judge interrupted Dolci to ask his weight and height. Dolci replied he weighed 210 pounds and was five feet eleven inches tall. "Every now and then, when the police got tired of carrying me, they dropped me on the ground, into the mud. I kept on urging the men to go on working but not to resist the police. I told them to sit on the ground if they were prevented from working—I admit urging the men to keep on working after they placed me in the police car. 'Keep on digging,' I shouted, 'keep on digging.' "

Dolci's imprisonment and conviction created a storm of indignation through Europe and heavy floods of argument in Italy, where he was both praised and denounced for his Gandhian tactics of protest. "His East Indian methods, which so many people find so disconcerting, are eminently suited to conditions in Sicily," declared the novelist Elio Vittorini. "Fasting and other forms of passive resistance might seem ridiculous in northern Italy; but

Sicily has much in common with India: the same class distinctions that exist in many parts of India are also to be found in Sicily."

Other intellectuals defended Danilo's position that, far from being a criminal act, the strike in reverse was a peaceable demonstration of Article IV in the nation's constitution which states that "The Republic recognizes the right of all citizens to work and insures the conditions necessary to render this right effective." His critics, however, abused Dolci for consorting with Communists, for working with Protestants, for permitting free love among his followers, and for defaming Sicily. Their hostility was shared by the authorities, who kept Dolci in a lice-infested cell for three weeks before according him a hearing. The cell, which housed forty prisoners, remained infested until a Sicilian princess, as a gesture of her admiration for Dolci, sent around four gallons of DDT to delouse it.

Dolci remained in jail for fifty days before his case came to trial. The burden of his defense was borne by two of Italy's most famous civil lawyers, Achille Battaglia and Piero Calamandrei, who gave their services free. During the final hours of the four-day trial Calamandrei (who was to die a year later) broke down under the power of his own eloquence, as did nearly everyone else in the courtroom. "This is not the trial of Danilo Dolci, nor the trial of Partinico, nor that of Sicily," he told the jury. "All of Italy is on trial here." Speaking as a Tuscan from Florence, he added: "Our agony is your agony." After six hours of deliberation, the jury acquitted Danilo and the others arrested of the more serious charges but found them guilty of "trespassing" and "inciting to commit an offense." Both sides appealed, the State because it considered Danilo's eight-month jail sentence too light, the defense because it contended that no law had been broken.*

On his release from jail, Dolci issued an impassioned statement to the press decrying the apathy of the nation over such pressing problems in Sicily as unemployment, destitution, and violence. "Are we to witness impassively our own suicide? Are we to accept all these evils simply because they are perpetrated chiefly by the 'strong,' those who have money and machine-guns on their side?

* Five years later the sentence was annulled by the Italian Supreme Court under the terms of an amnesty.

Should not each of us, regardless of his social or economic status, become a guardian of the highest moral laws?"

The wide publicity given to the trial in the European press led to frequent references to the "strike in reverse" as a novel and civilized technique for directing public attention to scandalous social conditions. And on the ancient image of Sicily was superimposed the bulky figure of Danilo Dolci, a trained architect from a village near Trieste who, for motives that confounded the average Italian, seemed determined to extricate western Sicily from the quagmire of poverty and ignorance that had entrapped it for centuries. Within a few weeks, the "Gandhi of Sicily," as a French journalist dubbed him, had penetrated the minds of thousands of Europeans who until then had neither heard of Dolci nor paid much attention to the postwar fortunes of the island, except perhaps to read about the Mafia.

The trial received scant coverage in the United States, but what I read kindled my interest in Dolci and made me determined to learn more about his activities. If my reaction to the man photographed in chains was probably stronger than that of most other Americans it was because Sicily was literally in my blood. My parents were born in Sicily, in towns that are a short train ride from Partinico, a Mafia stronghold where Dolci established his headquarters in 1954. Although I grew up in Rochester, New York, where my parents had met and married, the atmosphere in our home was so steeped in the culture of their past that my first language became Sicilian, that earthy admixture of Italian, Greek, Arab, and Spanish. Undoubtedly, it was this early influence on my psyche that led me to write two books about Sicilians: *Mount Allegro,* which was partly based on my first visit to Sicily in the dreadful days of Mussolini's regime; and *Reunion in Sicily,* which recorded the experience of my relatives and other Sicilians in the aftermath of a bitter war that had brought three invading armies to their shores.

In my campaign to gather more information about Dolci I began with my relatives in Sicily, but found they were of little help.

The few who had heard of Dolci sent me clippings from *Giornale di Sicilia,* which regarded him as a "strange and anachronistic

5

local phenomenon" who deserved to be jailed because "he disturbs the serenity of Sicily." These relatives could not understand my interest in him, since they were certain that he either had Communistic ties or was in the pay of some foreign power. "A person who carries on as Dolci does must have an ulterior motive," a cousin of mine wrote me. "Nobody in his right mind can be as altruistic as he pretends to be. Now I read that he has gone on a three-day fast in jail. . . . His photographs convince me that he could live on his own fat for a much longer time without any trouble. Who ever heard of a fat saint?"

My non-Sicilian friends were more helpful. One of them who is that rare phenomenon, an Italian Quaker, sent me a pamphlet about Dolci by Aldo Capitini, the noted pacifist and philosopher. Entitled *Rivoluzione Aperta* ("The Open Revolution"), the pamphlet equates Dolci's career in Sicily with the author's theme that acts of nonviolence and sacrifice, such as those practiced by Dolci, benefit the masses and express love for everyone, including those against whom they are directed.

The strike in reverse, I learned from Capitini, was only one of Dolci's acts of protest. Soon after his arrival in Sicily in 1952, while living among the poor fishermen of Trappeto, he moved into a hovel where a child had just died from lack of food and announced his intention to fast until the authorities came to the rescue of the village. "Rather than see another child die of hunger," he wrote to friends and officials, "I would prefer to die myself . . . If I cannot arouse people's love by living, I will arouse their remorse by dying."

After seven days, Dolci suffered a stroke which half-paralyzed his right hand and leg, and the village doctor explained that unless he ate he would die. Alarmed, a Milanese friend of his, Franco Alasia, who was to become his first and most faithful disciple, spread the news of Dolci's condition among the authorities in Palermo. At first he got nowhere but when he happened to mention that several of Dolci's poems had been published in a national poetry anthology, some of the officials, apparently out of fear that they would be criticized if they allowed a published poet to die, suddenly took an interest in his plight. On the tenth day of the fast a monsignor, a baroness, and a physician came to Trappeto with an offer from the authorities that would immediately furnish the villagers with some relief money and some funds for initiating a public works program; they promised that the rest of the 30 million lire requested would come a little later.* Dolci would not accept the offer until he had discussed it with the villagers. "Don't accept the offer simply that I may get better and live," he told them. "If you think it is a fair offer, then you can say yes; if you don't think it fair, feel free to say no." The villagers, weeping with relief, voted yes, and Dolci began to eat again. He was then twenty-eight years old.

The following year the notes he had written on conditions at Trappeto were published in pamphlet form. *Act Quickly and Well Because People are Dying Here* provided Dolci and Trappeto with their first nation-wide attention. A "J'accuse" documentary written in the dispassionate but effective style that was to characterize Dolci's other writings, it gripped the conscience of Italian intellectuals and made them sharply aware of the shocking disparity between the living conditions of southern Italy and those north of Naples. But it was not until the publication of *Report from Palermo* in 1956, a work which Dolci prepared with the assistance of a sociologically minded band of disciples, that he achieved international recognition as a new kind of social missionary immersed in the problems of poverty. Translated into six languages, the book took Dolci's voice out of the wilderness and sent it around the world. The story of Dolci began to transcend his efforts in Sicily and assume universal meaning for those concerned with the devastation of poverty.†

Report from Palermo, which won the coveted Viareggio Prize for its literary quality, provided a biting indictment of society for its indifference to human squalor; and in a world rapidly darkening from lack of spiritual values, established the author as a beacon of hope. One of its most affected readers was Aldous Huxley, who contributed a preface to the American and English editions that read in part: "In a society such as ours—a society of enormous

* The authorities did more than keep this promise. They spent 100 million lire in Trappeto during the next two years.

† One of the claims made by Dolci's friends is that *Report from Palermo,* or *To Feed the Hungry* as it was titled in England, provided the inspiration for the Peace Corps established by President Kennedy.

numbers subordinated to an overexpanding and almost omnipresent technology—a new Gandhi, a modern St. Francis needs to
be equipped with much more than compassion and seraphic love.
He needs a degree in one of the sciences and a nodding acquaintance with a dozen disciplines beyond the pale of his own special
field. It is only by making the best of both worlds—the world of the
head no less than the world of the heart—that the twentieth-century saint can hope to be effective. Danilo Dolci is one of these
modern Franciscans-with-a-degree."

This was not quite accurate, for Dolci had quit his studies in
architecture shortly before he was to receive his degree; but Huxley's statement completed the process initiated by the writings of
Aldo Capitini, and Dolci became a legendary figure. Bolstered by
the semantic magnetism of such phrases as "twentieth-century
saint" and "a modern St. Francis," his legend spread through Europe with astonishing speed and impact and created Friends of
Danilo Dolci committees in London, Paris, Stockholm, and
Geneva. Throughout the world men and women from all levels of
society were drawn to the image of a compassionate man of action
who knew what had to be done to prevent man's inhumanity to
man and who was even willing to die for his cause.

Dolci's aptitude for matching words with deeds reinforced the
legend. As soon as he had sent his publishers the manuscript of
Report from Palermo, he and fifteen members of his group began
an eight-day fast throughout the province of Palermo to protest
against the misery described in the manuscript. After its publication, Dolci used the Viareggio Prize money to organize a Congress
on Full Employment (which was boycotted by every government
official invited to attend). Three days later he and Franco Alasia,
his friend and disciple from Milan, began a long fast in a dank and
stifling cellar room of Cortile Cascino, a cesspool of a slum located
near Palermo's Palace of Justice. In their effort to move the conscience of the authorities, the two men did not eat for thirteen
days.

Although Dolci's stock in the world outside Italy kept rising,
most of his compatriots remained either unmoved or openly hostile. In answer to such international expressions of approval as
"the new Gandhi" and "the Colossus of nonviolence," the Italians

8

who were angered by the kind of publicity Dolci was creating for their country provided such harsh epithets as "fanatical visionary," "opportunist," "mad apostle," "impractical do-gooder," "misty mystic," and, most often, simply "troublemaker." The Government added fuel to their fire by finding *Report from Palermo* "obscene" in parts and giving Dolci another jail sentence; also by relieving him of his passport, and excluding from the country a number of foreigners who had come to join his staff in Sicily.

Some of the Government's harassment stemmed from Dolci's acceptance of the Lenin Peace Prize in December 1957, a sum of about $30,000 which he promptly invested in establishing "study centers for full employment," manned by teachers and agricultural technicians, in five strategically placed villages of western Sicily. To those friends and supporters who were dismayed that he would accept the prize, he pointed out that as there were no strings to it, he saw no reason for refusing it. He added that he would always be willing to accept money to help his work from any source whatsoever. "I am not a Communist," he said in a speech at Palermo. "I accept this peace prize and am profoundly thankful. I really believe in the need for peace—that is, in non-violent struggle and revolution, clean in method and without compromise."

While my researches on the subject of Dolci revealed a great deal about him, they left a good many questions unanswered. My notes included the following: Why would a man of Dolci's education give up an easy future to involve himself in the problems of Italy's poorest men and women? Why Sicily? I found frequent references to God in his early writings but none in his later ones. Did this mean he had lost his faith, broken with the Catholic Church? The year after Dolci arrived in Trappeto he married an impoverished fisherman's widow who had five children, then proceeded to have five more by her. Were the children brought up as Catholics? As a leader, how could he justify fathering so many children with all the poverty around him? Did he seriously regard himself as another Gandhi? Dolci believes that the *miseria* in Sicily, as well as in other underdeveloped regions, can gradually be overcome by education, modern farming methods, establishment

of industries, efficient government and an honest police force—
mammoth goals for a land as resistant to change, as steeped in
tradition, and as fatalistic as Sicily. How did Dolci expect to create
the revolution that would bring about these changes with less than
fifty persons on his staff, none of whom he permitted to engage in
any party politics? Who were his closest collaborators? What were
his and their relations with the Communists? In an area where the
Mafia had assassinated thirty-five union organizers, how did it
happen that Dolci was still alive? How did the man Dolci differ
from the legend that was rapidly enveloping him?

I was able to get a partial answer to the last question sooner
than I had thought possible. In 1961, when I read that Dolci was
coming to the United States in March for the first time, I invited
him to be my house guest while in Philadelphia. Probably because
our home is more centrally located in the city than the other
accommodations offered him, he accepted.

It was a time when American interest in Dolci was at its height.
A Friends of Danilo Dolci committee was about to be established
in New York, the first in the United States. The American edition
of his early book, *The Outlaws,* had just been published and was
receiving wide attention. In reviewing it in the *New Republic,*
Irving Howe expressed the respect that many American intellectuals had for Dolci when he wrote: "The great virtue of Dolci's
movement is that it breaks with the feeling that politics has become a specialized craft to be left to professionals and institutions.
. . . The challenge offered by Dolci's example is not so much a
saintliness with or without God, but the possibility of an active
goodness open to anyone, a 'saintliness' for which one need be no
more than a man."

In New York, which was Dolci's first stop, he was besieged by
men and women who wanted to work with him in Sicily. To the
reporters he said: "I came here above all to learn, to consult with
experts and interested groups, and to find qualified people to help
us in our development work, which is to make self-sufficient the
most miserable and bloodiest section of Sicily."

None of my reading had prepared me for the first impression I
had of Dolci when I met him at the train station. Instead of the
intense personality with the fanatical eyes I had conjured up in

10

my imagination (possibly because of all those references to Gandhi), the huge man in the beret I greeted struck me as a mountain of tranquillity, a calm and somewhat amused observer who looked at one with a directness that seemed to obliterate his spectacles. But if the general stance was that of a poised gentleman, the externals were not. The beret was absurdly small for so large a man, the suit so rumpled that I was at once reminded of the late Heywood Broun, as large a man as Dolci, who was once described as looking "like an unmade bed." And though Dolci's white shirt was buttoned at the collar, there was no necktie, a lack which somehow accented the bulk of his figure. The eyes were blue-gray, the thinning hair blond. He seemed more Teutonic than Latin, more like a seer than a saint.

Although he was bewildered at first by my brand of Italian, a peculiar mélange of Sicilian and fractured Roman, he soon got the hang of it, and began asking questions about me, the other members of the reception committee, and Philadelphia, which he recalled from history had been "a city of revolutionists." His general demeanor was that of a cheerful extrovert, which surprised me considering how dangerously he lived; but, unlike most extroverts I have known, he was highly intuitive and was adept in the art of listening. He also knew the art of modesty. "What does that say?" he suddenly asked, on the way to our house, where a group of newsmen were waiting to interview him. His finger pointed to the marquee of a movie house. On being informed it was the title of a Soviet film, "Ballad of a Soldier," he pronounced it a masterpiece and said we must not miss it. "What a shame that you are stuck with me," he sighed. "You would find the film much more rewarding than anything I have to say."

His traveling companion was Miss Victoria Bawtree, an ebullient, apple-cheeked young woman with a British accent and a firm grasp of Italian, who was both his secretary and interpreter, for Dolci spoke no English. Dolci, who towered over her, smilingly described her as his "protectress," as she scrutinized the heavy schedule arranged for him and decreed when, for the sake of his health, he must be allowed time off to rest. In the whirl of meetings and interviews that ensued in the next three days, she proved to be a remarkable interpreter. She had been one of Dolci's band

11

of volunteer workers in Partinico for two years and was so conversant with his attitudes and activities that she could convey the emotional impact of his statements, even though he spoke in a rather matter-of-fact, studiously precise style.

Except by Italian-Americans who could not bear to hear their homeland criticized, Dolci was warmly received wherever he spoke. Ironically, his first talk was in the Sicilian Pavilion of the Festival of Italy, an enormous exhibition sponsored by the City of Philadelphia and the Government of Italy to demonstrate "one hundred years of progress." The City's arrangement committee that chose the site either did not know of the official Italian attitude toward Dolci or ignored it. Relishing the situation, Dolci spoke frankly about the feudalistic conditions in western Sicily, its alarming percentage of illiteracy and crime, and the power of the Mafia. His opening sentence plunged into the heart of the matter: "How can you talk to people about the need of a dam when they do not know what a dam is?"

The only Italians who accepted invitations to the talk were two or three hecklers who tried repeatedly to interrupt Dolci, but were stopped by the audience. At the end of the meeting, one of the hecklers, who identified himself as an employee of Alitalia (the Italian air transport company) buttonholed Dolci and accused him of presenting a false picture of Sicily. Under Dolci's questioning, he finally admitted that he had been in Sicily less than a week, on his way to Ethiopia. "What did you do in Ethiopia?" Danilo asked softly, before turning his back on him. "Shoot Negroes?"

The same heckler, with a gang of his friends, appeared at a meeting of a Sons of Italy lodge two days later, where I acted as chairman. They kept quiet while Dolci showed the audience a BBC documentary film dealing with his work, "Murder by Neglect"; but as soon as he began speaking he was interrupted by the heckler and his friends, who protested that all of Dolci's talks stressed the poverty of Sicily without ever referring to its beauty. To this he replied: "If a man's liver is diseased and he comes to you for help, you do not tell him how beautiful his eyes are or how excellent his hearing is."

Halfway through the talk, the hecklers began shouting their objections to what Dolci was saying and were joined by several

12

other members of the audience. As chairman, I tried to restore order and when I realized I could not and was not getting any support from the audience, my Sicilian temper, which I usually manage to keep dormant in public, exploded. But the sound of it could not drown out the shouts of the hecklers. The meeting would have ended in chaos had it not been for a prominent judge, then the acknowledged leader of the Italian-Americans in Philadelphia, who, suddenly appearing from nowhere, took charge. For a few nervous moments those among us who were familiar with Judge Eugene Alessandroni's conservative political views were afraid he would side with the hecklers. Instead he summarized the main points made by Dolci and eloquently urged the audience to support his program. Then, addressing himself to the hecklers, he urged them to bear in mind that Dolci's intent was not to slander but to educate audiences to the economic and educational needs of western Sicily.

Although the meeting ended on a note of triumph for Dolci, there was no indication of that in the Italian-American press. The judge's remarks received no attention. Instead one newspaper called Dolci a "red dupe," and quoted the organizer of the Sicilian Pavilion, a local attorney, to the effect that "Dolci's arguments are not unlike those presented by the Communists." Another newspaper insisted that Dolci was doing Sicily more harm than good, and concluded: "Whether Christian or Communist, martyr or mountebank, Danilo Dolci remains a mystery."

The rest of his Philadelphia talks invariably aroused compassion, not criticism. Although Dolci made no appeal for funds, many individuals and several groups, Haverford College and the Unitarian Church among them, contributed money to his cause. Dolci was undisturbed by his experience with the Italian-Americans. "I have met the same kind of people in Italy. They are the blindly chauvinistic who resent any other image of Italy except that projected by the Italian Tourist Bureau."

In the three days that we spent together my understanding of the man blossomed rapidly, though most of my questions remained unanswered. His talks, private and public, were often poetic metaphors that expressed an obsessive concern about the underprivileged of Sicily. In a less disciplined mind this obsession

13

would have turned into fanaticism but in Dolci's, with its respect for accuracy and the amenities, it became an orderly, though unpredictable, process of expression. I found him more intellectual than I had expected a man with a mission to be, sometimes to the point of being overly abstract; yet underlying all of his utterances I sensed a clear and relentless devotion to humanity which amounted to a religion.

Between his public meetings and press interviews, we retired to the quiet of my home for meals, rest, and talk. He missed his children and his wife. Nearly every day she wrote him love letters in primitive Italian, from which he read excerpts, marveling at their poetry in the manner of a teacher who has become enamored of his student. There also arrived a copy of his newest book *Spreco* ("Waste") which he inscribed and gave to me, with the explanation that although human waste was his main concern, he was interested in examining all forms of waste wherever he went "as evidence of the insufficient planning that is the curse of both rich and poor countries." He added that the planning which does exist is often too theoretical and fails to take into account the realistic needs of the people for whom it is intended. This complaint, as I later discovered, was one of the major tenets of all his social criticism.

His conversation was devoid of small talk; yet there was little suggestion of the oracle about him. He was fond of asking questions, often the same ones. One of his favorite questions was based on his observation that wherever he went in the United States, he saw smoke coming out of the ground. "Where does the smoke come from?" he would ask nearly everyone he met. At first I thought this was nothing more than a conversational gambit, a way of amusing himself, but before long I understood that he had a serious motive in mind: to document the lack of precision among people, their readiness to present guesses as facts, their reluctance to admit ignorance. While dining with W. H. Auden in Manhattan, Dolci had put the question to him, and received an atypical response. Auden, to his delight, appeared to be horror-struck and muttered: "I dare not think about it."

Everything that Dolci said or did seemed to be geared to the challenges he had imposed on himself; there were few wasted

14

words and motions. Occasionally I found myself suspecting that he was not so much the master of himself as he was the servant of the ideals he had thrust on himself. This suspicion grew at lunch one day when, half-jokingly, I suggested he cancel one of the talks in his heavy schedule (six talks in three days) and go to a dancing party to which my wife and I had been invited. The proposal was enthusiastically endorsed by Victoria Bawtree, who declared that he owed it to himself to see Americans at play. When he did not at once say no, everyone around the table joined in the game of trying to persuade him to attend the party and forget the talk.

"It's kind of all of you to wish to provide me with entertainment," he said when we had finished, "but, alas, I am an inseparable part of the image that people have made of Dolci, a slave who is obliged to do what the image of Danilo Dolci dictates. There is no escape for me. How I envy your freedom to do as you please." He spoke lightly, in the jovial mood of the company, but there was no mistaking his seriousness.

Despite his crowded schedule, Dolci made himself available to anyone who wished to talk with him. Most were men and women who were eager to join his cause in Sicily. None of them had the particular skills Dolci was seeking. A few spoke Italian but lacked the emotional or physical stamina to cope with life in a Sicilian village. An elderly man and his wife, who spoke several languages and who had already written Dolci a number of times, begged him to let them bring music and dancing to Partinico. Dolci dealt with them gently but made it clear that he could not add them to his staff. "But we will pay our own way," the old man wailed in Italian. "You will never regret it."

One of his visitors was the local Italian General Consul. Shortly before Dolci was to leave the house for another meeting, the Consul, who knew me, telephoned to explain that as an official of the Italian government he could not very well attend any of Dolci's meetings. Would it be possible to make his acquaintance unofficially? Since Dolci did not object, I invited the Consul and his wife to join us at my home. They arrived within twenty minutes in their chauffeured official car. The Consul's wife, an elegant young woman with a vivacious manner and flirtatious eyes, was quick to break the ice after the introductions were made. "Signor Dolci,"

15

she scolded charmingly, "why do you insist on writing such depressing things about our beautiful Sicily? There is so much romance there yet you are so completely blind to it. Why can't you write about Sicily as Lampedusa does in *The Leopard?* Now there's a book that is worthy of Sicily!"

Dolci quickly got out of his chair and picked up *Spreco,* the book he had given me, which includes a report on Palma di Montechiaro, a notoriously impoverished town that had once been the residence of the Lampedusa nobility. Turning to a photograph that showed an open sewer in a muddy street, he shoved the book under the woman's pretty nose and said: "Madame, it was on this very spot that the Prince in Lampedusa's novel looked up at the sky and admired the stars."

The Consul's wife retreated into silence, like a reprimanded child, while her husband conversed with Dolci about contemporary Italian writers until it was time for Dolci to proceed to his next meeting. He must have fascinated the Consul, for the dapper official threw aside all governmental caution and invited Dolci to dine at the Consulate. He graciously declined, citing the tightness of his schedule.

In his final hour in Philadelphia, while we took a short *passeggiata,* I told Dolci that a publisher had recently offered me a contract to write a book about modern Sicily that would investigate the efforts of reformers who hoped to change its economic and spiritual situation; such a book, I pointed out, would necessarily deal largely with his own activities. Dolci urged me to accept the assignment and assured me he would gladly put all of his information at my disposal, but begged me to wait a few years. "People have such an exaggerated idea about the size of my achievements," he said. "A book that emphasizes my work at this time, no matter how truthful, would only add to that misconception. It would be better to wait a few years until we have done more." He sighed. "There is so much to do." Then he smilingly linked his arm into mine. "But I'm delighted that you want to write a new book about Sicily. For one thing, it will mean that you and your wife will have to come to see me . . ."

I saw him again briefly in New York, with a small band of supporters who had gathered in a Greenwich Village apartment to bid him farewell. He had just returned from Washington, where he had gone at Sargent Shriver's request to discuss the newly founded American Peace Corps, which was not unlike the small corps that Dolci directed in Sicily. Meeting with Shriver and his staff, Dolci had described the techniques he found most efficacious for working in an underdeveloped area; also the pitfalls he encountered. In an interview with the *Washington Star* that followed the meeting, he had, according to the reporter, used "down-to-earth words that had little regard for injured Italian pride in being classed an 'underdeveloped country.'" Dolci had called Sicily and southern Italy "a ball of lead" around Italy's feet, and added: "Until we Italians stop the stream of rhetoric about 'Rome, the cradle of civilization,' and start solving the problems of the South, none of Italy's problems can be solved."*

At the farewell gathering Victoria Bawtree announced that she would remain in New York to help organize the new Friends of Danilo Dolci committee there. She would also try to find a job that would help restore her finances, which were in a precarious state after two years of working in Sicily at subsistence pay.

Dolci seemed much more tired than he had been in Philadelphia. Yet his vitality easily surpassed that of anyone else around him; throughout the evening he dominated the group with his high spirits and pointed questions. With a straight face, he was still asking people what caused smoke to come out of the ground.

Four years were to pass before I could join Dolci in Partinico. Those were milestone years in his career, when he was openly declaring war on the Mafia and campaigning for the construction of two dams that could substantially improve the welfare of western Sicily.

In the course of arousing public opinion in support of his goals,

* In a 1965 issue of *International Affairs* (Vol. XIX, No. 2), Professor Gustav Schachter, an American economist, writes: "The Italian South contains 43 percent of the national territory and 39 percent of the population, but the average per capita income is half that of northern Italy." He adds that although regional agriculture in the South is proportionately larger than in the North, agriculture in the South is less developed. Commenting on the disparity in the industrial development of the North and South, he points out that "except for a few isolated large plants, 'industry' in the South often refers to small household units and artisan shops, which are usually family-run and rarely hire outside help or use mechanical power."

17

he also aroused the wrath of the Sicilian Establishment, to such a degree that the head of the Catholic Church in Sicily, Cardinal Ruffini, in his 1964 Easter pastoral letter denounced Dolci as a "publicist" engaged in "a giant conspiracy" to dishonor Sicily. A novel by a dead author, *The Leopard,* and the secret society, the Mafia, were cited as the other factors in the conspiracy—the novel for presenting "a false and antiquated image of the Sicilian people," and the Mafia for having a world-wide evil reputation that was out of proportion to its limited influence.

As Danilo Dolci was the only living person identified with "a giant conspiracy," the Cardinal's implication was deadly clear: Dolci was Sicily's extant No. 1 enemy; and the press bandied about the word "enemy" freely. The Cardinal's letter, and the wide publicity given to it when it was publicly approved by Pope Paul, shocked Dolci's friends and increased their concern for his safety. They feared that in an area rife with unsolved murders, the Cardinal's statement could easily be interpreted as official encouragement for the liquidation of Dolci.

More and more Dolci had been stepping on Mafia toes. In 1962, when he told the heads of various government agencies that they had to choose "between the Mafia and the dam," he was warned by the Partinico *mafiosi* to keep his nose out of their affairs. But Dolci, and his collaborator Franco Alasia, kept investigating their sabotaging techniques, and documenting the fact that, in the guise of representing the owners of the lands where the Government had agreed to build the Jato dam, the *mafiosi* were deliberately blocking its construction.

Two years had passed since the Cassa di Mezzogiorno, the government agency handling funds for the development of southern Italy, had appropriated money for the project and signed contracts with the construction firm. Yet, as Dolci pointed out, "not a stone has been moved, not a pick has been swung." He and his associates then launched an intensive campaign in the area to remind the public of the crucial benefits they would derive from the dam, and to emphasize the obstacles that were preventing its construction. In the final phase of the campaign, Dolci began a fast on September 7, 1962, at his home in Spine Sante ["Holy Thorns"], a disease-infested slum area where he and his family had lived for four

18

years. The fast, which received international attention in the press, was to have continued for ten days, but Dolci ended it on the ninth when the authorities, responding to pressures of public opinion, guaranteed that the construction of the dam would begin within five months. The work actually started two weeks after the deadline, in February 1963; and for the first time in many years there was the hope of steady employment for some of the Partinico men.

In October of that year Dolci began another fast, the eighth one in his career, in behalf of an unbuilt dam on the Belice River. The dam, which had been in the planning stage since 1930, was to be one and a half times larger than the Jato dam and affect an arid valley encompassing twenty-two villages. The Government had appropriated funds for starting the construction, but nothing more had happened. In August Dolci discovered the reason: for motives of political expediency, the funds had been diverted to other purposes.

This time Dolci fasted in Roccamena, a poverty-corroded village in the interior located some four miles from the site of the proposed dam. Seventy-five percent of the village's able-bodied men had been obliged to leave their families behind to search for work in other parts of Europe. Those who remained, both men and women, supported Dolci's action with a mass one-day fast of their own. Dolci also had tangible support from the British Committee of One Hundred. As a way of dramatizing its approval of Dolci's nonviolent tactics, it sent its secretary, Peter Moule, a young pacifist of international reputation, to fast with him.

For ten days the two men starved and slept in the same tiny room off the piazza, barely able to communicate, since neither one spoke the other's language. On the ninth day, weak from their ordeal, they got on horseback and led the villagers in a march to the Belice River. On the site of the proposed dam, in the presence of television crews and numerous Italian and foreign journalists, Dolci emphasized two central themes: the dam must be built to save the Belice valley from becoming a wasteland; only the dam could create enough jobs to stop the emigration of workers. In response to the demonstration, representatives of the Sicilian Regional Government came to Roccamena that same evening to

19

promise Dolci that the dam would be built. But they failed to specify when that would happen.

In the same year, the Mafia, whose crimes were becoming increasingly brazen and bloodthirsty, was responsible for the death of seven policemen and soldiers, who were blown to bits when an abandoned Alfa-Romeo they were investigating near Palermo exploded in their faces. In recent years it had become customary for the feuding *mafiosi* of the Palermo area to liquidate each other in that fashion, but this was the first time the technique had been used against the law.

Infuriated, the Palermo police department began filling the jails with hundreds of suspected *mafiosi*. Although many of the most powerful criminals immediately went into hiding, a number were caught in the police dragnet. Among them was Gaspare Centinaio, the *mafioso* of Partinico who had tried to sabotage the construction of the Jato dam. Another was his ally Luciano Liggio, one of Sicily's most ruthless killers, who made his headquarters in Corleone, the Mafia-dominated town where Dolci had established one of his five study centers.

The crime had significant national repercussions. With a speed that matched the heat of the public's indignation, the Italian government instituted a Parliamentary Commission of Inquiry into the Mafia's activities and, in September 1963, presented its first proposals for anti-Mafia laws. Thus began the Government's first long-range drive against the secret society that had been tyrannizing western Sicily for more than a century.

I noted with interest that, unlike Cardinal Ruffini, the Italian government was gradually relaxing its attitude toward Dolci as it adopted a more severe policy toward the Mafia. In 1964, the same year that the Cardinal attacked Dolci in his pastoral letter, Dolci was invited to Rome to testify before the Anti-Mafia Commission. It was the first time that his long and lonely crusade against the Mafia, which began in 1952, had been accorded official recognition.

In Rome Dolci made the most of his opportunity. Armed with thirty sworn affidavits, he charged that Senator Girolamo Messeri of Partinico, who had recently been appointed Under-Secretary of State for Commerce, had the electoral help of the notorious Italian-

American ex-gangster, Frank Coppola, while campaigning for office during the 1958 and 1963 elections. Amplifying on the activities of Coppola in a letter to his supporters, Dolci wrote: "From my observations I know that Coppola comes to Partinico before all senate elections and during any crisis, and he distributes voting slips of a kind that is illegal under Italian law. He is also closely connected with the Church, and when his voting slips run out, he has been known to go to the Church to get some more. On his visits to Partinico he has been received as a guest of honor in the houses of the most important citizens of the town. I have in my possession affidavits by various persons dealing with Coppola's activities . . ."

On his return from Rome, Dolci found Partinico flooded with angry posters flaying him as a "vulgar slanderer" and "a scoundrel with criminal tendencies." The poster was signed by Senator Messeri. Dolci promptly had it reproduced in hundreds of copies, which he sent to his supporters in Italy and abroad.

Not long after Dolci mailed me a copy of the poster, I received word that I had been awarded a Fulbright research grant to investigate social and economic conditions in western Sicily and ascertain what was being done to improve them. When I communicated the news to Dolci and did not hear from him for several weeks (later I learned he was away on a trip) I began to fear that he still had reservations about the timing of my project. But his answer, when it finally came, left no doubt as to his willingness to help me with my research as soon as I could get to Sicily. "We are delighted to think that in a short time you will be among us. As I wrote you a long time ago, of all the people I have ever met you are one of those who has made the deepest impression on me; the reading of your book *Mount Allegro* has underlined that impression . . ."

Dolci's letter augured well for the project. I decided to make Partinico my headquarters, and wrote back offering to do whatever work on his staff might be useful; I also asked him to find living quarters for me and my wife. In the meantime, I had learned that the New York committee that was organized to support Dolci's work was about to disband. Victoria Bawtree was no longer its secretary; two years before she had tired of New York and obtained a job in Rome. Before my departure, I tried to

21

determine why the committee had lost its interest in Dolci. The chief reason given was lack of communication—Dolci did not keep the New York group sufficiently informed of his activities. On the other hand, there appeared to be no lack of communication between the executive secretary of the New York committee and the executive secretary of the Partinico staff, a young American woman who, it developed, had become disenchanted with Dolci and had recently left his staff along with several other collaborators. It was clear that the grievances of Dolci's Partinico defectors had become the grievances of the New York committee.

Although the complaints I heard sounded reasonable enough, I was not unduly disturbed by them. After all, it was to be expected that the leader of an enterprise as idealistic and ambitious as Dolci's was bound to experience difficulties with his personnel. It also occurred to me that the label of "saint," as applied by Aldous Huxley, was now six years old—old enough to be faded by the glare of reality.

"Who Would Fast
For the Romans?"

Now AND THEN my Sicilian heritage rears its ancient head long enough to persuade me that the direct approach is not always the wisest one. This happened on the eve of our voyage; it suddenly seemed more feasible to approach Sicily by going first to Rome, the cradle of many of its crises. The decision, prompted by a reluctance to plunge headlong into a Sicily I had not seen for eighteen years, was not a difficult one; for some kind of prologue, however oblique, seemed required to prepare us (Patricia had never been to Sicily) for what promised to be a strenuous adventure.

The Italian ship, a floating recreation center dominated by vacationing professors and their wives who for eight days generated the atmosphere of an extended faculty club party, offered no useful clues to our immediate future. There was a singular shortage of Italians on board; the only one we knew was a countess in her fifties, a fading, hypochondriacal beauty who spent most of her time in the seclusion of her stateroom nursing her various ailments. After managing a de luxe beauty parlor in New York for several years, she was returning to her home in Florence. Although given to criticizing American vulgarity in vulgar excess, she was often in the company of an American, a sedate, elderly tycoon who, on discovering that the countess was traveling in third class, had insisted that she be transferred to first, and paid the difference. As an expression of her gratitude, the countess allowed

23

him the privilege of her company when she was not ill in her cabin, but turned a deaf ear to his plea for a Roman rendezvous.

The only other Italian passengers who engaged our attention were three swarthy men wearing black hats who moved together, like a dark cloud that constantly hovered on our horizon. Their fierce glances in my direction were unsettling. In my most paranoid moments I would imagine they were three *mafiosi* who, having got wind of my Sicilian project, were waiting for a propitious moment to hurl me overboard. But one morning, toward the end of the voyage, I fell into conversation with the swarthiest of them, and it turned out that they were three brothers who operated a spaghetti factory in Connecticut, on their way to Naples, their birthplace, where they each hoped to find a wife. Their persistent interest in me, I learned, had been dictated by nothing more than the striking resemblance I bore (documented by a snapshot shown to me) to one of their Neapolitan first cousins, who was also in the spaghetti business. On the strength of that, they insisted on buying us a drink.

Our first full exposure to Italians, on the train from Naples to Rome, was not nearly as heart-warming. The easy communication between passengers that had once been the distinctive feature of an Italian train ride was nowhere in evidence; instead there was a dourness as chilling as that of a New York subway at the morning rush hour. The faces around us were bored or worried and, if I made any overtures, grimly polite, as though they had all had their fill of foreigners. The only signs of amity I noticed were the smiles of a mother directed to the infant sucking at her breast, and the passing landscape, green and poignant with the early spring.

Our impression of the people's mood grew stronger during our Roman sojourn. There was prosperity and elegance, but little gaiety. Publicly, at least, the Roman soul had changed. No longer were there men on street corners singing out declarations of love to all passing women under sixty. Now they were whizzing around in their cars, defying other cars and barely missing pedestrians. The Roman's public obsession with the charms of women had taken second place to his obsession with the trappings of an affluent society.

The transformation was not without its compensations. Undistracted by the fascinations of a once outgoing people, one could finally concentrate on the beauty of the city. Once we learned to overlook the fact that every piazza had become a cluttered parking lot, the gates, walls, ruins, and pines of the ancient city asserted themselves in a bewitching montage of shapes and colors, occasionally embellished by piles of snow, remnants from the city's heaviest snowstorm since 1757, which had fallen a week before our arrival.

But if the Romans en masse seemed disturbingly aloof and excessively preoccupied with twentieth-century capitalism, their hospitality in individual encounters, though sometimes pat, was a welcome relief from the hotel we occupied overlooking the Villa Borghese, where a malfunctioning central heating system kept us in a state of chill that was only partly relieved by the antics of some elderly English and German guests.

Dining in the same room twice a day, they unashamedly paraded their loves and hates, and gossiped about one another with an acidity that destroyed any notion that mellowness is an inevitable feature of old age. The most memorable of them was a wine-loving octogenarian Englishman with three scarves wrapped around his neck, who kept the old ladies in a constant state of ferment by daily manipulating the attentions of several of them until they were beside themselves with jealousy. But divertissement is a poor substitute for bodily comfort, and to escape the harrowingly low temperatures of the hotel, we found ourselves accepting almost every invitation that would take us to other and warmer rooms, particularly when there might be an opportunity to discuss the fortunes of Danilo Dolci.

The first of our hosts was a friend I had known in Porto Empedocle, my father's hometown, on my last Sicilian trip. In those days of his youth Andrea Bellini wrote poetry, read Proust, and shyly talked of his longing to know the world outside Sicily. Now he had become a sophisticated man of the world, who wrote articles instead of poems, and who earned his livelihood as a television producer, but indulged in his yearning for imaginative expression by occasionally directing avant-garde stage and radio dramas.

"You never thought I'd ever escape from Sicily, did you?" he

25

asked, while we were dining with his wife and two children. When I admitted as much, explaining that most Sicilian sons seem to have trouble cutting family ties even after they are married, his wife informed me that soon after Andrea got his first job in Rome, his parents sold their house in Porto Empedocle and the whole family, including Andrea's grandparents, moved to Rome. They now occupied an apartment in the same building.

"So what makes you think you've escaped Sicily?" I asked Andrea.

"Because I feel like a Roman and I'm proud of that feeling. Sicily belongs to the past. To everybody's past. Believe me, it is far better to be a Roman, and to forget the past. Even my father is beginning to think so. He now speaks Sicilian with a noticeable Roman accent."

Yet Andrea was far from being a conformist. He expressed deep scorn for Italian television because of the tight censorship imposed on it by both the Government and the Catholic Church. The Church, he was convinced, was responsible for the increasing censorship. A play he had directed in Naples was shut down by the authorities; he was arrested and relieved of his passport. "It's enough to make a Communist of one, and that is what I'm rapidly becoming. Not that I really want to, but how else can you fight a government that is so heavily infested with Church authority?"

On the subject of Dolci, he knew little of his recent activities, but he had strong opinions about him. "The only important quality about Dolci is his honesty, which makes him a rarity among Italian leaders. But he will never get anywhere because he is too isolated from the mass of Italians. He'll remain that way as long as he persists in refusing to ally himself with any political party. When he accepted the Lenin Peace Prize, we all thought he would work for the Communist program, but he has made it amply clear that he is no Communist and will not collaborate with the Communist party. He doesn't seem to understand that alone, with only a handful of helpers, he can never solve any of Sicily's problems. The Italians all know this. That is why Dolci has to depend on foreigners so much for support. Foreigners, of course, don't realize how impossibly complicated the Sicilian problem is . . ."

One of the "complications" he discussed, of course, was the

26

Mafia, some of whose chiefs he had known while living in Porto Empedocle. In 1947 Andrea's father introduced him to one of them, Nicola Gentile, an ex-gangster from the United States who had been deported to his native Sicily. Three years later, while Andrea was in Rome attending school, they ran into one another, and Andrea asked him what brought him to the city. Gentile sighed and said it was all because he was the kind of man who was always trying to help people. His story was that the famous bandit Giuliano, "in a moment of stupidity," had tried to extort fifty million lire from a Palermo bank director, threatening to kidnap his son if the money was not delivered by a certain date.

The Director, who was unable to raise that much money, had described his plight to "friends," who in turn described it to other "friends." Eventually, the problem landed on Gentile's doorstep. Gentile promptly took care of the matter, and before long the Director received a note from Giuliano to the effect that he had no intention of either taking money from him or harming his son. The grateful Director sent for Gentile and, as an expression of his gratitude, placed a package of money before him. Gentile pushed the money away, and asked instead for "a small favor." His son had flunked a state examination in accounting three times. The Director assured Gentile his son would pass it the fourth time. Everyone was happy about the way the matter had been settled, Gentile told Andrea, but shortly afterwards when the police got wind of the fact that he had been in touch with Giuliano, he was summoned by the Police Commissioner of Palermo and asked about the bandit's whereabouts. Gentile denied any knowledge of the subject, but the Commissioner persisted with his questions, framing them within eloquent orations of abuse, which were interrupted only by his difficulty in remembering Gentile's name. Three times Gentile had to remind him what it was. The fourth time, while the Commissioner was groping for it, Gentile, in a spurt of friendliness, suggested he called him "Zio Cola"—the familiar form of address the Mafia chief was accustomed to. Instead of accepting the suggestion kindly, the Commissioner interpreted it as a grievous insult and after giving vent to his fury for several minutes ordered Gentile incarcerated. "If it had not been for that dear and noble gentleman, Cardinal Ruffini, I would still be in

27

that Palermo jail," Gentile told Andrea. "I don't particularly like Rome but I thought it would be a good idea to stay here for a while and give the Commissioner a chance to forget my name again."

Andrea said: "It is all well and good for Dolci to start denouncing people in the Government for their connections with known Sicilian criminals, but how does he expect to get anywhere when the Church and sections of the national government are all hand in glove with the Mafia? It seems to me that everything Dolci tries is bound to fail."

An Italian official of the Fulbright Commission echoed Andrea's pessimism about the value of Dolci's crusade. "Dolci really shocked the nation at first with his East Indian fasting and his strike in reverse, which was bolder than anything they had ever seen the Communists pull. Except for those eggheads who came to his support, most Italians followed his career for a number of years with the utmost nervousness and trepidation. And the authorities reflected their attitude by making Dolci's life as miserable as possible—arresting him on charges of pornography, kicking out his collaborators on the silly grounds that they were foreigners, etc. Then, a few years ago, the general attitude toward him changed. Suddenly everyone became indifferent to what he was doing. Even the Government stopped bothering him. This sort of thing is always happening in Italy. People are terribly scandalized about anything that disturbs their equanimity, but as soon as they become used to it they accept it as a regular part of their life. What keeps Dolci going is not the support of the Italians—not even that of the Sicilians who stand to benefit from his ideas—but the remarkable persistence of the man. Without the force of his personality, all of his projects would fall apart . . ."

In every living-room the mention of Danilo Dolci was certain to evoke a set of strong opinions about him. No one pulled any punches, the Americans in residence least of all. A magazine writer who had been living in Rome almost continuously since 1947, when I knew her as a wide-eyed young correspondent, gave a small reception for us in the bizarre three-story apartment she and her husband had constructed on the roof of a building in one of Rome's most ancient neighborhoods. In addition to the two children, a lemur, a parrot and three Siamese cats who shared the abode, the gathering included a bookish American in his mid-thirties who was known to me for his translations of Italian fiction, and a youthful free-lance journalist and his wife from Alexandria, Virginia, who had been living in Rome for four years. They were all enthusiastic Romanophiles, who hoped to live there indefinitely. The journalist and his wife were not certain their circumstances would permit them to, but they were glad they had remained long enough for their infant daughter to be born there. "It will be so much better for her," the mother explained, "to be able to say she was born in Rome than to have to give as her birthplace New York or Washington or any of those cities that have so little past."

From the rather diffident girl I once knew, my hostess had developed into an articulate worldly matron who was a fount of sharp observations. Compulsively witty, she was even able to joke about her husband's pancreas, which that very morning had unexpectedly landed him in a hospital bed, where, she said, "he lay thinking of all the gourmet goodies we had planned for dinner and groaning with pain and frustration, while they fed him intravenously."

When the conversation got around to Dolci, my hostess, who had published several articles about him which expressed a deep admiration, now declared flatly that she no longer cared for him. She offered no explanation of what had caused her change of heart. The translator, it developed, had also written about Dolci, being the author of one of the first articles about Dolci to appear in the American press. He had published it in *Esquire* under a pseudonym in the late fifties when the authorities were hostile toward Dolci. "I felt I had to use a pen name. I didn't want the Italian government to kick me out of the country just because of Dolci." Unlike the hostess's, his attitude toward Dolci was still friendly, but he too believed that as a social reformer he had lost his shock value.

The next evening we dined with the novelist Ignazio Silone, an old acquaintance of mine, and his Irish wife. Silone had been one of Dolci's earliest and staunchest supporters. In 1952 when Dolci was establishing his Borgo di Dio, a school and nursery for

29

the orphaned children of Trappeto, the novelist contributed a sizable sum of money toward the construction of the building. Later he raised his voice in vehement protest against Dolci's arrest for his strike in reverse. When Dolci was arrested a second time, in 1957, on charges of publishing pornographic material, Silone wrote a pamphlet in his defense.

A modest man, he made no mention of these facts when we discussed Dolci. He expressed a great deal of respect for him, but it was clear that he had lost confidence in Dolci's ability to change the Sicilian situation. "How can he get anywhere when the very people he seeks to educate to his point of view are leaving Sicily to look for jobs elsewhere? Most of the people left in the villages are old men, women, and children. What on earth can he do with them?" He had reached the conclusion that Dolci was "politically naïve." "He goes from one extreme to another," he continued. "On the one hand he gives the impression of cooperating with the Communists. On the other hand, he suddenly starts cooperating with the executives of a big industry like Montecatini, who play ball with him because they like the fact that he is trying to teach Sicilian peasants the advantages of using their chemical fertilizers. Yet I think you are wise in writing about him. Dolci is a fascinating phenomenon, a man of great integrity with a definite voice that touches the conscience."

Silone was interested to learn that one of our dinner engagements in Rome was to be with a Sicilian princess, who had stopped using her title when she became an ardent crusader for birth control in Sicily. Her name was Rosita Lanza. In New York I had been told that she operated a more or less clandestine birth control center in Palermo. Ruminating on the problem of birth control among the poor, Silone observed that, by some method still unknown to him, the size of families among the relatives and friends he knew in his native province of Abruzzi had greatly diminished in the past few years.

"They used to have as many as ten and a dozen children—one family I knew had eighteen—but now families seldom have more than two. These people still feel they are good Catholics; they simply use their common sense to vary the rules of the Church to suit their convenience. And they do this without hurting their conscience. Let me give you an example. As you know, there are usually several priests in a village who hear confessions. The questioning of the women in the confessional usually goes like this: 'How long have you been married? How many children do you have? So few? How do you explain the fact that in so many years of marriage there have been so few children?'

"The women do not dare lie to the priest while they are in the confessional. But occasionally there is a priest who, either out of neglect or for some reason of his own, does not ask this set of questions. As soon as one woman discovers such a priest, the news is circulated throughout the village and before long all the women are going to him with their confessions and ignoring the other priests . . ."

We had already had one encounter with the crusading Rosita Lanza, just before she was to fly to Palermo to visit her birth control center. She was a handsome middle-aged woman with luminous brown eyes that became stormy when she spoke about the plight of poor and ignorant Sicilian women. The most serious obstacle in her work to educate them, she said, was the opposition of the Catholic Church.

"It is sad how easily the poor can be intimidated by the Church," she added, and told how her attempts to draw women to meetings where she could discuss birth control with them were frustrated in Palermo by a priest who threatened the women in his parish with excommunication and eternal perdition if they set foot in any of her meetings. "For those who didn't take those threats seriously, he had another threat: he would ask the police to raid the meetings and arrest all the women present. As a result of all this, my meetings kept getting smaller and smaller. I was about to give them up altogether when I read in the newspapers that the same priest had eloped with a young woman in his parish.

"How terrible it is that priests have so much power. I keep telling the women who come to my meetings: 'Bear in mind that the priests cannot possibly understand your problems since they have not had any sexual experience. If they have had some, then they are hypocrites, for they must pretend not to have had any, and hypocrites are never to be trusted."

She blamed the Catholic Church for the continuation of "reac-

31

tionary Italian laws" which make family planning in her country illegal. "The same laws that served the Fascist government are still in the law books. And they are so unjust. For example, the Penal Code specifies that it is a crime for women to have abortions; yet the same Code makes it a crime to teach women how to avoid having unwanted children. Everybody knows how prevalent abortions are in Italy—at least a million a year—yet the law remains unchanged. That is what I consider evil: the legalized denial of truth. The rich, of course, have no trouble getting around the law. It is only the poor who suffer, the mothers who can't cope with all the children they already have."

From mutual friends, we learned something of Rosita Lanza's background. Like Florence Nightingale, she had become discontented with the prospect of leading an upper-class social existence, and at the age of eighteen had persuaded her parents to let her work as a practical nurse in a hospital. There, watching women sick with too much childbearing and children dying from malnutrition, she became impressed with the tragedy of poor families who are ignorant of birth control, and resolved to do something about it.

At first she tried to explain the rhythm method to mothers in the slums of Palermo, but most of them lost patience with it either because they found it too complicated—"It requires the services of a bookkeeper to keep track of things"—or because they could not rely on the cooperation of their husbands—"My husband wants to make love when he feels like it, not when the calendar says he may." Rosita Lanza then bought sponges, cut them into pieces, and explained how they could be used as contraceptives. Later on, she was able to import an obstetrician from London, a woman who was an expert in contraceptive techniques. Together, they taught several hundred women how to use the diaphragm.

"You would have thought that these women would have told other women about it," Rosita Lanza said the next time we met, in her elegant apartment overlooking the Forum. "But they hung on to the information as though it were a terrible secret that would create trouble if it became known. They're afraid of their priests, of course; but they are also very worried about what their neighbors might think . . ."

"What about Sicilian husbands?" I asked. "Do you include them in your educational program?"

She prefaced her remarks with a wry smile. "Unfortunately, too many Sicilian husbands have bigger egos than they have brains. In the poorer class especially, where people have so few satisfactions in life, the average husband is a self-indulgent creature who doesn't lift a finger to spare his wife the agony of a pregnancy she shouldn't have—a pregnancy she often has to stop secretly, at the risk of her life, so that her husband can keep his precious pride intact."

As we were parting, she said: "Please, when you talk with Danilo Dolci, try to convince him to support my work in Sicily. I supported him in the early days of his work in Trappeto, when hardly anyone paid any attention to him. Now he should lend his name to my birth control project. That is all I ask for—the use of his name."

Before the end of our Roman visit, I was given another message to give to Dolci, this one by Franco Restivo, who had been head of the Sicilian Regional Government when Dolci conducted his first fast to protest against the misery of Trappeto. Now Vice-President of Parliament, he represented the province of Palermo in the Italian House of Deputies.

As in the days of Mussolini, the approach to a high government official was designed to awe the layman. An armed guard read my credentials with such severity in his eyes as to suggest he might have to shoot me. I was then passed on to a receptionist with a gaudy uniform, who examined the credentials with a benign smile, as if to assure me I would not be shot this time. When he was done with me, I was asked to follow a guide dressed in tails, who led me through an up and down maze of red-carpeted hallways until we reached an enormous antechamber occupied by a half dozen glaring flunkeys. They stopped glaring when Restivo came out of a door to greet me. After ordering coffee for both of us, he led me into his office, another enormous room with a ceiling as high as that of the Sistine Chapel.

Restivo had a stocky body, horn-rimmed glasses, and a polished manner which I sensed had been acquired through years of prac-

33

tice. After some small talk about my age—I had told him I had been absent from Italy for eighteen years and he had said I must have been a child then—it developed that I was two years older than he. However, my seniority did not deter him from speaking almost incessantly during the next forty minutes.

His monologue dealt mainly with the character of the average Sicilian, his inclination to see too many sides of a question, and his propensity to distort his sense of reality with his fantasizing. Danilo Dolci, Restivo declared, is an intelligent man but is not Sicilian enough to realize what a complex people he is dealing with. "With his non-Sicilian directness, his demands for prompt action, he is constantly at odds with the very people he wants to help. By nature Sicilians are great procrastinators. And to some degree they are right. Some matters need considerable deliberation, such as deciding where a dam is to be built, but Dolci becomes impatient with any delays. The result is confusion . . ."

Having determined from my credentials that I was a writer of books, he sprinkled his talk with frequent similes and literary references. He likened Sicily to the anguished heroine of a novel who had lived in dire poverty all her life without complaint until someone gave her a pair of spectacles and she was able to see for the first time the horrors of her situation. Television, he said, provided the Sicilians with their first "spectacles"; now they can see enough of the outside world to understand how shocking their condition is.

To illustrate the tendency of Sicilians to talk rather than act, he recounted a "true story" about Luigi Pirandello, which the author himself had told him. After the Sicilian writer won the Nobel Prize for literature, he received hundreds of letters from people he had known in the past. Except for one letter from a former schoolmate, he was able to ignore all of them. The ex-schoolmate admitted he had never read any of Pirandello's writings but that his father-in-law knew most of his books and was a great admirer of his. "From the moment I mentioned the fact that you and I knew each other as schoolboys in Agrigento," he wrote, "my father-in-law, for the first time since I married his daughter, began to treat me as a person who deserves respect. But, unfortunately, the old man is a skeptic, and I am afraid that any day now he may start

34

thinking that I was bragging about something that isn't true." He begged Pirandello to visit him soon, so as to kill any doubts his father-in-law might develop.

Pirandello was so touched by the frankness of the letter that the next time he visited friends in Agrigento, he took a train to the small village near Caltanisetta where his former schoolmate now lived. Arriving after dark, he found that the village was completely without any lighting system. He stumbled around the darkness for more than an hour before he found his friend's house. As soon as he entered, he expressed his anger and disgust that in the twentieth century a village should permit itself to be without electricity. His vehemence persuaded his hosts to take the matter up immediately with the village mayor. After sampling Pirandello's ire, the mayor felt constrained to call an emergency meeting of the village's leading citizens.

The mayor opened the meeting with the proposal that electricity be installed in the village. A heated debate followed. Some of the citizens favored the proposal and said so at great length; others favored gas over electricity, and there was a third group who argued that any lighting system would impose too heavy a financial burden on the village. The arguments went on and on, and when there was no more kerosene in the oil lamps, the meeting continued in candlelight. At dawn nothing had been resolved, but they were still talking. Finally the mayor tabled his proposal on the grounds that they all needed some rest.

"Pirandello visited the village sometime during the mid-thirties," Restivo said. "Not until the fifties did the village acquire electricity. When you see Danilo Dolci, I wish you would tell him this story. It might help him understand that the Sicilian problem is not as simple as he thinks it is."

At Andrea Bellini's suggestion, we called on another Sicilian living in Rome, the artist Bruno Caruso, who for several years had been warring against the Mafia with all the savagery of his pen. The arresting drawings that stared at us from every wall in his studio were impressive evidence of Caruso's contention that art should function mainly as a weapon for social progress. According to several critics, his caricatures of *mafiosi* already had so functioned: in a nation that had long accepted the Mafia as a somewhat romantic phenomenon restricted to western Sicily, Caruso had "successfully unmasked and delineated its brutal and pervasive evil," and in that way helped to arouse public opinion against the "Honored Society" on a nation-wide scale.

The faces of his portraits were hard and shrewd, the eyes ferocious, and in almost every instance there was a show of teeth, with each tooth separately emphasized. One was the portrait of a *mafioso* who is cleaning his nails with the same dagger that he uses on his victims. Another was a *mafioso* with one thumb stuck in his belt, who is bragging that "we will kill anyone we wish and make you like it." A third showed a victim who had received a Mafia "warning," a slash of the knife extending from the forehead to the chin.

A fast-talking man in his thirties, whose excited temperament was belied by the tight control he exercised in his art, Caruso's feelings against the Mafia constantly spilled over into his conversation. The Italian government, he claimed, was "infested" with high officials who used *mafiosi* tactics to remain there, one of them a member of the cabinet who used hired gunmen to achieve his ends. When I told him I had interviewed Restivo, he said he had been conducting an attack against one of Restivo's colleagues who, at one point, summoned him to his office and showed him a thick batch of check stubs indicating payments to prominent Italians in all levels of society. "He wanted to prove to me that he had found all of them corruptible, willing to take his money. I think he expected me to become one of them . . ."

Danilo Dolci, he said, was a personal friend of his and a thoroughly honest man, but he lacked the "political savvy necessary to get what he wants." As an illustration of what he meant, he cited the fast that Dolci had conducted two years before in Roccamena as part of his effort to have a dam constructed on the Belice River. "His action received enormous publicity and persuaded the government to do something about it. But instead of making sure that the dam got started, he let the matter drop. And, of course, the authorities did the same. Now I understand that he is about to stage another campaign in Roccamena, but in the meantime two years have been lost."

Caruso could not speak for long without giving vent to his satirical nature. On the subject of Dolci's hunger strikes, he claimed that a number of the peasants who were committed to joining Dolci in one of the mass fasts he had led had secretly devoured huge sandwiches the day of the fast; then, in a spirit of guilt, had secretly added an egg to Dolci's coffee (the only form of sustenance he had agreed to receive on that particular occasion) in order to give him the strength they were certain he needed to cope with treacherous supporters like themselves.

Every morning at my typewriter, as I faced the gloom of the pines in the Villa Borghese, many of them broken and torn by the recent snowstorm, I tried to catch the sound and the content of the February voices that spoke to me about Dolci. The scene before me, as much as the cold of the hotel room, seemed to match the chilling mood of what I recorded. The temperature of the voices differed, according to the amenities dictated by the circumstances, but their veiled hostility and the standardized attitudes they expressed were all too apparent; I found myself wondering to what extent the voices represented a collectively guilty conscience spawned from being comfortable in Rome, while secretly aware that Dolci and his collaborators must be engaged in a far from comfortable mission.

Only once during our Roman sojourn did we encounter an enthusiastic and fully informed champion of Dolci, a native Italian woman who had spent part of her youth in South Philadelphia. Tonia, an author whose poetry and fiction had been widely published, was living with her alcoholic husband, an American would-be novelist who detested Rome. They had been married in New York a few years before, and moved to Rome in the hope that the change of environment would reduce his drinking and make it possible for him to continue writing his novel. But after a year it was clear to Tonia that he was worse off than he had been. His ignorance of Italian kept him in a state of sulking alienation, and he talked nostalgically about their life in New York, where they had many friends and no problems of communication. They were both anxious to leave Rome, but their lack of funds kept them imprisoned there. "I would go anywhere," he said, "even to Sicily. Rome doesn't wear well when you don't know the language. You're restricted to a bunch of phony Americans who think they are being fashionable by living here but who are as unhappy a group as you can find anywhere."

His resentment toward Rome had rubbed off on Tonia. "I used to dream of living here but now I find the city as cold as a museum. Even the artists in Rome have acquired the greediness of the times and seem to put monetary values ahead of everything else." She placed an arm around her husband. "How I wish we could go to Sicily with you. There is much ignorance there, I know, but there is also great human warmth and an understanding of basic values. Danilo Dolci knows this, and that is why every fast of his is an act of love . . ."

"Who would ever fast for the Romans?" her husband asked.

Although aware of all the criticism directed against Dolci, Tonia's admiration for him was unstinted: "You will hear people saying many cruel things about him. Some of them are the same people who used to say he was a saint. Apparently, he disappointed them by not dying, by not becoming a martyr. But no matter what they say about him, his value is tremendous. He is a constant shock on the Italian conscience. Everything he does keeps reminding the Italians how remiss they have been in trying to ignore the misery of Sicily."

On the eve of our departure from Rome we were dinner guests at the home of Dolci's former secretary, Victoria Bawtree, who two weeks before had married a Neapolitan economist and become Mrs. Giuseppe Lo Iacono. New York had not appealed to her—"it wasn't my cup of tea"—and after a few months she had returned to Italy to work for the Food and Agricultural Organization, a branch of the United Nations, editing a bulletin that deals with "the fight against hunger." The frenetic look I had noticed in Philadelphia was gone. Her apple-cheeked face was softer, and her eyes glowed, as though powered by some fresh secret.

She had two house guests, her parents, who through circumstances that could not be avoided, had arrived for their annual two-week visit in the midst of the honeymoon period, a situation which everyone concerned seemed to accept with good grace. "After all," joked Mr. Bawtree, as he proposed a toast to the newlyweds, "it isn't every father who can be present during his daughter's honeymoon." He was a tall, handsome gentleman with iron-gray hair, whose appearance matched his vocation, that of an English country squire.

The only subdued member of the group was the Neapolitan husband, a thin balding man with tired features, which he attributed to the frequent business trips he was obliged to make to Milan. "It would be much more convenient for us to live in Milan," he told us while we were alone with him. "Milan is a modern city with many more modern conveniences than Rome, but Victoria is enamored of this city's past and insists we stay here. I find it a very inefficient place." But if he could not influence his wife to leave Rome, he could influence her in other ways, especially in her attitude toward Dolci, which, apparently conditioned by her husband's criticism of him, had changed radically.

Victoria's staunch allegiance to Dolci as a heroic figure, so evident in Philadelphia, had become a thing of the past. Although she retained some feelings of friendship for him, she was now more willing to speak of his faults than of his virtues, particularly of "his lack of talent as an organizer." In the past she had accepted this shortcoming philosophically, as a flaw that could be overcome by the services of a dedicated and qualified assistant; but now she regarded it as a major handicap that seriously jeopardized the work of his group.

"Danilo is not capable of working with others," she said flatly. "He should work alone." And she told me what I had already heard in New York: that there had been a schism in Dolci's ranks, which led to a wholesale exodus headed by Eyvind Hytten, a former executive secretary of the Study Center in Partinico. The exodus had apparently been precipitated by the rebels' attempt to exile Dolci to Palermo and put Hytten in his place. I also learned that Hytten was now trying to raise funds for an institute in Palermo that would train young men to become leaders in underdeveloped countries. From the way that Victoria spoke of Hytten it was quite clear that she had become one of his sympathizers.

"Dolci is not a trained sociologist, though he tries to give that impression in his books," her husband said. "But Eyvind Hytten is a professional sociologist in every sense of the word. I don't know whether you realize that he has been a professor at several distinguished universities. That's what Sicily needs: experts, not a

39

Danilo Dolci, whose chief interest is to become more famous."

Before I could make any comment, Mrs. Bawtree, who was unable to follow the conversation since it was in Italian, intervened to invite Patricia and me to visit their country home in England, an invitation which was heartily seconded by her husband. That was the end of any discussion about Danilo Dolci. Although I was tempted to argue the points made by the Neapolitan, I managed to keep my mouth shut. Surrounded by newlyweds, who were bent on sharing each other's opinions, and by Victoria's parents, who kept declaring their pleasure to be with English-speaking friends of their daughter, the problems of Dolci seemed to become irrelevant to the congeniality of the company. Only when we returned to our chilly hotel room and looked at the broken pines in the Villa Borghese did I think of Dolci again.

Chapter

3

Danilo
Among Disciples

HE STOOD NEXT TO us at the rail of the ferry that was crossing the straits of Messina, somewhat amused by his discovery that we were foreigners, and took pride in pointing out to us those monuments of mythology, Scylla and Charybdis. His blue eyes and lanky body suggested he might be from the north of Italy, but his accent definitely identified him as a Sicilian. What interested me most about him was the color of his suit, which was not unlike that of the purple-blue mist obscuring the Sicilian coast in the distance. I associated it with that of a suit worn by a favorite uncle which had been made from cloth sent to him by a relative of Sambuca. It was a blue, faintly tinged with purple, that was to become synonymous in my mind with Sicily. Not the purple-blue of an eye or a flower, but a particularly Sicilian purple-blue, which for me evoked childhood memories as subtle and pleasurable as those which Proust could derive from a spoonful of tea.

Impulsively, I asked the man in the purple-blue suit whether by chance he came from Sambuca. He looked startled at first, as though I had accused him of committing a misdemeanor, but then smiled and explained that he had always lived in Catania. "I once went to Sambuca for a few hours but I don't think we could have met there. When were you there?" he asked.

I told him I had never been to Sambuca.

"You're fortunate. It's a miserable town," he said, and frowned.

"You mean it is poor."

41

"No, I mean it is miserable," he insisted. "That does not offend you, I hope. Perhaps you have friends or relatives there."

"A friend of mine came from there," I lied.

"And what made you think I did?"

"You look like my friend," I improvised.

He laughed. "The poor fellow." After a while he said, "If you want to see a part of Sicily that is both beautiful and progressive you should visit Catania, not Sambuca, which is a dirty country village in the Mafia district."

"Have you ever heard of Danilo Dolci?" I asked.

"No. Is he from Sambuca too?"

"He lives in Partinico."

He frowned again. "That's twice as miserable as Sambuca because it is considerably larger. You will find the eastern part of Sicily much better, more advanced. There is more water there and no Mafia whatsoever."

"I have heard it said that western Sicily is quite beautiful," I said, feeling defensive about that part of the island where my parents had come from.

"Yes, I suppose it is beautiful but it is also miserable. The people there keep it that way. People in eastern Sicily are more civilized. They really ought to give western Sicily back to the Turks . . ."

Before he could ask me where my relatives came from, I changed the subject by pointing to a news story on the front page of a Catania newspaper which told of "a crime of honor": a brother had killed his sister's lover to restore the purity of the family name. "I'm surprised that this kind of thing still goes on," I said. "Do you have many crimes of honor in Catania?"

"A few," he said. "They are usually committed by persons who were reared in western Sicily. People pay more attention to old customs there. However, you must understand that all Sicilians place a very high premium on honor. Even a civilized Sicilian is capable of murder if it means protecting his honor."

I was about to retort that murder, whatever its motive, is always an uncivilized action, but just in time my eye caught the headlines of another news story which told of civilian casualties in Vietnam, and once again I was able to restrain myself. By then the purple-blue mist had cleared, revealing the face of Messina in its early-morning glory, and it was time for all the passengers to return to their train compartments for the entrance into Sicily.

The first sign we noticed as we rode through the train yards of Messina bore the drawing of a skull and bones and the caption *Pericolo di Morte* (Danger of Death). But it proved to be nothing more sinister than a warning not to touch a highly charged network of power lines. The rest of the four-hour trip along the coastline to Palermo was a heady montage of mountains, sea, and farmland that was festooned with buttercups, almond blossoms, and orange and lemon groves. The gray and brown flesh of the mountains heightened the colors in the fields. Every now and then the eye would be startled by the sudden presence of a weirdly sculptured promontory jutting its wind-hewn head over the purple-blue waters, like some massive sea monster that had become paralyzed in midair.

The hypnotic power of the scenery would often be broken at each train stop by the antics of a man, most often the station-master. Though usually spacious of girth, he would race along the side of the train with the nimbleness of a ballet dancer, holding aloft an object that looked like a circular fly swatter but which he used like a magic wand. The purpose of his frenetic movements remained a mystery to me. Dressed in an opera-bouffe uniform of black and red, he suggested a performer on stage who had lost his sense of direction without losing his feeling of self-importance. There was no mystery about his importance. Only when he, and he alone, decided it was time to wave his wand could the train proceed.

Halfway down the coast we began to see telltale signs of the twentieth century that had been absent when I traversed the same area eighteen years before: an occasional industrial plant, two or three mechanical monsters mouthing the sea for oil, irrigation pipes snaking their way through cultivated fields, and the very first tractor I had ever beheld in Sicily. A shiny new truck arrestingly combined the present with the past. On its sides were depicted in raging colors and blood-curdling detail, traditional scenes of the Crusaders battling the Pagans, the very same theme that is often painted on the sides of Sicilian peasant carts. But the most emphatic evidence that the present had finally come to Sicily were

43

the galaxies of new, modern apartment houses in and around Palermo, tall structures of Mondrian colors and shapes, as amazing to the senses as the weird promontories on the coast. Nothing seemed more un-Sicilian to me at that moment, not even the couple in the next compartment babbling in German.

Before proceeding to Partinico, we spent two days in Palermo, talking with various American consulate officials about my Fulbright project, and indulging in the luxury of a hotel that could provide all the hot water we could use. None of the American officials evinced any enthusiasm for my plan to work with Dolci. They disapproved of the man for his leftwing connections, particularly for his association with the anti-American newspaper *L'Ora*, for which Dolci had recently begun to write a column. But though they were cool toward Dolci, their attitude toward me was friendly and helpful, and they extended courtesies which went beyond their call of duty, including the use of a car and chauffeur for our move to Partinico.

In our blind craving for hot water, a luxury we had not known in Rome, we selected a hotel which turned out to be the favorite haunt of top echelon *mafiosi*. The hotel was a ninteenth-century palace of a building on the Via Roma that was filled with antique ornaments and statuary. It was here, we learned soon after we registered, that the *mafiosi* chiefs met in informal sessions, sipping daintily their tiny cups of espresso while they determined who was to dispose of whom. It occurred to me then that we might have gotten into more hot water than we had bargained for, and every swarthy man in the lobby began to assume a sinister aspect, even the undoubtedly innocent hotel clerk who, though not swarthy, had a scar on one cheek.

But more disconcerting than our sense of apprehension was the acute embarrassment of having Danilo Dolci and his friend Franco Alasia unexpectedly appear at the hotel to welcome us to Sicily. "Whatever made you choose this place?" was the first question he asked after greeting us. But his concern was not the same as mine; he was simply thinking of the expense. The next time we visited Palermo, he promised, he would direct us to a hotel which was equipped with as much hot water and cost half the price.

Danilo, as I called him from then on, had lost a great deal of weight; he was no longer a fat man, his body moved with an alacrity it had not had in Philadelphia. He explained that he and Franco could only stay a few minutes; they were on their way to a meeting to discuss the formation of a new cultural group that would bring speakers, chiefly artists and authors, to Palermo. "This city is a cultural desert," Danilo said. We sat on a divan near a cluster of men in black suits who sipped on espresso cups; like snakes sizing up their prey, they could not take their eyes off Danilo. Except to lower his voice, he ignored them as he asked me if I would consent to be one of the speakers for the new group.

At that moment I would have consented to anything he proposed, so strong was my guilt at having the "Gandhi of Sicily" catch me inhabiting this excessively ornate Mafia hangout. Later it developed that my promise to be a speaker for his group was to be the most serious error I was to commit during my association with Dolci.

Before we parted, Danilo gave me a press release issued by the Swedish Friends of Dolci and a copy of a clipping from the *Manchester Guardian,* suggesting that I read the material at my leisure, so that we might discuss it in Partinico. As we rose from the divan, Franco's eyes traveled over the opulent décor of the lobby, and with a nervous smile he said: "I'm afraid there is nothing luxurious about the house we've rented for you. To begin with, it's in a slum . . ."

"Don't worry about the Mangiones," Danilo interrupted crisply; then raising his voice, as though to make certain the black-suited men nearby heard him, he assured me that either he or Franco would meet the U.S. Government car when it arrived at the main piazza of Partinico the next morning. His emphasis on *"U.S. Government car"* was unmistakable.

The clipping from the *Manchester Guardian* was headlined "Attempt to Replace Dolci in Sicily"; it consisted of an interview in London with Eyvind Hytten, who told of his split with Dolci and described his plans for establishing an institute in Palermo to train development workers. He was quoted as saying: "We did not want to be instruments for maintaining Dolci's fame. We wanted his fame to be an instrument for our work for Sicilians. I think that we, more than Dolci, now represent the possibility of doing

45

something for Sicily." Speaking of the institute, Hytten added that Sicily was "an ideal place" to give practical training to development workers from all parts of the world. The writer of the article concluded: "It is not yet certain that the institute will come into being. Nor is it certain that the decline of Dolci's organization is irreversible. But there seems to be some logic in the progression from Dolci the saint to Hytten the technocrat."

The Swedish committee's press release, however, indignantly denied any logic to the situation. "We deplore the manner in which Hytten has publicly taken a stand against Dolci," it said; then fully washing its hands of Hytten, whose work with Dolci the Swedish group had originally sponsored, it declared: "We will in no way participate in Hytten's plans, but will continue to support Danilo Dolci in his tireless campaign to release Sicily from the grip of poverty and a powerful Mafia." Another part of the statement sharply criticized the *Manchester Guardian* for giving its readers the false impression that Hytten had become Dolci's legitimate successor in Sicily.

Early the next morning the longest and blackest American car I had ever beheld arrived at the hotel to take us to Partinico. To my joyful surprise the driver was Salvatore Gangi, an old friend, who on my previous venture in Sicily had accompanied me on a leisurely journey that took us all around the island in a station wagon. His assignment then had been to show in scores of villages American documentary films sponsored by the U.S. Information Service. He was still doing film work for the U.S.I.S., but when he heard that his office was providing a car for us, he had insisted on being the chauffeur. "Today, being Saturday, is my day off and I could think of no happier way of spending it," he said pumping my arm.

I recognized him at once. But though his face had little changed the once powerful body that resembled that of a wrestler seemed to have shrunk.

"For a while I didn't think I would live to see you again," he told me as we left the center of Palermo. "I was dying of a heart condition and the doctors gave me no hope. It was only a blessed miracle from heaven that saved me."

"Don't tell me you believe in miracles?" I teased.

46

"Of course I do," he said quickly.

He had changed, I thought. During the month we had traveled together through Sicily I had been struck by his pragmatic view of life; though he had little education, he seemed to be completely free of the superstitions that plague many Sicilians.

"A man of your education may not be able to have faith in miracles," he added, "but I do. And so does my son. One day, while I was at the hospital still in my pajamas, we got into my car and drove day and night until we got to Lourdes. I prayed for two days, and then I was cured. I think that having my son with me helped. I have not always been a good father but he has always been a very good lad. If God is willing, he will become a priest one day."

"Then you are no longer anti-clerical?"

"Of course not," he replied. "There are many things I understand now that I did not know eighteen years ago."

Once we had passed Monreale, the hilltop town next to Palermo that houses a cathedral famous for its great Byzantine mosaics, we began to drive through territory I had never seen before, first along the sumptuous valley known as the Golden Shell, a fertile expanse that extends from the sea to the mountains in undulating terraces thronged with orange and lemon trees. Beyond the valley, we traveled through harsh mountain scenery, bald and forbidding under the gray scowling sky, constantly beset by breathtaking hairpin curves, which Gangi handled with ease. "This used to be bandit territory," he said, and pointed first to the mountain village of Montelepre where Giuliano had come from, then to a number of caves that had served as hideaways for his band. Next to Montelepre were three or four other villages, all perched on mountain tops like a family of sharply-beaked white birds.

I asked Gangi whether he considered Partinico a dangerous town.

"There used to be a murder there nearly every day but during this past year, for the first time in many years, no one has been murdered yet. But you and Mrs. Mangione have no cause for worry. The Mafia never bothers with foreigners. In Sicily they only kill people they know well. . . . Forgive me for asking, but why have you chosen Partinico to live in? There are so many other

47

towns in Sicily that are so much more beautiful. The only attractive thing about Partinico is its wine, which is the best in the province. But surely that can't be the reason you chose it . . ."

As I described my project, it became evident that Gangi had never heard of Danilo Dolci. After explaining what Dolci was doing to encourage Sicilians to free themselves of their misery, I noticed that Gangi was grinning. "Ah," he said, "then I am not the only one who believes in miracles." A little while later while we were passing through a notorious Mafia stronghold called Borgetto, Gangi nodded toward an extensive tract of houses huddled on a plain between the mountains and the sea, and we began to descend toward Partinico. The road became broader as we entered the town, then narrowed again before we reached the main piazza, which was flanked by the Cathedral on one side and a line of sundry shops opposite it. The area between them was crowded with small and large knots of men in black caps who, apparently immersed in their conversations, were indifferent to the rain that had just begun to fall. From one of the knots emerged Franco Alasia, unshaven and bareheaded, smiling as he extended his hand to us through the car window. I noticed that his face had the chalky pallor of a sick man's.

We followed his small Fiat down a main thoroughfare until we reached the police station, then turned sharply into a narrow street bumpy with cobblestones, through which ran a narrow cement trough that served as a drain. This was the Via Emma, where we were to live. Old women in black and children stared at us through open doorways. From both sides of the street radios shouted the news of the day and Italian versions of jazz. We passed an intersection with a public fountain where women bearing water jars were clustered in the rain. At the same intersection a group of chickens and a mangy mongrel were feeding from a soggy mound of garbage. Nearby a group of young boys, among them a one-armed ragamuffin, were pitching marbles against a wall.

About fifty feet beyond the fountain Franco pulled up before a four-story house with balconies on the second and third floors and a sun terrace on the fourth. Our apartment, which included the balconies and the terrace, consisted of three rooms and a pink tiled bathroom (without hot water); it started on the second floor and extended upwards, one room at a time. The pink bathroom and the terrace were the apartment's most impressive features. From the terrace we had three enticing views of Partinico. In front of us were spread hundreds of red rooftops which, even in the rain, took on the aspect of a gaudy tablecloth. To our left, at the entrance of the town, a sentinel in the shape of a mountain gleamed blue through the gray mist; to our right, less than five miles away, the Mediterranean curved sensuously into a border of green fields.

There was no time to dally; Franco had orders to take us to a meeting of Danilo's Consiglio Technico (Technical Council) which was to begin in a few minutes. Gangi, who seemed reluctant to leave, finally took me aside and whispered what was on his mind: if Partinico should prove too unpleasant, he would be glad to take us away, any time of the day or night. I promised to bear that in mind, and he left, heading for a wineshop recommended by Franco.

Obviously relieved that the apartment had met with our approval, Franco became cheerful and informed us that the sight of the U.S.I.S. car, "so big and so American," had sent a shudder through the *mafiosi* assembled on the piazza that morning. "I could see the expression on their faces as the car drove up and you called out my name. Anything, of course, that makes the Mafia think that our group has important connections is all to the good."

Danilo, intent on greeting us and making certain we found our living quarters satisfactory, barely listened as Franco repeated the observation for his benefit. Seated behind his desk, he was in his most efficient mood, as he handed me a list of the purchases he suggested for making the apartment more comfortable, issued an invitation to his home for both the midday and evening meals, in order to relieve Patricia of cooking chores "on this first and probably most difficult day," and tactfully determined that I had not changed my mind about working for him, an exercise in caution that made me wonder if he was afraid I had come under the influence of Hytten or his friends. Once assured I was still on his side, he explained that I could be most useful as an English translator and interpreter since none of his present collaborators knew that language.

"Why don't you learn English?" I suggested. "I might be able to help you."

He shook his head. "There are too many things to do now.

49

Someday perhaps after one or two more dams get built. After today's meeting you will understand how many things must get done in a relatively short time . . ."

Before the meeting began, he showed me a small room with a desk, chair, and typewriter that was to serve as my office. On its door was a card with my name typed on it. "You see," he said, twinkling, "I had already counted on your help . . ."

We returned to his office where staff members, representing the study centers in western Sicily under Danilo's jurisdiction, were gathering around a long conference table. I noticed for the first time what a barn of a room it was, with walls at least fourteen feet tall. The one opposite Danilo's desk bore a series of posters dominated by three headlines: "The Dam is Prosperity," "The Dam is Progress," "The Dam is the Future." The wall nearest to the desk displayed large photographs of Einstein, Gandhi, and Lenin, arranged below each other in that descending order. The hugeness of the room accentuated its dampness and cold; the only heat came from a small circular contraption fueled by butane gas. As we sat around the conference table studying the agenda Franco had given each of us, I saw small clouds of vapor issuing from the mouths of the assembled, and I could not help thinking of the early Christians holding secret meetings in the damp catacombs of Rome.

Symbolically enough, there were twelve persons at the table. To my surprise, all of them, with the exception of Patricia and me, were either Sicilian or Italian. Evidently all of Dolci's chief foreign collaborators had left the Center with Hytten. Danilo introduced us to the group, then asked me to say a few words about my reasons for being in Partinico. After that the group concentrated on the main purpose of the meeting: to resolve the final details of what was undoubtedly to be the most ambitious action the Center had ever undertaken: a campaign entitled "Week of Mourning" to bring pressure on the authorities for the construction of the dam on the Belice, the same cause for which Danilo and the English pacifist, Peter Moule, had fasted for ten days two years earlier.

The operation, as described, would open on Sunday noon in Roccamena with a deliberate act of civil disobedience—the occupation of the main piazza by a group of volunteers headed by Danilo and his lieutenant, Lorenzo Barbera. After a forty-eight-hour fast, they would be replaced by a second group of volunteers who would also fast for forty-eight hours. The end of the fasting would be marked with a mass march to the Belice River that would include representatives of the twenty-two villages in the "dying Belice valley." As an expression of the mourning theme, all electricity in the valley would be turned off that night. In the final event of the campaign, a representative group of mayors would accompany Lorenzo and Danilo to Rome, and stage a silent march from the railroad station to the Parliament.

Barbera, who had been designated to coordinate the events, reported that he had been traveling through the valley during the past week making certain that the mayors of the villages would participate in the demonstrations or send delegates to take their places. All political parties except the neofascists, he said, would be represented. "As far as I can determine, only the police and the priests are opposing the demonstrations. Everyone else thinks they should be supported." In many of the villages, he added, the police were carrying on a systematic program of intimidation, trying to discourage people from taking part in the campaign. Some of the priests were trying to do the same from their pulpits. One priest had refused to listen to Barbera, saying: "My business is saving souls and nothing else."

Although Barbera spoke authoritatively about the role that each person around the table was to play in the operation, I sensed a certain reluctance to assume as much leadership as Danilo had thrust upon him. He may have felt too inexperienced to do justice to the responsibility, or he may have been afraid that Danilo might regret sharing the limelight of publicity with him. At one point he startled the group by declaring flatly that he would not go to Rome with the delegation of mayors.

"Why are you saying that?" Danilo asked, obviously put out.

"Well, for one thing," Barbera said, "it would save us some money. For another, I believe it would be wise for me to remain in Roccamena after the demonstrations—just in case something should go wrong there."

But no one, not even his Roman wife Paola, with whom he managed the Study Center in Roccamena, agreed with him. It was

51

"psychologically important," his wife insisted, that he accompany Danilo and the delegation to Rome. With his closely cropped curly brown head and cherubic lips, Barbera resembled a scowling angel as he listened to her and the others. There was nothing angelic about the rest of him. His short, powerful body and broad shoulders were those of a Sicilian of the soil, which is what he once had been.

I already knew something about him from reading his recently published documentary study, *The Dam at Roccamena,* which is largely based on personal encounters with the residents of that village. The biographical note in the book revealed that he was born of peasant stock in Partinico in 1936, and received enough schooling to qualify as an elementary school teacher. At the age of twenty, while waiting for a teaching post, he became acquainted with Danilo, and helped him investigate the extent of prostitution in Partinico. Pleased with his work, Danilo encouraged him to attend a social work school in Rome. There he met and married Paola, a fellow student, and on completing his studies in 1960 took charge of the Study Center at Roccamena. *The Dam at Roccamena,* which followed four years later, is obviously influenced by the style of Danilo's earlier books, but it reveals one advantage Barbera has over his mentor: a native grasp of the Sicilian dialect, which enables him to extract confidences that few Sicilians will share with a non-Sicilian. Temperamentally and physically, the two men are quite unalike, but they both have two qualities that bind them in a firm alliance: a passion for improving the lot of Sicilians, and a courage that knows no fear of any man.

Outvoted, Barbera quietly agreed to go to Rome. A little later there was more disagreement between him and Danilo, this time over the wording of a statement that was intended to memorialize the purpose of the march to the Belice. Danilo proposed that one of the sentences in Lorenzo's text be eliminated for its lack of clarity. Now the majority of the group sided with Barbera; the sentence seemed clear enough to him. But Danilo held to his point of view, and announced that if the text remained as written, he would refuse to take responsibility for it, and abruptly turned to the next piece of business.

As I was to learn from later meetings, Danilo would conscientiously follow democratic procedure only up to a point; if the group favored a decision which he considered unwise or contrary to the interests of the Center, he would just as conscientiously veto it. Yet he was obviously anxious to have his colleagues in agreement with him. *"Siamo d'accordo?"* (Are we in accord?") was a favorite rhetorical question which he used repeatedly, sometimes in the face of open disagreement.

Danilo next announced that all members of the Council, with the exception of Paola Barbera, "who has to look after her children," and Dr. Vincenzo Borruso, "who has business elsewhere," had agreed to participate in the fasting on the Roccamena piazza. On hearing this, Dr. Borruso, who had left the table to warm his hands over the heater, appeared embarrassed and started to say something but changed his mind. He was the physician who supervised the Partinico health clinic, which the Center sponsored. A small, thin man with features that looked more Oriental than Sicilian, he was one of the most articulate of the collaborators but not the most popular. The young man sitting next to me whispered in my ear: "The doctor doesn't believe in fasts, except for his fat patients."

While Danilo spoke, Franco suddenly clutched his stomach and began to tremble. His face turned white, and his half-opened mouth was gasping. No one seemed particularly concerned. My neighbor explained that Franco often had such attacks. "It's his ulcer. He should go to the hospital in Palermo for a cure but he keeps putting it off."

"The most crucial time during the entire demonstration will come on Sunday noon when we try to occupy the piazza," Danilo was saying. "The police may try to create confusion among the demonstrators by engaging us in individual actions. Those of us who are accustomed to such tricks must remember to hold our ground firmly, no matter what happens. While it is hard to predict exactly what the police will do, each one of us must know what he intends to do."

The final point on the agenda was on another subject. Danilo raised the question as to whether the Center's forthcoming bulletin should announce the recent opening of a new hospital in Corleone, which Mafia interference had kept closed for many months after its completion. The collaborator from Corleone argued that the Center should take full credit for the hospital's opening, indicating that had it not been for the investigation of the Mafia interference which he and his associates had conducted, at considerable personal risk, the hospital would still be closed. Dr. Borruso vehemently disagreed, declaring it would be downright dishonest to suggest any connection between the activities of the Center and the opening of the hospital.

Danilo doodled as he listened to the doctor's oratory, while Franco, now recovered from his attack, glared at the speaker, hardly able to wait for his turn to disagree. No one supported the doctor's point of view. Danilo closed the discussion by emphasizing that the Center had no intention of taking credit for something it had not done, but he believed that the bulletin should carry an announcement of the hospital's opening. This he considered justifiable because, whether the public knew it or not, the Center's investigation of the Mafia interference "had undoubtedly contributed to the pressure that finally opened the doors of the hospital."

It was then almost one o'clock. Danilo apologized for the length of the meeting and the cold in the room, and, after inviting everyone present to lunch at his apartment in a half hour, declared the meeting ended, though not without first asking, *"Siamo d'accordo?"*

Once they left the meeting, the mood of the group changed. Barbera shed his sober manner and, while we stopped for an espresso on the way to the lunch, he and his wife and Michele Mandiello, the head of the Study Center at Menfi, bantered with one another and exuded friendliness toward Patricia and me. Mandiello, one of Danilo's earliest collaborators, was a tall, congenial Neapolitan in his early forties who, as an agricultural expert, was said to have performed miracles converting the peasants of the Menfi area to twentieth-century farming techniques.

Judging from the uninhibited way the two men joshed one another, he and Barbera were old friends. "Why do you always bring us to this café when you know very well it is infested with *mafiosi?*" Mandiello demanded.

"For two simple reasons," Barbera replied. "The coffee here is the very best in Partinico. Secondly, were they to poison you with it, we would immediately know who had done it."

It was still raining. We sloshed along the main street, the Corso delle Mille (so named because Garibaldi and his 1,000 liberators were said to have traversed the same route), past the shopping district until we arrived at the building where Danilo occupied an apartment with his wife and five children. Their first home in Partinico had been in the town's worst slum because Danilo had held that they should not live any more comfortably than the poorest Sicilians, but after a few years, when his children contracted worms and other infectious diseases because of the unsanitary condition of the area, he had been persuaded to move.

As we entered the third floor apartment (Franco Alasia, we were told, lived in the apartment above with his wife and two children), Vincenzina, Danilo's wife, was setting food on the table. She was a small, wiry woman with a poignant smile who said little yet managed to convey a great deal of warmth. The Arabic coloring of her skin as much as the clarity of her deep brown eyes reminded me of my mother, who was born less than a hundred miles away from Vincenzina's birthplace, Trappeto. Four of the five children she had by Danilo (the five she had by her fisherman husband were now grown up and out in the world) romped around the guests, joking and giggling. The oldest one, Libera, who was born during the first year of the marriage in 1954, helped her mother with the serving. With their blue eyes and fair hair, most of the children resembled their father. All spoke proper Italian, in marked contrast to their mother's Sicilian inflection, but Daniela, the youngest, who had an impish sense of humor, liked to pepper her talk with outlandish Sicilian idioms, a technique for teasing adults that seemed highly sophisticated for a child of five. Daniela was the only one of the children with a conventional name. A third girl was named Chiara (clear); the two boys, who followed Libera in order of birth, Cielo (sky) and Amico (friend).

The food was simple but plentiful and tasty: a fennel soup, followed by boiled artichokes, so small and tender they could be eaten whole, and a variety of local cheeses—all served with homemade bread and a strong white wine. From where I sat I had a comprehensive view of the main room and the kitchen. Except for a piano, a television set and a portable phonograph, the furnishings were drab and sparse. The walls were stuffed with books, pamphlets, and albums. In the kitchen I could see a small refrigerator and a stove with an oven, which was turned on full force to provide some warmth for the guests. As I discovered later, there was indoor plumbing, but it was out of order.

At the end of the meal Danilo announced that Vincenzina would accompany us on our shopping tour that afternoon before preparing the evening meal. Patricia protested it was too much work for Vincenzina to cook for us again, it would be more simple for everyone if we went to a restaurant. But Danilo would have none of it. And his wife, taking her cue from him, insisted it would be no trouble at all. "Please tell your wife she must have supper with us, so that she can start teaching me English," Libera pleaded.

"*Siamo d'accordo allora?* Danilo said with a smile.

Patricia responded with a faint "*Si.*"

Later we became quite fond of Partinico but on that first day everything seemed irremediably dreary, as we went from shop to shop buying blankets, sheets, and food. The rain and the noise added to our gray state of mind. The Corso delle Mille, as dangerous a street to cross as any in the center of Rome, was crowded with screaming scooters and roaring motorcycles weaving through automobiles and peasant carts returning from the fields. Under each cart, tied by a short cord to the axle, was a dog that trotted along at a weary pace which barely prevented it from being strangled to death. It was impossible to keep one's mind off death. Signs of mourning were everywhere: black stripes on the sleeves of men, placards announcing a death in the family on the doors of homes and stores, and wherever I looked there were women draped in black from head to toe. Every now and then there was a refreshingly incongruous note: a pair of spiked heels on a woman totally in black, as if to hint that beneath the lugubrious costume beat a feminine, cheerful heart. The placards on the doors usually commemorated the memory of a husband, wife, sister, brother, daughter or son; but I saw one which read "In memory of my son-in-law." Vincenzina told me she had never seen one that commemorated the memory of a mother-in-law or a daughter-in-law.

She said that it is customary to leave the placards on the doors for years, until the winds and the rains have destroyed them.

Mourning, as I already knew from my own Sicilian relatives and from reports in Dolci's books, is a serious matter in that part of the world. Some women go through life without ever shedding their mourning costume (one of my aunts did just that, though most of her life was spent in the United States). A widow's mourning duties, often enforced by the severity of public opinion in the community, are especially exacting. In some villages widows are not expected to leave their houses for a year after the husband's death. During that period the marriage bed remains unmade, the mattress is not beaten, and the sheets go unwashed. "If a woman is seen washing herself during the first months after her husband's death," a Sicilian once told Dolci, "people will speak badly of her."

As we trudged along the Corso in the rain, our arms jammed with purchases, I spied another woman in black wearing spiked heels. When she caught me staring, she turned her face toward me and I got a glimpse of a furtive smile, which ended abruptly as her companion, an older woman also dressed in mourning, nudged her along by the elbow.

Vincenzina and all five of the children helped carry our parcels. Before we could reach the Via Emma the rain began to fall in torrents, and we were obliged to stop every few minutes to salvage the foodstuffs that kept dropping through the wet wrappings. It provided an entertaining game for the children to retrieve such rolling objects as cans and oranges; for the rest of us it was a watery nightmare, which continued until a friend of Danilo spotted us from his car and gave us a lift to the Dolci apartment. The rain suddenly stopped as we entered the building.

Danilo arrived shortly afterwards, dry and serene. Although he had been up since 4:30, his customary rising time, he showed no signs of fatigue. When I marveled at his stamina, he briskly informed me that there was one more item on his agenda for the day: a *passeggiata* before supper that would give us an opportunity to talk without being interrupted by the children. The children began squealing their objections, begging to come along; he quelled them by promising to take them for a ride later that evening.

Near the center of town he bought six newspapers published in Palermo, Catania, Milan, and Rome and scanned their front pages to see whether there was any substance to a radio broadcast he had heard earlier which claimed that the Cassa di Mezzogiorno had allocated funds for the construction of the Belice dam. There was no story to that effect in any of the newspapers. "Just as I thought," he said. "The broadcast was an effort to make people think that there is no need for next week's demonstration."

A bleary-eyed acquaintance with an obsequious smile waited until Danilo had completed his inspection of the newspapers, then approached him for money. Danilo hesitantly handed him a few lire. As the man moved away mumbling thanks, Danilo explained that he disapproved of alms but that the man had a large family and was one of those who had recently lost his job at the Jato dam. "Besides," he added, "it is carnival time," and he pointed to some children in masks and costumes who were throwing confetti at the passing strollers. A number of other men stopped him as we walked, not for money but to inquire when they could expect to get back to the jobs they had held at the dam. Danilo assured them he would make it his business to find out. "Instead of hiring more men, as they should be doing, the construction company has been releasing them. They claim it is because of the poor weather. We'll see . . ."

Not until we reached the outskirts of the town were we able to converse without interruption. He spoke first about the exodus led by Eyvind Hytten. The schism, he said, had been brewing for some time but did not come to a head until he was out of the country for ten days. In his absence the staff, at Hytten's instigation, decided to write a book dealing with the economic aspects of the Center's projects, a manuscript of some 250 pages which they planned to enter in a contest sponsored by an American publisher. For ten days the staff abandoned all its other work to concentrate on the preparation of the manuscript. On Danilo's return, the work was presented to him for his approval. He refused to give it on the grounds that no book with any quality could possibly be completed in such a short time, thereby precipitating a storm of resentment that led to the exodus.

Danilo said: "Hytten is a brilliant man with many good ideas—

and some bad ones—and I was sorry to see him leave. But perhaps it is just as well that the staff consist mainly of Italians, instead of foreigners. We'll always welcome persons from any part of the world who have special abilities to contribute to our projects, but now it seems to me highly desirable to have most of the work done by natives of this country. After all, in all underdeveloped areas the work must finally be conducted by the people who belong to those areas. . . . What do you think of Lorenzo Barbera?"

I answered that I had been favorably impressed by both his book and his personality.

"Lorenzo has come a long way since he joined our staff, and he will go even further as he becomes more experienced. Lorenzo is a good example of the kind of native leadership that can be developed . . ." He was interrupted by the roar of a passing truck. "When there are enough Lorenzos and enough dams," he said, after a while, "then perhaps I can move on to some other underdeveloped area."

"To some African country?" I asked, knowing he had recently visited Senegal and Ghana.

"Yes, or perhaps somewhere in South America. There is so much to be done in so many places. . . . Here in Sicily we're trying to establish some effective principles that can be applied to any of the underdeveloped areas."

As we walked along the narrow roadside, he must have divined my fear of the cars that were bearing down on us from behind, for he insisted on changing places with me, so that he would be the one next to the road. "I am so large that they are bound to notice me," he said. Observing how oblivious he was to the danger of being hit, I now began to fear for him. "Tell me, Danilo," I said, "do you ever take any personal precautions against the Mafia?"

"For the past year, ever since there have been direct threats made to me, I've taken the precaution of not going out alone at night."

When I asked whether it had occurred to him that any one of the cars speeding toward us could inflict as much damage as any *mafioso,* he laughed. One of the pleasant things about our relationship was that I could make him laugh. "You're still nervous about the cars then?" he said.

"I certainly am," I replied. "Why don't we face the traffic instead of letting ourselves be at its mercy? In that way we might have some chance of jumping out of the way if we see a car coming too close to us."

"That's a very intelligent suggestion," he said. "I knew you were wise from the first day we met . . ."

"Not so wise," I said. "Only nervous."

We moved to the other side of the road, and Danilo remarked: "It is certainly better to look at danger straight in the face."

We returned to the subject of his staff. When I pointed out that it was now about half the size it had been during the early years of the Center, he said: "We don't want to become too large or ambitious. All we want is a small group of high quality that will be able to plant a few good seeds. We must never become so important as to feel we are doing things *for* the people; we must always try to do things *with* people. That is the most important of all our principles, the one that sets our group apart from all political parties . . ."

I told him about the criticism I constantly heard in Rome over his failure to associate himself with a political party. "Ah yes, that criticism has existed for many years," he sighed, "but it has never made much sense to me. To do our work properly we must be able to act independently, without being tied down to any political line. This sometimes enables us to engage in actions which are more extreme than any political party can afford to take. No party, for example, not even the Communists, would dare agitate for a new dam by committing an act of civil disobedience. Their hands are too tied by complicated political considerations. Yet nearly all support our programs of pressures. Whatever effectiveness our group has comes from *not* having any official connections with a political party."

"But aren't there Communists within your group?"

"Two or three, perhaps, but there are also Christian Democrats and Socialists. We don't care how they vote as long as they don't engage in any political action. No one in the group is permitted to run for any political office, and whenever there is an election, all the study centers shut down. We don't want the voters coming to us for advice about voting . . ."

60

We turned back toward the town. Bone-tired and eager for food and rest, I was relieved that we were returning to the apartment, but Danilo made several stops on the way, one in a store crammed with gaudy furniture—the ribboned flower arrangements everywhere attested to the newness of the business—to congratulate the proprietor on his "beautiful store" and wish him luck. "I shall need it," the proprietor said gloomily, looking about at the empty store. Although I did not doubt the sincerity of Danilo's gesture, only fatigue prevented me from questioning it on grounds of aesthetics. No one willing to sell such ugly furniture, so pretentious that it must degrade the sensibilities of those who lived with it, seemed deserving of congratulations.

A little later we entered a wineshop where the owner informed him that his good wine was gone. "I wouldn't want to sell you an inferior wine," he added.

"Such wonderful honesty!" Danilo exclaimed when we were on the sidewalk. "People are essentially good, aren't they—even people who sometimes behave as though they were one's enemies?"

Unwilling in my weariness to accept so large and benign a generalization, even from a staunch believer in the philosophy of nonviolence, I said: "What about Cardinal Ruffini? There is someone who has behaved like an enemy by denouncing you as an enemy of Sicily."

"It is true that the Cardinal and I have been in sharp disagreement for many years," he answered gravely, "yet I am certain he is a man of honest intentions who sincerely believes he is acting in the best interests of Sicily."

I was too tired to argue the point.

At the apartment I found Patricia engaged in the project of trying to teach Libera some English words, with only fragments of conversational Italian to help her. "Hello, goodbye, yes, no, how are you, skirt, leg, hair, girl, boy," Libera recited at the top of her voice, spilling out everything she had learned. She stopped showing off her newly acquired vocabulary long enough to help Vincenzina serve the supper. Between courses Amico and Cielo entertained us by mimicking American wild West characters they had watched on television. With handkerchiefs drawn over their faces bandit-style, the two brothers took turns mowing down everyone

61

at the table with their make-believe shotguns. "To think," Danilo groaned as he watched the massacre, "that these are the sons of a pacifist."

The meal had barely ended when the children began demanding that their father keep his promise and take them for a drive. "The lights, the lights," they kept chanting in unison. "We want to see the lights." Longing to get rid of my damp clothes and stretch my weary body on a bed, I had somehow expected that Danilo would postpone the ride until he had taken us home. An expression of shock came into his eyes when he understood the nature of my hope. "But you can't go home now," he protested, "not until you have seen the lights of the city from the top of Monte Reale. I had carefully planned this as your introduction to Partinico. I promise you and Patricia will not be disappointed. *Siamo d'accordo?*"

"Yes," Libera shouted in triumphant English.

At first it seemed impossible to squeeze four adults and five children into one small Fiat, but the Dolci family was undaunted by the challenge, and within minutes we were on our way up Monte Reale, the same mountain we had seen that morning from our terrace. The darkness had no quieting influence on the children. All the way to the top the members of the family, led by Danilo, presented a varied program of Sicilian and Italian folk songs, sung with a skill that could only be developed through repeated performances. The curves were numerous and treacherous but the family kept singing together, pausing only for occasional solo parts by Chiara and Daniela. As we whizzed around the curves, I was relieved that Danilo was such an expert driver; only when both hands would abandon the wheel to applaud at the end of each song did Patricia and I clutch one another in terror.

At the mountain top we got out of the car and looked down on the lights of Partinico, a myriad of stars in an upsidedown sky. A few miles to the east, shining through the dark like two mammoth Christmas trees planted in space, were the hilltop villages of Borgetto and Montelepre. "Isn't it beautiful? Isn't it enchanting?" Danilo kept exclaiming to each of us until the children, becoming chilled in the cold mountain wind, slipped back into the car for warmth. The cold did not interfere with Danilo's exultation. "Aren't you glad I persuaded you to come?"

I wanted to say *"Siamo d'accordo"* but my teeth were chattering, and I could only nod.

On the way down I learned that Monte Reale derived its name from the fact that the Bourbon king Ferdinand II built his castle there. Ferdinand did not remain long; his rule became so unbearably tyrannical that the people of Partinico rose against the Bourbons in the area a month before Garibaldi arrived to liberate Sicily from its foreign rulers. It proved to be a false liberation; shortly afterwards the landowning barons, using gangs of *mafiosi* as troops, resumed their feudal powers, and continued to keep the majority of Sicilians in a subservient state.

But Danilo was in no mood to discuss history. Before reaching the base of the mountain he was struck by what he said was "a great idea"; amid shouts of approval from the children, he proposed that Patricia and I sing a program of American songs. Though neither of us has any more talent than is minimally necessary for secret solo singing, it was impossible to refuse. Our performance abounded in sour notes but the Dolci family kept applauding and demanding more. We arrived at the Via Emma as we were limping through "When the Saints Go Marching In," and just in time, having exhausted both our repertoire and our voices.

"Golden dreams," each member of the family sang out to us as we stepped into our new abode.

Chapter

4

Partinico Scene

No GOLDEN DREAM would ever be possible. Or so it seemed during those first days. Not on a mattress that had the sharp and rugged contours of a jagged mountain. Not in an unheated stone house with stone floors that exuded a dampness that rotted the plaster in the ceilings and penetrated with ease our monumental bedcovers of blankets, clothes, and newspapers. Not with a bathroom which, though a model of pink opulence, could emit only an occasional stream of icy water. And even if a pleasant dream had been possible, golden or copper, it would have been ripped to shreds at dawn by the ferocious clamor of neighboring church bells, whose assault on the eardrums sounded more like a battle alarm than an invitation to worship.

Yet, miraculously enough, within two weeks a certain degree of adjustment had been gradually achieved. Our bodies discovered the valleys in the mattress and learned to stay within them; a *bomba* was bought which, fed by a cylinder of butane gas, dispelled some of the chill some of the time. We even acquired hot water on tap by persuading the landlord to share the cost of an electrically operated heater, a rare luxury in that part of Italy where power was so expensive that our monthly electric bill invariably exceeded the rent. And although we never became accustomed to the four-times-a-day insanity of the church bells, they no longer had the effect of catapulting us out of bed at dawn.

Even without the church bells, morning sleep on the Via Emma would have been difficult. An hour before dawn we would be awakened by the grating noise of wheels over cobblestones, as the

64

peasants rolled their carts out of their hovels into the street, where they were hitched to horses and mules for the long trek to the fields. As soon as dawn came, the *vaccari* with their cows would take possession of the street to sell milk to the housewives. The milk was squeezed directly from udders into tin buckets which the twittering women lowered from their balconies with ropes. Nearly always, in the midst of these proceedings, a cow would utter a roar of hopeless grief.

Later came the street peddlers, chanting their wares in inflections that were unmistakably Arabic. Some used peasant carts, some small trucks or motorcycles with sidecars, and twice a week from Trappeto came a blue-eyed peddler on a bicycle with a basketful of fresh fish. His was the most enthralling of all the chants, for it rang with the sound of the sea. The bigger vehicles from Palermo, piled high with kitchenware or drygoods, would arrive toward the middle of the morning, equipped with loudspeakers that could be heard through the whole neighborhood. I noticed that the bigger the truck the more handsome the salesman who manned it. With their silky voices and Adonis features, they were undoubtedly selected for their ability to lure housewives to their wares.

At all hours of the day there were the voices of our immediate neighbors, shouting conversations from doorways, or exchanging insults with persons farther down the street, who were generally regarded as inferior and unfriendly. The loudest of the voices belonged to Peppina, a chunky middle-aged woman who had the vitality and stance of a bull. When enraged, she could easily overcome any opponent with the speed and fury of her verbal onslaughts. The rest of her immediate family, her bedraggled husband who worked the land and her two beautiful sons who were apprenticed to a mason, were the essence of meekness. Luckily, Peppina took an immediate liking to Patricia and on learning that we had decided to move the kitchen equipment from the second to the fourth floor, ordered her sons to do the job.

A quieter but more aggressive neighbor was Maria, who lived in the house adjoining ours with a husband who was a truckdriver. Her eloquence was as impressive as Peppina's but it lacked her friend's speed and ferocity. The day after we arrived, she came to

65

our door bearing a bottle of wine, and offering to teach Patricia the art of embroidery. She was motivated by neighborliness but also, as we eventually gathered, by the need to brag that she could consort with Americans. When I informed her that Patricia already knew how to embroider, she said, "But how can she if she is an American?"

The most visible of our neighbors were Donna Vincenzina and her husband who, with their bachelor son, lived in a hut opposite our balcony. All morning she would sweep dirt into the street or scrub clothes in an ancient washtub shaped like a child's coffin, which sat in front of her doorway. Her skin was so deeply wrinkled that I assumed she must be in her eighties and marveled that so steady a flow of applied energy could come from so old a woman. I later learned that she was in her early sixties. Like Maria, she never wore anything but black; the black kerchief that was always tied around her head gave her the aspect of a benevolent witch. Unlike Maria and Peppina, she was rather shy and quite inarticulate; but her gray eyes and quick smile conveyed a depth of goodness and charm that no stream of language could ever suggest.

Her husband was a cheerful, toothless extrovert with the grin of a satyr, who invariably occupied a chair next to the washboard, watching Donna Vincenzina go about her chores but never lifting a finger to help her. He had migrated to St. Louis early in the century but had been obliged to return to Partinico because he could not find a job. Whenever he saw me, he would call out the few American phrases he still remembered: "Howsa world treating you?" "All bosses no damn good." "You betch your life." And once I thought I heard him say: "Lay 'em and leave 'em." He told me that his biggest mistake in life was to leave St. Louis.

"It's better to be poor in America than miserable in Sicily," he said. "There is no hope here." He was bitter that his son had said no to a cousin in Detroit, who offered to smuggle him into the country and marry him to a rich girl. "My son claims he likes it here. He prefers to be a miserable *contadino* bachelor than an American gentleman married to a rich girl. Can you imagine anything more idiotic?"

Our landlord and his family were as prosperous as anyone on the Via Emma, a distinction that was emphasized by an enormous television set in their living room. The owner of extensive vine-yards, he manufactured wine which he sold wholesale in Partinico. Unlike most Sicilian men, he was a devout Catholic, a pillar of the neighboring church, which he attended faithfully. His greatest hope in life, he once confided, was that his son, who was now in the Italian army, would marry a good woman and move into the rooms we now occupied. That wing of the house had been recently built as his son's wedding gift.

The landlord's wife, a woman in her fifties as alert and bouncy as a robin, spent most of her time mending and sewing. Except for her compelling language of hospitality with which she would frequently entice us into her living room, she seldom had anything to say. Not able to cope with any emergency requests we made for advice or repairs, she would hurriedly summon her married daughter Teresa, who lived in another wing of the house with a husband and two children. Together they would appear at our door breathless from rushing, usually with a bottle of wine as a token of their good will, and I would repeat the problem to Teresa, trying to keep my eyes off the close-fitting lounging gown she usually wore. Even in street clothes, Teresa was a joy to be-hold, a brunette beauty whose sensuous speech and movements were accentuated by a melancholy view of life, which I ascribed to having a husband who was her physical and mental inferior. Un-like her mother, Teresa was intelligent and helpful and, on those few occasions when I encountered her alone on the terrace, which her family shared with us, appealingly frank-hearted. I could not help suspecting that were it not for her mother's strict surveil-lance, Teresa might have become the Madame Bovary of the Via Emma.

Her husband, though a capitalist in the technical sense of the word since he owned the barbershop where he worked, made no bones of his allegiance to the Communist party. His favorite sport was taunting his Christian Democrat father-in-law, raising a clenched fist near his face with every pro-Communist statement he delivered. He ridiculed the older man for being "enslaved" to the Church, and liked to brag that the last time he had been in a church was to be married; he saw no point in going again. Yet his house was filled with photographs of him and his wife partici-

pating in baptismal and christening rituals, which could only have
been performed in a church. Teresa, although she did not contra-
dict him, took her children to church every Sunday, and in his
presence expressed pride in having been asked to be a *madrina*
(godmother) six times in the past two years.

The two men were in complete disagreement on the subject of
Danilo Dolci. The only fault the barber found with Danilo was in
his refusal to join the Communist party. To this, the father-in-law
retorted that Dolci might as well be a member of that party since
he worked so closely with it. But his chief objection to Dolci was
that he had presented Partinico to the world as a horrible town.
"If Partinico were as horrible as he claims it is, do you think any of
us would live here? Why doesn't he tell the world about the prosperity we have here?"

"Where is this prosperity you're talking about?" asked the son-
in-law. "There won't be any real prosperity here until the dam
gets finished. And were it not for Danilo, there wouldn't be any
hope of a dam . . ."

"A dam is a waste of money," the father-in-law interrupted.
"The problem is not to provide water to grow more crops. The
problem is to find people to pick the crops we now grow. Everyone
is leaving the land to find work in foreign countries. Danilo would
be doing Sicily a real service if he used his efforts to get industries
established here, so that men didn't have to migrate to find work."

"Where do you get such phony arguments? From your friend,
the priest?" The little barber was stretching his neck like a bantam
rooster preparing to attack, but Teresa interceded to point out
that he had forgotten to serve us anything.

Despite the heat of their disagreements, the two men spent most
of their leisure time together, not through any feeling of affection
but because it was an ordained ritual for all members of the landlord's family to dine together every evening and remain in each
other's company until it was time to retire. The group also included another married daughter, somewhat younger than Teresa,
who lived at the other end of the Via Emma with her carpenter
husband and their infant daughter. The infant was the chief play-
thing for the entire clan. All evening she was passed from one
person to another for hugging and kissing, tossed high in the air

until she responded with screams of delight or fright, and each time she dissolved in tears returned to her mother or father to be smothered with affection. This family scene, interwoven with television programs, was repeated every evening until midnight. From our bedroom we could hear the noises of their togetherness.

Danilo's headquarters were a fifteen-minute walk from the Via Emma. They occupied a large, ramshackle building that had once been the manor of a baronial family. The Baron and his wife were now reduced to subsisting on the rent they collected for the building, and what had once been a courtyard where elegant horsedrawn carriages drew up to the entrance had become a desolate lot filled with mud holes and reeking with the stench of sewage and garbage.

Except for the size of the building, there was little in its exterior to hint at its aristocratic past. Its present function was identified by a modest wooden sign near the entrance: Centro Studi e Iniziative Per La Piena Occupazione, a name that had recently been shortened by eliminating the last four words. As Danilo explained the change, "We don't want to spread ourselves too thin. The problem of 'la piena occupazione' (full employment) will take care of itself if we do our work well."

There was nothing baronial about the staff's main offices, which were situated on the ground floor in a twentieth-century mundane appendage to the original building. Only the palatial rooms upstairs, lovingly ornamented with baroque cornices and fresco painting, expressed its original nineteenth-century splendor. Now that they were utilized as auxiliary offices, meeting halls, and storage chambers, their obscured glory intimated the mixed sense of triumph and embarrassment that the toughest of revolutionists must experience when they establish their plebeian quarters in lavish palaces recently inhabited by the vanquished.

A few of Dolci's staff members expressed a certain deference toward the building because of its connection with the past, but most of them might as well have been working in tents, so indifferent were they to it. This was especially true of the young clerks, who were among the first members of the Center whom I got to know well. The oldest of them was Vittorio, a thirty-year-old mimeograph operator who, as the father of five children, drew the same subsistence pay as Danilo. Vittorio had a thin body and a large head with a hatchet-shaped jaw. Endowed with the worst temper I had ever encountered, he could not speak on any subject without swearing obscenely, a characteristic which he prudently suppressed in Danilo's presence by saying virtually nothing.

The other clerks were barely past twenty. A tall, pretty fair-haired girl named Rosalba supervised the newspaper files and helped with the mail. She had no interest whatsoever in the goals of the Center, but she did her work diligently and with such a serious demeanor that only the most lecherous of the bachelors who visited the offices dared flirt with her. The payroll and other bookkeeping matters were handled by Marusca, who spent half the week in Palermo studying at a social work school. A Roman, she was the only one of the clerks not a native of Partinico; she was also the only one of them to volunteer for the fast at Roccamena.

The most personable of them was Osvaldo, the diminutive office manager, mail supervisor, and chief typist, who had worked at the Center from the time he was sixteen. Despite his extraordinary industry, his enormous hazel eyes and long black eyelashes, set in a sensitive, pale face, made him the living image of a languishing Jean Cocteau hero. His remarkable sense of efficiency and enterprise, which were in marked contrast to the apathy and dourness of the average Partinico male, he proudly attributed to his mother's Roman heritage. "The best thing my father ever did for me was to marry my mother."

His association with the foreigners at the Center had extended his horizons and made him determine to pursue a career, still undefined, that would take him away from Sicily and provide him with riches and social status. To this end, he took a correspondence course in art and studied English with whatever Americans and Britishers came to the center. He lost no time enlisting Patricia as his new English teacher, and from time to time he would use my services to ghostwrite love letters in English, passionate epistles accompanied by ravishing photos of his poetic visage which he directed to several young women in the Eastern and Western Hemispheres, with whom he maintained a steady correspondence. His dream of glory was that one of his pen pals would some day offer to marry him and maintain him in luxury, outside Sicily.

Despite his ambitious nature, he was deeply devoted both to his work and to his friends. And when these two sides of his soul clashed, Osvaldo would become swathed in gloom. One of these clashes had taken place since the exodus of Hytten and his group, which included some of his best friends. The episode had left Osvaldo critical of Danilo, but he had been unwilling to join the exodus nor would he permit his criticism to interfere with the quality of the services he performed for the Center. At the same time he could not bear to give up his friendship with the men and women who by now had openly become Danilo's adversaries. In an effort to resolve this dilemma Osvaldo took to visiting his friends in Palermo secretly. Danilo, sympathizing with the young man's conflicts, did his best to help the situation by pretending he was not aware of the visits.

With Franco sick at home and Danilo in Rome preparing some of the groundwork for the forthcoming "week of mourning," Osvaldo became my chief guide during those early days at the Center. He produced the batch of letters in English that needed to be translated and the English galleys of Danilo's newest book, *A New World in the Making*, which Danilo had asked me to examine. In taking me on a tour of the offices, Osvaldo called my attention to a current correspondence file, which contained all the letters that had been received and written at the Center during recent months. The file was available to every staff member, in order that anyone could inform himself about the Center's business.

When I commented on how democratic this practice seemed to me, Osvaldo's only response was a smile. Later, when we became friends, he said that the system always worked to Danilo's advantage but not always to the advantage of the rest of the staff. "This file enables him to know exactly what the rest of us are up to, but it doesn't prevent him from writing or receiving letters which no one ever sees." I defended Danilo on the grounds that some of his correspondence, particularly that dealing with his investigations of the Mafia, probably had to be kept secret. Osvaldo politely agreed with me, then hastily dropped the subject.

71

The file was a mirror of the aspirations and disappointments that constituted the Center's existence. There were letters to and from the various Dolci committees in Europe, reporting every degree of success and frustration; letters from young idealists begging to work at the Center; letters enclosing small money donations and apologizing for not sending more, many of these from England written by semiliterate adults and grade-school children; letters promising to pray for Dolci's success in Sicily. There were also reassuring letters from Danilo's friends: Bertrand Russell, Laurence Olivier, Carlo Levi, Salvatore Quasimodo and other famous men. And also angry letters.

A letter from the Mayor of Corleone asked Danilo how he would answer the enclosed note he had received from an Italian in Milan. The note read: "Dear Friend: We can say with absolute sincerity that we Italians have one horrible disgrace: the dirty people of the South. All the South stinks, but most of all Sicily, land of the sun, oranges, and bandits. The Sicilians are a mass of delinquents; the police are obliged to spend most of their time trying to control them. I speak of Corleone especially, where all the people are brigands. Poor Italy. Sicilians are the shame of Italy and of all the world."

There was no indication of what Danilo had written the mayor, but in the file was the copy of a manuscript he had written titled *The Psychology of Misery*, whose view of the Sicilians would have served as an apt rebuttal to the bigotry expressed in the note. "Because the Sicilian peasant has known misery for so many centuries," Danilo wrote, "he takes it for granted that it is his way of life and he sees no point in trying to do something about it. When the news was broadcast on the radio that a rocket had struck the moon, many of the peasants expressed disbelief. 'The moon and the stars are the flesh of God and cannot be touched,' they said. 'Up there is the unattainable perfection of the stars; down here are the sad days of man's life on earth. We are but worms . . .' "

There is more conviction than sorrow in this lament, Danilo added; there is also a profound sense of resignation. "When I don't work, I am in the dark," a peasant told him. "And I become ashamed to be seen idle. But what can I do? It is up to those who command us to provide us with work." But the problem of the

Sicilian, the manuscript pointed out, is more complicated than that of earning a living. He needs to emerge from the closed society in which he has lived so long; he must start believing that a change in his situation is both possible and desirable. Only then will he rid himself of the superstitions that have become encrusted on his brain through long centuries of ignorance.

The building of a dam is a significant step in the right direction, the manuscript concluded. "Any Sicilian who has seen how impossible it is in the summer to cultivate a land that is scorched by the sun will soon become aware of how a dam can transform the land and create a green summer filled with crops, fruit, and butterflies. And he will think: 'The land can be changed,' and he will begin to understand that a dam can not only provide him with new work and new bread but also nourish a genuine hope about his own personal development."

When Franco had been sick in bed for five days, I decided to call on him. I found him alone, with the door of his apartment wide open so that Danilo's wife on the floor below could hear him if he required help. His wife Anna, a dressmaker, was in Palermo trying to line up some work; his two children were in school. He lay in bed clutching a hot water bag to his stomach, his white face strained with pain, but he smiled, voiced his pleasure at seeing me, and apologized for not being at the Center when I started to work there. In answer to my question as to whether he was receiving medical attention, he said he did not want to see a doctor until the demonstrations at Roccamena were over. "After that I'll go to a hospital at Palermo and find out what is wrong with me."

Not wishing to tax his energies, I made a move to leave, but he begged me to stay. "Why don't you ask me some questions about our work?" he suggested. "In that way you will be getting some information for your project and I will be feeling useful for the first time this week." I sat down again, and asked him how his association with Danilo began.

They had met in Milan in 1947 while Danilo was teaching an evening class in literature in which Franco was enrolled. He was then twenty years old, three years younger than Danilo, and had a good job as a mechanic in an automobile factory; but he aspired to be an engineer. "I thought I'd have an easier time interesting beautiful girls if I had a real profession." He first attracted Danilo's attention with a writing assignment on the topic "Who am I? What do I want to be?"

"The grammar was atrocious but the content interested Danilo, and he discussed it with me. It was the first time that an intellectual had treated me, a worker, with respect. We were quite different then. I considered myself a Communist, Danilo was a Catholic. Without trying to convert me to anything, he opened my mind to ideas which had never occurred to me, and we soon became friends. It may surprise you to know that Danilo was a very busy athlete in those days—rowing, running, skiing, he did all those things—but he was always reading too. Sometimes he wrote poetry, and every day for at least an hour he would play the piano. Yet what impressed me most about him was that he treated everyone as an equal."

As Franco reminded me, Danilo was then completing his studies in architecture, but a few weeks before he was to receive his degree, he left Milan and went to work for Don Zeno Saltini, a priest who had established a settlement for destitute children called Nomadelfia, near Modena. "There never has been a priest like Don Zeno," Franco said. "Even the most dogmatic Communists loved and respected him. On a building in Modena I saw with my own eyes a slogan which read: 'Death to all priests, except Don Zeno.'

"I used to visit Nomadelfia fairly often because Danilo was there and in that way I got to know Don Zeno well. He is one of the three men I most admire in this world. The other two are Girolomo Li Causi, the head of the Communist party in Sicily, who isn't afraid to fight the Mafia, and, of course, Danilo. They all have guts and they all battle for things that matter . . ."

Observing Danilo and Don Zeno go about their work with the destitute children, Franco said, caused him to become dissatisfied with his way of life. Except for earning him a salary, his job seemed a waste of time. "I wanted to do something that would have some meaning but I did nothing until Danilo asked me to join him in Trappeto for a few months. This was in 1952. By that time I had married Anna and we had our first child. We were married in church because I felt friendly toward the Catholics then, as a result of knowing Danilo and Don Zeno. But later on I regretted it. And when I became aware of how indifferent the Catholic Church was to the misery of the Sicilian people, I refused to have either of my children baptized. If they want to get baptized when they are old enough to have opinions of their own, they can baptize themselves.

"By the way, did you know that Danilo at one time seriously considered becoming a priest? At Trappeto he used to play the church organ and I used to pump it for him. I remained with him for four months, until my money ran out, and then went back to my family and job in Milan. In 1954, when I was laid off and it was hard to find work in Sicily, I wound up working in a factory in Paris. That didn't last long because the job they wanted me to do was related to the making of bombs. Although I explained I was a pacifist and had been one ever since I saw the Americans bomb a school near Milan with two hundred children in it, they insisted that I either do the work or leave. So I left.

"My next job was with an American company that was building an oil refinery in North Africa. It was an unforgettable experience because I never ate better in my whole life. Those American breakfasts, with all the ham and eggs and butter you wanted! It was a fine job but then the political situation of the country suddenly changed and the whole enterprise came to an end. I tried Paris again, and this time landed a first-class job with the Citroen company. Anna joined me and found work at Christian Dior. I can't say I was very happy; yet everything seemed very promising for us. After a year and a half Citroen was so pleased with my services that they offered me a free house in the suburbs." Franco paused to drink some water. I suggested he tell me the rest of his story some other time, but he insisted on continuing it.

"It was strange, Jerre," he said, "at that moment when economic security was really within my grasp, I found that I didn't want it. The idea of committing myself and my family to a standardized middle-class existence depressed me. Not knowing exactly what I wanted, we went back to Milan and I worked there until February 1956, when I got a telegram from Danilo saying he had been arrested and jailed. I left for Palermo at once and for a few

75

days did what I could to help him. On returning to Milan, I decided that I must try to change my way of life; that I must go to Sicily and work with Danilo. Before the end of the year, I was back with him, that time for good . . ."

A wave of nausea stopped him. He vomited into a pan, trying to apologize as he did so. After I had cleared away the mess, he tried to tell me about the first time he had fasted with Danilo, but I urged him to keep quiet, and he sank back into the pillows. His daughter returned from school a little later. She was a brunette with exquisitely delicate features, and of such small stature that I mistook her to be a child. When her father informed me she was fifteen, the poor girl blushed a deep crimson, as though a shameful secret had been revealed. "She will suddenly shoot up one day," Franco said, watching the girl tidy the room.

I got up to leave. "I'll see you at the Center toward the end of the week," he said as we shook hands.

I told him it would be wiser if he remained in bed and put himself in the hands of a doctor. I offered to get him one.

"I'll be all right," he said with a wan smile. "The German nurse at the clinic will be along this afternoon to give me a shot of vitamins. That usually helps. By Monday I should be ready for Roccamena . . ."

"Surely you're not considering taking part in the fast?" I said, though I could sense that was exactly what he was planning to do.

"I'll be all right," he repeated.

On the way home, I picked up a copy of *L'Ora* and read on the front page that Danilo Dolci had been nominated for the Nobel Peace Prize by the Swedish Parliament. The leftwing newspaper jubilantly identified Danilo as one of its regular contributors.

Chapter

5

The Occupation
of the Piazza

DANILO RETURNED FROM Rome two days before the "week of mourning" was to start, and immediately the office staff began to move with an agility that had not been evident during his absence. "It isn't that we are lazy," Osvaldo told me, "but we seem inclined to take it easy when Danilo is away. When he is here, it is like working with a lighted firecracker under us."

On being told that Vittorio was home in bed with a fever, Danilo insisted that, fever or not, he be summoned to the Center to mimeograph a press statement he needed that morning. "He can go back to bed the moment he's finished the job," he said. Vittorio arrived at the office, unshaven and glum, and mimeographed the material. Danilo then praised him so lavishly for being a conscientious worker that he decided to remain the rest of the day.

"Danilo is always wanting things done in a bloody hurry, no matter what the hour may be," he growled, and he recalled that one morning he woke up at four, dreaming that Danilo was knocking at the door demanding entrance. His wife opened her eyes at that moment and he told her his dream. "That's strange," she said. "I was dreaming the very same thing." While they were marveling at the coincidence, they both heard a loud knocking on the door. "I opened the door," Vittorio said, "and there sure enough was Danilo, apologizing for getting me out of bed but ordering me to come to the Center so that I could mimeograph a news release he wanted to take with him to Palermo."

Danilo had not returned from Rome alone. With him were two men and a woman, a magazine photographer who looked like Vittorio Gassman, a journalist of Milan from the influential Christian Democrat newspaper *Il Giorno,* and a chic woman of Rome in her thirties, who was a television producer. They had all been assigned to cover the events at Roccamena. Danilo had persuaded them to spend a day at Partinico before proceeding there, in order that he might show them a dam that was already under construction. I was invited to come along.

The visitors were tough-minded, worldly Italians, with all the sardonic attitudes typical of their tribe. But Danilo handled them with such aplomb (he would make a first-rate diplomat) that by the time we set out for the Jato dam, their questions had become less cynical, their involvement with Danilo's remarks more convincing. Danilo, always the educator, tried to imbue the group with the significance of a dam in an area where people are victimized as much by geography as by history. In Sicily there are excessive rains during the winter months, frequently resulting in heavy floods; but there are no rains whatsoever in the summer, and the countryside becomes as brown as a desert. The rivers are few and small (all the rivers in southern Italy put together do not have the capacity of the Arno) yet Danilo believes they represent the major hope of Sicily. The Jato river travels only a few miles, from the village of S. Giuseppe Jato to the Gulf of Castellammare and is absurdly small even at its widest point, yet he is confident that the dam will raise the living standards of all the Sicilians who live in the dozen villages of the river area. "Nearly 25,000 acres of land will be irrigated and over 1,600 acres reforested. The number of working days and the gross yield of the land will be trebled and quadrupled . . ."

He swung off the main road onto a dirt road that had been constructed for the purpose of transporting building materials for the dam. "The first day the road opened," Danilo said, "I was greeted by a man I had never seen before who tipped his hat and addressed me as 'Signor Dolci.' I made some inquiries and learned that he was a local *mafioso.* He and his friends were already trying to get a foothold on the project. We've been able to get rid of some of them, but not all. One of the security guards on the job is a well-known *mafioso,* a killer, hired by the construction company. We haven't been able to do anything about him so far."

Some three hundred men were at work with picks, shovels, and dynamite, and with bulldozers and caterpillars. There was still much to do but the general outlines of the dam were clearly visible. Danilo, who was once described as "the perfect mediator between the hopes of the population below and the apathy of the politicians above," was greeted by scores of workers who shouted and waved and insisted on shaking hands. "Some of these men never had a regular job before this one," Danilo said. "The dam may open a new world for them. In western Sicily the people have become prisoners of a static world. Even though they work better and harder than any other people I've known, they haven't been given the education and technical means to break out of their prison. They are an intelligent people and the dam will give them a real chance to live as an enlightened and democratic group . . ."

"What makes you so optimistic about these people?" the photographer broke in. "Even though they are intelligent, how can they understand what a democratic life is really like when they've never had one?"

"People learn rapidly when they find it is to their advantage," Danilo replied, "and the Sicilians are no exception. Already a good part of the population in this area has had clear proof that when a large enough group works together with determination and a spirit of nonviolence, some very important things happen, such as getting a dam under way. And one democratic development follows another. For example, for the first time in their lives the workers on this dam are organized into a trade union. And for the first time the sharecroppers and landowners, both of whom stand to benefit from the dam, are getting together to make certain they will get their fair share of water; not, as in the past, the share that the Mafia would or would not let them have."

We had left the dam and were taking a roundabout route back to Partinico. "There are many healthy signs of progress," Danilo continued, "but of course there is the danger that while the surface of the situation may seem to be changing, the structure may remain the same. If the Mafia should succeed in diverting the huge sums of money being spent on the dam to the usual Mafia

channels, then the old traditions of violence and apathy will survive and perhaps even become stronger."

"Do you blame the Mafia then for most of the troubles in this
section of Sicily?" the woman, whose name was Silvania, asked.

He disregarded her question and pointed to a public fountain
near the road; water was pouring out in a thick stream, muddying
a large tract of ground around it. "Here you see how the water is
wasted," he said. "In a few minutes we'll get to a place where there
is no water whatsoever, though it is desperately needed . . .

"To answer your question, Silvania, I would say that the Mafia
is only a symptom of the misery in western Sicily, a very destructive symptom but a symptom nevertheless. The people here must
come to realize that the reasons for their miserable situation do
not lie primarily in the evil of others but in their own confused
ideas, in their lack of organization and unity of purpose."

He brought the car to a sudden stop. "This is the place I wanted
to show you." We left the car and saw a group of new houses and
four peasants at work ploughing the ground near them. Danilo
and the journalist spoke to the men, while the photographer took
pictures. The peasants identified themselves as residents of Piana
dei Greci, an ancient Albanian settlement some fifty miles away.
The land and the houses had been granted to them by ERAS, the
government agency concerned with Sicilian agricultural development.

"What a gift," the older of the peasants said. "This place is so far
from our village that unless we can borrow a car, we can't get here.
If they had bothered to look at a map, they would have realized
how far it is from where we live."

"You should also tell these gentlemen," another peasant said,
"that there isn't enough land here to support a family with children. Maybe a bachelor, if he didn't eat too much, but not a
family . . ."

"What about the houses?" the journalist asked. "They look quite
attractive. Why don't you live in them or rent them?"

The older peasant bridled. "We aren't that crazy. The houses
are no good to anyone, not even to animals. They're built without
either water or electricity. Who would want to live in them?"

The third peasant said: "The only use we have for them is for storing our tools and for getting out of the wet when it rains . . ."

"Did you get all the pictures you wanted?" the journalist asked the photographer as we drove away.

"Yes, but who in hell is going to believe that such new houses were built without water or electricity? I'll be lucky if I can get my editor to believe it . . ."

Near Partinico the woman from Rome said: "Sicily seems like such a foreign country to me, though I must say I like it." She turned to the photographer coquettishly. "Weren't those the most delicious artichokes we had at lunch? Not even in the most expensive restaurants of Rome have I tasted anything as good. I hope we can have another feast of them in Roccamena."

Danilo drew a deep breath, and stepped on the accelerator.

Roccamena is twenty miles from Partinico, and thirty-eight miles from Palermo, but the roads are very bad and hardly anyone ever goes there. The nearest village is Corleone where, according to Lorenzo Barbera, one can easily hire a killer for about eighty dollars. From its superior height, the village commands overwhelming views of a long plain encircled by a necklace of mountains, but it itself is devoid of beauty. Its historical interest is minimal. Founded by a land baron in the late nineteenth century to provide homes for his peasants, it consists of little more than a huddle of rudimentary buildings that have long since fallen into a bleak state of disrepair, a condition that reflects the general mood of its residents.

"When I first arrived in Roccamena," wrote Lorenzo in his book, "I was immediately identified as a foreigner, even though I was a Sicilian from Partinico, and regarded as somebody one could freely insult, even in his presence, as he wasn't likely to understand the dialect. Because my predecessors at the Center had included a Belgian and a Swiss nurse, who spoke French to one another, they were convinced that all Center workers were incapable of understanding them."

Determined to be understood, Lorenzo first made friends with the young men of the village who were on summer vacation from school. "The students of Roccamena, like those in other Sicilian villages that summer and all other summers, would leave their bed at eleven in the morning, have lunch at one, and return to bed. When the heat had subsided, they would wander around, tired and bored, until sunset, heckling one another and swapping dirty jokes and tales of their amorous adventures. After their evening meal, they would meet again at the village bar and play a game of *briscola* to decide who was to pay for a round of soda pop. From ten until midnight they paced up and down the main thoroughfare, ending their *passeggiatta* at the edge of town, where they would all urinate as a group. But not even that act was performed in harmony and with a sense of satisfaction: there was always someone who would try to urinate on the others, and there would be quarrels. . . . At midnight, they would all go home to bed, still unhappy.

"Some of these same young men would tell me, 'Here one dies of boredom and heat. There is nowhere to go, nothing to do.' Another used to say: 'I'm getting out of this town as soon as I can and never come back.' And another: 'As far as I'm concerned, there is only one way of dealing with this town: a bomb powerful enough to make ashes out of everything and everybody. We're all poisonous weeds. One bomb and the thing would be done.' "

Lorenzo asked why they did not initiate some action that would shake them out of their apathy. They replied that if someone were to propose anything, he would be unmercifully badgered. " 'What do you expect in Roccamena? Here the skulls are more impenetrable than the rocks. Our greatest talent is making fun of one another. If something useful is tried, it fails. Associations, cooperatives, even religion fails because everyone wants to do things his own way . . .' "

Yet, as I learned from Danilo on the way to Roccamena, Lorenzo had succeeded in establishing serious discussion groups among the young men and, later, a citizens' committee for the development of Roccamena, which was becoming the nucleus of an organization involving all the villages in the Belice valley.

We were all squeezed into the Fiat once more, Patricia and I along with the seven members of the Dolci family. Halfway to Roccamena two policemen stopped the car to point out that there were too many of us in the front seat. "That is quite true," Danilo admitted, but after consulting with one another privately, the police returned his identification card and waved him on. Fearing that other policemen on the road would not be as lenient and would prevent him from reaching Roccamena in time for the occupation of the piazza, I offered to leave the car with Patricia, so that there would be a legal number of passengers; but Danilo would not hear of it. "If the police want to detain me, they can always find some excuse. Don't be concerned."

At the outskirts of Roccamena we were stopped again, this time by a half-dozen policemen, but they merely asked to see Danilo's driver's license. "Let's hope the law will be as nice to us the rest of the day," he said as we rode into the main street, a narrow thoroughfare that passed through the whole village. Above the street, strung high between the buildings, hung a series of black-bordered banners which, in chronological order, cited the broken promises of the Italian government to build the Belice dam. The first was dated 1928. The only banner without a black border read: "Water Means Life for the South." The words were from a telegram Danilo received during his 1963 Roccamena fast from Giuseppe Saragat, shortly before Saragat became President of Italy.

Danilo parked the Fiat near the office of the Center, and we went upstairs to a room jammed with press and television representatives and the demonstrators who were to occupy the piazza. Lorenzo and Franco met us at the door. Franco, looking more haggard than ever, escorted Danilo to the only empty chair in the room. As the rest of us found places on the floor, Danilo pushed his chair against the wall to make more room, joking: "It can finally be said that I have my back to the wall."

In opening the meeting Lorenzo identified the various mayors and village officials who were to participate in the demonstration. To indicate the international interest it had aroused, he also introduced the journalists and television workers who had come from a number of European countries to cover the event. After that he read messages from a batch of telegrams, all expressing enthusiastic support for the week of mourning. One of them, from the executive secretary of the Dolci Committee in Stockholm, announced that 130 Swedes would fast for forty-eight hours in sympathy with the proceedings at Roccamena. Another telegram informed the group that Peter Moule, the British pacifist who had fasted with Dolci at Roccamena for ten days in 1963, would arrive from London the next day to take part in the demonstrations.

Danilo spoke next: "It is a small thing that we are about to do but if we do it well, it will be useful to the villages in the Belice valley, to the country, and to our children. There is the risk of having our heads broken but there is also the risk of going backwards. We must assert ourselves as persons of responsibility who want to go forward.

"We are here to be of service, to join together people of various political beliefs toward one common cause. We shall fast not to ridicule the police, not to be photographed. Ours is a position of reason that emphasizes the distinction between force and truth. By our nonviolent action we shall show that truth has its own strength. Ours is a strategy based on love, not hate, and should result in a chain reaction of discussion and insight.

"In our fast we shall drink water, in order not to endanger our health. Some of us have been fasting since yesterday. What will be the effect of not eating for forty-eight hours? The peasants already know the answer from past experience. There will be a certain weakening of the body; therefore it is well not to talk much, to preserve one's strength. And, of course, there should be no singing since our theme is that of mourning.

"Anyone who is not completely persuaded about our nonviolent action must speak out now. We must know clearly what we must do and why we must do it. Ours will be an act of civil disobedience, for it is the law of this village that the main piazza must be left open for traffic. It is a sensible law. We shall be breaking it because we want to say, in effect, that matters have proceeded in the wrong direction for too long a time; that they need to take a new direction. That is why we shall try to block the square by remaining seated on it.

"We shall proceed in orderly fashion toward the piazza, three abreast, and when we get there, I shall give the signal for seating ourselves. At no time during the occupation of the piazza should more than three or four of us rise at the same time. If you meet with opposition from the police and they try to carry you away, keep your heads up. You will find that more comfortable. No matter where they carry you, keep on returning to the piazza together or singly. Remember, there is no need to be either afraid or excited. We hope that this action of ours may result in civilized police behavior. That would be as important as bread."

He turned to Lorenzo and asked if he had anything else to add.

"One or two things," Lorenzo said. "We are not troublemakers and we don't want any troublemakers among us. If any of us has a knife in his pocket, however small—or any other weapon—let it be deposited here now." He paused a moment and when no one produced anything, he continued: "Just one more point. If you have any ideas of your own that you would like to express on the poster you carry, then do so by all means. You'll find crayons and all the other equipment you need at the piazza . . ."

"Don't you want to say a word about what to do after the fasting?" his wife asked.

"Oh yes, that is important. When you have finished your fast, don't start eating like wolves. Eat very lightly at first. Otherwise, you may become ill."

Danilo looked at his wristwatch and said that it was time they started moving toward the piazza. Since I was closest to the window, he asked me to see if there were any police on the street below. There were none. As we all moved toward the door, a young girl asked: "If the police take us away from our parents, what should we do?" No one answered her question, but an unshaven man who was probably her father picked her up and held her tightly.

Three abreast, led by Danilo, Lorenzo, and Franco, about one hundred men and women began to approach the piazza, less than eighty yards away. Lorenzo held high a poster which said: "Whoever wishes to pursue the old road of waste, exploitation, and the Mafia must pass over our bodies." After they had taken a few steps, the bells of the church in front of the piazza began to clang dolefully, causing one of the demonstrators, a mayor, to laugh and say: "Well, at least we have the church with us." Lorenzo corrected him: the bells were ringing to summon the villagers to high noon mass; the clergy had made it quite clear they wanted no part of the demonstration.

On reaching the edge of the piazza, the demonstrators were confronted by two groups. On one side waited a swarm of photographers and television crewmen, one of them carrying a piece of equipment that looked like a machine-gun. Their eyes were riveted on the other group, the eight policemen and half-dozen officials who were a few feet away. One of the officials was the Mayor of Roccamena, a thin-lipped, chain-smoking Christian Democrat who, after passionately promising to be among the demonstrators, had suffered a severe case of political jitters during the night and decided to be a spectator instead. Next to him, in civilian clothes, were the police commissioners of Roccamena and Corleone.

There was an ominous hush as the demonstrators quietly, as though they were tiptoeing into a forbidden room, advanced to the center of the piazza and waited for Danilo to provide the cue that would initiate their act of civil disobedience. "Let us be seated now," Danilo said calmly. As he lowered himself to the ground, he smiled affably at the Mayor of Roccamena and said *"Buon giorno"* to the two police commissioners. Neither one returned the greeting. The demonstrators all sat on the ground with him, except for an ailing ex-mayor of Salaparuta, who had left a sickbed to fast with the group. The ex-mayor occupied a tiny chair placed next to Danilo, one hand flat against a huge paunch, the other holding up a placard which read: "Enough broken promises. We want results."

With the photographers and television crews waiting for the police to act, the only sounds heard were the murmur of conversation and the sound of a loose blind flapping against a stone wall in the cold wind. The police stared at the demonstrators, saying nothing. The officials kept whispering to one another but gave no order. The two Dolci boys, seated near their father, turned their placards in the direction of the policemen. The slogans they had improvised were inspired by all the talk they had heard of men leaving their families behind to seek work abroad. "Children should be with their fathers," Amico's poster said. "Fathers should be with their children," read Cielo's slogan. The police continued to stare, as though hypnotized.

The tension remained unbroken until a young man, out of

86

breath from running, arrived at the piazza with the news that the policemen stationed at the outskirts of the village were now directing cars to follow a detour that would circumvent the piazza. The talk among the demonstrators instantly surged into a noisy crescendo and one of them, who had prepared for this moment of truth, wildly began waving a placard on which he had scrawled: "Even the police are with us!"

Once it became evident there would be no adverse police action, everyone became more relaxed, except the police commissioners, who went on conferring in whispers. Two peasants arrived on the piazza carrying bales of straw, which they distributed to the demonstrators "so that their bottoms wouldn't wear out." With typical peasant prudence, they had made certain first that the group would be permitted to occupy the piazza before presenting their gifts. The whole square suddenly became filled with throngs of shouting children who chased one another in a happy holiday mood, interfering with the work of the photographers trying to get closeups of the demonstrators. From the church rose the soprano voices of a choir singing of the glory of God.

Above all the noises, the reporters tried to interview some of the demonstrators. "Even though I am illiterate, that doesn't mean I don't know what is right," I heard one peasant say. "I've been hearing about agrarian reform for years but I haven't seen anyone lift a finger to get us out of the dark cave we live in. Danilo and Lorenzo are the first to give us any hope that something good might be accomplished."

Ugo Palma, a professor of biochemistry at the University of Palermo whom I had met earlier that morning, engaged the police commissioner from Corleone in conversation. Palma expressed his appreciation for the authorities' decision to let the demonstrators occupy the piazza peacefully. "Don't you agree," he asked, "that it is best for everyone concerned to make this a nonviolent action, both on the part of the police and the demonstrators?"

The commissioner sniffed the air disdainfully. "It's best for everyone but the police," he replied curtly. "It makes us look like a bunch of damn fools . . ."

A little later when we spoke to Danilo about the lack of police action he said: "The fact that I've been nominated for the Nobel

87

Peace Prize may have something to do with it. I would say that while there is a certain element of morality in the police's decision not to interfere with us—an element that is certainly welcome—there is also an element of opportunism about it and perhaps even one of conformity. But from the point of view of what we are trying to accomplish, this new kind of behavior from the police is a wonderful thing that is bound to create a great deal of constructive discussion."

"Although the Mayor of Roccamena changed his mind about participating in this demonstration," Lorenzo was explaining to a reporter, "there are other Christian Democrats involved in it, among them the Mayor of Partanna. The only party that has officially boycotted this action are the Socialists, and that is all because of one man—a former collaborator of the Center who got sore when the Center parted company with him because he had been engaging in political activity. This same man now heads a Sicilian government agency that is supposed to take the initiative in developing the resources of this area. If he had done his job properly, the dam would already be under way and we wouldn't need to have this demonstration . . ."

As the high mass ended, the doors of the church were flung open and the parishioners poured out into the piazza. They were nearly all women and children. The women turned their faces away from the demonstrators, as though fearing the Devil might be among them, and hastily scurried home. The youngsters remained to join the other children, and their combined shouting crushed all hope of trying to achieve an atmosphere of mourning.

While I chatted with Danilo, I heard Patricia calling out my name. The voice, somewhat muffled, seemed to come from within a circle of children, who were shoving and yelling trying to reach the center. I tore my way through them and found Patricia seated on a small wooden box, with a sketchbook on her knees and a crayon in her hand, totally engulfed by pushing children. An old man wearing a black shawl and holding the blonde child Patricia had been trying to draw was cursing the children for not allowing her enough room to work. At first the children heeded my entreaty to stand back and provide Patricia with the space she needed, but in a few minutes they were again crowding her, vying

88

with one another to see what she was doing. Patricia was obliged to stop. She gave the old man the half-finished sketch of his grandchild and gathered her materials.

Most of the children then resumed their pandemonium in other parts of the piazza, but a few remained and plied her with questions about artists. They had never seen an artist in action before. In the meantime, the grandfather was proudly displaying the sketch to his friends on the piazza. The Community Guard, an elderly villager in a gaudy red and blue uniform, came over to congratulate Patricia on her work and inform her that he too was an artist. "The last time Danilo came to Roccamena to fast for the dam, a recitation I gave in pure Sicilian was broadcast on television all over Sicily." If we would lend him our tape recorder, he would be happy to recite the saga of the mice who invaded a home and took possession of everything, including the people in it.

On being told that we had no tape recorder, he said I must be joking. "All Americans have tape recorders." I convinced him I was not joking, and he invited us to accompany him to his home, where he would give us a private performance of the mice saga.

Before taking us to his home, Don Salvatore introduced us to a demonstrator who was his son-in-law. Luzzu Amato was a slender, almost pretty young man with a heavy black mustache. "You're the first American I've known who can speak Sicilian," he said, and asked where we were planning to have dinner. He and his father-in-law were vastly amused when I replied that we would eat at the nearest restaurant. "There's never been a restaurant in Roccamena," Amato said. "If you don't object to eating in a poor man's home, come and have a meal with me and my family this afternoon."

When I started to protest that it would be too much of an imposition, he said: "If you talk that way, I shall become offended."

What about the demonstration? I asked. Shouldn't he remain on the piazza? He had a prompt answer for that. "I'm free to come and go as I please. I didn't sign up for the fast. If I were to go without food for forty-eight hours, my wife would be a widow in a week." Don Salvatore promised his son-in-law he would deliver us to his house at five.

The saga of the mice, some fifty verses long, was mildly humorous for the first ten verses, then it became a bore. The ordeal was prolonged by Don Salvatore's insistence that I translate each verse for Patricia. After the recitation, as further evidence that he was an "artist," he beat out a mazurka on an ancient and out-of-tune upright piano. He played the composition twice, and then announced that he was also a prolific inventor. Most of the inventions he described sounded like Rube Goldberg contraptions held together by indomitable optimism and serving purposes which were neither desirable nor necessary. The simplest one would release the scream of a siren whenever anyone knocked at the door. "Think of all the deaf people who could profit from this," he said. His most recent invention had a practical purpose: a mask to protect the eyes of men working with fire and metal. "If I could get to Milan I could sell the idea to a big industrialist, I'm sure, and make a fortune." I did not have the heart to tell him that his invention had long been in use.

He took us next door to meet an eighty-two-year-old invalid who had once lived in Cicero, Illinois. The crumpled old man asked if the depression was over in the United States. I told him it had ended some years ago, and he groaned. "I should have had more patience and waited." His daughter, a stocky young woman dressed in black, was a geyser of complaints. "My American relatives used to send me clothes but now they send me only Christmas and Easter cards. What good are those to me? I need their help, not their greetings."

Her loudest lament was that her husband, to whom she had been married only two months, was obliged to go to Switzerland in search of work. "And now he writes that the Swiss are furious at having so many Italians in their country and are treating them like dogs." She dug into a drawer and found her husband's most recent letter. "They can't stand Italians here," she read. "There are signs everywhere which say, 'Italians, go home.' They treat us like dogs. I sometimes feel that I have died and gone to hell."

She cut short our expressions of sympathy by pointing to huge cracks in the walls and ceiling and shouting: "Are these conditions fit for human habitation?" To emphasize this point she took us upstairs to her bedroom, where part of the ceiling had collapsed.

Under it stood a large and shiny chifferobe, a gaudy monument to bad taste which must have cost several hundred dollars. "Isn't it beautiful?" she asked, noting my fascination with it. "We bought it with my dowry money. Now there is no money. None has come so far from Switzerland, though my husband has been gone a month. I don't even have money enough to buy oil for our spaghetti sauce."

Suddenly thrusting her husband's letter into my hand, she cried: "Take it. Take it and publish it in America so people will know what terrible things are happening to us . . ."

On the way back to the piazza Don Salvatore, realizing how shaken we were by the experience, said: "You mustn't mind Dunnietta. She is in a bad state because she needs her husband. He should not have left her so soon after their marriage."

I saw her again later that afternoon when the old man led us along the muddy and smelly alley where his son-in-law lived. She was standing at her door staring at us with such hostility that it hardly seemed possible we had been in her house earlier. In her fierceness, with her long, uncombed hair hanging around her shoulders, she was the picture of a frustrated Medea. In the mistaken impression that Dunnietta was a close friend of the family I had brought a liter of olive oil as a gift for my host, expecting he would share it with her. As it turned out she was simply a neighbor and, according to Amato, "a real bitch." He was astonished to learn that Don Salvatore had taken us into her house. "That father-in-law is a genius of an inventor but he is completely stupid about some things."

I felt badly about the woman's lack of olive oil, and thought I would buy another liter later on to give to her. But after spending a couple of hours with Amato, I changed my mind, fearing I would make an enemy of him if he found out. In a country where poverty has deprived men of everything but their pride, it is easy to make enemies.

Luzzu Amato, his wife, and their three small daughters lived in a second-story room which contained a table, three chairs, and two beds, one for the children, the other for the parents. The cooking was done in a small alcove on a gas burner. The ground floor of the hut was for storing a mule and a cart, but Amato had been jobless for eight months and had been obliged to sell both. There was no water in the house, except that which was sometimes available from a public fountain. The toilet facilities consisted of a bucket, which was kept on the ground floor.

Amato's wife and Don Salvatore's wife were huddled over the gas burner when we entered, but we were not introduced to them until the food was served. One of the Amato children, an infant, was in the arms of his sixteen-year-old sister, a brunette with flashing eyes but otherwise plain features. The two other children, one four and the other six, sat on the bed in white, starched lacy dresses that rustled whenever they squirmed. No one spoke to us except Amato, who was obviously the king of his roost, thoroughly accustomed to obedience and silence from all members of his family except the infant daughter. On her he lavished kisses every few minutes, smothering her with his thick mustache until she cried.

When the food was served, we were appalled to find that we were eating alone. Amato insisted they had all dined earlier, but the children's eyes told me that was not true. He apologized for being too poor to serve us meat, but assured us that the eggs which his wife had poached in a tasty tomato sauce cost fifty lire each and came from the hens of trusted friends. Without much urging, Patricia and I persuaded both little girls to share our eggs.

All through the meal Amato talked a blue streak about himself, while his family sat and stared at us. I learned that, despite his participation in the demonstration, his deepest aspirations had little relationship to Danilo's philosophy of nonviolence. "What we need," he pontificated, "is less conversation about what should be done and more direct action. Another Salvatore Giuliano could solve all of Sicily's problems in no time. Believe me, if such a man were to come along I would be the first to join him."

Giuliano, I protested, had been a villain who had the false reputation of stealing from the rich to help the poor. He had been responsible for killing and wounding many innocent persons, nearly all of them workers and peasants.

"If you will forgive me for disagreeing with you," Amato said, "that's the story the authorities would like to have people believe, but the real villain was his cousin Gaspare Pisciotta, the same bastard who betrayed Giuliano to the police and then shot him to death. If you can return to Roccamena after the demonstrations, I'll be glad to introduce you to some *mafiosi* in the village who can tell you how Pisciotta, in trying to save his own skin, worked hand-in-glove with the police . . .

"I must tell you that I had the great honor of knowing Giuliano in person." He waited with a proud smile while I translated the announcement for Patricia. "I was a kid of ten working on a dairy farm near Roccamena with my father. Giuliano and some of his men walked into the place one morning and robbed it clean. I guess I must have looked scared. As he was leaving, he came over to me, patted me on the face, and told me not to be afraid. Then he put 100,000 lire in my pocket and told me to be good to my parents. What a great man he was!

"There are some people who think it is wrong to rob at any time, but I don't agree with that. Many honest Sicilians have turned to robbery as the only way they could find to feed their families. Here is how I see it: If I have a piece of bread and I see that you don't have any, I naturally give you half of what I have. But if you have a piece of bread and you know I don't have any and yet you don't give me a piece, what else can I do but resort to robbery?"

I resisted the temptation to ask whether he would be willing to share his bottle of olive oil with his neighbor Dunnietta, and asked how he was able to support his family.

He shook his head sorrowfully. "We live on borrowed money and a few lire I earn from time to time doing odd jobs for the municipality. I suffer from severe arthritic pains in the back, and can't work in the fields or do other strenuous labor. The job that would suit me best is that of chauffeur. Although I don't own a car, I do have a driver's license—don't ask me how I got it—and I'm the most skillful driver in Roccamena. If you ever hear of anyone who could use my services as a chauffeur . . . Signore Mangione, do you know what I keep dreaming at night: that Giuliano is still alive and I am his chauffeur, driving him up and down the Via Liberta in Palermo."

I turned to his wife, who had not said a word, and asked if she had ever been to Palermo. Startled to have me address her directly, she glanced at her husband as though to find out whether she had his permission to speak. "Annichia has never been to Palermo," he answered for her. "And that, of course, is the way it should be. We Sicilians do not like to expose our women to the general public. Their place is in the home with their children and nowhere else."

The heavy woman with cowlike eyes gave no indication of whether she agreed or not. Patricia wanted to know if Amato would ever take his wife to a dance.

With the question, his whole demeanor changed. For the first time his speech and gestures became passionate. Never would he take her to a dance, he answered, because if he ever saw a man making the slightest advance to her that man would be dead. He must have noticed the expression of shock on Patricia's face when I translated his statement. "Please explain to your signora that in Sicily we do whatever is necessary to protect our honor, especially when a wife or a sister is involved . . .

"At a dance there are likely to be present men who would feel superior to me simply because they are rich; these are the ones who would try to take liberties with my wife—or with my sister, if she were along. It is the way rich people often are, but they are also very stupid. What they don't realize is that although poverty keeps you hungry, it also makes you very crafty—so crafty that it would be possible for me to kill a man without being caught. And, believe me, I wouldn't hesitate to kill him if he tried to make a cuckold of me or threaten the honor of my sister."

"Is he angry with us?" Patricia asked before I translated the statement.

"I hope not," I said. "But he's beginning to make me very nervous."

His face had become flushed; his fervor gleamed in his dark eyes as he turned them on every member of his family one by one, apparently to emphasize that he had uttered a warning which they must now memorize or pay dire consequences. I watched his sister wince, as though she had been directly accused of some shameful action. The next moment she was trying to quiet the infant in her arms who, possibly incited by a premonition of what she could expect when she was older, had burst into tears.

My nervousness grew after I had watched him toss down his fifth full glass of wine, especially since I became aware that I had been studying his sister from the moment we sat down at the table. A number of times her eyes had deliberately met mine, with such complete lack of embarrassment that I could not help thinking that she was prepared to flirt with any male she encountered, regardless of the consequences. After hearing Amato's harangue I did my best to avoid looking at her but did not wholly succeed.

"Let me tell you to what extent we Sicilians will sometimes go to make certain that our honor is kept intact," Amato resumed, suddenly intense again. The newspaper account he described concerned a bachelor of Reggiocalabria who lived with his sister. "Reggiocalabria is so close to Sicily that its men have the same principles about honor that we do." One day the sister reported that a married neighbor, the father of two children, had leered at her. Although she swore that was all that had happened, the brother murdered the neighbor and his wife as well as their two children. Still furious, he continued to kill everyone he could find who was connected with the family, including two pregnant women. "So far he has killed a total of forty-two persons. Only three members of the family are left. My guess is that he'll get to them before the police get to him. In the meantime, his sister has become insane. I imagine he is also insane."

Despite the last statement, it was evident that Amato relished the grossness of the crime, and I began to worry about any suspicions he might have about my attitude toward his sister. Patricia had once warned me that my habit of looking intently into people's eyes might get me into trouble. Would the sister tell her brother that I had leered at her? Had he told the story of the Reggiocalabria madman with some sinister purpose in mind? I announced it was time for us to leave, pretending there were a couple of matters I had to discuss with Danilo before returning to Partinico.

Amato urged me to have one more glass of wine. "Danilo can wait. It will be a long time before those people in Rome start building his dam."

But I was determined. Firmly, I disengaged myself from the arm on my shoulder, and Patricia and I began saying good night to each member of the family. As I shook hands with the sister, I had an irresistible compulsion to look into her eyes once more. This time they were blank.

A cold mountain wind was blowing over the piazza. Danilo and his wife and the rest of the fasting demonstrators began to prepare for the long night. Danilo's portable phonograph was playing Vivaldi as we arrived on the scene. Some of the villagers had just finished building a bonfire near the blanket-draped demonstrators. The police, who up until now had watched the group from the edge of the square, now moved into it and warmed their hands over the blaze. One of them chatted with a pretty girl, a teacher attached to the Center who was taking part in the fast. "I'm glad that there was no need for violence today," the policeman told her. "I hate to get rough with people who aren't criminals . . ."

In the firelight, an old deaf mute named Piddu, a peasant who was a talented mime, began to entertain the group by enacting his encounters with various villainous members of the animal kingdom. Later a shepherd began to play on his wooden flute, a bittersweet tune that evoked beauty and sadness. The shepherd was still playing when Patricia and I left the piazza to return to Partinico.

March for
a Dying Valley

THE NEXT MORNING I drove to Roccamena with Franco, while Patricia remained in bed nursing a bad cold. Franco still looked ghastly but claimed he was feeling much better, well enough to participate in the second forty-eight hours of fasting. We bought copies of all the Italian newspapers available in Partinico, and spent most of the trip reviewing the coverage they had given the occupation of the piazza.

The most comprehensive and sympathetic account appeared in the *Giornale di Sicilia,* the Christian Democrat newspaper with the largest daily circulation in Sicily. The frontpage headline read: "A Quiet Fast in the Piazza of Roccamena While the Police Stand by and Watch." A photograph of Danilo showed him next to the paunchy ex-mayor of Salaparuta on his tiny chair. He was identified as "Giuseppe Di Girolama, a fat and sick man who breathes with difficulty, who participated in the fast against doctor's orders, so as to show his disagreement with his party's [Socialist] attitude toward the demonstration."

As was to be expected, the most hostile report was published in *Telestar,* a neo-fascist Sicilian daily, which tried to convey the impression that the whole affair had been a fiasco. "Only a Few Demonstrate with Danilo Dolci," read the big headline. Under it was a photograph of Danilo seated on the piazza with Vincenzina and two other demonstrators; his facial features had been cleverly distorted to resemble those of a hippopotamus. The story began:

"Danilo Dolci with seven men and a woman yesterday occupied the street that crosses the main square of Roccamena." Franco found the final paragraph amusing: "Yet Danilo Dolci, when appraised for his efforts over the years, deserves everyone's respect, even that of his adversaries. What is it that makes this man live so humbly, even when he is not fasting, when he could, if he wished, live luxuriously outside of Italy, where his books are bestsellers and where he would be revered?"

"It will be news to Danilo that his books are bestsellers," Franco said.

The headline in *L'Ora* read: "Half of Europe Watches the Protest at Roccamena."

"Half of Europe," Franco complained, "but nowhere in Italy." Although the event had been taped for Italian television, the telecast had been killed. "That's what happens in a country where television is run by the government and the government is run by the Catholic Church," he grumbled.

"In the Piazza on the Straw They are Fasting in Roccamena" read the headline of the *Il Giorno* account written by the journalist of Milan. Typical of Italian newspaper style, the story was a mixture of straight reporting and shameless editorializing. The writer sneered that the demonstration was held "virtually under the protection of the police" and also that the shouting of the children in the piazza transformed the event from one of mourning to that of a *festa*. But not all of the report was unfriendly. One paragraph read: "On Wednesday there will be a march to the banks of the Belice, the river whose waters go to waste in the sea, the river which for thirty years has nurtured the dream of the peasants that with a dam and proper irrigation they will be able to get rid of their misery. On Wednesday evening, according to the schedule, all lights in the valley will be turned off. 'The outside darkness,' says Dolci, 'can illuminate the inside of man—his conscience and his intelligence.'"

"Not so bad for a Christian Democrat snob," commented Franco. "Maybe his experience at Roccamena will produce some internal illumination in him."

The story that pleased him the most was published in the Roman newspaper, *Il Messaggero*. It was a brief and straightforward account on an inside page. Of all the news stories, this one, Franco said, was most likely to be read by members of the Italian Parliament:

At Roccamena has begun the "week of mourning" in behalf of a dam on the Belice, initiated by the Study Center, of which Danilo Dolci is the major exponent. "The waters of the Belice," reads a proclamation issued by the Committee for the Week of Mourning—"despite the perennial promises of government authorities, continue to go to waste in the sea. Every year there are wasted more than 60 million meters of water, and about five billion lire in potential agricultural revenue. While thousands of families remain destitute, and twenty-two villages starve, eroded and suffocated by confusion and exploited by the *mafiosi*, the valley is dying . . ."

The week of mourning has these three objectives:

(1) Taking immediate steps toward the building of the dam.

(2) The enactment of laws against all vestiges of agricultural feudalism.

(3) The establishment of an agency for the development of the region that will take into account the individual needs of all the villages in the region.

The piazza had the desolate air of an abandoned picnic ground. Pieces of straw and gray remnants of the bonfire were scattered everywhere; there were no children about. Pale and drowsy, the demonstrators were huddled close together, some still under blankets and coats. From Vincenzina, who was rubbing Danilo's back, I learned that he had not fared well; he had sciatic pains in his back, a cold in his head, and he was running a temperature. Despite his coughing and sneezing, he declined my offer to find him some medication, preferring to wait until his fast was over and he could return to Partinico. His spirits improved when he saw the large headlines in the newspapers Franco handed him. "All this is bound to create discussion, and that is all to the good," he said. He shook his head dolefully when he saw the *Telestar* headline and the hippopotamus version of himself. The day before, the writer of the story had assured him he intended to write an "honest" account.

Gradually the piazza began to fill again, with demonstrators who had spent the night at home and with idle villagers who came to talk. Peter Moule, the British pacifist, arrived at noon, accompanied by his fiancée, Rosalie. They were to have been married that week but when the news of the week of mourning reached them they decided to postpone the ceremony and join the demonstrators. The girl was quiet and beautiful; the schoolteacher spectacles did not conceal the poetry of her sea-blue eyes or detract from the firm delicacy of her mouth and nose. Moule, who also wore glasses, was a tall and lean young man. His red beard and thin figure gave him the aspect of an anchorite, but an anchorite who smiled, which he did frequently as it was his only means of communicating with the Sicilians.

A steady stream of villagers shook hands with Moule and eagerly asked if he remembered them. They had affectionate memories of him when he fasted in Roccamena with Danilo the first time. They said to him: "Now there is mourning but two years ago there was singing and a very famous movie actor came to speak to us. There was also a poet, the first ever to visit this village. Do you recall him?" They had to make sure there was still a bond between them. Moule smiled and nodded at all the comments and questions, and handed out a pocketful of buttons bearing the words "Committee of 100." The significance of the message was beyond them but they felt honored and wore the buttons proudly, as badges of their friendship with the young Englishman.

As soon as school let out the piazza became a screaming jungle of racing children. The teen-age boys stopped racing when they discovered Rosalie and formed a crowded circle around her, enthralled by her willingness to converse with them, even with her fiancé close by. Living in a culture that makes virtual prisoners of its female members from the time they are twelve, the opportunity of being near to so lovely and congenial a girl, without fear of censure or punishment, intoxicated them. Some of the boys became small tornadoes of pidgin French, the only language they had in common with her.

In my wanderings near the piazza I encountered Paola Barbera, who invited me to lunch at her home along with a friend from Stockholm who was covering the demonstrations for Swedish television. Lorenzo, she explained, would not be present, since his fast would not be over until late that afternoon. Having been fearful all morning that I might run into Luzzu Amato and be inveigled to his home for another meal (in the night I had dreamed he was

100

forcing me to marry his sister at the point of a breadknife), I accepted her invitation with alacrity.

The apartment was a large dingy one at the edge of the village. Shyly, Paola said she had asked me to come a little early because she had been wanting to speak to me alone ever since my arrival. The year before Danilo had lent her the Italian translation of *Mount Allegro;* the book had made a deep impression on her and raised "a serious question" about Sicilians which she was anxious to discuss with me. She began by explaining that when she married Lorenzo in Rome she had been encumbered with the usual prejudices that central and northern Italians have about southerners; despite all of Lorenzo's efforts to explain what Sicilians were actually like, she had been extremely apprehensive at the prospect of living in a miserable Sicilian village, away from the sophistications of her native city, among the uneducated and illiterate.

At Paola's request I followed her into the kitchen, so that she could prepare the lunch while we talked. "For quite a while after we came to Roccamena," she continued, "I was quite unhappy. They called me 'The Foreigner' and with reason. I couldn't understand their language and, like most foreigners, I tended to judge everyone too superficially. But gradually understanding began to come, and it came more quickly when I read your book. I began to appreciate the same things you do in that book—the remarkable wisdom of these people—I find it even among the most ignorant peasants, their great love of family life; and most of all, I think, their passionate attachment to life itself. There is despair among them, to be sure, but it is despair that comes from economic poverty, not the despair so prevalent in the north that comes from spiritual bankruptcy. If you give a Sicilian a chance to earn a livelihood, he becomes a happy man, a much happier one than the more educated and more affluent Italians can ever be . . .

"You know all this from having grown up among Sicilians. Even though your Sicilians lived in America, their way of life and their attitudes were exactly like those I encounter in Roccamena. What I would like to know from you is this: What is going to happen to these people? Suppose we do succeed in getting enough dams built and making them prosperous? What then? Will they retain the

101

wonderful qualities they have now? And are they really wonderful qualities, or am I just being a romantic?"

We both laughed over her observation that her "one serious question" had multiplied into a questionnaire. I told her I had often meditated on similar questions, without arriving at any satisfactory answers. What made all her questions difficult, I said, is the fact that many of the qualities we both admired in Sicilians stemmed from situations which were basically evil, such as the stranglehold which feudalism had on Sicily for so long, which encouraged ignorance, class differences, and the subjugation of women.

"I've met a few unhappy women in Roccamena," she said, "but on the whole they are happier than most women I've known. They seem to enjoy being overprotected by their husbands . . ."

"To the point of being their prisoners," I said. "Would you enjoy being married to a typical Sicilian husband?"

She smiled. "I guess not. If my husband were a typical Sicilian, I could not have invited you to lunch with me."

I told Paola about some of the major changes I had observed among Sicilians living in the industrialized society of Americans. At first they were shocked by the freedom American women enjoyed, but gradually they came to accept many of the same liberties they had once condemned as "immoral," not for themselves but for their daughters. Their American experience also ended the despotic rule of the father, and his custom of selecting spouses for his children. And because it is not uncommon for couples in the United States to live away from their parents, Sicilian families were no longer as closely knit as they once were. "Sicilian culture, as you know it here," I said, "is vanishing in the United States. In a couple of generations there won't be any trace of it, except for a few Sicilian names that Americans have trouble spelling."

"Is all that desirable?" Paola asked. "If people lose their sense of being Sicilians, they will lose the qualities that make Sicilians so attractive. They will become like everyone else, like the Italians who live in an industrialized society . . ."

We were interrupted by the arrival of her Swedish guest, a small, spry man in his thirties with a bushy mustache and a cocktail party ebullience that seemed startling in Roccamena. His

102

name was Lars; he spoke English as easily as he did Italian.

"Why aren't you dressed in black, Paola?" he asked, giggling. "Don't you know it is your duty as the wife of Lorenzo, who sits in the piazza with his hunger pains? Furthermore, are you not a collaborator of Saint Danilo, the savior of Sicily and the inspiration of all masochists?"

Paola went on with her cooking. "Simmer down," she said. "Lunch will be ready in a few minutes."

On learning that I had come to Sicily to write about the activities of Danilo and his group, he said: "What activity? What do those collaborators do with their time? There are twenty of them now. Have you found out what they do?"

I replied that I was beginning to. "It seems to me they do quite a bit."

"They don't do a damn thing except eat, sleep, fornicate, and answer the telephone. The Center used to get some work done when there were foreigners there. But now that Danilo is working with natives very little gets done."

"Lorenzo gets a great deal done," Paola said quietly, serving the omelette.

"That is only because of your un-Sicilian influence on him," he said. "Danilo's willingness to work with so many Sicilians on his staff is just one more proof of his genius for suffering."

"Why are you so bitter about Sicilians?" I asked.

"Because one of them married the only girl I'll ever love." He laughed, and tried to put an arm around Paola.

"You must have had something to drink," she said.

He denied it. "It is your presence that makes me feel so exhilarated. But to return to your question, Mr. Mangione. You haven't heard how bitter I can be on the subject of Sicilians. They are a cruel and heartless people who care only for their precious egos . . ."

"If you go on that way, I'll put poison in your food," Paola said.

"Their philosophy is to do nothing," he continued. "They believe in death, not in life. They pay more attention to their cemeteries than to their homes and villages. In fact, the only beautifully maintained places in Sicily are the cemeteries."

Paola tried to change the subject but did not succeed. The Swede began to tell us that when he first came to Roccamena after the war he noticed a large stone blocking the road; it had apparently fallen there from a bombed building. On his second trip, ten years later, he found that the stone had not been moved. "The first thing I did when I arrived here on Sunday was to investigate the stone. It was still lying in exactly the same spot blocking the road. Another monument to Sicilian inertia."

"Why don't you stop talking and eat for a change?" Paola suggested. "Don't you like my food?"

"Paola, my dear, if you were not the most beautiful woman in the world but the homeliest one, I would marry you anyway because of your superb cooking. Lorenzo is too stupid to deserve you. Imagine giving up food like this to fast for a dam that will only create new problems for the Sicilians. How can they cope with new problems when they haven't been able to do anything about the old ones?"

"If Lorenzo were here, you wouldn't dare talk this way," Paola said.

"If he were here, I would ask him why in hell he hasn't done anything about that stone. Three people could easily remove it, but they won't because there is no hope of change in Sicily." He turned to me. "There is only one thing that changes in Sicily, Mr. Mangione. The holes in the road. Every year they get larger . . ."

"You are a dour, Nordic pessimist with no faith in anything," Paola said.

"Ah, but you are wrong," he replied rapturously. "I have utmost faith in you." He held out his arms imploringly, while grinning. "Let me take you away from this annex of hell, where the land and the people are as hard as rock, where there are never any flowers in the fields even when it is spring."

"You are a madman," Paola said calmly, serving the fruit course.

Later, while the Swede was in the washroom, she said: "Please don't take Lars seriously. He's really not as bad as he sounds. He used to be a member of the Dolci Committee in Stockholm but then he had a fight with the head of it and resigned in a huff. He's been saying bitter things about Sicily ever since. I hope he hasn't offended you . . ."

I assured her he hadn't.

"Basically," she said, "he is like any typical member of an industrialized society: alienated and unhappy."

"What about the rock on the road?" I asked.

"I don't believe that story, but I'll have Lorenzo look into it." After a moment she added: "He's dead wrong about the flowers. They are late this year, but they always come and they are the most beautiful wild flowers in Italy."

The Swede and I left together shortly afterwards. He was obviously embarrassed, and said very little as we went toward the piazza. On our way out Paola had revealed that, although I was an American, I was also a Sicilian.

Danilo and Vincenzina were preparing to leave the piazza as I arrived. They and twenty-eight other demonstrators had been fasting since Saturday; now the fast was to be resumed by a new group. With Danilo and his wife were their two oldest children, Libera and Amico. As Danilo rose from his bed of straw, I noticed with what difficulty he moved, and also that his body was trembling. I put my scarf around his neck but that did not stop the trembling. Crouched over in pain, with his arms around Vincenzina and Libera, both of whom barely reached his waist, he limped toward his car, like some broken warrior leaving a battlefield. The rest of the children, who had spent the night at the home of a Roccamena friend, were waiting for him near the car. One of them was holding a bag of fruit. As soon as they saw Danilo, they rushed up to him, kissing his face and clinging to his body. The youngest one cried as she hugged him, unaccustomed to seeing her father in pain.

On the road we were stopped by a policeman, at almost the same point where we had been stopped the day before. But it was a different officer, a suave young man whose voice sneered as he glanced at the identification papers and exclaimed, "Ah, Signore Dolci in person." He leisurely counted the number of passengers, and noted various irregularities in the condition of the car. "There are at least four reasons why I could have you fined," he finally announced, "but I've decided to be generous with you this afternoon, Signore Dolci." He returned Danilo's papers. "This time you may proceed."

"*Antipatico,*" was Danilo's only comment when we were out of earshot. But Cielo had a great deal to say about the villainous nature of all policemen. Danilo cut him short, saying that he loved policemen as much as other people, though he was not always in agreement with them. "Policemen often behave badly only because they have been commanded to do so. I am certain that if jobs were easier to find, fewer men would wish to become policemen."

"But you said he was '*antipatico,*'" Cielo argued.

"He was," Danilo admitted, "but perhaps if I were to know him better and learn what he is like when he is not being a policeman, I might find him *simpatico.*"

"I don't think so," Libera said. "He had no humor."

"It is true," Danilo said, "that a sense of humor and an appreciation for silence are among man's best assets."

"In that case," Vincenzina said, "shouldn't you be silent now? You're ill. You should preserve your strength."

No one said anything for some time. Then Danilo broke the silence by proposing that a division be made of the bag of fruit that had been given to the children. Addressing the children with the same seriousness with which he addressed his staff meetings, he said: "I would like to suggest that I be permitted to eat an orange and an apple and that the rest of the fruit be divided equally among the rest of you. *Siamo d'accordo?*" I tried to give my share to Vincenzina and then to Danilo, and when they both refused it, to the children, but got nowhere.

We parted at the Via Emma after arranging to meet at the Center on Wednesday morning, when we would return to Roccamena for the mass march to the Belice. But I encountered Danilo an hour later in a drug store, where I had gone to buy some aspirin for Patricia, who was still ailing. Exhausted and feverish, he was describing his symptoms to the pharmacist and asking him to prescribe an effective antibiotic. The medicine cost more lire than Danilo had with him. I had expected that the pharmacist, an old acquaintance of his, would give some consideration to the reasons for his illness and make him a gift of the medicine. But it soon became clear enough that he had no such intention, and I supplied the rest of the lire. "I'll be cured after a day's rest," Danilo said, thanking me. "I never allow an illness of this kind to continue for more than a day."

On Wednesday morning at 7:30 when I arrived at the Center, I found Danilo looking wan but hard at work. "I'm practically cured," he assured me. He had been up since 4:30, his customary rising hour, preparing the statement he was to deliver at the end of the march, and now he was immersed in trying to telephone people in Rome and Milan. While Osvaldo typed his speech, Danilo worked on a news release and kept urging the operator to try again. I had already heard of Danilo's habit of telephoning people while they were still asleep. As an early riser, he found it incredible that people would still be in bed, ignoring their telephones, as late as seven-thirty.

None of the half dozen calls he tried to make that morning was completed. Nothing seemed to go right at first. At the garage where we stopped to have a soft tire checked, the only attendant was a ten-year-old boy who insisted it had not been punctured, that a little air would fix everything. As we hurried to Danilo's apartment to pick up his family, we heard a fierce explosion under us which sounded like a blowout. Rushing to another garage, we were told by an adult attendant that he could find nothing wrong with the tires. "What then caused the explosion?" Danilo asked. The attendant said it would take him one hour to figure out the cause. There was no time for that, Danilo replied, and sped to his home, where the family was worriedly waiting for us.

Despite all our fears, nothing went wrong on the road. A policeman stopped the car to inform Danilo that there were too many persons in the car, but waved him on. At the outskirts of Roccamena another policeman, who did not recognize Danilo, politely explained we would have to take a detour into the village since the "main piazza was blocked."

The area around the piazza was already crowded with journalists, photographers, and Sicilians who had arrived by bus from the villages in the Belice valley to take part in the march. They were nearly all men, dressed in their Sunday blacks; their leaders carried huge red banners with the name of a village or trade union embroidered on them. The sun was in view, but it had rained

107

hard during the night, and the demonstrators on the piazza had been soaked to the skin. Their weary faces contrasted sharply with the fresh and vibrant men who kept arriving every few minutes on buses, and taking their places solemnly behind the banners of their leaders.

While Danilo and Franco went into a huddle to check the final details of the march, I joined Lorenzo Barbera, who was organizing a contingent of demonstrators to parade through all the streets and alleys of Roccamena and urge the residents to join the march that was about to start. I found myself in the front line of the parade, next to Lorenzo. As we sloshed through the mud, the paraders yelled out slogans and asked the women and old men on the balconies to participate in a march that would help bring about a better world for their husbands and children. Lorenzo, who usually spoke in Italian, exhorted them in Sicilian, addressing himself particularly to the women.

"Don't be ashamed of joining the march," he shouted at them. "There will be other women in the march, many of them. Remember, the march is for the benefit of your families. March with us!" Ordinarily a quiet man of few words, he now became an impassioned orator with a big voice that belied the size of his body. He brought the parade to a dead stop in front of a half-constructed building where there were three men working. "Are you going to let others march for you?" he demanded. "What kind of men are you who can ignore an event like the march? Don't you want a dam that will bring prosperity to this valley?" The men listened sheepishly, and when he paused for breath, one of them said: "Since when has it become a sin to work, Lorenzo?" An older worker spoke up hastily. "Don't mind him, Lorenzo. I promise we'll all be there when the march starts."

The next stop was at the village school. Lorenzo urged the principal to dismiss all classes for the day, in order that the students could join the march. Speaking in Italian this time, he told the woman that although official permission to close the school that day had been sought and denied, she as the principal had the authority to permit the students to march, with the understanding they would make up the lost classroom work at some other date. Though claiming to be in sympathy with the purpose of the

108

march, the principal rejected his suggestion. "If you had not tried to get official permission, I could have acted on my own, but since official permission has been denied to you my hands are tied . . ."

If she were truly in sympathy with the march, Lorenzo replied, she would find a way of untying her hands. "This march has great significance for all the children of the village, even for those who are yet too young to understand its implications now. Nothing they can learn in the classroom today can be nearly as important as their participation in the march, which expresses a hope for their future."

But the woman was adamant. She said she had talked with her superior the night before on the telephone and he had been outraged by newspaper reports which indicated that on Sunday the children had turned the demonstration into a carnival, instead of doing their homework for the next day.

Lorenzo, dropping his politeness, accused the woman of being against the march. "I know," he said, "from conversations I have had with all your teachers that the children have been threatened with reprisals if they are absent on the day of the march. Do you deny that?"

Without denying anything and without any loss of glibness, the principal said she would telephone her superior and find out whether he would grant the children special permission to be in the march.

"Fine," said Lorenzo. "Why not telephone him right now?" He pointed to the telephone on her desk.

"I'll have to wait a half hour," she said. "He doesn't get to his office until then."

Outside, Lorenzo said sorrowfully, "She has no intention of phoning anyone. She'll pretend that she phoned and that the answer was no. I know what she's like."

The march, called for 10:30, started only a half-hour late, a miraculous feat of timing considering the congenital lack of punctuality among Sicilians and the complications of gathering together at one point representatives of twenty-two villages. Some two thousand persons, a surprising number of them women with infants in their arms, marched nine abreast. The only other children present were those too young to be in school. Danilo, taller

109

than anyone else that morning, was in the front line, flanked on both sides by eight mayors, four of them Communists, three Christian Democrats, and one a political independent from Gibellina. Most of the marchers were on foot, but some rode horses, asses and mules. Three of Danilo's youngest children were perched on a peasant's gray mare that had been fitted with wooden seats. A number of jeeps filled with heavily armed policemen drove alongside the march, without disturbing anyone. All along the line it was relatively quiet. The only loud sounds came from a native of Roccamena who, during the first mile, kept running up and down the sides of the road shouting slogans through an electrified megaphone. There was no sign of him after that.

The Belice River is more than three miles distant from Roccamena, over a rough, jagged road which twists around a barren tract, land that will one day become the bed of a lake once the dam is built. I wore rubbers (an unknown luxury in Sicily) which protected me from the muddy surface at first, but as the road became rougher its sharp stones sliced through the soles and let in the water and mud. A number of the marchers, whose feet were poorly protected, took to the fields, in an attempt to avoid the stones, but the mud was too deep for walking; some of them became mired, and had to be pulled out.

The farther into the valley we advanced the hotter it became. The marchers began to remove some of their clothing and, also, to walk at varying speeds, so that the crisp orderliness present at the start of the march gradually disappeared. By the time they had reached the halfway mark, they resembled a wandering horde. Looking back on the road that twisted in great curves around the treeless and rocky landscape, I saw a scene that belonged to Biblical times: a line of old peasants and mothers with babes in their arms, some on foot, some on mules, traveling single file across the rim of a hill, their lonely figures silhouetted against the hot sky.

I walked with Peter Moule and his girl, and a five-year-old child named Nina who had attached herself to Rosalie early in the march and fiercely clung to her hand. The child's dark curly hair was matted with dirt; the eyes in the pale face were pitch black. In her compassion for the child's frail body, Rosalie wanted to carry her, but Peter would not allow it, pointing out that as she had been fasting for thirty hours she needed what strength she had left to complete the march. Another man and I offered to carry the child, but Nina let each of us know with a flash of her eyes that she would have none of us. Rosalie alone she trusted; on those few occasions when Nina said anything, it was only to her that she would speak. I was puzzled by the coarseness of her voice and the crudeness of her dialect until a woman near me explained that Nina was the only child of a widowed shepherd who lived in a remote mountain shack; she seldom saw anyone but her father.

While we marched, Peter spoke of his first fast in Roccamena. "Danilo and I had a regular routine. We would rise at six in the morning, and open the doors of our ground floor room about forty-five minutes later. We were right on the piazza, and there were always people waiting to talk with us, anxious to know how we were. At two o'clock we would close the doors and take a two-hour siesta. The doors were opened again at four and kept open until nine, when we retired for the night. In the evening some of the men would bring guitars and mandolins and we would all sing together.

"Many of the visitors were schoolchildren. They were very friendly and talked a blue streak. The girls would soon leave but the boys would remain and go on talking. Sometimes they arrived chewing on candy or cookies and offered us whatever they had. Danilo would explain why we couldn't accept their offerings. They learned quickly. At first I found it very aggravating to watch food being eaten in my presence, but after a couple of days I became quite indifferent to it.

"As the days passed the adults came in increasing numbers. At first they were all men but gradually they began to bring their wives and toward the end of the fast the women actually came on their own. The women had been warned that if they cried in our presence, they were to leave. One old woman had tears streaming down her face but she had shaped her lips into a smile, so that she could stay. The women were far more reticent than the men, except for a housewife who had heard that Danilo was a saint and demanded that he perform a miracle for her sick husband. I guess the most surprising caller we had was the local police chief, who arrived one evening to pay his respects and wish us 'courage.' Con-

111

sidering how much the Sicilians despise the police, I admired him for his own courage. He was quite embarrassed and stayed only a few minutes.

"Even though the promises made by the authorities at the end of our hunger strike were not kept, the fast was a successful one, I thought, because nearly all the people in the village became involved in the reasons why we were fasting. Toward the end of the fast some 130 villagers, to show that they were in sympathy with us, stopped eating for twenty-four hours. I haven't seen many of those people on this trip. I suppose they are in various countries working or trying to find work . . ."

I asked Peter what physical effects the fasting had on him and on Danilo.

"Provided you don't move around too much, fasting for the first couple of days is fairly easy," he said. "Around the fourth day you begin to feel the effects, mainly in the legs, which become weary and cumbersome. About that time you begin to dream of food. I kept dreaming of my favorite dish—a vegetable curry. My mind didn't seem to become affected; throughout the fast I felt alert and quite able to concentrate. Danilo had a tougher time of it physically. Possibly because he is a little older than I am, he tired more often. After the first couple of days we both experienced some kind of urine poisoning; to counter it, we both agreed to take a certain amount of sugared water every day, and this stopped it. Danilo also took certain drops prescribed by the doctor for his heart condition . . ."

The march came to a stop. Before us rose a steep hill; one side of it formed a sheer cliff of red rock. Beyond the hill lay the Belice, an unprepossessing stream at this time of the year, yet one that becomes swollen with flood water in the fall and winter. The floods had depressed a large tract of land near the river bank and given it the shape of a giant horseshoe. A peasant who heard me exclaim at this quirk of nature called my attention to the huge cracks within the horseshoe which had been caused by erosion. He said: "Ordinarily a horseshoe is a sign of good luck. But this one is a sign of misfortune. Summer, fall, and winter these lands suffer. Floods and landslides in the cold months and too much sun and no rain all summer long. Most of the year our earth belongs to the Devil."

112

Danilo had planned to hold the meeting of the marchers on the hilltop, but the hill was too steep for the tired men and women, and only a few of us followed him to the top. The rest of the marchers seated themselves on the grass, their big red banners resting among them like wilted flowers.

One of the highlights of the day was to be the "unveiling" of a dedication cut into the face of a cliff overlooking the Belice, but the man charged with the assignment had failed to carry it out. In a feverish effort to compensate for the failure, Paola Barbera printed the words of the dedication on a rock imbedded in the hilltop: "Here the people of the Belice valley came to affirm their intention to contribute to the birth of a new world that will be without waste, without Mafia, and without exploiters." Studying her handiwork, Paola said sadly, "On the cliff the words would have been seen for miles around. This is a poor substitute, but at least it gives the photographers one more thing to photograph."

Danilo waited on the hilltop, hoping the marchers would join him after they had rested a while, but when he saw that they had no intention of moving, he decided to hold the meeting in the field where they were already seated. He was the first to speak. "All we need to do is to look around us," he began, "to see what the earth is saying. The eroded hills show us their bones; the cracks in the soil tell us that the river is devouring the land in the valley. Before us is a road that was begun but not finished. The houses of Caparini [a settlement built by the Italian government, plainly visible across the river] are empty of people, just as its faucets are empty of water, its electric wires without current. In this valley, where twenty villages are rapidly becoming empty, the teachers are without students, the illiterate are without teachers. There are stationed at Roccamena five policemen and only two teachers . . .

"We have resolved that these hills will be reforested, that the water, gathered in a lake of the dam, will be used to enrich the valley instead of destroying it; that children will grow up with their fathers and fathers with their children; that there will be more teachers than policemen in all the villages. We have resolved that the valley and its people will cease to be in the grip of a feudal situation; that they will pledge themselves, through the

113

work of each individual, of each group, of each region to improve themselves, availing themselves of new machines, new techniques and of new industries, without ever becoming enslaved to them.

"Many wonder how it happens that our effort, a relatively minor one, has attracted the attention of so many people throughout the world. I do not believe that it is only because of the suffering in this particular land; for every country has its share of that. If we are watched with interest it is mainly because we have discovered that economic development must be accompanied by the prospect of peace; and that the effort for peace, in order not to become abstract, must be dedicated to the resolution of specific social and economic problems.

"More and more people are realizing that in order for humanity to survive and achieve a new kind of world, it is necessary to recognize that there is an indispensable link between economic planning and nonviolence, between redevelopment work and nonviolent revolution . . ."

In a few sentences Danilo expressed the basic credo of his group, while adapting it to the specific situation confronting the inhabitants of the Belice valley. There were no gestures; the delivery was free of rhetorical flourishes, almost to the degree of monotony. Yet he spoke with all the firmness and poetry of his convictions and if the general tone of the talk was too intellectual for the peasants and workers, it did not fail to impress the students, teachers, and journalists in the audience, those who would be most likely to repeat what they had heard. The next three speakers engaged in the histrionics and clichés of the professional orator; the last one, a spellbinding mayor, was frequently interrupted by loud applause, something that had not happened once during Danilo's talk.

Peter Moule was to have announced at the conclusion of the meeting that as a gesture of their support for the week of mourning, the pacifists in London were picketing the Italian embassy all that week. But in the euphoric aftermath of the mayor's oratory, Lorenzo, who was chairman of the meeting, forgot to call on Moule. Distressed by the blunder, Danilo tried to stop the audience from dispersing, but it was too late.

The march back was more arduous; the road was mostly uphill, the marchers were tired and hungry. Inasmuch as the return to

Roccamena was not an ordained part of the march, as many as could avoided walking. Danilo and his family returned on horseback. Peter Moule and his fiancée received several offers of rides, but declined them. Although I was tired, I felt obliged to follow their example, my conscience arguing that if they, who had been fasting, walked, I, who had not been fasting, should also walk. Nina was still with us, still clutching Rosalie's hand. Observing the child's devotion to the English girl, some of the peasant women began asking Rosalie whether she would take Nina back to England with her. "The Virgin Mary would bless you all your life if you were to do such a beautiful and charitable thing," one of them said.

Acting as interpreter, I explained that neither Rosalie nor Peter Moule was rich; that supporting the child would present many difficulties for them. To that, one of the women said: "There would be no problem. All English people are richer than we are." "And, of course, the Americans are the richest of all," her friend added.

From their persistent urging, I had assumed that the women were related to Nina, but it developed that she was a complete stranger to them; they were simply promoting an idea which appealed to their imaginations. Would they be willing to give one of their own children to a foreigner? I asked them, and they became indignant at the suggestion. "Of course not," the older one said. "We would never part with our children. We Sicilians love them too much."

"Isn't it possible that the father of this child feels the same way about her?" I asked.

"It's possible," the woman agreed. "But perhaps her father doesn't love her enough to deserve her. Just look at her poor starved face . . ."

A sixteen-year-old boy, overhearing the conversation, told me that three years before an Italian American from Texas had taken a liking to him and promised he would return to Roccamena shortly and bring him to Texas to live. "He kept saying I had a very American face and would have no difficulty living among Texans, but I never saw him again."

115

"It's better that you remain with your family," one of the women said.

"My family is in Germany, but I can't join them until they've found a large enough house to live in."

A vigorous old man with a white handlebar mustache entered the conversation. "You wouldn't want to go to Texas," he told the boy. "That's where the Mafia killed Kennedy, *bon arma*."

"What makes you think the Mafia did it?" I asked.

"I know they did it because we Sicilians are experts on the subject of the Mafia."

I was too tired to pursue the point, but the old man was intent on talking, and asked if I was the American who had come all the way from Philadelphia to join the march. I said I had come to Sicily for a number of reasons. "Your country's government is a pretty good one," he continued, "but it should be destroyed, along with all other governments. There isn't a government that isn't evil. If there were no government in Rome, there wouldn't be any problems in Sicily. Don't you agree?"

I expressed the opinion that government would probably be necessary for a long time.

"What you say proves that you don't have enough faith in people," the old man exclaimed. "Now Danilo Dolci has plenty of faith in people but he doesn't always understand them. For example, tonight everyone in the valley is supposed to turn off his lights. Yes? Danilo believes this will show that we are all in mourning for the dying valley of the Belice. But he overlooks a basic point: overpopulation, the curse of Sicily. As a man who has a wife, he should certainly know what happens between couples when it is pitch dark and there is nothing else to do. Mark my words. Nine months from tonight there will be hundreds of newborn Sicilians in this valley that might never have been born . . ."

The women were glaring at him. The old man nudged me and grinned. "I like to shock them," he said in a whisper they could all hear. "If you can't lay them, shock them."

"Dirty old man," one of the women hissed. About a half-mile before we reached Roccamena Danilo drove up with his Fiat, accompanied by his children, and asked us to get in. As we were piling into the car with Nina, Danilo pointed out there was no room for the child. I began to explain that Nina had marched with us all day, but Danilo was obliged to be firm: a friendly authority had warned him that the police would now be looking for any excuse to detain him; he could not afford to take any chances. Peter and Rosalie regarded each other steadfastly for a moment, caught in the miserable conflict of choosing between the child and Danilo, but there was no time to deliberate—Danilo was in a rush —and expediency prevailed. Sunk under the weight of our guilt, none of us dared look back at Nina as we drove away. Only Danilo, who for all his idealism has a pragmatic mind, was not stunned by the parting. Long ago in Trappeto, through ordeals far more traumatic, he had learned the fallacy of compassion without purpose.

As we sped toward Partinico, he said: "Except for forgetting to ask Peter to speak at the close of the meeting, I would say that the week of mourning has been successful so far. Please tell Peter that he will have his opportunity to speak at the press conference we'll be holding in Rome." He beamed at both of us, then concentrated on the road ahead of him.

Chapter

7

Days in
Western Sicily

MARCH 12, 1965

THE MARCH to the Belice received even more space in the press
than Sunday's occupation of the piazza. Only *Telestar* reported
the event in a disparaging fashion, claiming that it was nothing
more than a picnic attended by a few hundred persons, and that
almost no one bothered to turn off the lights that night. One of
the villagers was quoted as saying: "Why should we be in mourning? Nobody's dead."

MARCH 13

The newspapers are filled with photographs of the "silent
march" in Rome from the railroad station to the Chamber of
Deputies at Montecitorio. Danilo is in front, flanked by Peter
Moule and Carlo Levi, the senator and author of the famous
book *Christ Stopped at Eboli*. Behind them marches Lorenzo with
the mayors, who wear sashes around their stomachs.

Following the meeting with Sicilian representatives of Parliament, at which Danilo presented the demands of the delegation,
there was a press conference at the Teatro Goldoni, where Peter
Moule finally made his announcement. At the close of the conference Danilo said: "I return to Sicily with the hope that in Rome
everything possible will be done to start the construction of the
dam on the Belice. The crisis in that valley affects all of the na-

tion. Everyone is agreed that the dam is necessary but no one seems to have the power to take the first step. We keep watching a game of tug of war between the government in Rome and the one in Sicily . . ."

This morning the delegation was to have conferred with the head of the Cassa di Mezzogiorno, the agency that finances the building of all dams in southern Italy. But in a telephone conversation with Franco, Danilo reported that the agency head left word that he was "not available;" the delegates talked with his assistants instead.

MARCH 14

It is Sunday but all the stores are open. The men here do nearly all of the family shopping; it is another way, I suppose, of keeping the women indoors. In any grocery or meat store you can hear them jabbering away while they wait their turn. I go into an empty shoe store to buy a pair of warm slippers that will protect my feet from our icy marble floors. Moments later a gang of children, searching for their father, swoop in and out of the place. The blond and squat proprietor comments on the large number of poor children there are in Partinico, and we are soon launched on a discussion about birth control.

He knows about rubber condoms (the Italians call them *guanti*—gloves) but he has never heard of diaphragms, and asks me to draw a picture of one. His face reddens when I tell him I can direct him to a place in Palermo where he and his wife can get full particulars about birth control techniques, and he explains that as he has been married only a few months, he has no need to think of such matters yet. The most common form of contraception in Partinico, he informs me, is self-abortion. He knew a woman who tried to abort herself by placing parsley into her vagina, stems and all. She had done this several times before but this time she became ill and died before she got to a hospital. "The doctors found a bed of parsley inside her. I'm certain the woman knew that parsley could poison her blood stream, but she was willing to take her chances. I'm told that many women do the same thing to themselves, and count on God to help them survive."

Finding me attentive, the proprietor began to talk about the

119

excessive devotion that Sicilian women have for the Church. "Their attitude amounts to insanity. It is all right to go to church once a week but to go every day is madness. The priests have far too much power over our women. They are very sneaky: they dress the way they do, in black skirts, so that women will feel more comfortable with them and be more inclined to succumb to their influence. Often that becomes an evil influence . . ."

His voice shrills with emotion. I try to find out how often his wife attends church, but he is too busy denouncing to hear me. "All priests under the age of seventy should be compelled to marry. As matters now stand, they can have almost any woman they want without any of the responsibilities of marriage. A priest is constructed like any other man, and I can easily understand his desire to go to bed with a woman. But why should he be given every advantage to prey on some other man's wife?"

He begins to tell me about a Partinico priest who has been carrying on an affair with a married schoolteacher, but is interrupted by the entrance of a customer, and I am able to make my exit.

MARCH 15

Not all of Danilo's enemies have left his staff. A German nurse who has been attached to the Center-sponsored Partinico health clinic for the past two years makes no bones of her hatred for him. She is a small, wiry blonde in her late thirties, with rather severe features and a torrential style of talking. We met this morning after Dr. Borruso, who runs the clinic, had taken me on a tour of its four immaculately clean rooms. The nurse was leaving with her bicycle to call on an expectant mother who had become too ill to come to the clinic for her weekly vitamin injection, but when she learned that I was a writer and spoke English she put her bicycle aside.

At first she spoke of some of the problems that Dr. Borruso had already described to me, the main one being that although the clinic is trying to educate the women of Partinico in matters of health, it is constantly thwarted by the twenty-six doctors in the town. "They are only interested in making money and taking every possible shortcut, such as giving penicillin to patients for whatever is wrong with them. They won't bother explaining any-

120

thing to these poor people. For example, they ask mothers to use powdered milk without explaining that for children over a certain age regular milk, which is less expensive, may be used safely. Their main idea is to take whatever money they can get and get rid of their patients as quickly as possible . . ."

I suggested we talk some other time, when a patient was not waiting for her. She agreed but at once resumed her monologue, this time about Danilo. "If you are going to write about him, you should tell the truth. You have the opportunity of setting people right, of letting them know what he is really like." We had just met but already she sounded as if she were scolding me. "I pity all those who believe Danilo to be some kind of a saint or prophet who can teach people what to do. The only thing I have learned from him is how corrupt he can be. He doesn't care about improving the lot of the Sicilians. He cares only about his ego. His books, his fasts, his demonstrations—everything he does is for his own glory. He has made a career of being an egomaniac."

Her English was broken but headlong; I could not get in a word.

"When I first came to Partinico he was conducting weekly discussions with the people of Spine Sante on all kinds of fascinating subjects. It was a very useful thing to do because it encouraged Sicilians to think about a good many subjects that have become too fixed in their minds . . ."

I recalled reading transcriptions of some of the discussions in Danilo's book *Conversazioni*. They dealt with such topics as: "Is it right or wrong to murder?" "What are the qualities of a good woman?" "What are the qualities of a good man?" "Should an infant be baptized? Why?" "If a man is called to war, should he go?"

"All the discussions were constructive and should have been continued," the nurse was saying. "But what happened? As soon as Danilo had tape recorded enough material to fill a book, he stopped the discussions. He wasn't really interested in opening the minds of the Sicilians. He just wanted to publish another book that would make him more famous."

While she paused to catch her breath, I asked: "If he makes you so unhappy, why do you stay here?"

"Why? Because there are many sick people in Partinico who

121

need my services. The other reason is that it is my duty to stay here as long as I can and warn all foreign visitors about Danilo Dolci's character. If I don't, they are liable to be deceived by his charm. When there is time, I would like to tell you more about him . . ."

She mounted her bicycle and rapidly rode away, but I could still hear the sound of her anger. It was the anger of an obsessed mind. "Maybe she was once in love with Danilo and he rejected her," Patricia said when I gave her an account of the meeting.

March 17

Franco goes to Palermo tomorrow to enter a public hospital. His stomach trouble has been diagnosed as an ulcer. He tried to discuss the diagnosis with the doctor who examined him but was told that such matters are never discussed with patients. This will be the second time he has tried to enter the hospital; he reported earlier in the week, as requested by the doctor, but was told there was no room for him. Apprehensive about the kind of treatment he will get, he hopes that the "American method" will be used: eliminating an ulcer by freezing it. Why it is called the "American method" neither one of us is certain. "Perhaps it is an outcome of the cold war strategy," Franco jokes. Despite the diagnosis, Franco goes on smoking, eating fried foods, drinking coffee, and suffering.

March 18

As I am leaving the house to buy some wine, my landlord notices my empty bottle and tries to press two liters of his excellent wine on me. I accept only one, and extract from him the address of a shop where I can buy wine of similar quality. The address belongs to a house that is adjacent to the church with the noisy bells. The woman who responds to my knocking is suspicious at first and fires questions at me through a half-opened portal. Who sent me? What am I doing in Partinico? Am I married? The significance of the last question escapes me; the other two may be prompted by caution, for she probably has no license to sell wine. Both portals are opened at last, and I am admitted into a gloomy cave of a room holding two giant vats.

The woman is middle-aged with Arabic-dark, fine features and a figure that is alluring, even by American standards. Although the place is in semidarkness, I can see her uneasiness. Her fingers nervously fondle the empty wine bottle I have handed her; her big oval eyes keep darting from me to a closed door in the room. Removing my beret seems to have a reassuring effect on her; her lips part over shiny false teeth in a smile. *"Scusi,"* she murmurs; then opening the door she has been eying, she tilts her head back and shouts, "Alfonsa."

Within seconds a tall, gawky girl joins us. Her skin is sallow, her features are out of proportion, and her shoulders are stooped from the embarrassment of being too tall. "Your mother is no good at siphoning wine," the woman tells her. "You do it."

Without saying a word or glancing at me, the girl sulkily sinks to the cement floor on all fours, and the woman sticks the end of the rubber tube in her mouth. She begins to suck but nothing happens. "Harder, you aren't sucking hard enough," the woman says. The girl keeps trying, while the woman berates her. "You should use more force." The girl's knees dig into the cement; it is obvious from her bulging eyes that all her energy is concentrated on the tube. But no wine appears, and the exasperated woman lashes her with more scoldings, even accusing her of pretending to suck. The girl says nothing; now and then when she stops to catch her breath, I can see the skinny body shuddering with the effort. "You want me to do it," the woman snarls. "That's what you want." In her resentment over the daughter's failure, she has forgotten about me. "Suck, Alfonsa, suck," she cries.

The situation is saved by the arrival of a boy in his early teens. Immediately enlisted for the job, he takes the tube from his panting sister and within seconds the wine is pouring noisily into a dishpan. After there is enough to fill my bottle, the woman orders him to keep on sucking. "It is not the kind of thing your mother likes to do," she whines.

I pay and am ready to leave, but the girl suddenly becomes animated on realizing I am an American, and begins to question me about my work and about my impressions of Partinico. She appears anxious to have me confirm her dislike of the town. One day she would like to live in a large city, she tells me. She is twenty years old and is taking a secretarial course in Palermo. English is

123

one of her subjects. "But my teacher is terrible. Even if I knew all
the English she does, I still wouldn't be able to speak the language
well." She regards me steadily for a moment without speaking.
"I'm sure that you could teach me English in a short time . . ."

"My daughter doesn't know what she is saying," the mother
intercedes hastily. "She gets absurd ideas from these trips she
makes to Palermo. If your wife could teach her English, that
would be a different matter, of course."

I explain that Patricia knows no Italian, a fact that astonishes
both of them. As I leave, I feel the girl's brooding eyes on me.

Patricia and I visit the local police station to register, as required by law. This means answering dozens of questions about
ourselves and our antecedents. Our replies are laboriously recorded in pen and ink by a police chief who smacks his lips every
time he completes a word. While he concentrates on his penman-
ship, Patricia nudges me and secretly points to a fat folder on his
desk. Across the face of it is written the name "Danilo Dolci."

A tall, blue-eyed blond detective enters the office to pick up
some papers, and the police captain stops writing long enough to
introduce him to me as a *paisano*. His hometown is Porto Empedocle, where my father was born and raised. I inform the detective that we shall be going there for the Easter weekend to visit my
uncle. Delighted to encounter an American who has ties with his
hometown, he insists on treating us to an espresso at a nearby bar,
then proposes that he drive us to Porto Empedocle since he will be
visiting his own family at Easter. A little later, as he realizes perhaps that it might be embarrassing for everyone to have an associate of Danilo Dolci traveling with a member of the police force,
he remembers that he has promised to take his wife's parents
along, which means there would not be enough room in his car for
us.

I ask him about the Mafia in Partinico, how active it is at this
point. "You and your wife need not be afraid," he replies. "No
one will harm you. You are safer in Partinico than you would be
in Philadelphia." I tell him that I am relieved to have this assur-
ance, but point out that I was asking the question in a more
general sense. "This is a quiet period," he says. "Thanks to the

activities of the Anti-Mafia Commission, the *mafiosi* are either in hiding or in jail waiting to be tried. We haven't had a murder in Partinico for the past year and a half. Yet we work just as hard as ever. You have no idea how much paper work we are obliged to do . . ."

I have no doubt that as part of his paper work he will write a summary of our conversation and add it to Danilo's file.

MARCH 19

Today is St. Joseph's day, the most celebrated saint's day in Sicily, when everyone named Giuseppe or Giuseppina receives gifts. Although no one in his family bears the saint's name, Danilo invites us to a supper at his home that will feature Vincenzina's *cassatedi,* a special St. Joseph's day pastry that stirs up childhood memories for me. Before we get to the Dolci home, we taste the *cassatedi* made by our landlady's daughter, which are superior to Vincenzina's because they are abundantly filled with the correct ingredients, *ricotta,* candied fruit and chocolate. In the interests of economy, Vincenzina is obliged to substitute a chickpea paste for *ricotta,* which is expensive. But her children gobble up the pastries, and demand more.

Supper keeps being postponed while we vainly wait for another guest, Bill Taylor, one of the original founders of the Danilo Dolci Trust in London, who is visiting the Center for a few days on his way to England from Africa. Danilo has known Taylor since the first time he visited London in 1957 when he made such a favorable impression on his English audiences that a Danilo Dolci committee was quickly established, headed by Professor Ross D. Waller, of Manchester University. Bill Taylor came to Sicily the next year as a representative of the committee to determine how the group could best assist Danilo's work. Out of Taylor's recommendations came the Committee's decision to assume financial responsibility for the Center's office at Menfi.

Taylor, a shy and slender man in his middle thirties, arrived this afternoon carrying a knapsack and sleeping bag, and attired in shaggy camping clothes and rough boots. He comes from the Bechuanaland Protectorate* in southern Africa, where he has

* Now called Botswana.

been doing a one-man job of social work for two years, under the sponsorship of the Quakers. At Danilo's suggestion, we invited him to use one of our rooms during his stay in Partinico. Unlike Peter Moule, he has the traditional reticence of the Englishman, and at first it is difficult for me to reconcile his personality with an incident which Danilo described to me this morning: After one of his London speeches, it was Bill Taylor who delivered such an impassioned plea for funds that an audience of seventeen hundred persons contributed more than two thousand dollars to the work of the Center.

While we wait for Taylor, the children demand I regale them with American jokes, but I cannot remember enough that are suitable for youngsters, and they soon wind up telling their own. After that, they imitate the sounds of barnyard animals. Danilo outdoes the children with his fierce rendition of an angry dog.

The missing guest does not appear until we have finished the meal. The excuse he gives is that he got lost, but later when we are alone, he confides that he was button-holed by the German nurse, who convinced him that a seven o'clock invitation at the Dolci household usually meant eight o'clock (probably maliciously, since the woman must know what a great premium Danilo places on punctuality).

Danilo, using my services as interpreter, questions Taylor closely about his Bechuanaland experience. He shows particular interest in the country's religious history. "Christianity came there about the middle of the last century when Dr. Livingston personally converted one of the tribal chiefs," Taylor says. "But sometimes the people forget their Christianity and revert to some of their old pagan customs. During a long dry spell not long ago an unconverted medicine man let it be known that no rain would be forthcoming unless there was a sacrifice of human blood. As a result, four men kidnapped a young baby and killed it in a ritualistic ceremony. The whole thing was a dreadful failure. No rain came, and the four men were arrested by the British and, in true Christian fashion, sentenced to death . . ."

Taylor adds that Christianity has brought monogamy to Bechuanaland but that the country was better off with polygamy. "As matters stand, the balance of life has been severely disturbed because it is a country where there are far more women than men. To compensate for the restrictions of monogamy, girls are allowed to have all the children they want before they are married. The father of an unmarried girl never objects because every time she has a child he will receive cattle from the man who impregnated her. A father can accumulate quite a herd of cattle that way."

"Do those girls ever find husbands?" Patricia asks.

"Without any trouble. The men like to marry girls with lots of children since the children will provide them with an easy means of support. Everyone profits, except the women."

"One way or another women always fare badly in underdeveloped countries," Danilo says. "In Sicily they can become victims of social patterns that sometimes lead to murder." He begins to tell the story of an eighteen-year-old girl he knew in Trappeto who was in love with a young man of a well-to-do family. As soon as the boy's family learned of the situation, they ordered him to stop seeing the girl. Although the boy loved the girl, they could not permit him to marry the daughter of a poor fisherman. The girl and her parents soon became resigned to the verdict. But not their neighbors. They began to criticize the girl openly for having permitted the young man to besmirch her honor. And they told her that the only way she could restore her honor was by killing him. They argued that the murder might cost her a few years in jail but that on her release the villagers would hail her as a decent person, eligible for marriage.

The fisherman father was a peace-loving man, but he gradually succumbed to the propaganda of the neighbors. One day he bought a loaded pistol and presented it to his daughter. By this time, the girl had also become convinced that there was only one course of action open to her. She sought out the young man in a café, and killed him while he was drinking a cup of espresso.

"The girl became an assassin simply because the group to which she belonged demanded it as the price she would have to pay to keep her place among them," Danilo says. "This sort of thing happens again and again in Sicily. Violence is condoned not because the Sicilians are more hot-blooded than other people or because they are criminal by nature, but only because violence is an accepted feature of a long established social pattern. Yet the pat-

tern can be changed; the custom of assassination can be eliminated. The proof of this is that there are seldom any crimes of
passion among Sicilians who migrate to more advanced countries,
such as the United States or England."

Someone asks why the Church has not done more than it has to
discourage crimes of passion among Sicilians.

Danilo replies: "The Sicilians are generally suspicious of their
church. In other parts of the world religion usually means goodness. Here it is associated with the comfortable lives of monks and
priests, who are resented. Sicilians go to church with the hope of
getting help from God, not to learn anything from the priests."
He pauses while Vincenzina leads the two youngest children,
whose eyes are drooping, toward the bedroom. "Carlo Levi was
right to call his novel *Christ Stopped at Eboli*. Christianity does
not exist in Sicily any more than it really exists in Bechuanaland.
The religion here is a kind of paganism with Catholic trappings.
The saints who are most revered are not the Christian saints of the
north who represent morality, such as St. Francis, but the saints
who can perform useful miracles. St. Lucia, for example, who can
restore sight to the blind; or St. Calogero, the saint of good diges-
tion, or any of the various saints that fishermen rely on for larger
hauls. In Trappeto, every summer for three months, a priest of
considerable education leads his congregation with Latin chants as
they invoke the heavens for rain.

"The Sicilians have a strong sense of morality but it is a primitive morality; it is not based on Christian ethics. It does not encourage the ideal of working together for the common good. In
Sicily the ideal is minding your own business, not helping others.
There is a Sicilian proverb which says: *Chi gioca solo non perde
mai.* (He who plays alone never loses.)

As we are leaving, Danilo asks Bill Taylor whether he plans to
visit the Center's office at Menfi. Taylor says he will be traveling to
Menfi in a day or two; he is eager to see what has been accomplished there since his last visit. What he fails to tell Danilo is that
he is taking the German nurse along to be his interpreter.

MARCH 20

This morning I attend my second meeting of Danilo's "cabinet."
It begins quietly enough, but ends in an explosion. First there is a

discussion of the Center's plan for establishing an institute at Trappeto that will train young Sicilians to be leaders in community development work. About twenty carefully selected students, each representing a different village in the area, will participate in a series of seminars administered by Lorenzo Barbera. They will first learn the basic principles of sociological research, so that they can recognize the most prevalent forms of waste in their villages, as well as unused resources that can be utilized for the benefit of the whole community. After a thirty-day training period, the students will return to their respective villages and begin applying what they have learned in the citizens' committees which the Center is trying to establish in each of the villages. The hope is that eventually each trainee will take the lead in developing a specific plan for the educational and economic advancement of his village. All this is in accordance with Danilo's constant emphasis on grassroots planning.

As I listen to these plans, it occurs to me that the training school is not unlike the one that Eyvind Hytten would like to establish in Palermo, and I wonder whether Hytten's ambitions have acted as a spur to Danilo. If he can get the Center's institute established first, it will place Hytten in the inglorious position of a would-be imitator. The Center doesn't yet have enough money to finance its institute but it hopes to get a grant from Oxfam, the English foundation, which is sending a field representative to Partinico shortly to take a close look at the Center's activities. I am to be his interpreter.

The next point on the agenda, a review of the Center's efforts during the week of mourning, is disposed of quickly. Except for the delegation's failure to meet with the head of the Cassa di Mezzogiorno, there is general satisfaction over the results. All agree that in the future there will be no more delegations to Rome; every effort will be made to compel the authorities to come to Sicily instead.

The explosion is touched off a few minutes later when Michele Mandiello, the good-natured chief of the Menfi office who accompanied the delegates to Rome, asks Danilo's permission to reveal "some important personal information" he picked up on his way to Sicily. "The information I have can help us save Lorenzo's life," he begins ominously.

129

"Does it need saving?" Lorenzo asks, smiling.

"Lorenzo, you are in profound danger," Michele says. "I speak to you as a friend, with my heart in my hand." In the stress of his emotion, his Neapolitan accent seems even stronger than usual. He tells how on the boat from Naples to Palermo, one of the delegates who lives in Roccamena and is a friend of Lorenzo, confided that there are definite plans afoot to have Lorenzo murdered by a hired assassin. The informant is so certain Lorenzo will be killed that he has decided to avoid his company in the future, so as not to risk his own life. "He even knew how much the assassin would be paid for the murder—50,000 lire." Michele pauses and stares at Lorenzo with worried eyes.

Lorenzo grins. "50,000 lire is the minimum rate. Is that all my life is worth?"

"Please, Lorenzo," Michele exclaims. "This is no joking matter. I entreat you for your own sake and for the sake of your wife and children to pay serious attention to what I am saying . . ."

"Was there any motive given?" Danilo asks.

"It is Lorenzo's book that has caused all this trouble," Michele says angrily. "The book said some nasty things about the Baron Tizzio and now the Baron, along with some people who were called *mafiosi* in the book, are out to get him."

"Everything I wrote is true," Lorenzo says.

"True or not, you're in danger," Michele explodes. "Don't you understand? You and your family must leave Roccamena as soon as possible."

"That is absurd," Lorenzo's wife says.

Her reaction shakes him. "Paola, you don't know what you are saying. This is Sicily, not Rome."

"I am certain," Paola says, "that if Lorenzo's life were in danger, we would know about it. We have some very close friends in Roccamena who know exactly what goes on every minute of the day. One of them would have told us by now . . ."

"I've been in Sicily for eight years," Michele says, "long enough to know that close friends are absolutely no help in a situation like this one. Please take my advice and leave Roccamena. At least for a while. I implore you."

"I have a question for you," Lorenzo says. "If you heard that someone was threatening your life, would you leave Menfi?"

When Michele says nothing, Danilo comments: "If it is true that Lorenzo's life is in danger, moving away from Roccamena isn't going to save it. There are hired assassins available everywhere."

"The immediate danger is in Roccamena," Michele says. He turns his pleading eyes toward Lorenzo.

"I'm grateful for your solicitude, Michele," Lorenzo responds. "But you must believe me when I tell you that I am in no danger. I have antennae. I know everyone in Roccamena. If any danger existed for me or for any member of my family, I would be aware of it."

Danilo wishes to proceed to the next point on the agenda, but Michele has more to say. "I would like to know why Lorenzo's book was not discussed carefully before it was sent to the publisher."

"It was discussed," Lorenzo says, "but not by *mafiosi* or by anyone else criticized in it."

"I don't recall discussing it," Michele says. "Recently I read it for the first time and, frankly, I was surprised by some of the language. There are words in it that should not appear in any book, words that children should never read."

"The book was not published for children," Danilo says.

"But the book might be seen by children. Or a parent might find himself reading from the book to his children."

"If a child becomes corrupted," Paola says, "it isn't because of any dirty words in a book."

"Let's consider what the dirtiest words in my book are," Lorenzo says. "One of them is the word 'asslicker.' Surely, Michele, you'll have to admit that word is used everywhere, even when there are children present. Another phrase I use is 'son of a bitch.' That's a common expression, often used by mothers. Another is the threat 'I'll break your balls.' Certainly, there are many fathers who use that expression when they get sore at their sons . . ."

"I've used worse language than that in my writings and even been arrested for it," Danilo says. "But I was cleared because the court realized I was using the language honestly in a documentary manner. Lorenzo does the same in his book. If we do something which we believe is right, we should not be concerned about the opinion of those who disagree with us."

"I agree with Danilo," Lorenzo says. "There was no point writ-

131

ing pleasantly about the Baron simply because he is considered an important man. If we try to win the friendship of important persons, we will isolate ourselves from the ordinary people."

Michele insists on having the last word. "It makes sense to risk your skin for something important, some principle you believe in, but to endanger your life for the sake of a few dirty expressions doesn't make any sense to me."

After the meeting Dr. Borruso informs Danilo that he has just learned that the German nurse is accompanying Bill Taylor to Menfi. Danilo asks me if I know anything about it, and I confirm the information. "Oh, that's terrible," he says with a mournful smile.

"The woman is a mess," Dr. Borruso says. "She often contradicts me when I make a diagnosis, right in front of my patients. I'm sure that many of them think she must be my mistress to take such liberties. I'll be glad when her contract expires in August."

Surprisingly, Danilo's attitude toward the German nurse is quite benign, though he is fully aware of how harshly she criticizes him. "She is very hard on everyone. Once she accused a German collaborator of ours of falling asleep during a meeting. She did it at the top of her voice in German, right into his ear. The poor fellow wasn't asleep at all; he was simply concentrating on what was being said with his eyes shut." Danilo says he has the highest respect for her as a nurse. "She has a thorough knowledge of medicine, and a born talent for giving injections. I shall hate to see her leave in August, but I wish she weren't going to Menfi with Bill Taylor."

MARCH 21

The siphoned wine is the finest I have bought in Partinico, and today I return to the cavelike room with a bigger bottle to fill. The woman regards the bottle unhappily. She is alone this time, and I wonder if she will deign to get on her hands and knees to suck on the tube. Instead she begins to talk about a son who is studying in Monreale to become a missionary priest. To prepare himself for his vocation, he is trying to learn several languages, some by himself, and is corresponding with missionary priests in

132

various countries. Her eyes gleam as she describes his virtues. "It costs money to write to all those people but my son would make any sacrifice to get the money he needs to buy stamps. Believe me, he is a saint. The other day he told me that when his allowance came to an end, he went without soap and tooth powder for a while so that he would have money for stamps." She comes closer to me and her eyes pierce mine. "I couldn't help crying when he told me that. I begged him to let me know whenever he needed more money and I would do everything in my power to get it for him. I don't want him to suffer in any way. But my son has always been a saint, always helping people, and there is nothing he can do about it." The tears flow down her cheeks, but she makes no effort to wipe them away.

My instinct tells me my effort to comfort her with a few cliché phrases is not enough; she expects me to dry the tears, to console her in a more tangible way. In my reluctance to oblige her, I can only offer to do whatever siphoning is necessary. She won't hear of that, nor will she siphon the wine in my presence. I resolve the impasse by leaving the empty bottle with her, while I do some other shopping chores.

On my return, the bottle is ready for me, and so is she. Trapping me with her eyes, which come even closer now, she expounds on the brilliance and saintliness of her son with all the emotion of a criminal lawyer addressing a jury. At one point, during one of her more forceful statements, her false teeth start to fly toward me. She shuts her mouth just in time. I take advantage of the moment to retreat to the door, but she is talking again before I can get it open, insisting I must make her son's acquaintance and discover for myself what an extraordinary human being he is. I promise to see him the next time he comes to Partinico, and flee.

MARCH 22

Danilo has requested a biographical sketch of me which he can use to publicize the Palermo talk I have promised to give in June. "During your stay in Sicily we want to enhance your prestige all we can," he says.

Valorizzare is the word he uses for "enhance." It is one of his favorite words; in both his writings and his conversations he uses it in reference to anyone or anything whose value, he feels, should be increased or recognized. Sometimes he gives the word universal scope by applying it to any people who need to be educated to the possibility of change and improvement. In a large sense *valorizzare* is a key word in the goals he is trying to achieve.

His other favorite word is closely linked to *valorizzare* in its ideological implication: *pianificazione*. Although its last two syllables sound like a familiar Sicilian obscenity, the word means "planning," and when it is used in connection with grassroots planning, it is music to Danilo's ears. He protests when I confess that the word has no appeal for me: it is too Germanic, and it has a rasping sound. *"Pianificazione* is a beautiful word," he insists, but I suspect it is Danilo the social reformer, not Danilo the poet, who makes that claim.

MARCH 23

Ever since my arrival Danilo has been setting aside one hour of his time every morning for answering my questions. Today's session extended for three hours as he talked of his early life. I am not surprised to learn that most of his antecedents are not Italian, for temperamentally at least he is unlike any other Italian I have ever known. His Italian father had German and Italian parents; his Slav mother had parents who were German and Slav. This makes him half German, one quarter Slav, and one quarter Italian. As a boy, his mother spoke to him in Slovenian and made him say his prayers in that language twice a day.

The village where he was born, Sesana, which is near Trieste, was once Italian but is now part of Jugoslavia. He was born during its Italian years on June 28, 1924, and grew up in a lower middle-class atmosphere, with a severe father who was a station master for the Italian State Railways, and an intensely religious mother who was intolerant of non-Catholics. "One of the greatest shocks of her life came when I broke with the Catholic Church," Danilo says. His father did not share her attitude toward religion. He went to church only to be married, to have his children baptized and christened, and to attend funerals. He refused to attend the rest of the time.

Danilo felt closer to his father than he did to his mother—"he was far more intelligent than his work indicated." Yet it was his mother who instilled in him an early love for music. She was the first to give him piano lessons. Later his teacher became Marusi, the famous organist of the Milan Cathedral, who came to the village to teach the children of a wealthy family and was persuaded by Danilo's parents to take their son on as a pupil. By the time he was fourteen, he was a skillful performer on the piano, the organ, and the accordian, and had developed an abiding devotion to Bach.

Marusi would rap his knuckles when he played badly but his father would often beat him on the slightest provocation. Danilo ascribes his father's severity to the fact that he was subjected to the strict discipline of a German mother and felt duty-bound to inflict a similar discipline on his son. The memory of the beatings has influenced Danilo's policy for disciplining his own children. Trying to avoid inflicting any physical punishment on them, he reasons with them; but if they persist in doing something that he considers detrimental to their welfare, he spanks them a few times.

His father was an extremely nervous man who would sometimes scream for no apparent reason. Totally dependent on cigarettes, he would begin to tremble as soon as he was in need of one. As a result of watching his father during such moments, Danilo has never been tempted to smoke. He believes that his father's temperamental difficulties may have been the reason why as a child he told many lies and engaged in a great deal of fantasy. Because books were another form of escape he soon became a compulsive reader. Often in the classroom when he was supposed to be listening to the teacher, he would secretly be reading a book.

He began with the Bible and the Koran and went on to Buddha, Confucius, Tao, and all the seven hundred verses of the *Bhagavad Gita.* He devoured the Greek classics next, even Aristotle's *Ethics,* which he barely understood then. Plato made the deepest impression on him, but he particularly enjoyed the Greek plays. He would time himself and find that he could read a Greek drama in two hours. He also read the forbidden books which his father kept under lock and key; he found he could easily get to them by removing the unlocked drawers above them.

At the age of fifteen he had become a systematic reader, who

135

rose at four and read until it was time to go to school. "It was then that I learned to understand the importance of silence. Those morning hours of reading and thinking, before anyone else was out of bed, were the most beautiful ones of my youth." He soon became acquainted with many of the world's greatest writers. While still in his teens, he had read all of Shakespeare, Tolstoy, Schiller, and Goethe. Thoreau he has never read, he says in answer to one of my questions; Gandhi he did not read until journalists began to refer to him as the "Gandhi of Sicily."

Despite his father's severity, Danilo believes that he led a fairly normal and contented childhood. "I played the piano every day, I read, and I engaged in sports. I was no champion, but I enjoyed tennis, skiing, and swimming. I had no close friends, but I felt closely bound in friendship to the authors I read. The only time I remember crying was when my father would beat me."

In school he was a rather ordinary student. The one subject he excelled in was writing. As early as the age of eight, his compositions would be circulated among members of the faculty as superior examples of student writing. Written in expository prose on topics assigned by his teacher, these papers in no way reflected his private excursions into fantasy. Only later, in his teens, did he engage in imaginative writing. "I began to write poems then because I decided that prose was inferior to poetry." (He kept on writing and publishing poems until 1955. The following year, as he came out of prison after the strike-in-reverse experience, a publisher gathered his favorite ones into a single volume, *Poésie*. The last three of the poems, written while living in Trappeto, are in Sicilian.)

Danilo has one sibling, his sister Miriam, who was born when he was eight years old. "We never had much in common. She conformed to all the expectations of our parents. Now she is a married woman with children who lives a bourgeois existence in Aquila. We seldom correspond." Unlike his sister, he was a bitter disappointment to his parents, failing to accomplish any of the things expected of him. He did not become an architect, nor marry the daughter of a prosperous building contractor to whom he was briefly engaged, nor ever earn enough money to support a wife and family in circumstances that were at least as comfortable as their own.

136

They began to have serious worries about him from the time he was eighteen when, in protest to the war, he began tearing up all the Nazi posters he could find. That was the year 1943, while Danilo was in imminent danger of being drafted into the Fascist army. "I had never heard the phrase 'conscientious objector' and I had no idea there were such persons in the world, but I felt strongly that it was wrong to kill people and I was determined never to do so."

To evade the authorities, he left school (he was then a first-year student at an architectural school in Milan) and with some money he had saved from part-time teaching, purchased a train ticket to Rome. En route there was a train check by the Nazis, and Danilo was arrested and jailed. "I think they suspected I was the one who had been ripping up the Nazi posters." He was placed in a verminous cell occupied by nine other persons, most of them thieves. "A board divided into ten sections served as our bed."

Danilo's powers of persuasion saved him. At the prison hearing, ten days later, he happened to mention the name of an obscure German sculptor while conversing with a Nazi interpreter. The interpreter, who knew of the sculptor, was impressed by Danilo's extensive knowledge of his work. Pressing his advantage, Danilo somehow convinced him that he was a brilliant student of architecture who had no interest whatsoever in political affairs. In a few minutes he was handed a pass that permitted him to leave the prison scot free.

Avoiding the trains this time, he traveled by foot and hitched rides from truck drivers until he reached a snowy village in the Abruzzi mountains called Poggio Cancelli. There he was sheltered by a peasant family, along with some escaped British and American prisoners. In exchange for the Latin lessons he gave the children he was provided with one meal a day. Diseased dead hens which the peasants refused to eat augmented his diet; he made the hens edible by skinning and boiling them. He remained in Poggio Cancelli until early 1944, when the Nazis were being driven out of Italy, and then returned north to resume his studies as an architect.

For the first time since his education began he developed into an outstanding student. By the time he was in his fourth year he had already published two architectural monographs of professional quality, *The Science of Construction* and *The Theory of Reinforced Concrete*. He was also winning various commissions. Everything pointed to the prosperous career his parents had wished for him, but when he was within weeks of obtaining his diploma, he was assailed by an avalanche of doubts as to the wisdom of devoting his life to the goals of a materialistic society which was still steeped in fascist psychology. "I began to ask myself, 'Why build houses for the rich?' 'What is the point of becoming a conforming member of a society controlled by forces for which I have no sympathy?'

"I had spent a year examining nature closely, trying to understand its meaning, and trying at the same time to correlate my observations and my thoughts with my reading. And I saw that the life I would lead as an architect would have little or no relationship with what I felt and thought. For by now I had become convinced that all men should be brothers."

The decision to renounce a career in architecture and live according to the dictates of his conscience was a painful one, Danilo says. "I felt guilty about it, knowing how hurt my parents would be, but there was nothing else I could do." From Milan he went to Nomadelfia, the communal village established by the Catholic priest Don Zeno to provide family living for abandoned children. Built by some of the children themselves on the site of an abandoned concentration camp where five hundred Jews had died, the village was an expression of Don Zeno's belief that Christian Communism could work. On his arrival there in 1949, Danilo found 1400 children under the care of sixty women who served as their mothers.

He became Don Zeno's secretary but many of his duties were quite unsecretarial. "I worked in the fields with the youngsters, and handled latrine chores. I got to know the children well. When they would first arrive some of the children's faces were monstrous but as soon as they were treated well the children became beautiful. I learned that by loving people they become lovable; that the life of a human being can be molded, just as clay can. I began to sense the possibility that life was a science and an art and that human beings could be dealt with as materials of nature. People, like mountains and plains, are themselves landscapes and can be-

138

come the finest of all works of art. For the first time I realized how people might be changed for the better . . ."

Danilo fell in love with Nomadelfia. "There was such perfection in the atmosphere that you felt you could touch it." He was a success as Don Zeno's chief lieutenant, and after a year he was assigned the task of building another village on two hundred acres of a wild and desolate tract which Don Zeno had purchased on a site in Tuscany known as Ceffarello. With the help of forty boys, Danilo began the task of clearing the land, and building. "The earth was filled with snakes, vipers, and stones. We ploughed the ground, eliminated the stones and roots, and cultivated the soil. After a year the vipers and snakes left, the wheat grew, and the stones became materials for buildings that sheltered families."

Danilo describes Don Zeno as a peasant at heart, with cultural limitations (to this day he does not write Italian well), but a man of profound intuition and love. "He hated the idea of orphan asylums; he understood that children need parents. Although he was no intellectual, what he knew he knew thoroughly. For example, he read the New Testament one paragraph at a time, not proceeding to the next paragraph until he had completely assimilated the one he was reading. I loved and respected him both as a teacher and as a friend."

In 1951 Danilo's work at Ceffarello was interrupted by a belated stint in the army. He made his position clear to the authorities: he would accept the summons but would refuse to do anything of a military nature. Fortunately for Danilo, the commanding officer was a benign and cultured person who had read some of Danilo's poems. He let him have his way. Danilo spent the next three months in Siena participating in fire drills and gymnastics and, with the commanding officer's permission, taking weekend leaves to assist Don Zeno at Nomadelfia. As his final army assignment, he was ordered to design a new regimental standard for his company. The emblem he produced was a caricature festooned with grotesque eagle heads and talons, but no one objected to it.

In the meantime, Don Zeno was being harassed by creditors and by the Minister of Police, a Sicilian-born Christian Democrat by the name of Scelba who regarded the priest as a dangerous Communist and was determined to close down Nomadelfia and send

139

its children to orphan asylums. By the time Danilo returned from the army, Don Zeno had lost Ceffarello, buildings and all, to the creditors. In desperation, the priest appealed to the Italian government for financial assistance. Through Scelba, he was informed that the government would pay all of Nomadelfia's debts, provided the community ceased to exist.

Scenting imminent danger, Don Zeno began moving the children to a 200-acre wilderness called Rosellana, near Ceffarello, which had been donated to him by the daughter of a tire magnate. Before he could evacuate the community, the Police Minister's forces swooped down on Nomadelfia and made off with one thousand children in a single day. At the same time, the Vatican, deciding it had had enough of "the mad priest," began recalling all the assistant priests assigned to him.

Don Zeno refused to give up. Invoking a law which protects any priest from becoming bankrupt, he began liquidating his assets. After winning the court case that ensued, he turned layman and bent all of his energies, as well as Danilo's, into transforming the wilderness at Rosellana into a new Nomadelfia. In 1962, through the intercession of a kindred spirit, Pope John XXIII, Don Zeno became a priest again. Nowadays Nomadelfia is a thriving community of 2,000 inhabitants, with the doughty priest still in charge.

Danilo parted company with Don Zeno early in 1952. "A paternalistic Christian community based on a foundation of love is certainly an admirable creation," he says, trying to explain his reasons for leaving, "but I felt that Nomadelfia had certain limitations, and that I needed a broader outlook. Then, too, I felt I had assimilated as much as I could. I began to experience a sense of claustrophobia, an urge to be as free as the air and the sun."

He points out that even while he worked with Don Zeno, he had certain reservations about the Catholic Church. He believed, for example, that the Vatican should become a museum of antiquities, and that the Pope should live in Trevestere, the slum area of Rome. Nor could he accept the Church's conception of the Ascension. "No, I couldn't wholly agree with the Church in matters of dogma and theory, but I could be a friend and participant, as I was during my association with Don Zeno, and as I tried to be when I went to Trappeto in 1952."

MARCH 24

A two-hour session with Danilo as he tells me of his early days in Sicily.

"I went to Trappeto because until then it was the poorest village I had ever seen." He had first known the fishing village in his seventeenth year while visiting his father, who was station master there during the war years. As a teen-ager the poverty of Trappeto struck Danilo as more picturesque than tragic, but after his experience with the children of Nomadelfia he understood it for what it was. He went there with the hope of doing something that might alleviate its misery. He had no grand design in mind; he wanted to do whatever seemed possible.

The warm welcome he received from the villagers was due, to a large extent, to the memory of his father who, during the war period when food was scarce, had taken it upon himself to release a sizable store of grain in Trappeto, which the authorities had placed under lock and key before departing. "Basically, my father was a good man," Danilo says. "He had no use for the work I chose because he was convinced I was wasting my time. He would often tell me that my ideas were invalid because he believed this to be a world of wolves whose chief interest is to destroy one another. Yet there was a great deal of humanity in him."

He arrived in February, with thirty lire in his pocket, and set about familiarizing himself with the villagers and their condition. An account of his early days in Trappeto, written by two fishermen, describes how, from the very beginning, he became immersed in the problems of the sick and the needy. "Whenever he saw that the case was a bad one, he would go as far as Balestrate to buy the medicines for them. He would go whether he had any money or not, and he would tell the pharmacist in Balestrate that he would pay him as soon as God sent him the money. Often, he would get the medicines on credit, but when he didn't, he wouldn't give up. He would go around the town asking everyone he knew whether they had what he was looking for. The villagers watched him and wondered, and asked themselves why in

141

the world so intelligent a man should have come among us to live a life which was even harder and poorer than ours, who have nothing. When he sees a child with a running nose, he takes his handkerchief out of his pocket and wipes it; then he gives the child a kiss. The villagers would often talk to him, and ask him what he planned to do, and he would explain patiently what ought to be done. God, he told them, wished the world to be a place where all men lived together in brotherly love, in a world without wars, murders, robberies, unemployment, children dying of hunger, and waste. Our Lord, he said, did not want to see these things that were wrong, and so everyone in the community must live as brothers. At first the people did not understand too well but little by little they began to realize what he had in mind."

At first the plight of the children made the deepest impression on Danilo. Soon after his arrival in Trappeto he began to borrow and beg money to establish a home for the neediest of them. At the end of six months he succeeded in building the Borgo Di Dio (The House of God), which housed all the children it could hold, thirty boys and girls, most of them children of fathers who were in prison for banditry. The story of the two fishermen includes a vivid account of some of the difficulties Danilo had with creditors, particularly with the owners of a Palermo store that had supplied the furniture for the home. When they learned he could not meet the promissory notes he had given them, "they seized him by the shoulders and began to shake him and shout that if he did not pay them the money at once, they would knock his brains out." The women in the house became frightened when the men wanted to take Danilo to Palermo with them and hand him over to the police. But he remained calm and said to them: "These children have no fathers and mothers. Do you want to see them die too? You can take my motor scooter, if you like, since I have no money to pay you." So the men took the motor scooter and went back to Palermo. Four months later, Danilo paid them their money and they returned the motor scooter. Later he bought the bathroom and toilet fixtures from the same store. It was the first house in Trappeto to have a bathroom in it, and the whole town came to the Borgo to admire it.

Vincenzina, whom Danilo first knew as a cleaning woman in a

house where he had roomed, moved into the Borgo di Dio to become its housekeeper. With her came her own five fatherless children. Some of the villagers, her relatives in particular, were scandalized because Danilo also lived at the Borgo. They became even more scandalized when he and Vincenzina declared their intention to marry. Her relatives were outraged that she would dare think of marrying while still wearing mourning for her dead husband. One of them symbolized their fury by spitting into her face. The union was also bitterly opposed by Danilo's parents, who were horrified that their highly educated son should consider marrying an uneducated woman with so many children. After several months of delay (caused chiefly by pressures Danilo's mother brought to bear on the local clergy), they were married in the village church in August 1953, when Vincenzina was two months pregnant with their first child. "I married her," Danilo says, "because I felt it was the right thing for me to do."

Even before the Borgo was completed, Danilo realized that feeding and training a few children would have little or no effect on the plight of the many villagers, who were desperately in need of jobs. A broader effort, one which went beyond the scope of charity, was called for in order to help alleviate the increasing poverty in the village. At first he appealed to the authorities in Trappeto and Palermo, asking them to establish public work projects so that men might feed their families and the physical state of the village itself might benefit. "Many of the houses are such a deplorable state of repair that any vet would declare them unfit for cows," he wrote. "The worst season of the year is just ahead of us, and there are many men without jobs. Are we to wait until they are so driven by hunger and misery that they will rise in revolt? . . . Are we to wait until they are mown down by the machine-guns of the *carabinieri?*"

His pleading met with indifference. "If one goes to the town hall," he observed in his diary, "he discovers that Councilor 'X' is still on vacation, that his private secretary 'Y' cannot be reached. More often than not, the doormen behave like lazy dogs assigned to guard the tranquillity of their masters."

When a child in Trappeto died of malnutrition, he began his first fast, vowing that he would not eat another mouthful of food until the authorities came to the rescue of the village. The eight-day fast, which almost cost him his life, committed him irrevocably to his crusade against misery, and provided him with an intellectual father in the person of Aldo Capitini. In his first letter to Danilo, the pacifist philosopher scolded him for having endangered his life without notifying those who would be most sympathetic to his cause, himself and his friends. "You had no right to think of dying without letting everyone know what you had in mind . . ."

The two men met and became good friends. Danilo, the man of action, became the hero of Capitini, the philosopher of nonviolence. In his writings Capitini began to champion him as a reformer who, like Gandhi, uses nonviolence as an expression of love for his fellow man and as a weapon against social stagnation and oppression. During the next six momentous years of Danilo's life, Capitini became his first serious explicator (*Rivoluzione Aperta*) and his biographer. As Danilo's mentor, Capitini gave him the courage to be religious without depending on the Catholic Church, as well as the insight to conduct his battle against misery from a democratic point of view that encompassed the concept of grassroots planning. Thus, under his guidance Danilo became less of a religious-minded thinker immersed in acts of individual charity, and more of a sociologist with a faith in group activity. In the process of this change he acquired a surer sense of direction which, abetted by an immense will power, contributed to his development as a social reformer with a well-defined ideology.

I inquire about Danilo's present concept of "God," pointing out that the term appears frequently in all of his early writings but seldom occurs after 1954. He replies: "There is a rhetoric dealing with the love of God which can be very confusing to the reader. More and more as I try to clarify my own thinking, I try to use less confusing words." Trying to ascertain his personal definition of God, I point out that when Albert Einstein, one of his heroes, was asked whether he believed in God he responded that he believed in Spinoza's God which revealed itself in the harmony of nature and man rather than in a God that was concerned with the fate and actions of man. Einstein's definition of God is not his, Danilo says. "I have not tried to define God. If ever I felt a need to clarify my feeling on the subject, I would try to do so by thinking through it and perhaps writing about it. That I might do when I am older and more experienced. On the other hand, it may never be either necessary or desirable."

On the subject of Catholicism, he says he stopped attending services when he discovered what a negative role the Catholic Church played in Sicily. "The priest in Trappeto had little use for people in trouble. He would say that one should keep away from sinners just as one should shun lepers. The Church in Sicily doesn't seem to be interested in goodness for its own sake. I have never heard a priest say that one should not kill. No priest has ever said 'enough' to the murders committed in this zone. The Church of Pope John XXIII interested me; but not the present one."

Danilo's second fast did not take place until three years after the first one. After living in Partinico for a year and discovering that conditions there were even worse than those in Trappeto, he fasted for a week in November 1955. He had two purposes in mind: to draw attention to the violence and misery in the area and to promote the building of a dam over the Jato River that could provide irrigation for the entire valley. The fast was a preliminary skirmish in a carefully planned campaign that was to be climaxed by the famous "strike in reverse" in February 1956. As part of that campaign, one thousand persons from the three neighboring towns of Partinico, Trappeto, and Balestrate engaged in a twenty-four-hour fast to protest both the unemployment situation and the failure of the authorities to stop illegal fishing by trawlers—a Mafia-controlled operation in that area which had continued undisturbed for a dozen years, ruining the possibility of earning a living by legal fishing.

Danilo smiles as he recalls the discussion among the fishermen and farmers that preceded their decision to stage a mass fast. "Their first idea was to stop all the trains that arrived in Partinico by stretching their bodies across the tracks. They discarded the plan as soon as they realized how few of them would be willing to risk their lives that way. Then they got the idea that it would help our cause if I could fast for a thousand days. When they understood the impossibility of that, they substituted the plan that was followed.

145

"I believe it was the first time in Europe that such a mass fast had taken place. The police tried to stop it, claiming that public fasting was against the law. As if private fasting is within the law! The people weren't frightened by the threats of arrest because there were too many of them to put in jail. 'The worst thing they can do to us,' some of them said, 'is to force us to eat.' "

The fast took place on the beach at Trappeto, at the port in Balestrate, and in the office of the Camera di Lavoro in Partinico. "I remember that as I drove from one place to another to see how things were going, I was followed by a group of police trucks bearing down on me as though I were some kind of a beast they were tracking . . ."

MARCH 25

Bill Taylor, back from his excursion with the German nurse, had dinner with us last night. He is elated with the progress he observed in the Menfi area, which he had not visited since 1958. "Michele Mandiello has accomplished wonders in winning the peasants over to modern farming techniques. In 1958, the year before he went to work there, Menfi was an arid area, despite the presence of a beautiful irrigation scheme served by the Carboi dam. The peasants, who had no idea what a dam was supposed to do, were letting all the water go to waste. The authorities hadn't lifted a finger to teach them how the dam could improve their economy. The cynics were saying that the government deliberately ignored the educational aspect of the project in order to promote the impression that trying to improve the agricultural situation in that part of Sicily was a waste of money. Thanks to Michele's missionary work, the irrigation system has been used to its fullest extent and has made Menfi one of the most productive areas on the island . . ."

Another significant difference Taylor noted was the general change of attitude toward the Mafia. "People talk about it openly now, but in 1958 they would refuse to discuss the subject with me or would cut me short by saying, 'Don't believe those exaggerated stories.' There was a good deal of Mafia stealing then, particularly of goats and sheep. Everyone seemed to know who the thieves were but the police would never make an arrest."

146

Taylor told us of an accidental encounter he had that same year with the corpses of a prominent Mafia leader and one of his henchmen. "I was on my way back to Partinico from Menfi, with an economist, an engineer, and a social worker. We had gone there to make a socioeconomic survey of the zone but weren't able to get any help from the local officials. Shortly after a thunderstorm, when we got to a mountain road near Corleone, we saw a Volkswagen lying on its side with three big holes in it. A truckful of dam workers just behind us also stopped to see what was wrong. We all went over to the car and found in it two passengers still sitting upright with their hats on. They were both dead. The workers seemed terribly frightened; before we could talk with them they ran back to their truck and drove off.

"Not knowing much about electricity, my friends and I stupidly assumed that the men had been killed by lightning. But the next day I read in the newspapers that the three holes in the side of the car had been made by three hundred machine-gun bullets and that the dead men were *mafiosi*. The driver was the notorious Dr. Michele Navarra, a physician of Corleone, whose gang had been responsible for a good many murders in that area. Apparently he had been killed on orders of another Mafia bigwheel of Corleone, Luciano Liggio, who had been feuding with Navarra over a conflict of interest in the irrigation system of the Carboi dam. I gathered that Liggio and his gang were being paid to terrorize the workers who were trying to complete the irrigation system, and Navarra and his gang were being paid by the construction company to protect its workers from Liggio's men . . ."

Liggio, I recalled from my researches on the Mafia, represented the new and younger Mafia, and had been a key contact man working closely with Joseph Profaci of the American Mafia. He had recently been jailed by the Sicilian police. Navarra was chiefly memorable for his political shenanigans on an election day in Corleone when, determined to help elect the Christian Democrat senatorial candidate, he created a corps of "blind electors," hundreds of men and women who pretended to have lost their sight so that Navarra's men could escort them to the polls and control their vote.

Toward the end of the evening Taylor spoke briefly of his expe-

147

rience with the German nurse. Evidently he had remained un-
affected by her bitter propaganda. "I've met Germans like her,
and understand her well," he said. "She is an emotional woman
with a rigid mind. She is incapable of accepting any deviations
from the kind of behavior she has been trained to consider
proper." He spent a great deal of time on their journey trying to
refute her criticism of Danilo and his chief lieutenants; he thinks
he may have changed some of her ideas.

MARCH 25

Franco returned to Partinico today without having done anything about his health problem. After waiting a week for the doctor's decision as to whether or not he required surgery, he quit the
hospital this morning, disgusted and frightened by the conditions
he observed in his ward. "The place was filthy. People around me
were dying from lack of attention. Nobody on the hospital staff
gives a damn what happens to the patients. If they are poor and in
a ward, they are regarded like animals. I decided I couldn't stand
another day of the filth and horror, and walked out."

The day after tomorrow he will travel to Milan, where he knows
of a good hospital clinic that is clean. "I won't be as nervous
there," he says with his Charlie Chaplin smile.

"Did the Palermo doctor say anything to you about the American way of treating an ulcer?" I ask.

"As far as I could tell," Franco replies, "he didn't even know
about the Italian way."

If Bill Taylor has had any softening influence on the German
nurse, there is no sign of it. As soon as she spots me at the Center
this morning, she plunges into another diatribe against Danilo. Of
the thousands of words she emits, I note two specific grievances.
The first is that Danilo has dipped into funds allocated for the
clinic in order that Michele and some of the other staff members
might purchase cars they need for their work. The other is a more
familiar one: that Danilo runs the Center dictatorially though he
pretends to be democratic. "I often criticize him at the monthly
meetings of the Center but he glosses over all criticism—my own
and everyone else's—with banal statements that kill any possibility

of discussion. The reason for this is that he can't face the truth
. . ." Her eyes flash, her voice crescendos.

I try to learn her impressions of Menfi but she is not listening.
"I'm going to denounce Danilo at the next general meeting," she
announces. "You will be able to see and hear for yourself what I
am talking about. Will you come to it?"

I tell her I shall try to be present.

MARCH 26

Kenneth Bennett, the man from Oxfam, arrives for a three-day
visit to determine whether the foundation should contribute funds
to support the work of the Center. A previous Oxfam subsidy was
for a project to encourage the breeding of rabbits. Enthusiastically
endorsed by Eyvind Hytten and merely tolerated by Danilo, that
undertaking proved to be a fiasco. This time Danilo hopes that
Oxfam will help subsidize the newly planned Institute for the
training of community leaders, in which he has a deep faith.

Although there is no advance description of Bennett, I quickly
identify him among the passengers leaving the plane. Danilo is
amazed that I can, but there is no mistaking the distinctively British quality of Bennett's clothes and his stance. When I greet him
by name, Bennett regards me with the wariness one might have for
a confidence man but relaxes as soon as he recognizes Danilo from
photographs he has seen. Bennett is a short, balding redhead in his
middle years; he has a prominent nose, and quiet blue eyes that
radiate intelligence. Since his Italian is not fluent, he is relieved to
hear that I shall be with him during his sojourn to do whatever
interpreting is necessary.

Danilo, who tends to sound more efficient than usual in the
presence of Englishmen, at once begins to discuss the Center's
projects and aspirations. By way of documenting what he is saying,
he takes us on a comprehensive tour of the Partinico area that
includes a visit to Montelepre, the hill town of the bandit Giuliano, and to the site of the Jato dam.

At Montelepre, Danilo points to an old woman in black seated
in front of a doorway and identifies her as the mother of Giuliano.
At the edge of the town we see a beautifully kept cemetery that
provides a sharp contrast to the dilapidated houses in the village.

149

Giuliano is buried there, next to the man who claimed to have killed him, his cousin Gaspare Pisciotta. "Giuliano recruited many members of his band from Montelepre," Danilo says, "particularly during the forties. They were men who used banditry as a way of protesting the terrible conditions around them; also as a way of feeding their families. They were not men with criminal mentalities. Nowadays the men in this village either migrate or find occasional work in Palermo."

At the dam we leave the car, and Danilo leads us on a spirited hike to each of the key features in the construction. Everywhere the mud is thick and slippery. An engineer accompanies us but there is actually no need of him; Danilo knows as much about the technical aspects as he does and is able to describe them far more clearly. Indefatigable, he guides us into a dimly lighted, partially built tunnel where the uneven ground is treacherous with potholes. Bennett follows Danilo willingly, undisturbed by his zeal; I less willingly. By the time we emerge on the other side of the long tunnel Bennett has slipped and skinned his knee badly; but he makes light of the injury and insists Danilo continue the tour.

On the way to Partinico, Danilo summarizes the psychological and material benefits that the eighteen villages in the valley will derive from the dam. "Montelepre will be one of the beneficiaries. In all the villages there will be more jobs, less migration, and less delinquency. Sicilians thrive when they have work. But there is a good deal more to be done besides completing the dam and reforesting the hills around it. The people need to be educated to the possibilities that exist around them and inside them. We at the Center can do some of this educational work but the bulk of it must be done in the villages themselves, with the help of trained community leaders who can determine what steps need to be taken. That is why the Institute we are about to start can be the most important project the Center has ever undertaken . . ."

Bennett asks what, specifically, the graduates of the Institute will do to improve the economic situation of the villages.

"At first their chief value will lie in their technical ability to ascertain the resources as well as the problems of a village," Danilo replies. "There is a distressing lack of information everywhere in this part of Italy. By making himself an information expert in his

150

village, the community leader learns, for example, what economic help can be obtained from the government. There are a good many laws that have been passed for the benefit of Sicily but very little is done to take advantage of them because few persons know they exist. You might think that a mayor would know what those laws were, but a village mayor is usually a part-time official, with very little education. Even if he knew that such laws existed, he would have difficulty trying to figure out what they meant. A community leader would make it his business to learn those laws and to show his village how it can profit from them.

"Properly coordinated information can mean gold to a village, but there is very little of it available. Although hundreds of engineering tests have been conducted in Sicily, no one except the technicians who conducted them are aware of the results. In a village near Partinico there were some petroleum tests made not long ago; instead of petroleum, the engineers found water. But they never bothered to let the village know of the water, although there was a desperate need of it there. There simply is not enough coordination between local, regional and national offices. The people we train would try to find out what information is available and how it can be exploited to benefit their villages."

Anxious to brief Bennett as fully as possible before he begins his tour of the zone the next morning, Danilo heads for the Center even before the Englishman can register at the hotel, and furnishes him with complete details about the Center's personnel and budget. To my surprise, the annual operating budget amounts to less than $70,000. More than half the amount is derived from Dolci-supporting committees abroad; the rest comes from private sources and Italian groups. The money is spent largely for rent, employee insurance, and study and research projects. Less than half of the total budget is used for salaries.

The salaries are so low that I wonder how they can be stretched to meet basic living costs in an area where food prices are almost as high as in Philadelphia. Vegetables are cheaper, but meat and eggs cost more than they do in large American cities. The average monthly salary of a Center worker is approximately $75. The budget statement Danilo shows us includes the following method for determining monthly salaries: "Very young collaborators re-

151

ceive $48; older and experienced collaborators lacking a formal education $64; collaborators with experience and professional training $96. In addition, each collaborator receives annually $8 as a salary increase; another $8 for each child in his family; and $32 for his wife.

"Naturally," says Danilo, "toward the end of each year we are nearly always in the red, both the Center and its collaborators. Yet we manage somehow . . ."

"We're not interested in a large staff," he says discussing the fact there are twenty collaborators now as against the sixty there were two years ago. "Quality of staff rather than quantity is our aim. Of course, we can manage with a smaller staff now because many of the services the Center used to perform, such as operating *dopo-scuola* [after school] classes in various villages, are now being done by the government. Thanks to the examples established by the Center, the municipalities now provide their own *doposcuole*. The four teachers on our present staff are used to train the *dopos-cuola* teachers hired by the municipalities. More and more, we succeed in obtaining the collaboration of experts who are employed by the government. For example, two years ago the Center was paying for the services of an agricultural expert in Partinico. This year Partinico has four agricultural experts, all of them on the payroll of the Cassa di Mezzogiorno . . ."

By now, even Danilo is tired, and we part. Laden with information and statistics, Bennett finally gets to his hotel. Later in the evening Patricia and I dine with him in a restaurant run by a fisherman in the coastal village of Terrasini.

Chapter

8

Artichokes,
Hope, and Violence

MARCH 27

THE NEXT MORNING Bennett, Patricia, and I journey toward Menfi
with Michele Mandiello and his new car. It is my first opportunity
to know Michele away from the Center, and I soon begin to ply
him with questions about himself and his experience in Sicily,
which began in 1959.

Born in 1926, Michele is two years younger than Danilo. He
grew up among peasants, in a small farming town in the province
of Salerno, where his father ran a small grocery and seed store.
His interest in the problems of small farmers led to his formal
education as an agriculturalist, which in turn led to a job as a
trade union worker among the peasants of La Spezia in northern
Italy. In 1948 he participated in an event which, he says, had a
deep influence on his thinking. "The farm workers in our union
joined hands with some factory workers of Melara who had been
fired because of their refusal to manufacture cannons. The men
won the support of the factory's technicians and, under their guidance, began to manufacture tractors and railway cars instead of
cannons. It was a pretty successful enterprise for three months;
then an army of policemen descended on the factory and drove
everyone out."

On the death of his father in 1953, Michele was obliged to return to his village to support his family. In his spare time he and a
former school companion organized the peasants in the area to

153

campaign for improved road conditions. By the time he came to Sicily in 1958 at Danilo's invitation, to explore the possibility of working for the Center, the peasants had achieved their goals.

"I had read of Danilo's work among the peasants and fishermen and had become an admirer of his, but it was the first time I had seen Sicily. When I arrived in Partinico, I was horrified by the poverty around me. There were dirty, half-naked children everywhere, piles of garbage on the streets, and millions of flies. It was the month of August, the worst of all the Sicilian months. Near Menfi I got another shock when I saw miles and miles of irrigation ducts filled with water that wasn't being used, while all around the earth was brown with thirst, and not a blade of grass able to grow. What a terrible and sinful waste, I thought. Seven billion lire had been spent to construct a dam with a capacity of some 35 million cubic meters of water, yet for two years all that water had been permitted to flow into the sea. As I listened to Danilo talk to me about the Center's determination to educate the peasants so that the waste could be stopped, I decided in my heart that my mission in life would be to work in Sicily . . ."

He interrupts himself to point to an empty building with some tracks running in front of it. "We call that the fantasy railroad," Michele says. "It is a monument to fascist corruption. The Fascists started building the railroad but somehow the money for it got diverted into mysterious channels and the idea was abandoned. In Sicily there are a number of such monuments. A few kilometers from here there is an entire village built in Mussolini's regime— houses, school, town hall, everything. But no one has ever lived there. Even if people were to occupy the houses, they would have no means of earning a living in that area. No one ever bothered to figure that out—not until the village was completely built . . .

"In Menfi we had to start from scratch, with a hole in the wall as an office. I began by making a large wall map showing all the water ducts in the area and all the parcels of land that they could irrigate. The next step was to find farmers who would listen to what I had to say. There were two attitudes to overcome. One was the general hostility toward the irrigation system. The other was the old habit of growing nothing but wheat and beans, the traditional Sicilian crops for centuries . . ."

"What kind of beans?" Bennett asks.

"The kind that peasants feed to their horses and asses. Not the kind that people eat. Sicilians consume a great quantity of vegetables, but they are not grown in Sicily; most of them are imported from the Naples area. It is little wonder that the cost of living in this predominantly agricultural island is almost as high as it is in the industrial north. There is a great deal that the Sicilians could do to improve their economy by changing some of their habit patterns. I agree with Danilo when he says that the problem in Sicily is not so much of poverty as of ignorance."

I ask Michele how long it took him to win his first Menfi convert.

"The first person to listen to me with any seriousness was an intelligent young farmer who helped me make my map. Ciccio Sanzone didn't need to be converted—he already knew about the value of irrigation and crop diversity. But, fortunately for me, he was having trouble—insect trouble—with his artichoke crop, and I knew exactly what to do about it. When I couldn't find the required insecticide in Sicily, I wrote to the company that made it, and they sent me a free sample. That gave me a great idea. From then on I got free samples of almost everything I needed to demonstrate that with irrigation, fertilizer, and chemical insecticides you could accomplish wonders.

"The first two years were the toughest. We had more enemies than friends then—some of them the town's leading citizens, who couldn't bear the idea of changing the status quo in any way. They called me and my associates Protestants and Communists and said that we had evil ulterior intentions. They warned families not to send their children to the *doposcuola* an Englishwoman by the name of Ilys Booker was establishing for the Center, claiming that the children would be kidnapped and sent to England, the United States, and Russia. As proof that we were dangerous revolutionaries, they told of the bearded foreigners who hung around our office—actually they were our own British technicians—and described how they went spying around the countryside with mysterious maps in their hands.

"Despite all the antagonism, we began to make progress. We got the ex-mayor, a surveyor, interested in our cause and began to

155

have weekly meetings with the peasants and some of the more enlightened citizens of Menfi. We discussed with them ways and means of utilizing the irrigation water, and also to experiment with crops that were new to the area. We began to establish crop demonstration areas. In 1959 there were thirty-nine of them. Gradually we increased their number until there were two hundred by 1962. They were essential because they proved to the peasants that what we were advising them to do really worked . . ."

He stops, suddenly embarrassed. "I hope Mr. Bennett doesn't take me for a braggart. Please explain to him that I had a great deal of expert help for what was accomplished. And, also, that there is a great deal more to be done."

It never crossed his mind that Michele was bragging, Bennett says. He already knows of his successes in Menfi, and recalls a statistic to the effect that the peasants in the area who used to earn 150,000 lire per hectare from growing wheat now derive one million lire by growing other crops on the same ground. Encouraged, Michele augments the statistic with the more general one that in the four years after the Center opened its office in Menfi the total agricultural income in that area had more than doubled. In the same period, the consumption of meat had tripled. That reminds him that it is almost lunchtime.

We dine on a terrace facing the Mediterranean, a few hundred yards from the ancient Greek city of Selinus.* It is warm enough to swim, but the long stretch of wide beach in front of us is completely deserted. "This whole sector could easily be made into one of Italy's great resorts—the ruins at Taormina don't begin to compare with those at Selinus," Michele says. "But rich Sicilians hate to invest their money in Sicily, and the government does nothing about it except talk."

Bennett, still interested in Michele's early years at Menfi, asks him what "unexpected problems" he encountered.

"There were too many of them," he replies with a smile. "One was in connection with our effort to encourage the wholesale production of eggs. As you may know, despite the large consumption of eggs in Sicily, most of them come from eight foreign countries and, of course, are quite expensive. This has always seemed absurd to me. It occurred to me that if I could show the farmers how to

* Called "Selinunte" on modern maps.

raise corn, the ideal food for hens, they could easily increase their egg production. At first everything went fine. The corn I planted grew to a height of nine feet; the peasants were impressed. But then a peculiar thing happened: the hens refused to eat the corn. I was dumbfounded. All other hens in the world eat corn, I told myself; why shouldn't Sicilian hens do the same? I didn't know what to do about it, except worry. Luckily, a friend of mine, a shrewd peasant, had faith in me. Without saying anything about it to me or to anyone else, he locked up a group of hens for several days and fed them nothing. When he released them, he fed them corn. They gobbled it up as though it were ambrosia. The other hens, watching them devour it so greedily, decided to try it. After that, it became the daily food of all the hens.

"That first corn we grew created another unexpected problem. As soon as it reached its full growth, all the caterpillars for miles around converged on my corn field for a big feast. We could have easily killed them with a chemical insecticide, but I was afraid that at that early stage of their education, the peasants might consider the chemical poisonous. You must remember that these were peasants whose farming habits had been ingrained into them by centuries of tradition. One of my assistants solved the problem but it cost him a great deal of sleep. For nearly a week he stayed up every night and destroyed most of the caterpillars by hand. It was a noble thing for him to do, but for months afterwards, he told me, his dreams were filled with murders."

Before continuing to Menfi, we ramble through the streets of Selinus, which the Greeks built more than 2500 years ago on a site that is totally encircled by sea and mountain. The abandoned city has the disquieting silence of distant history. On a main thoroughfare, which Michele nicknames Broadway, some of the history is plainly stamped into the pavement by the wheels of the chariots. Most of it has to be imagined from the piles of gray stones neatly lining the sides of each street, the broken skeletons of buildings that were once homes and shops. The stones still harbor life: a vast colony of lizards that sun their green crocodile bodies with the aplomb of first families; and, miraculously, a variety of glorious wildflowers spawn in unseen soil. There are buttercups, white alyssum, and beds of purple and pink sweet peas.

At the outskirts of the city is a massive graveyard of crumbled

157

temples. They appear to have been struck by an earthquake but Michele has been told by archaeologists that most of them were destroyed by Carthaginian conquerors who used ropes and teams of horses to pull down the columns. "The Carthaginians did it to show what contempt they had for the traditional Greek gods," Michele reflects. "At Menfi I have sometimes felt like a Carthaginian, but I get rid of the feeling by telling myself that I am replacing old ideas with new ones that are more constructive."

Menfi is only a few miles beyond Selinus, on a flat inland area. Michele's face, registering pink excitement, becomes the map that informs us we have reached the lands where he has been doing his work. On both sides of the road we begin to see stretches of green fields, most of them bursting with artichokes. Above them, to the height of a man, is a skinny network of irrigation ducts that bear the waters of the Carboi dam. In the surge of his excitement, Michele stops the car at the edge of a field, picks four artichokes, and with a pocket knife swiftly pares them to the heart. As we each bite into their rawness, we agree they are tender and savory; Bennett, a vegetarian, is especially lavish in his enthusiasm. "With a little olive oil and salt," Michele tells him, "they are more delicious than any meat."

In addition to artichokes, which have supplanted wheat as the area's chief source of income, we note tobacco, lettuce, tomatoes, string beans, and grapevines. Now that the Center has achieved some of the main objectives it has had for the Menfi area, Michele informs us, it will start concentrating on the long-range goal of promoting the expansion of the irrigation system to other villages near the Carboi dam; it will also help establish cooperatives to provide farmers with increased profits and more efficient distribution of their products. Michele is presently helping to organize a grape growers' cooperative. "It isn't easy. The history of cooperatives in this part of Sicily is an unhappy one and the farmers are naturally leery about forming a new one. But as the crop situation has improved, their confidence in the Center's recommendations has grown, and I think we are finally ready for a successful wine cooperative that will father others."

Bennett and I express surprise that Michele and Danilo, who must be aware of the damaging effects of smoking, have encouraged the cultivation of tobacco. Michele says there were two reasons for it: The first was to provide easy outdoor work for women, who are usually confined by tradition to their homes; the second was to provide farmers with a guaranteed source of income. "Cigarette manufacturing being a government monopoly, the State buys all the tobacco our farmers raise. Of course," Michele adds tactfully, "had we known in 1959 what we know now about the harmful effects of smoking, we probably would never have introduced the crop. But we can't stop it now. If we did, we would be accused of taking bread away from the mouths of children."

Although the countryside around Menfi is greener than it ever was, the town itself has the same seamy look it had when I saw it in 1947. There are more motorcycles, scooters, and cars now, but they do not detract from the general bleakness of the scene. Now and then I catch a glimpse of a woman sitting in the doorway peeling vegetables, but invariably her back is turned to passersby. Except for those few who have been lured into the tobacco fields, the women of Menfi are still committed to the influence of their Arabic ancestors.

The Center's office is at sidewalk level on the main thoroughfare, a simply furnished room decorated by the wall map Michele prepared when he first arrived. There are three men waiting for him as we enter. He quickly gets rid of one of them, a senile shepherd who visits him every day in order to repeat the same old story of how the Mafia ruined him by kidnapping his sheep one by one until there were none left; each time the old man complained to the police, the *mafiosi* would burn down his mountain shack. "It is too late for me to help the old man," Michele said, "but he reminds me of my grandfather; so I listen to his story whenever I have time."

The two other men are farm laborers who are helping Michele organize the wine cooperative. While Michele rushes off to see the Mayor on some urgent business related to the cooperative, the men ask us if we are representatives of a canning company that has been exploring the possibility of establishing a factory near Menfi. They are keenly disappointed to learn that we are not.

"Michele believes they have decided to build the factory in Siracusa," the younger one says, "and we keep hoping he is mistaken.

159

A canning factory is desperately needed in this zone." He explains that while irrigation has solved production problems, little is being done about problems of marketing and distribution. "What good is it raising a big crop if we can't get enough money out of it? Sometimes it doesn't pay us to pick all the stuff we grow. We either have to sell our crops for too little money or let them rot in the fields. Either way we suffer. The profits we should be getting land in the pockets of the middlemen. They are like the parasites on our plants, except that we can't get rid of them as we do the insects."

The two men agreed with Bennett that cooperatives might be the answer to their problems. "But do you know what it means to get a group of Sicilians working toward the same aim?" one of them asked. "It isn't easy. We Sicilians are cursed with a distrust of one another."

"The wine cooperative will be the test," the older man says. "If that works out, then we'll be able to organize other cooperatives. But in the meantime, if you gentlemen encounter any wealthy persons in England or America, please tell them that there is a fortune to be made with a canning factory at Menfi."

The two men disagree on the question of whether the presence of the Mafia in the Menfi area explains the reluctance of manufacturers to build there.

"Manufacturers aren't afraid of the Mafia," the younger one says. "Why should they be? They can buy or sell anyone."

"The Mafia can intimidate anyone," the other insists. "If I were a manufacturer, I would hesitate to tangle with the Mafia. Who wants complications of that sort?"

The two men are still arguing the point when Michele returns with the news that the Mayor is ready to submit the final application forms for the cooperative to Rome. "We've been filling out forms for a whole year but I think these are the last of them. If all goes well, we'll have the cooperative established within a few months."

After a tour of the countryside and a feast of raw artichokes at the local trattoria, Michele drives us to Sciacca for the night, since Menfi has no hotel. On the way he reveals that he and his family left Menfi a few months before and rented an apartment in

Sciacca. "The main reason we moved was because of the lack of drinking water in Menfi. Although there is plenty of water for the plants, there is not enough for people. Sometimes we would have no water for a whole week." He sighs. "As I told you and Mr. Bennett, we still have serious problems in Menfi . . ."

On both sides of the road we see caravans of men on horses and mules riding toward Menfi after a day's work in the fields. In each caravan there are six or eight peasants. In the twilight, with their long bright scarves covering half their faces, they look like the Arab tribesmen of a Delacroix painting. Michele asks me to examine their faces closely. "Do you notice how young many of them are? That is a sign that things are going fairly well in Menfi. When things get bad in a Sicilian village, the young men are the first to leave and look for work in other countries."

Michele installs us in a motel on the edge of Sciacca that is equipped with surprisingly modern conveniences, but the comforts of our room are lost on me as an army of cold germs attack me during the night. The next morning Michele, noticing my condition, expresses sympathy for what he terms my "fever" (the name given to most ailments in Sicily, whether there is a fever or not), and promises me "an almost immediate cure." After showing us the main sections of the seaside town, which have a sensuously Spanish atmosphere, we drive up a near-by mountain to a grandiose hotel below which Sciacca gleams like a giant topaz. The fashionable hotel, where the wealthy come to enjoy the views and bathe in sulphuric water, is closed during the spring but Michele finds a running fountain and urges me to drink from it. The foul flavor of the water nearly costs me my breakfast. Michele glances at his watch and prophesies that within one hour I will be over my "fever."

On the same mountain we visit a country schoolhouse where Michele's adopted daughter assists an older teacher in conducting elementary grade classes for twenty students. Aurora, he explains, is actually his niece. Her father was his brother, and had been killed in the war. As Italian brothers often do under similar circumstances, Michele married his brother's widow. The girl is a pretty Neapolitan brunette in her early twenties. Her superior, a balding Sicilian with Svengali-fierce eyes, chain-smokes while conducting his class, a fact which shocks Bennett, Patricia, and me but leaves Michele undisturbed. Aurora takes over his class while he shows us around the school building, which is less than five years old. Although it contains a kitchen and shower, there is no water or electricity and, apparently, little hope of acquiring either. There are also no toilet facilities; the bushes serve for that purpose for both students and teachers. We are told that the children do not mind, probably because their homes have the same lack of conveniences. Actually, the general atmosphere is quite cheerful; the children have enhanced it by planting flower beds all around the building. As we are leaving, some of the students hold up a gaily painted sign which they had made during our brief visit: "The children of this school warmly greet you."

From Sciacca we drive to the Carboi dam and its adjoining reservoir, Lake Arancia, listening to Michele's exclamations of joy as we pass one artichoke field after another. Bennett pronounces the dam a marvel of engineering efficiency, but asks why a hydro-electric plant has not been built on the site to reduce the forbid-dingly high cost of electricity in the zone. The government authorities have given the idea a great deal of consideration, Michele replies, but little else. "Many intelligent ideas that would help Sicily are smothered to death by endless governmental talk. That is one reason why Sicily continues to be an underdeveloped region . . ."

More surprising than the lack of a hydroelectric plant is the total lack of irrigation around the village of Sambuca, though its outskirts are within plain sight of the Carboi dam. As we approach the hill town there is a drastic change in the appearance of the land. Ravaged by erosion and neglect, the arid and uncultivated fields are filled with rocks, brambles, and deep ruts. Under the hot noon sun, the ruts glisten like scarlet wounds.

"Twelve hundred men, more than half of Sambuca's popula-tion," Michele says, "have been obliged to leave the village be-cause of its dead economy. Only the money they send home keeps the place alive. Yet Sambuca could have had the same prosperous agricultural development that Menfi had if, instead of talking, the villagers had taken action while the dam was being built. The Christian Democrats are mainly to blame. They have been fight-ing the Communists tooth and nail ever since the first Communist mayor was elected in 1946. The Christian Democrats have been more interested in trying to weaken the political power of the Communists than in worrying about the economic welfare of the village. I am a Catholic but I deplore opposition that is simply for the sake of opposition."

The village is not so high as Roccamena but it has the same remote and desolate atmosphere. While we stop at a café for an espresso, Michele dashes out of the place to greet an old friend who is passing by. He returns with the explanation that his friend is back for a brief visit after working as a stone mason in Germany for two years. "The poor fellow doesn't want to leave his family again but he has no choice in the matter. How else can he provide for them? A dreadful thing happened a few minutes after he arrived in Sambuca the other day. He had not reached his house yet when he met his youngest son on the street. The boy walked right by him, not realizing he was his father. Poor Ignazio had to introduce himself . . ."

"Not being recognized by their children isn't the only heartache our migrants suffer," the man behind the espresso bar says. "I talk to many of them. You have no idea what indignities they suffer in the hands of foreign bosses. They treat Sicilians like dirt and give them the most dangerous jobs to do. If there were enough jobs available in Sambuca, all the men who have left would be back within two days."

We return to the car and head toward the interior, in the direction of Corleone. Michele glances at his watch; two hours have passed since we left Sciacca. "How is your fever?" he asks.

"Frankly, not much better."

"You probably didn't drink enough of that water," he says. "Shall we go back for some more?"

The emphasis with which I say no makes him laugh. I tell Michele I will try to cure my fever Danilo style, mainly by willpower.

"It would certainly be useful for all of us to have Danilo's willpower," he remarks.

"And courage," Patricia adds.

Bennett observes that it must take a great deal of courage to denounce the Mafia as openly as Danilo has. "It is amazing to me that he is still alive. Why hasn't the Mafia tried to kill him?"

"That is a question he often asks himself," I report. Michele recalls that in 1963, when Danilo denounced Senator Girolamo Messeri before the Anti-Mafia Commission for his connections with the criminal Frank Coppola, an ex-Partisan leader published an article warning all politicians in Rome with Mafia connections that if any harm came to Danilo or to any of his assistants, the politicians would have to reckon with the fury of all the ex-Partisans.

I ask Michele whether the Mafia had ever tried to harm him.

"Not so far," he replies. "I don't think they will try anything. The Mafia is still fairly strong in Menfi but so is the Center. We've made many good friends around there who feel as the ex-Partisans do."

Observing that neither Michele, Danilo, nor Franco is a Sicilian, I suggest that the Mafia may be reluctant to kill an outsider because it would be too difficult for them to foretell what repercussions would follow. This is evidently one of the reasons why the Mafia does not disturb foreign visitors.

"That has occurred to me," Michele says. "I also think that Danilo's fame protects him and his associates, though I am not at all certain that this protection extends to our friend Lorenzo. They could easily kill Lorenzo in a village like Roccamena and make it look as if the murder was unrelated to his work at the Center." After a moment he adds: "The better known a man is the safer he is from the Mafia. If they had killed Danilo when he first came to Sicily, no one would have paid much attention to the murder; but in those days the Mafia had no idea that he could possibly become a threat to them. By the time they realized what he was up to, it was too late; he had become too famous, not only in Sicily but internationally."

We are now in the heart of the big Belice valley, an overwhelming panorama of treeless plains and hills encircled by sharp-toothed mountains whose bare skin is feverishly red in the afternoon heat. At first the eye is enthralled by the monumental elements; they intimate the unfolding of a Greek drama in which sky and earth vie for supremacy. But there is no movement whatsoever in the scene; it is as if the drama has become paralyzed at the very moment when the chief protagonists are at each other's throats, with no hope of resolution. Watching the relentless sun in

164

the hard sky as it burns into the naked landscape, the initial excitement turns into premonition; the mind becomes oppressed by the likelihood of finding oneself stranded in the valley, with not an inch of shade anywhere for comfort.

For a long time none of us says anything; with no other car or person in sight, we may be silenced by the same fears. Then Michele, less affected than the rest of us by his long familiarity with the valley, predicts that one day there will be trees growing on the hills and mountains to replace those that had been lost many years ago through man's greed. "The trees will come when there is a dam to feed the valley and when all vestiges of feudalism are gone. The big landowners like the valley to be without trees; it makes it easier for them to control the area. A single *mafioso* guard can observe exactly what is going on for miles around. We are probably under observation this very moment." He turns toward me. "But tell your wife not to be frightened. With two Americans and one Englishman in this car, we are in no danger."

It is a relief to come upon the next village, Santa Margarita di Belice, and see people and buildings again. Michele stops the car to direct our attention to a huge baronial structure which he identifies as "Donnafugata," the summer palace of the Salinas family in Lampedusa's novel *The Leopard*. "It is not in Piana di Montechiaro, as many tourists think," he insists. The building is now a slummy apartment house with scores of ragged children running about in the courtyard. Above the main entrance is the Lampedusa coat of arms with the central figure of the *gattopardo* (the Italian title of the novel which means *serval* but was romantically mistranslated in English as *leopard*). When I venture the opinion that Lampedusa may have wished to be ambiguous about the location of the summer palace, Michele cannot agree. "If fiction is written to give the impression of truth," he says, "why would a writer want to confuse his readers about the location of a building that is important to the story?"

We both agree, however, that *The Leopard* conveys a misleading image of the Sicilians. "They are not as helpless or as resigned to death as Lampedusa would have us believe," Michele observes. "They are a people who can take action when they have the opportunity to do so. Think of the millions of Sicilians who left their

165

families at the beginning of the century and traveled to North and South America to find work. That was hardly the action of a people that is resigned to dying . . ."

Bennett, who has been in India recently, tells of a survey made there which reveals that most of the natives are perfectly satisfied with their lot, despite their acute poverty. "They have no wish for more money or property; they see little possibility of happiness in either of those commodities."

"I have known Sicilians who are like that," Michele says. "They are the weaker ones who accept the misery of this world in the hope that things will be better in the next. Yet even they are capable of changing. Lampedusa's low opinion of poor Sicilians is pretty typical of the landowning aristocrats who have been exploiting the peasants working for them. I suppose that attitude enables them to exploit with an easier conscience . . ."

We climb the same mountain road where Bill Taylor had seen the bullet-ridden corpse of the infamous Dr. Navarra, and a little later drive into Corleone, a village that has become synonymous with Mafia terror. With the assassination of Navarra and the arrest in 1965 of his rival and murderer, Luciano Liggio, crime in Corleone has diminished, but the memories of the days when the town had the highest homicide rate in Sicily are still fresh enough to provide surviving *mafiosi* with effective powers of intimidation.

In his book *Mafia and Politics* Michele Panteleone reports that in the four years following the end of the war "no fewer than 153 murders were recorded in the Corleone countryside—an average of one murder every twelve days." That was the period when the Mafia, which had been crippled for twenty years by the enmity of the Fascist regime, was returning to a stronger position of power than it had ever had. The ironical story of how the American military command, by enlisting Mafia aid for its bloodless invasion of Sicily in 1943, became an unwitting accessory to the Mafia's rehabilitation has been told in full detail by Panteleone and other writers. Here it is sufficient to recall that following the collapse of Italian Fascism, all the *mafiosi* jailed by Mussolini were released (with the apparent consent of the American occupation forces) on the spurious grounds that they had been imprisoned for their antifascist activity. Villainy further triumphed when these same "anti-fascist" *mafiosi* were given key administrative jobs in postwar Sicily. Catapulted into the arena of politics, the Mafia was quick to form alliances with the party in power, the Christian Democrats, and by its techniques of violence and intimidation became an effective vote-getting agency for the party.

Simultaneously, members of the Mafia were also strengthening their hand as the police force (and sometimes partners) of the large landowners, who were confronted by militant peasants demanding their share of the uncultivated parcels of land allotted to them by law. In its bloody campaign against leaders of the peasant movement, the Mafia assassinated thirty-five secretaries of agricultural unions who were asking for nothing more than the enforcement of land reform laws that were already on the books. The pervading influence of the Mafia can be gauged by the fact that not one of these crimes was ever punished.

Among the victims was a trade union leader of Corleone, a young war veteran named Placido Rizzotto, whose corpse was found in a deep gully in 1950, two years after he had been kidnapped in broad daylight on the town square. If each person who saw the kidnapping had picked up a stone, one witness told Danilo, the kidnappers could have been easily routed.* "They seized him, trampled him down as though they were stomping on grapes and threw him into a car. He shouted for help but no one paid any attention. Nobody wanted to hear. Do you think it is right that a man should get himself killed for the sake of people who become deaf and blind when it suits them?"

The same witness said: "Placido understood that in this backwater everything is rotten. It is like being in a stagnant pool; things rot, insects breed and spread epidemics; the corruption pollutes all things. Placido wanted change, progress; that is what he was aiming for. I myself don't know what to think: he is dead and if he is dead he must have been wrong—I can't help looking at it that way . . ."

Luciano Liggio was one of the *mafiosi* accused of the crime but no one was ever convicted. As in most crimes involving the Mafia, the case was thrown out of court "for lack of sufficient evidence." There was a witness to the actual murder but he did not live to

* As reported in *Waste* by Danilo Dolci.

tell his story. He was Giuseppe Letizia, a young shepherd of thirteen, who was so horrified by what he saw, that he became delirious as he tried to describe the murder, and was taken to the local hospital for treatment. There he was given an injection by Dr. Navarra, who was then working hand in glove with Liggio, and Giuseppe died shortly afterwards.

Despite all the murders in Corleone, Navarra was never once interrogated by the police during its numerous investigations. As a white-collar Mafia leader who was a power in local Christian Democrat politics as well as a highranking officer in several of the town's administrative agencies, he was considered untouchable. Liggio, who began his criminal career by stealing cattle which were clandestinely slaughtered for the Palermo market, was the terror of Corleone for more than twenty years. The blatant Al Capone of his area, he and his henchmen conducted steady guerilla warfare on all farm laborers around Corleone who tried to assert or extend their rights as sharecroppers. In his extensive intimidation campaigns, which sometimes victimized landowners as well, he set fires to haystacks, killed hundreds of mules and horses, and decreed assassinations.

The arrest of Liggio has not ended his influence in Corleone, we are told by the young social worker in charge of the Center's office. "Despite the fact that the Mafia has been lying low, the people are still afraid of showing too much initiative. Some of them believe it won't be long when the Anti-Mafia Commission goes out of business and Liggio is released from prison. They are afraid he will come back to Corleone and carry on as he did before . . ."

At lunch the young social worker discusses some of the most pressing problems in Corleone: bad roads; insufficient water; poor housing, a great deal of it unfit for human habitation. He is trying to organize a citizen's committee to try to cope with the problems but is meeting with considerable resistance. "With so many of the men gone off to work in foreign countries, morale is low and there is plenty of fear."

As he turns to have a whispered conversation with Michele, I remember that this is the same young man who conducted the Center's investigation of the new hospital at Corleone which, for reasons best known to the Mafia, remained closed long after it was built. Now the hospital is open, but the young man's parents, having heard some ominous Mafia grumblings about the investigation, are insisting that he give up his job with the Center. "He wanted my advice as to what he should do," Michele reports to us later. "I told him he would have to make up his own mind."

On our way out of the restaurant Michele is greeted effusively by a rotund police marshal who embraces him, kisses him, and, on being introduced to us, insists on buying all of us an espresso. He is the personification of ebullient grace. He inquires about the health of Michele's family, directs tactful questions to Bennett and to me about our presence in Sicily, and extols the fine qualities of the young social worker.

As we are leaving Corleone, I tease Michele about his chummy relations with the law. "I'm just as puzzled by the Marshal's sudden burst of affection and respect as you are," he says. "It is the first time any police officer has treated me as though I were a close relative. What it means I do not know. Let us hope it wasn't intended as a kiss of death for me or for our young social worker friend. As you may know, the Mafia—and sometimes the police—put on a great display of affection for their intended victims just before they are about to do them in."

After a few miles he reconsiders. "Perhaps I am being unduly unfair to the Marshal. Who knows? His display of good will could simply be his reaction to our demonstration at Roccamena. I must tell Danilo about it . . ."

Driving through the hot, parched landscape, we pass through the village of Piana dei Greci where Albanian, the language of its original settlers, is still spoken after seven hundred years. The name of the village, as I explain to my companions, will always evoke for me (and for most Sicilians) the memory of a massacre that was perpetrated nearby at a May Day workers' picnic in 1947, while I was living in Palermo.

In accordance with a long established annual custom, the people of three neighboring villages—Piana dei Greci, St. Giuseppe Jato and San Cippirello—jointly celebrated May Day with an outing at Portella della Ginestra, a large clearing in the country that is almost equidistant from the three villages. The picnickers were in a jubilant mood. Only ten days before the Popular Front had won an unexpected victory in the first election of representatives to the new Sicilian Regional Government. From this show of leftwing strength, the peasants believed that, despite the opposition of the Mafia and the landowners, they would finally be permitted to occupy the uncultivated portions of the large estates, as specified by law. What happened at Portella della Genestra that day smashed that optimism to bits.

Shortly before noon the picnic grounds were swarming with villagers who had come on foot or in their gaily painted peasant carts, bearing food, wine, and mandolins. As they listened to the opening sentences of a local shoemaker who was to make the first speech, several machine-guns from a nearby mountain began pouring a steady stream of bullets into them. Within three minutes, which was the length of the attack, the ground was covered with eleven dead and fifty-six wounded. No one bothered to count the number of casualties among the animals, whose screams were said to have been heard above those of the people.

There were loud and eloquent expressions of mourning and indignation in all parts of Italy, and even louder demands for the arrest of the assassins. For several weeks the police put on a good show of rounding up suspects and interrogating persons who were at or near the scene of the disaster. Nothing came of it, except that one of the police trucks capsized on its way to Piana dei Greci and several policemen were killed. In the months that followed, it became evident that the authorities were either in the dark or (as some of the leftwing newspapers insinuated) were unwilling to bring the murderers to justice for fear of treading on too many toes.

The day after the massacre the police refused me permission to visit Piana dei Greci, but allowed me to talk with some of the wounded who had been taken to a Palermo hospital. They were a simple and kindly people, of various political affiliations, who were certain they had been gunned down by hirelings of the large landowners and their *mafiosi* farm managers. The purpose of the massacre, they explained, was to put the fear of God in the peasantry and in that way kill the land reform program.

Three years were to pass before it became clear that this judgment was quite close to the truth. In June 1950, at a trial in

Viterbo, it was established that the bandit Salvatore Giuliano and his band had perpetrated the crime on behalf of the Mafia elements within the Christian Democrat party. It was also shown that the massacre was only the first of a planned series of terroristic acts directed against peasants' and workers' unions. Partinico was one of the nine villages included in the campaign. Two Molotov cocktails, hurled into the offices of the local peasants' association, killed two of its members. But the most significant revelation that emerged from the Viterbo trial was the existence of an extensive network of intrigue and collusion between the Mafia, the politicians, Giuliano, and certain segments of the police force.

Patricia asked Michele if the three villages still observe May Day together.

"Yes," he replied, "but there is no longer any celebration; it is now treated as a day for mourning."

Michele is interested in my interview with one of the wounded peasants, who said: "They think that by killing some of us they can prevent us from earning our bread on land that is rightfully ours. But they will soon understand that what has happened will bring us closer together."

"It should have," Michele says, "but it didn't. The trade union movement was broken, and the Mafia became more powerful as it exercised greater influence over politicians, landowners, and voters. After the massacre the peasants got a few parcels of uncultivated land, but they were too small and too arid to contribute to their welfare. About ten years ago the peasants began to abandon the land and look for jobs in other countries . . ."

We arrive in Roccamena, the final stop in our tour. Michele leaves us to return to Sciacca. The rest of us meet with Lorenzo Barbera in the office of the Center, where Bennett asks a series of pointed questions about the new Institute. While furnishing the answers, Lorenzo shows us a chart he has prepared which indicates how a village can benefit from the services of a trained community leader. "He will become a key man in the citizens' committee of his village, the man who can educate others to recognize the problems of the community and their solution. The citizens' committee, in turn, will become part of an intercommunity committee that will work for the benefit of the whole area. It will be up to the Institute to start this whole process of growth by nourishing its first seeds."

The Mayor of Roccamena enters the office during the discussion, and is invited to remain. Listening closely to what is being said but never saying a word, he smokes one cigarette after another until he has no more. When he realizes that no one else smokes, he shakes hands with each of us and departs. A little later Lorenzo drives us back to Partinico.

Uneasy Spring

MARCH 28

DURING THE WEEK Danilo works without pause, like someone who cannot tear himself away from his work. But on a Sunday he can become as gregarious as any Sicilian and, on the slightest pretext, will gather together his family and whatever visitors are about to indulge in his favorite recreation—a picnic outing to one of the paradisiacal scenic points near Partinico.

Today, being Bennett's last full day in Sicily, provides the occasion for such an outing, this one to Scopello, a fishing settlement about an hour's drive away, which Danilo describes in terms that are as shamelessly rhapsodic as those of a travel folder.

Halfway on the journey, we stop at the edge of Trappeto and climb a dirt road to the plateau where Danilo built his famous Borgo di Dio in 1952, which served as a shelter for destitute widows and orphans until a squad of armed policemen shut it down in 1954 on the specious grounds that it was "unsanitary." The other two buildings on the grounds, which were also constructed during Danilo's early years in Sicily, consist of a ramshackle auditorium and a single-story house of several rooms, where he and Vincenzina lived after their marriage. The grounds will become the campus of the new Institute, with the auditorium serving as the school building and the house as the dormitory and mess hall.

Few campuses in the world enjoy as idyllic a view. Below us the white houses of Trappeto and the purple Gulf of Castellammare, ringed by rosy-tipped mountains, fuse into an image of such palpable tranquillity that it is difficult to relate it to the devastating

173

misery described in Danilo's writings about the village. From this distance the only possible fault one can find with Trappeto is that the houses are too closely crowded together. Noticing how much free space there is in the hilly area surrounding the village, Patricia wonders why some of the families do not move to higher ground to avoid the congestion and enjoy the view.

There are a number of reasons, perhaps the most basic one being that Sicilians, who have been invaded by many enemies in their long history, have a subconscious need to live close together. A more practical reason is that water is scarcer on the hilltops than it is in the village. Danilo has still another explanation: "How can the people know that the views from their hilltops are extraordinarily beautiful when they have never known any other views? Besides, how long can a view remain beautiful in the minds of parents who are harassed by the need to feed their children?"

As we wander around the flower-covered grounds with Vincenzina, she expresses her nostalgia for the place. It was here that her children, Libera and Cielo, were born. "We gave our strength and our hearts to these buildings and to these grounds. Danilo and I have a great love for it; yet we could not keep on living here. It was so beautiful that I became uncomfortable—ashamed—to be living here while my friends and relatives lived in terrible conditions."

"Perhaps you can come back here someday when things are better in Trappeto," Patricia says.

Her eyes light up. "I would like that. After all, this is my village, the place where I was born."

"When I first came to Trappeto I figured out that it would be possible to have irrigation here by simply using pumps to raise the water level of the Jato, which is close by," Danilo is explaining to Bennett. "That is what we began to do, but as I studied the idea further a better idea developed. I realized that if a dam were built near Partinico it could serve all the villages in the Jato valley. That was another reason for moving to Partinico . . ."

At the bottom of the hill, Danilo looks back at the dirt road we have descended, and recalls that there was no road there when he arrived in Trappeto. "We built it," he says, and for the first time since I have known him I hear a note of pride in his voice.

At Scopello, to Danilo's surprise, we encounter a busload of Italian students on the verge of leaving. From the bus windows they notice the Anglo-Saxon faces of Bennett and Patricia and jeer at them with anti-American remarks shouted in broken English. Their unfriendliness is to be expected; even the conservative press is filled with anti-American sentiment these days. "No one used to come here," Danilo says in a disappointed voice. "Someone must have written an article about the place."

The wonder is that it is not swarming with tourists, for Danilo has not exaggerated its enticements. The most captivating aspect of Scopello is a unique sculpture show rooted in the aquamarine inlet, consisting of rocks that have been shaped by wind and sea into man-beast creatures. They stand in a variety of suggestive poses that baffle and delight. The fishing settlement, which looks out on these progeny of Poseidon, fronts a coastline that is strewn with wind-eaten boulders resembling big sponges. Behind the fisherman's shacks, the boathouses, and a pink palazzo extends a long green slope that is riotous with wildflowers. All these elements somehow combine to form a masterpiece of harmonized colors and shapes, such as nature seldom achieves on so intimate a scale.

As it is too cold and windy to eat outdoors, we repair to an abandoned shack where Vincenzina, assisted by a fisherman's wife, roasts over an open fire a large mess of freshly caught sardines. She also serves an egg and fennel salad, chunks of first salt cheese, and a mature wine of Partinico. Watching Bennett nibbling on a sardine I think of how consistent a gentleman he is, though at the cost of being an inconsistent vegetarian. Fish, as Patricia and I accidentally discovered during our recent journey, is usually excluded from his diet along with meat. Although he gave no indication of this fact the first evening we dined together, I noted a curious fact: of the four species of fish that made up the meal, Bennett ate only one. Later, when we learned about his fish taboo (suspended that first evening to relieve us of any embarrassment), he explained he had settled for one species of fish because he would have felt more guilty partaking of all four.

After the meal we wander among the fishermen, who are busy preparing for the tuna season, which is only a few weeks off. A half dozen men are mending enormous nets, and repairing and painting boats. Their work is supervised by a Sicilian with distinctly Semitic features whose title is *reis,* the Arabic word for "leader," which has been in use in Sicily since the Arabic occupation ten centuries ago. The *reis* and Danilo are old friends, and they talk nostalgically about the old days when Danilo was a neighbor in Trappeto.

As I listen to Danilo expounding on the beauty of Scopello and of the entire Castellammare coastal area, I point out to him that none of his love for the natural beauty of Sicily ever enters into his writings. He replies that when he writes he is concerned with Sicily's social and spiritual problems, not with the scenery. Yet I cannot help reflecting that his vision of Sicily, as expressed in his books, might emerge even more powerfully if, occasionally, the problems were contrasted with the extraordinary beauty of their natural setting.

On the way back to Partinico, Danilo is all business as he discusses with Bennett the long-range effect that the new Institute will have on shaping the work of the Center. Bennett interrupts at one point to ask whether it would be possible for him to inspect the Center's health clinic in the morning before he leaves, a request which leads me to believe that the German nurse has spoken to him. Danilo replies there would be no problem making the arrangement, but quickly makes it clear that the clinic, which may become a state institution shortly, occupies a secondary place in the Center's plans. "It is easy enough to get money for enterprises like clinics and health education and they are certainly necessary," he says, "but the money spent on them will not be nearly as fruitful in the long run as that invested in a school to train community leaders." When Bennett makes no comment, Danilo adds: "The actions at the Center must be strategic in nature since they are on such a small scale. We try to provide the yeast in situations that have the maximum potential so that the potential can rise to the top . . ."

Bennett nods, but says nothing. Then Danilo talks about the enchantment of Scopello, and says: "Please tell Mr. Bennett that he must return to Sicily soon so that we can have another fish roast at some other beautiful spot."

MARCH 29

This morning, on my way to the Center, the voice of the wine woman nabs me from the balcony where she is hanging clothes. Her son, she screams, is home on a vacation from the seminary and will come around to the Via Emma to see me. Shortly before our evening meal, he appears at our doorway, a tall, thin, spectacled Julien Sorel endowed with the mother's fine features. His black robe, adorned with red piping, reaches to his ankles; his headpiece is a black broadrimmed affair similar to the one worn by cardinals. Although his manners are better, he has his mother's oral aggressiveness. As soon as he enters, he begins to ply me with the very same questions asked by his mother and his sister. On learning I am a writer, he becomes so delighted that he rises and shakes my hand again. When I explain my reason for being in Partinico, he exclaims in an incredulous voice: "But surely, you're not going to write anything favorable about Danilo Dolci, are you?"

I reply that I am gathering as much material about him as possible, with the hope of presenting it objectively. "In that case," he says, "I can be of tremendous help to you because I know what he is really like." At one time he had been "a profound admirer" of Danilo but after discussing him with the priest at Trappeto, who knows Danilo well, he had suddenly lost his respect for him. The priest had told him that Dolci came to Trappeto pretending to be a Catholic in order to influence people more easily. Soon after his arrival he showed his "true colors" by seducing the widow who used to clean his room. "I feel my face becoming red when I think and speak of these things," the young seminarian says, "but you are interested in the truth and I must tell it to you. When the widow's brothers discovered their sister was in the family way, they told Dolci that unless he married her he would be a dead man. Danilo saw that they meant business and did as he was told. But instead of keeping his mouth shut about it, as a man would have done, he told the press he was marrying a poor widow with five children to show his solidarity with the people of Sicily."

I express surprise that a priest would gossip about such matters with a student.

"But the Catholics aren't the only ones who know the truth about Dolci," he says, ignoring my opinion of the priest. "His own

177

collaborators have told me they have no use for him. A compatriot of yours, a young woman, told me she had always dreamed of working with Albert Schweitzer in Africa but decided to come here to work with Dolci because Sicily was closer than Africa. She was soon sorry; she said Dolci was an egotist who paid too much attention to his personal affairs. She was one of a group of foreigners that washed its hands of the Center. They were all disillusioned with Dolci, just as I was."

The people of Partinico are also fed up with Dolci, he adds, because he offends their civic pride. "Dolci publishes lies about Partinico so that he can persuade people in foreign countries to give him money. Once, while he was taking photographs for one of his books, he dressed some children in rags so as to give the impression that the children had nothing else to wear."

Commenting that children in rags are a common sight in Partinico, I ask him whether he thinks the Partinicans are well off.

"They certainly are," he says enthusiastically. "Have you noticed how many hairdressing salons there now are in Partinico? I know of at least three. And look at all the television antennae you see in the poorest sections."

Television sets are not necessarily a sign of prosperity, I point out; in the United States, as elsewhere, they provide a form of escape from the troubles of poverty. He expresses surprise that there should be any poverty in the United States. Then, returning to the subject of Dolci, he predicts that one day someone will kill him "for sticking his nose in other people's affairs." He obviously relishes the idea.

"It is best for everyone to mind his own business," he adds, "but Dolci has never done that," and proceeds to inform me of his "foolish denunciation" of Senator Messeri for his connection with Frank Coppola. "All that Signor Coppola did was to tell people to vote for the senator. What is wrong with that?"

When I reply that in the United States we would consider it bad form for a senatorial candidate to have the public backing of a notorious gangster, he exclaims: "But how can that be when I know it to be a fact that Frank Coppola helped your President Truman become elected?" Noticing my skepticism, he adds earnestly: "I know that is true because Frank Coppola himself told me." With more pride than embarrassment, he reveals that Coppola and his relatives, who live in the vicinity of the Via Emma, are quite friendly with his family. "Signor Coppola has done many generous things for the Catholic Church," he says. "People should bear that in mind before maligning him . . ."

Our conversation is interrupted at this point by Patricia, who comes to notify me that supper is ready. The seminarian apologizes profusely for detaining me, then asks if I will correspond with him when I return to the States. I explain I am not much of a letter writer, but give him my address. As he shakes my hand, he makes a final statement: "Unlike Dolci, I have a great and sincere desire to help the poor people of Sicily and I am constantly trying to think of how that can be done. But first I must become a priest. If God permits, I will be ordained in two years' time."

"Isn't he good looking?" Patricia comments as he shakes hands with me again.

"What did your wife say?" he asks.

"She says you are very handsome."

He blushes and, not knowing what to say to that, puts on his hat and leaves.

APRIL 1

Last night through the portals of our balcony we watched Peppina in the startling role of a female Prometheus as she scurried through the darkness and rain holding aloft a brazier of hot coals intended for her married daughter, who lives a dozen houses away.

Our heavy schedule of work leaves little time for socializing with her or the other neighbors. My encounters with them usually take place in the mornings when I go down to the street to await the trashman. If there is more than one woman outdoors then, they surround me like the fates of a Greek chorus, eager to talk on any subject. The husbands, with the exception of Donna Vincenzina's who does no work, are rarely in sight. We see them only on Sunday when, attired in neckties and black suits, they recline on chairs tilted against the front of their houses. Their hands are idle, they speak only when spoken to, and eventually they fall asleep. The women, on the other hand, are never idle outdoors. They peel vegetables, embroider, sweep away dirt (without gathering it) and, whenever possible, talk.

The exception is Teresa, our landlady's daughter, who, partly

179

out of snobbery and partly because she is busy with her two young children, seldom mixes with the other women. Once a week she hangs her delicately colored wash on a clothesline that extends over the width of the street and advertises, like a banner, the superiority of her sensibilities. But even this she does aloofly, controlling her clothesline invisibly from an upper window of her home, by means of a pulley.

This morning, while we wait for the trashman, Maria and Peppina complain of how little they see of Patricia. I realize it is futile to offer her lack of Italian and Sicilian as an excuse since they are too gregarious to admit to any barriers of communication. Instead I explain that in addition to housecleaning and cooking, Patricia is busy painting her impressions of Sicily. Maria promptly offers her services as a model, but I point out that Patricia never uses models, mainly because she prefers to work alone.

"Alone?" Peppina exclaims incredulously. That anyone would eschew human company to be solitary is beyond the ken of the average Sicilian, and both women jump to the conclusion that I am being a strict Sicilian husband who will not permit his wife to leave her house, except in his company. "You should be more generous with her," Maria says gently. "You should allow her to see other people."

They urge me to take Patricia to the forthcoming festa for the favorite local saint, the Madonna del Ponte, who is celebrated for her powers to cure the sick and the maimed. "I myself saw her perform a miracle," Maria says. "On my twelfth birthday my family took me to her shrine for a visit. As they lifted me up to kiss her feet, I saw the Madonna shift the infant Jesus from one arm to another . . ."

Despite their great admiration for the Madonna, neither woman believes she is capable of producing a miracle powerful enough to improve the lot of the Sicilians. "Not even she can overcome the faults of the Sicilian character," Peppina says. "Take, for example, this matter of the garbage. Most families throw it everywhere without caring how much it stinks or how many flies it may bring. In the summer there are so many flies in the Via Emma that it isn't safe to open your mouth."

Maria blames the garbage situation on the town authorities. "Like all government officials in Sicily, their main interest is getting rich as quickly as possible. They don't care what happens to the poor."

"The trouble is we don't complain enough," Peppina says. "And there is so much to complain about. Our men work themselves to the bone, yet we are always in terrible debt . . ."

The trashman finally comes into view.

"That lazy good-for-nothing," says Donna Vincenzina, who has just joined us. "Look how slowly he moves."

"He's slow because he picks up gossip wherever he goes," Maria says. With a grin, she adds: "I'll bet there is more dirt in his head than you'll see in his cart."

APRIL 2

During breakfast the doorbell rings frantically. It is the German nurse, breathless from bicycling too hard, asking if I shall be present at the Center's general staff meeting scheduled for this morning. "Please," she begs. "Come to it. I am going to denounce Danilo to his face in the presence of everyone."

Ever since Kenneth Bennett left Partinico without visiting the clinic, her crusade against Danilo has assumed fresh vigor. I inform her I cannot attend the meeting; a new member of the American Consulate staff in Palermo has made an appointment to visit me this morning. "Bring him," she pleads. "It will be useful for him to hear what I have to say." When I tell her that it is impossible, she suggests I break the appointment and arrange to see the Consul some other time. That too is out of the question; he is already on his way.

"You *are* interested in knowing what I am going to say in my denunciation?" she asks anxiously. On being assured that I am, she promises to let me have a verbatim copy of it. "You won't find it included in the minutes of the meeting. Danilo always makes certain that no criticism of him is ever mentioned in the minutes." With that, she shakes my hand in military fashion, and goes off on her bicycle.

The Consul arrives an hour later with his Italian-born wife and their small daughter, who at the age of eight already moves with the grace of a ballerina. Charles Stout has a quick mind and a passion for information, but I find that his attitudes toward Danilo, gathered chiefly from the reports of his predecessor (a

181

Sicilian who had filled the post temporarily), reflect the standard prejudices prevalent among rightwing Catholic spokesmen. But he has been in Sicily less than two weeks, not long enough to form any judgments of his own. He is frank about his mission to the Via Emma: he wants to hear what I have learned about Danilo so far.

There is not enough time for that, of course, but we discuss some of the views passed on to him by his predecessor. The dominant one, that Danilo is inclined towards Communism, I try to refute by pointing out that the basic principle in his ideology— social revolution through nonviolent group action—is at odds with Communist party dogma. While it is true that Danilo and the Communists share certain goals of social reform, which make them temporary allies, there is an irreconcilable difference in the techniques used to achieve those goals. Moreover, the Communists are chiefly motivated by political considerations. Danilo's motives are educational rather than political.

When Stout reminds me that Danilo has been a frequent contributor to the pro-Communist newspaper *L'Ora,* I quote from a conversation I recently had with him on this very subject. *"L'Ora* provides me with the forum I need, an opportunity to say what I wish. No other Sicilian newspaper has offered me such a forum. The articles I write for it express my own ideas in my own language. I have a strict understanding with the editors that not one word I write for them may be changed or deleted. Should there be any breach of that understanding, our relationship would end."

Stout and I continue our discussion at a picnic lunch amid the red poppies and buttercups of the grounds surrounding the Borgo di Dio. "Why not meet with Dolci directly?" I suggest to Stout. Since he speaks fluent Italian, such a direct confrontation would surely contribute to his understanding of him. Dolci, I assure him, would be happy to be interviewed, especially by an American Consul; he is at his Socratic best when he is answering questions without the intervention of an interpreter. "Later perhaps," Stout replies, and I sense that first he would like more time to study the man and his writings more thoroughly.

The statement that the German nurse read at the general meeting is under the door when we return to the Via Emma. Neither the temper of the denunciation nor the style of the writing seems characteristic of the nurse, and I can't help wondering which one of the Center's ex-collaborators was her ghostwriter. The opening paragraphs describe a recent interview she had with Danilo during which he asked her to refrain from passing judgments on work of the Center that is outside her own field, especially when in the presence of visitors. When she replied that she would express her opinions freely to whomever she pleased, Danilo suggested she leave the Center at once. He told her that a person of her intelligence should realize that in any organization there are certain rules of behavior to follow in dealing with visitors; he added that she was an "anarchistic person."

Admitting there was some truth to that charge, the nurse recalled that she had always managed to be late at the Hitler Youth meetings and that during their singing she sang out of tune and used words of her own. Working at the Center, she said, made her feel as though she were still living under a dictatorship. She then accused Danilo of refusing to tolerate any criticism of the Center. "Every collaborator who criticizes the Center is considered immature, ignorant of fundamental principles, and even neurotic, even though they may have been highly regarded at first."

The nurse wound up her denunciation by declaring her "feeling of solidarity" with the ex-collaborators who "tried to make the Center a democratic structure, a more authentic base for work . . . They tried to fight against the waste there is of people and possibilities, and against the cult of personality. But they tried in vain."

During the *passeggiata* I run into Osvaldo, who was present at the morning meeting, and ask him how Danilo received the nurse's statement.

"I think he stopped listening to it after a few seconds," Osvaldo replies. "When the nurse was finished, he went on to the next order of business as though nothing had happened."

APRIL 4

Franco returns from Milan in a state of elation. All of his abdominal troubles, his doctors assure him, can be banished by simply adhering to a prescribed diet. Unlike the Palermo doctors,

183

they find no trace of an ulcer, no cause for surgery. He looks rested, and there is actually some color in his cheeks. "I feel resurrected," he says, "like Lazarus."

On learning that Patricia and I are about to leave for a brief stay in Palermo, he insists on being our chauffeur and, for a few hours at least, our guide. To show us an area we have not seen he takes the sea route, which is somewhat longer than the mountain one, and we pass through a series of coastal towns which he terms "the narcotics zone"—Terrasini, Cinisi, Carini, Isola delle Femmine, Sferracavallo and Tomasso Natale. Here drugs arriving from Syria and Turkey are transferred to motor boats and fishing trawlers, and then forwarded to European points (sometimes inside dummy oranges) for shipment to the American market.

"The Mafia has no trouble recruiting poor Sicilians to help them with their drug traffic," Franco says. "The average Sicilian has no idea of the evils of drugs for the simple reason that he can't think of drug addiction as a social problem. In Sicily no one, except a few aristocrats who lead the *dolce vita,* ever takes drugs. The peasants and fishermen engaged in the drug traffic don't consider their work any more evil than handling contraband cigarettes, which is another one of their sidelines. For them it is just another way of earning a little money. When I once asked a peasant how he was getting along, his answer was: 'I manage to make enough to feed my family, *grazi diu,* what with the small piece of land I cultivate and the powders I handle on the side.' "

In Palermo Franco is eager to show us some of the slum areas in the center of the city, where some 150,000 persons live in congested squalor. But first, by way of contrast, he takes us to the Palace of Justice, which is near the worst part of the slums. Built in 1958 at a cost of almost three billion lire, the Palace is an architectural extravaganza, obviously modeled after the overbearing government buildings constructed during the Mussolini regime. It is Sunday, when the Palace is closed to the public, but Franco smooth-talks his way through the guards and gets us inside. "Who needs such a building?" he mutters as he leads us through the vast emptiness of one palatial hallway after another. "It is an expression of arrogance, a way of telling the little people who get in trouble with the law that they don't stand a chance against the might of government. They ought to rename it 'The Palace of Injustice.' "

As we walk toward a slum area called Cortile Scallila, Franco points out the nearby Cathedral of Palermo and the adjoining residence of the Cardinal: "His Eminence needs only to look out his window to see this cancer of misery. If he had felt any compassion for the people living in such squalor, he would have insisted that the authorities do away with the slums before building a palace of justice . . ."

At first the main difference I note between this slum and those I have known in New York, Philadelphia, and Chicago is the narrowness of the streets, which are little more than alleys. I also see more congestion and hear more noise. Street vendors, stationary and ambling, add to the din with their blaring histrionics, as they vie with one another to attract customers. Some of them promenade through the alleys with a cluster of money pinned to their shirts, hawking raffle tickets for prizes that vary from outright cash to a piece of meat or a half-dozen fish.

Franco knows the area intimately, not only because of his activities with the Center but also because he wrote the text for a book of photographs dealing with the Palermo slums entitled *Voices and Faces*. He introduces us to a portly sixty-year-old woman and her emaciated cobbler husband, who works outdoors, his mouth full of tacks. They live with ten children in one room, for which they pay 5,000 lire a week. The woman assures me that her housing situation is no better or worse than most of the families on the street, but she is in no mood for complaining. She is eager to inform us that she has three half-brothers and three half-sisters in Chicago whom she has never seen. Her father deserted his family early in the century; he migrated to the United States and married a full-blooded American Indian woman. "It took my mother thirty years to find out where he had gone and what had happened to him, and by that time he was dead. How I would love to meet my Chicago brothers and sisters before I die! Don't you think it is a sin to have such close relatives without ever setting eyes on them?"

The atmosphere on the street is astonishingly cheerful. On this Sunday morning, at least, the men and women with whom we talk

185

have none of the dourness and apathy I associate with dire poverty. The only note of bitterness comes from a fat young woman bearing an infant in her arms. On hearing me comment on the television set in her room, she turns on me angrily and asks: "Don't you think we are entitled to some distraction from all this ugliness?" With her chin she gestures toward the dilapidation around us. She calms down after I assure her I intended no criticism, and tells us she was born in this neighborhood and has seldom left it. "Where would I go in these rags, with my children to look after, and a husband who treats me as though I were his slave?" Were she to go anywhere, she says, she would like to go to the country and look at nature. Pointing to the small piece of sky visible to us, she adds: "That represents the only connection I now have with nature. They tell us that someday the government will move us out of here and put us in *case popolare* where the air is better and there is plenty of sky. But who can believe that? As I see it, the only way any of us can ever leave this place is inside a coffin."

Cortile Cascino, which is exactly two hundred yards from the Cathedral, has smaller buildings and more sky, but poverty here is at the most obscene level, and the desperation of the people more obvious. As we roam through the squalor, children clutch at our sleeves and follow us, begging for money. Men and women in tatters glare at us. In *Report from Palermo* Danilo wrote of this quarter: "No matter how often one has seen it before, the sight of swarms of naked children playing in mud and filth or scrambling about on railroad tracks, comes as a fresh shock. The walls of the broken houses and squalid shacks sweat with damp, and the rooms are infested with scorpions, fleas, and cockroaches. There are no water taps. Only one family has a toilet. All the other families work, eat, sleep, and do their business in their one room . . ."

We go down a small stairway past thousands of flies, to the door of an abandoned windowless cellar room where Danilo and Franco fasted together for thirteen days in November 1957 to protest the failure of the authorities to abolish the slum. Franco is disappointed to find the door padlocked. A woman in black, who has been watching us, reminds Franco that she is the one who cooked the chicken broth which he and Danilo ate immediately after their long fast.

186

"But what good did all that fasting do?" she asks. "Do you think we are any better off than we were then?"

Franco dolefully shakes his head. Later he tells us that although there has been some slum clearance in the city, some of the worst slums still remain. "The filth in these places is so great that children die of infectious diseases continuously. *Pozzi di morte* [death holes] the newspapers call them, but nothing happens. Did you notice that a few days ago the *Giornale di Sicilia* called Palermo the dirtiest city in Europe?"

Across the street another woman in black calls out Franco's name. "Don't you remember me?" she shouts. She is seated behind a small table selling candy. She is probably the largest woman I have ever seen outside a circus. As we approach her, I note an even more remarkable feature: her upper lip bears a fully blossomed pepper-and-salt mustache.

"Of course I remember you, Signora," says Franco. "You haven't changed a bit."

"You're still too thin, Signor Alasia," she scolds. "Haven't you stopped fasting yet?"

When he assures her he is eating regularly, she presses some free candy on him.

Before we part Franco advises us not to return to either of the slums alone. "They are apt to take advantage of foreigners. They wouldn't hurt you, of course, but they would try to steal whatever they could by all sorts of tricks." He sighs as he shakes hands with us. "You can hardly blame them, can you?"

Patricia and I take a *carrozza* to the home of a bookdealer from whom I have been ordering books by mail for several years. Not until my arrival in Sicily did I discover that Marco Pasquale was a member of Danilo's staff for three years. Pasquale's most recent letter, which came as we were about to leave Philadelphia, had urged me to visit him in Palermo at my earliest opportunity as he has "something of vital importance" to tell me.

We find Pasquale ensconced on two floors of a badly deteriorated baronial mansion, surrounded by thousands of books and enough pieces of Sicilian folk art to start a small museum. With him lives a tall Junoesque Norwegian artist, who is introduced to us as Erica. Pasquale is a cyclone of cordiality, a small man who hides his shyness behind a barrage of talk. Whenever he mentions a book title, he rushes to his bookcases to find the book and present it to me as a gift. At the end of his opening monologue he has given me five books, all of them dealing with Sicily.

The matter of "vital importance" has to do with Danilo. Did I realize what a "rank opportunist" he is? "Everything he does is for the sake of getting more publicity, so that the Center can get more money from its foreign supporters. He has no plan and no sense of direction. For years he has been talking about the necessity of producing an economic plan for the western zone of Sicily. Yet when such a plan was started by Michael Faber, the English economist, and Carlo Doglio, the Sicilian city planner, Danilo squelched it. He can't stand the idea of anyone on his staff doing something that might steal the show from him . . ."

I already know that Pasquale, along with Faber and Doglio, were part of a dissident group of collaborators that broke with the Center in 1961. Differences of opinion over the value of the Faber-Doglio study, together with Danilo's refusal to give the Center a political character, contributed to the break. It was in the ensuing reorganization that Eyvind Hytten, then a staunch ally of Danilo, emerged as the General Secretary of the Center.

When I mention the most recent exodus led by Hytten, Pasquale makes a gesture of contempt. "They didn't show much sense. Hytten and his friends actually proposed taking over the direction of the Center and sending Danilo off to Palermo in exile. That is pure stupidity. Danilo owns the Center, and nobody can kick him out. Hytten was a fool to think he could . . ."

Pasquale's indictment of Danilo, though lacking the German nurse's hysteria, is so comprehensive as to be suspect.

"Despite his personal faults," I ask at one point, "despite his difficulties with personnel problems, wouldn't you say that Sicily is far better off with a Danilo Dolci to expose its misery?"

He answers with an emphatic no, arguing that Danilo's activities tend to "muddle" those that the leftwing parties are conducting for the benefit of Sicily. "As long as he refuses to work with a political party, he is bound to create more harm than good . . ."

In disagreeing with him, I point out that many of Sicily's most serious problems might still be unknown to the general public except for the powerful spotlight that Danilo has fixed on them with his demonstrations and his books. Pasquale grudgingly agrees with this.

"I must say this for Danilo," he adds, "his sense of strategy is so sharp that he knows precisely when and where to take an action in order to create maximum publicity. I remember that once when we were planning a march to demonstrate for the building of the Jato dam, the staff members wanted the march to start in Partinico, but Danilo said no to that. 'The march,' he said, 'will be from Montelepre to the Jato.' He was shrewd enough to realize that Montelepre, being famous as Giuliano's birthplace, would get far bigger headlines than Partinico."

While Pasquale goes out to buy some beer, we have a talk with Erica, who seems starved for the opportunity to speak in English, a language she speaks more easily than Italian. She tells us that she had first come to Sicily at the suggestion of Lorenzo, who, while in Oslo, proposed that she represent the Norwegian Dolci committee at a forthcoming demonstration in Roccamena. An airline gave her free passage from Oslo to Genoa in exchange for one of her paintings; she traveled all night the rest of the way in a third-class train that was jammed with returning Sicilian emigrant workers. "They behaved as though they had never set eyes on a blonde girl before." She tried to stave off their amorous advances by inventing, with the help of a Norwegian-Italian dictionary, a story about her husband and four children waiting for her in Palermo. "I think that made them all the more excited about me," she says. "But luckily there were so many of them that no one could do anything very bad . . ."

In Roccamena she experienced similar difficulties. When she decided to go for a walk along the outskirts of the village, she was pursued by a pack of lecherous young men with motorcycles and cars. She was rescued in time by an older man driving with his sister, who told her in French that only insane women dare walk alone in the Sicilian countryside. Lorenzo, sensing the difficulties she would have in a small village like Roccamena, arranged to have her join the staff of the Partinico Center. The idea appealed to her at first since her immediate superior was a fellow Norwegian, Eyvind Hytten. But she found the work dull, and the quality of the staff "appallingly poor."

As an escape from boredom, one afternoon she accepted an in-

189

vitation to go swimming with a visiting English writer who had a
motorcycle. The episode brought her association with the Center
to an abrupt close. The spectacle of the big blonde girl astride the
motorcycle, with her arms encircling the Englishman for support,
scandalized the townspeople as well as some of her Center colleagues. The next morning Erica was summoned to Hytten's office
and ordered to leave the Center at once. Her sex life was her own
affair, Hytten told her, but it could not be conducted at the expense of the Center's reputation.

Hytten's castigation disturbed her deeply. She was crushed that
a fellow Norwegian, on whom she had counted for understanding,
would not believe that her excursion with the Englishman was
entirely innocent. For two days, she says, she wept and even con-
templated suicide. Then a friend introduced her to Pasquale and
his establishment, a former flour mill at the edge of Partinico
which he had converted into a bookstore and rooming house.
"Everything was better for me after that." Except for occasional
visits to Norway, she has been with him ever since.

Erica assures us that she loves Pasquale and would like to be
with him the rest of her life; she is less certain about her feelings
for Sicily. She is depressed by its mores, particularly by the feudal
code of behavior it imposes on women. "In Palermo I feel suffocated. In Norway I would often go for a ten-mile hike alone without thinking about it twice. Here I cannot go anywhere alone
without being mistaken for a prostitute. I am a free spirit. I need
freedom. How can I paint and write poetry unless I can be close to
nature and breathe freely? And if I cannot paint and I cannot
write poems, what use is it being alive?"

Once a week, as an expression of sympathy for the plight of
Sicilian women, Erica is a volunteer worker at Rosita Lanza's
birth control clinic. Her job is simply to keep children occupied
while their mothers are consulting with the clinic head. "It is
unimportant work but it is work that has to be done, and there is
no one else to do it. So I do it, even though Pasquale keeps warning me that if the authorities ever find out, they will throw me out
of Italy."

A previous dinner engagement obliges us to leave shortly after
we finish the beer. Pasquale urges us to dine with him and Erica

on our next trip to Palermo. "There are so many things I need to know about your fantastic country, things that cannot be found in books. Also, I'll be interested to learn whether your opinion of Danilo changes after you have watched him in action a little longer . . ."

"Please come back soon," Erica interjects. "It was so refreshing talking with you. There are so few congenial souls I can talk with in Sicily." She puts her arms around Pasquale, and proclaims in Italian: "Tonight I will be able to write a beautiful poem."

The next morning we visit the offices of the United States Information Service to talk with its local chief, Robert Jordan, a big handsome ex-newspaperman with abundant silver-gray hair and a Barrymore profile. Jordan is not in his usual cheerful mood. Some of his unhappiness is caused by the latest edition of *L'Ora*, which has again stooped to flagrantly dishonest tactics to create anti-American sentiment among its readers. His mood is also affected by the shenanigans of the Mayor of Porto Empedocle. The Mayor is scheduled to head the ceremonies for the commemoration of a square to be known as "Piazza John F. Kennedy," but he keeps frustrating Jordan's office by changing the date of the ceremonies to suit his personal convenience. For the fourth time he has asked Jordan for another change of date, though perfectly aware of the complicated negotiations Jordan must undertake each time with numerous American and Italian officials, including the administrative personnel of a United States Navy ship and its band.

The chief purpose of my call is to advise Jordan of the talk I am slated to give in June in the series of cultural meetings sponsored by the Center. As I am a Fulbright research fellow, it seems proper to advise him of any public appearances I plan to make. Inasmuch as the printed announcement for the series lists a number of sponsors that are unknown to us, Jordan summons his Sicilian press consultant to identify the names. With a glibness that brings back memories of the McCarthy era, the aide labels all of the names either as "Communists" or as "undesirable persons who would like to see drastic changes made in the Italian government." The contempt in his voice spurs me to comment that the latter group must include millions of persons, myself among them. The aide, who had obviously assumed that I would be receptive to his damning generalizations, regards me with horror. Afterwards, I wonder how much of what he tells his chief is what he believes and how much of it is what he imagines an American official might be pleased to hear.

The conversation with Jordan ends on a pleasant note, with an invitation to Patricia to exhibit in the gallery of the United States Information Service the series of oil pastels she has been working on entitled "Impressions of Sicily." A date in mid-May is chosen for the show.

In the final event of our excursion we dine with an old friend, Corrado Niscemi, who spends six months of each year in Philadelphia as an ordinary American citizen and the rest of the year in Palermo as a Sicilian prince residing in his ancestral home, the Villa Niscemi, on the outskirts of the city. He is presently living there alone with his staff of servants, while waiting for his wife to return from a tour of Greece.

The chauffeur who has picked us up at our hotel honks his horn at the entrance of the villa until a withered old woman appears, with an enormous bunch of keys fixed at her waist, and unlocks the heavy iron gates. We drive through a huge bouquet of a spring garden, and are greeted at the palace steps by an old acquaintance, the former Niscemi chauffeur I knew twenty years ago, who has since been elevated to the post of general manager. After expressing condolences for the death of my father, whom he knew when my parents were guests at the villa in the fifties, Parella leads the way up a scarlet-carpeted stairway and past a series of splendorous rooms (one with lavish baroque frescoes on the ceiling, another displaying a collection of old Spanish pistols, a third studded with gilded furniture and portraits of ancestors set on easels) until we emerge on the outdoor terrace where Corrado is waiting for us, dry martini in hand.

He greets us affectionately, while murmuring phrases of endearment for my father who, he explains, is often in his thoughts, as are all of the dead he has ever loved. "In Sicily we live with the dead," he adds. "They are more present than the living, for Sicily is an island of magic where people fantasize so much that the only true reality becomes death . . ."

192

Corrado is wearing thick glasses which magnify the pupils of his brown Spanish eyes grotesquely. In recent months he has had two cataract operations, and has lost partial sight in one eye. The ogre effect of the oversized pupils is somewhat diminished by a newly acquired mustache with saucy tips that bend skywards into a playful salute; but the mustache is misleading. There is less joy in the man than it might lead a stranger to expect. Although he is capable of laughter, it is easily smothered in the deep sighs of his essentially melancholy nature. What usually emerges is a distillation of irony and sorrow. His most natural role is that of a contemplative observer, a philosopher without a thesis.

From the terrace it is easy to understand why Corrado favors this place over his Rittenhouse Square apartment for his exercises in contemplation. The villa exudes the seductiveness of protected beauty. It is surrounded by mountains of diamond-hard brightness, but its grounds are a sensuous bed of spring flowers. The walls of the villa, just high enough to keep out the tallest intruder, accent the impression that for generations this private paradise has successfully isolated its residents from any unpleasant Sicilian reality.

As we drink our martinis, which are perfectly concocted by a peasant servant girl he has trained in the art, Corrado drapes his long body on a chaise lounge and discourses on Sicilian history and folkways, of which he has a vast knowledge. But, as always, his words are obscured by his failure to pronounce them sufficiently, a congenital habit which frustrates the keenest of ears. After knowing him for more than twenty years, I am still unable to decide whether this failure is derived from innate apathy, or from an instinctual preference to communicate more with himself than with others.

Although he is adept in a number of languages, his speech is predominantly Sicilian, a fact which once gave rise to the quip that Corrado is a man who speaks many languages—all of them in Sicilian. Not all of what he says in our two hours together is lost on me; I have little difficulty following him when he talks on his favorite themes, such as the Sicilian addiction to fantasy. "In Sicily all sense of time is suspended; the people prefer to live in a world of fantasy, as they have done for centuries, on the increment of

193

ancient superstitions. That is why they have such a steadfast allegiance to the status quo. Their souls are committed to their imaginations . . ."

I ask him what he thinks D. H. Lawrence meant when he declared Sicilians to be a "soulless" people.

"He probably meant that they do not have human souls, and he was right. They have universal souls derived from the ancient gods who first populated Sicily. Certainly, there is something divine in your mother, for example, with her extraordinary wisdom and her appreciation of the force that gives life."

Long ago I noted that Corrado's affection for Sicilians extends only to those he personally knows and likes. He finds fault with the mass of them for their laziness (despite all evidence to the contrary) and for their habitual backbiting. "Most of the talk you hear among Sicilians consists of gossip and criticism of neighbors expressed on a very imaginative level. This is the game they like to play most because it sustains their sense of drama about everyday living and also because it prevents them from being bored with one another. Their penchant for fantasy makes the game possible and pleasurable. It is no accident that the writer who has most effectively questioned our conventional concept of reality is a Sicilian—the playwright Luigi Pirandello, who was your father's *paisano* . . ."

He turns to Patricia and asks her whether she has had any great surprises during this first encounter with Sicily. The greatest one, Patricia answers, is that in general the people seem fairly content, despite their desperate poverty. As for those who have acquired any material goods, such as our landlord and his family, they seem much happier than persons of similar wealth in the United States.

"That is because Sicilians haven't yet been harmed by the values of industrialized society," Corrado says. "But things are changing, even in Sicily. Take your landlady's daughter. In the old days she would have been a baroness and no one would have known the extent of her wealth. Now she belongs to the lower middle class and makes no effort to conceal the fact that she is better off than her neighbors. This is a significant change because it has been a strong and ancient habit among Sicilians to hide their wealth as much as possible, in order to avoid envy and having someone put a

194

hex on them. The houses with the worst exteriors were often the most lavish inside. You can still see this attitude among peasants who decorate their carts and their horses fancily in order to detract attention from the contents of the carts . . ."

We retire to a dining room and are served by the same girl who prepared the martinis; this time she wears white gloves. Pursuing the theme of a changing Sicily, I ask Corrado what is the greatest single change he has observed in the past twenty years. He answers: "Increased dependence on the State for economic support for families, accompanied by a decrease in the sense of family responsibility. This is beginning to change the entire fabric of Sicilian life. There is no longer gratitude to God for finding something to eat; there is, instead, bitterness toward the State for not providing more than it does.

"At one time the Sicilians were among the proudest people in the world. But their sense of dignity has been undermined by too many invasions of the island. Too often the Sicilians have been unable to say no. Have you noticed that Sicilian women are like that? You can rape them with your eyes, and they know exactly what you are doing. And often they will encourage your desire by raising their skirts and inviting you in. Sex is without love in this country; it is an act of rage and bitterness, not tenderness. The man pins the woman to the bed with the attitude: 'I work hard to support you; the least you can do is to give me a male child.'

"How can birth control make any inroads among a people with that psychology? I have asked this question of Rosita Lanza, who is a cousin of mine, but she cannot answer it. Once I asked a peasant woman why she had so many children—there were nine of them running around in the one filthy room that was their home and she had another inside her—and she said to me: 'Because there is no misery in the hay.' Mind you, she didn't say *sheets;* she said *hay.* They live like beasts, they think like beasts, and they fornicate like beasts—on the hay."

Changing the subject abruptly, he asks: "Now tell me, what the hell are you and Patricia doing in Partinico?"

Although he is a devout Catholic, Corrado is sharply critical of the Church for its attitude toward Danilo Dolci. "He is a good man, one that the Catholic Church should have encouraged, not berated—the Cardinal is such a fool. Dolci impresses me as a kind of Quaker. He is impressive because he is the first social reformer to be concerned about the fate of Sicilians. He has done a few things, but he will get nowhere. As an outsider, he will never be able to understand the mentality of Sicilians, no matter how many Sicilian widows he marries. And after a while he will get tired of butting his head against a stone wall, and Sicily will go on in its old way as though he had never been here. Only one thing may change Sicily: television. Once the Sicilians become absorbed in the fantasy of television, their own fantasy will begin to fade, and they will become like everyone else. Fortunately, that is not likely to happen in my lifetime."

Over our coffee cups I ask the same question I have been asking him perennially: Why doesn't he write a book about Sicily? He dismisses the question with a deep sigh and his customary excuse: "You should know, my dear, that many of the most significant things in life can never be written down." But for the first time he speaks to me about his good friend and first cousin, Giuseppe di Lampedusa, who unlike Corrado rose above the stagnation of his social environment by writing *The Leopard*. "I do not care for the novel as it was published, but I had great respect for the original version." He adds that the original manuscript was twice as long as the published one and a far worthier contribution to letters. "The editors changed the meaning of the story drastically by making cuts they should never have made. And they got away with it because the author was dead and there was no one to defend his version."

As if to explain why it was Lampedusa and not he who had become the writer, he says that his cousin, unlike himself, preferred books to people. "He felt uncomfortable among people, particularly among women, possibly because he had a mother fixation. He had a genuine fear of big women; yet he married one. But to be a writer you have to be lucky as well as neurotic. His good luck was to have an extraordinary uncle whom he loved, and who was one of his chief literary inspirations. This was his Uncle Giorgio, a man who believed in democracy for the Sicilians and was elected a national representative in Rome. You will find Uncle Giorgio in many pages of *The Leopard*."

196

Corrado sides with Michele Mandiello in the belief that the house known as Donnafugata in the novel is the one at Santa Margarita di Belice. "Lampedusa loved that house mainly because his mother had loved it, and he wrote about it with love." He pauses as he glances about the sumptuous room, then says, "I love the memory of my mother, *bon arma,* and I love this house; yet I shall probably never write about it . . ."

While we both ponder over the complex question of why one man's love produces a novel and another man's love does not, Parella enters the room bearing a bouquet of orange blossoms for Patricia. It is a gracious cue for our departure. "Come back soon, and watch your step in Partinico," Corrado says as he kisses both of us goodbye.

Parella accompanies us to the car which is to return us to our hotel. Before we drive off, he instructs the chauffeur to pick up some Easter greeting cards for the Prince. "They should be of simple elegance and verge on the religious," Parella says. The chauffeur nods, as though he knows exactly what is meant.

Late that night we arrive at the Via Emma, and find a telegram from my Uncle Pitrinu, who lives in Porto Empedocle. He is my father's eighty-six-year-old brother, whom I have not seen for eighteen years. Although he is no Uncle Giorgio, he is fascinating in his own way, and I have written about him in some of my books. "What has gone wrong?" the telegram reads. "Are you sick or in trouble? Why haven't you visited me?"

The next morning, ridden with guilt, I send him a telegram promising that Patricia and I will spend the Easter weekend with him.

APRIL 9

At today's conference with Danilo he dismisses the German nurse's denunciation as "not unexpected," and voices his concern about another personnel problem: the young man in charge of the Center's office in Corleone has bowed to his parents' fear of Mafia recrimination and submitted his resignation. Danilo hopes a replacement for him can be found among the students who will attend the new Institute.

Since he expresses curiosity about my meeting with Charles

197

Stout, I let him know that the American Consul's office has the definite impression that he, Danilo, has allied himself too closely with leftwing groups, particularly with *L'Ora*. Danilo expresses appreciation for my attempt to defend his position, then calls my attention to several articles he has published in *L'Ora* recently which state ideas that are contrary to Communist philosophy. "Although I need to use *L'Ora* as a forum, your American friends should realize that I could never be a Communist. I would be happy to discuss this point with Mr. Stout and any of his colleagues. The previous American Consul and I were good friends; we played tennis together and talked frankly with one another. That's the way it should be . . ."

While on the subject of Americans, I translate a letter I received this morning from Morris Garnsey, an American professor of economics of the University of Colorado, who had called on me a few days before to ask questions about Danilo's projects. He had first gone to the Center to talk with Danilo directly; when Danilo found he knew no Italian, he sent him to me.

The letter is postmarked Palermo, where Professor Garnsey is delivering a series of lectures.

April 8, 1965

Dear Mr. and Mrs. Mangione:

Mrs. Garnsey and I wish to thank you for receiving us so cordially when we arrived unannounced at your door. We regret that the impromptu nature of our trip made it impossible to stay longer. I am sure we have much to talk about.

In my lectures at the Instituto Superiore per Imprenditori e Dirigenti de Agienda I stress that Howard Odum was a great man because:

1) He had a burning sense of social injustice concerning the regional underdevelopment of the South, and he was able to communicate it to others. Note: In 1930 when Odum started his work the per capita income in the South was 54 (if per capita income in the United States is given a value of 100) and in some Southeastern states it was as low as 36. In New York it was 160!

2) He believed that the problem of low income in the South could be solved only when its nature and causes could be determined *scientifically* and the remedies developed on an equally scientific basis. He felt that these steps were necessary to overcome opposition to reform from vested interests in the South, and persuade people in other regions and in the nation to support regional development.

Surely there is much similarity between Dolci and Odum with re-

198

gard to the first point. As for the second, it seems to me that Dolci so far has not developed a scientific (sociological and economic) basis for his reforms. I agree that it does not take much, if any scientific analysis to say that people are hungry and they should be fed. But in the period of 1965–2000 it will require advanced scientific planning and a high degree of technology to achieve a socio-economic organization that will both realize (1) efficiency in production and competitiveness in a world economy and (2) equity in distribution or sharing of output among all the people.

In my opinion, these two goals of welfare—high productivity and equitable distribution—have been realized adequately, even superbly, by the Tennessee Valley Authority. Their emphasis on multiple-purpose, coordinated, pervasive economic growth has resulted in a steady rise of income in agriculture and industry and in a great improvement in the welfare of the people. Today the TVA area per capita income is 80% of the U.S. average.

I would hope that Dolci could convert to his cause and that of Sicily a small group of qualified, expert, regional economists, social anthropologists or cultural sociologists fully conversant with the latest techniques of planning—devising plans, setting specific targets, and persuading the people of the region to understand and cooperate in the planning process. This happened in TVA. It could happen in Sicily.

Thanks again.

Sincerely yours,
Morris E. Garnsey

Danilo comments that although he agrees with the basic points made in the letter, Professor Garnsey fails to take into account the psychological differences between the feudal mentality of the Sicilians and the twentieth-century mentality of the Americans in the Tennessee Valley. The Americans, he says, were already open to the possibility of social change and economic improvement; the Sicilians, handicapped by attitudes ingrained into them by centuries of oppression and servitude, have yet to recognize the possibility of change. As for the task of actively involving planning experts in the Center's goals, that remains an unsolved problem, mainly because of the difficulty of attracting to Sicily qualified experts who know the language and are willing to accept the small stipends paid by the Center.

APRIL 10

Lorenzo and his wife drive us to Palermo to attend the first of the Center-sponsored cultural meetings, with Leonardo Sciascia,

Sicily's leading writer, as the featured speaker. On the way I discuss the contents of the Garnsey letter with Lorenzo and am rewarded with a pithy appraisal of the various experts who have been associated with the Center in the past.

The outstanding one, in his opinion, was Dr. Silvio Pampiglione, a professor of parasitology at the University of Rome, who in 1960, at Danilo's suggestion, conducted an inquiry among 600 families (3,000 persons) into the sanitary and hygienic conditions in Palma di Montechiaro. In the introduction of his report Pampiglione wrote: "Sanitary and hygienic conditions in Palma di Montechiaro are quite unbelievable. Yet, from official figures available, it would not appear that they differ greatly from those existing elsewhere in western Sicily, although they are undoubtedly among the most evident and spectacular."

The findings of the report scandalized sociologists and government authorities alike and led to a three-day international congress to discuss the pressing social problems of Palma di Montechiaro and of other underdeveloped areas of the world. As the president of the Congress, Danilo insisted it be held in Palma, a town without restaurants, hotels, and plumbing. He wanted to make certain that the shocking information in the Pampiglione report was not lost on the delegates; he wanted them to see and smell first-hand human misery in its rawest state.

"Pampiglione was an orthodox Marxist who was always spouting quotations from the writings of Lenin," Lorenzo tells us, "but he was an excellent scientist and a generous human being. He would have conducted other studies for the Center except for a political complication, which caused him to leave. He became firmly convinced that the Center should back Silvio Milazzo, the rightwing Christian Democrat president of Sicily, who was trying to govern the island with a coalition of right- and leftwing parties. Danilo was equally convinced that the Center should not form any political alliance with Milazzo or anyone else.

"Pampiglione developed at least one strong disciple while he was here. She was a woman who, when she first arrived at the Center, was such a fanatical vegetarian and pacifist that she would refuse to wear shoes made with leather. After coming under Pampiglione's influence for a couple of months, she became a militant Communist who ate all the meat she could get and wore nothing but leather shoes. She left the Center because of its refusal to engage in power politics . . .

"We also had some English experts. One was Ilys Booker, a remarkably talented community development specialist who worked in Menfi for eighteen months until it became too much for her. She left in the middle of 1961 and wrote a report which, I'm told, has the most penetrating observations of Sicilian life ever written by a non-Sicilian. We also had a young economist, Michael Faber, who came to Sicily that same year. He was extremely able but was handicapped from the start because he spoke no Italian. On top of that, he was resented by the other members of the Center because he insisted on being paid 250,000 lire a month instead of 35,000 lire, which was the salary most of us were receiving. He didn't last long . . .

"Faber was to have worked with Carlo Doglio, an experienced community developer. Together they could have come up with a useful plan for the entire region, but it didn't work out that way. Doglio was a brilliant man but filled with contradictions. Although he was nonviolent in his philosophy, he often expressed destructive impulses toward the Center. And although he was enamored of the idea of helping to create a new world, he sometimes defended the old social structures. He was a man who seemed to embody the best and the worst of all current cultural trends. He had hoped to direct the Center but his relationships with collaborators were not rational enough; he had difficulty making a concrete point. He left at the end of 1962 because he wasn't able to cope with the power struggle of which he had become a part.

"The man who won that struggle was Eyvind Hytten, who had come to us from the University of Stockholm where he was teaching philosophy. He was with us from 1960 until the middle of 1964. There were so many conflicts among the staff during that period that I decided to steer clear of them. So I remained in Roccamena and tried to do something about the problems there."

I ask Lorenzo whether the Center's plan to train community developers and establish citizens' committees will obviate the need for established community planners, such as Faber and Doglio.

"We'll always need the experienced planning experts, but not to the extent that some experts think they are needed," Lorenzo replies. "We'll need them chiefly for guidance. The planning itself

201

should stem directly from the people who are to be affected by it. In other words, *pianificazione dal basso . . ."*

The Leonardo Sciascia meeting becomes an alarming experience as I imagine myself in his place six weeks from now. There is no lecture, as I expected there would be. There is simply a brief statement by the speaker in response to three questions put to him by Danilo at the outset of the meeting. The rest of the evening is devoted to coping with questions from the floor. Some are not questions at all but bellicose orations peppered with leftwing slogans and sneers.

The architecture of the auditorium, which is a replica of an austere medieval chapel, reinforces my impression that the event is nothing less than an inquisitorial drama, with orthodox Communists in the audience playing their role of inquisitors to the hilt. That Sciascia is able to give a good account of himself is of little consolation to me; he has two advantages which I lack: a magnificent command of Italian, and prestige enough as Sicily's most esteemed living writer to forestall outright abuse.

Danilo, a vision of bourgeois respectability in a dark suit and necktie (the first I have ever seen him wear), asks Sciascia the three questions that are to provide themes for the discussion: Who are you? What has been your main work until now? What direction will your work take next?

With engaging candor, Sciascia identifies himself as "an elementary school teacher who began writing books, probably because I realized I am not a very good school teacher." He describes his books as "a series of libels which are intended as constructive actions," and emphasizes that he has no interest either in making a contribution to literature or in becoming known as a literary figure. He says that he writes as one who is dedicated to the proposition that Sicily is a disturbing reality that needs changing.

The inquisitors lose no time pouncing on him, eager for blood. They demand he be more specific about his sense of responsibility as an author; they criticize him for not participating in the political scene, and they attack the characters in his books for not having more "positive" personalities.

Sciascia, unperturbed, holds to his position that he is a writer, not a political activist, that he presents problems as he sees them, without any thought of suggesting how they might be solved politically. He is not always on the defensive. He attacks the ruling establishment in Sicily as "incapable," expresses disgust with both leftwing and rightwing political parties, declares that Sicilian autonomy has proven itself a rank failure in its twenty years of existence, and bemoans the fact that the breach between Sicily and the rest of Italy is widening instead of closing.

At no point during the evening does anyone call attention to the fact that Danilo, unlike Sciascia, is a prime example of a writer who is also a man of action.

APRIL 11

The more I ponder over last night's event, the more qualms I have about my participation in the cultural series. This morning I try to bring up the subject, in the hope of convincing Danilo I should withdraw. But we are on our way to Terrasini where the Dolci family are to be our guests at a restaurant celebrated for fish dishes, and Danilo is in a rare Sunday mood, unwilling to discuss anything but the beauty of the Terrasini coastline which he promises to show us by motorboat. His only comment about the Sciascia meeting is that it was "gratifying" both for the "quality" of the discussion and for the size of the audience.

At Terrasini we place our restaurant reservations and select our main courses from a spectacular assortment of freshly caught fish displayed before us like a procession of Courbet still lifes. We then proceed to the village port to engage a motorboat. The brisk wind and the unusually choppy Mediterranean drown all the enthusiasm for the expedition that Danilo has inspired. Patricia and I, being nonswimmers, are less enthusiastic than anyone else, especially after noting that the motorboat Danilo has selected is without life preservers. I suggest the expedition be postponed to some other Sunday when the waters are calmer but Danilo, whose sense of determination remains undiminished even on Sundays, firmly declares the waters serene enough, and promises the experience will be "a delightful and memorable" one.

"I'm sure it will be memorable," I mutter to Patricia as we step into the boat.

203

Once we move out of the inlet the waters become even choppier and the boat begins to bob up and down in an unsettling rhythm that sprays the air with the nauseating fumes of hot fuel oil. But if Danilo has underestimated the discomfort of the expedition he has not exaggerated the remarkable beauty of the red cliffs that inflame the blue clear waters of the Terrasini shoreline with crimson shadows. One stretch of cliffs, more than two hundred yards in length, is imprinted with clearly defined layers of beige, red, and pink, somewhat in the manner of Giotto's Florentine tower. Although the cliffs are not tall, they form a monumental sculpture covered with snarly lines of stone that suggest a giant epitaph in secret language paying homage to the drowned. Beyond this stretch, the cliffs become even mightier and more demoniacal, and are fissured by deep caves which, according to our navigator, extend as far as Partinico. (Later on Danilo explains that the people of Terrasini are notorious for the flexibility of their imaginations.)

The boat trip, lasting for more than an hour, is particularly harrowing for the children who, unimpressed by the red cliffs which they have seen before, are constantly on the verge of illness. Danilo, cheerful and attentive, manages to divert them sufficiently with his teasing so that no one gets sick, except for the navigator's grandson, who vomits over my shoes.

The restaurant, manned by ten members of the same family, bustles with a steady influx of diners, most of them prosperously dressed families who have driven from Palermo for their Sunday repast. There is no hint of Sicilian poverty here. In our two hours of dining Danilo counts over one hundred customers. It is the only sociological effort he permits himself. He and Vincenzina are in a euphoric state of mind, as are the children once recovered from the effects of the motorboat trip.

On the way home while he drives, Danilo plays a newly invented game with his two youngest children, who are in the back seat. When Daniela puts her arm around his neck, he tells her that the more she hugs him the faster the car will travel. Soon both children have their arms around him, and Danilo keeps exclaiming at the "fantastic speed" we are moving. Vincenzina, who usually watches and says little, enters into the spirit of the game, suggesting to the children that the car will gather the speed of a racer with each kiss they give the driver. During the rest of the journey the children compete with one another hugging and kissing their father as he marvels at the velocity of the car.

We pass a magnificent beach which is totally deserted, and Danilo identifies it as one of his family's favorite summer haunts. When he suggests we all go swimming together in a few days, I inform him that I can't swim and Patricia barely can. "How is that possible?" he asks. I explain that my father, who was a superb swimmer, inculcated all of his children with a fear of water. Having learned to swim in the buoyant salty waters of the Mediterranean, he was convinced that only a powerful swimmer like himself could survive the unsalted waters of Lake Ontario. Whenever we visited the shore, we became infected by the loud anxiety he expressed for our safety as soon as our feet touched water.

Danilo claims he knows exactly how to expel my fear of water; he has made swimmers of many persons who were deathly afraid of drowning. "I am not only a first-rate swimmer but also I have a psychological understanding of people's fear of water. If I were not so interested in my present work, I could earn a good living as a swimming instructor."

Vincenzina recalls how Danilo's zeal for teaching the children of Partinico to swim once earned him the wrath of a mother. He remembers the incident well. "One or two of the Center's teachers and I used to take some of the neighboring children in Spine Sante to the beach every week to give them swimming lessons and also to open their eyes to the beauty of the sea and the coast. One evening, after such an excursion, Vincenzina and I heard a woman in the street screaming invectives against me. It was the mother of one of the boys we had taken swimming that day. She was berating me for having corrupted her son by exposing him to a 'nude' woman. The woman in question was a schoolteacher who had worn a swimming suit that was quite conservative, but as the boy had never seen either of his parents in any state of undress, he told his mother that the teacher was nude."

"No one in Trappeto and Partinico ever went to the beach until Danilo got here," Vincenzina says. "Now there are some who go regularly because he taught them that the beach is beautiful and swimming is enjoyable. I am one of them."

APRIL 12

A black letter day. My qualms about participating in the Center's cultural series have been justified. Now Danilo and I find ourselves engaged in a conflict that seriously jeopardizes the project that has brought me to Sicily.

It begins with a telephone call this morning from Robert Jordan, who informs me that he and the American Consul General are of the opinion that I should withdraw as a speaker in the Palermo meetings. Their fear is that no matter how well I acquit myself in the course of the discussion, the leftwing press will distort my statements to conform with its anti-American campaign, which the war in Vietnam has accelerated. Jordan only hints at their deeper concern: as a Fulbright fellow, appointed under the auspices of the U. S. State Department, my statements might also be represented as those of an official spokesman.

My first reaction to Jordan's words is one of resentment: Fulbright grant or not, I feel that no American government official should try to infringe on my freedom of speech, even by suggestion. Yet even as we talk, I realize that Jordan is actually echoing my own private reservations. Regardless of the merits of his request, I know I must try to avoid a situation from which I cannot possibly escape unscathed. As an American, I am far more vulnerable than Sciascia; the inquisitors would surely draw a great deal of blood, and the leftwing press would finish me off. I promise Jordan I will try to persuade Danilo to release me from my promise to appear in the series.

In my session with Danilo later in the morning, I devote the entire hour to this effort. I begin by explaining that the Sciascia meeting took me by surprise. In agreeing to speak in the series, I had no idea that instead of delivering a lecture I would be expected to spend most of the time answering extemporaneously any questions which the audience might bring up. Neither from a linguistic nor a political point of view do I feel qualified to engage in that kind of performance. As I point out, one of the subjects which the audience will certainly insist on discussing with an

American is the Vietnamese war, a topic about which I know only what I have read in the Italian press.

This is the gist of my appeal to Danilo, but I may as well save my breath. As soon as he hears about the phone call from Jordan, his eyes harden and his jaw tightens; it is doubtful that he hears the rest of what I say. He waits until I am finished; then announces in a chilling voice that he fully intends to hold me to my promise to speak. If I refuse, he adds, he will issue a statement to the press declaring that the U. S. State Department has forbidden me to do so.

I try to make him understand that my wish to withdraw as a speaker, although triggered by the phone call, is actually my own. His only response is to repeat the threat, explaining that his conscience will not permit him to act otherwise.

What about my conscience? I am tempted to ask him; but I desist, having no wish to quarrel with a champion of nonviolence.

APRIL 13

Franco is the Mafia expert at the Center. Under Danilo's direction, he is constantly digging up evidence of Mafia exploitation, terror, and political influence. It was he who helped to elicit depositions from usually close-mouthed citizens of Partinico, which Danilo presented to the Anti-Mafia Commission to indicate the Mafia-client relationship existing between Senator Girolomo Messeri and his ally Frank Coppola. It was also Franco who prepared a carefully documented report issued by the Center which exposes the efforts of the Partinico Mafia to impede the construction of the Jato dam. A few days ago I accidentally learned of another dangerous assignment he has received from Danilo, this one more difficult perhaps than any of the others: to help him collect evidence indicating the Mafia-client relationships of one of Sicily's most powerful political figures, Senator Bernardo Mattarella, the present Italian minister of foreign commerce.

In a country where minding one's own business is the basic law of the land, Franco's extraordinary ability to ferret out facts which may endanger the personal safety of his informants (not to mention his own), has been a constant source of wonder to me. But watching him in action today, after he had decided I should interview a woman of Partinico whose son had been murdered in her presence, I begin to understand what makes him such an expert investigating reporter.

"I can't guarantee that the woman will be willing to talk about the murder," he says as we begin our search for her, "but if she does, you owe it to your project to listen to her."

The woman is not at the address he has; her neighbors disclaim any knowledge of her whereabouts. We go to two other addresses, where the woman's children live, yet no one will admit knowing where she may be. Franco, with the acumen and persistence of a born sleuth, questions relatives and neighbors until he is able to deduce where the woman is now living. Almost three hours after our search began we find her and her husband in a one-room hovel surrounded by seven young grandchildren and their mother. The room is not unlike others I have seen in Partinico. The plastered walls are streaked with rain stains; there are holes in the roof large enough to see the sky. The floor is of dirt; the place reeks with the smell of chicken excrement. Four adults and seven children live here, along with five hens.

The grandparents and I sit on the only chairs in the room; everyone else, except the mother, sits on boxes or on the edge of a bed. The mother informs me she had eleven children but that four died. "I keep praying there will be no more sickness for a while. Just now I am the only one who is sick. I should go to a doctor but my husband is out of work and we already owe the doctor a good deal of money." I offer her my chair, but she insists on standing and hovers over me and her mother-in-law, anxious to hear everything.

The most pitiful figure in the room is the grandfather. A recent stroke has deprived him of his power of speech. He clings to a cane with both hands all during the interview, a mummy of a man with burning eyes. His wife, the mother of the murdered man, is a small, gaunt woman with strong facial features and gray hair. Tears well up in her eyes as she listens to Franco tactfully describe the purpose of our visit. Then she quickly wipes away the tears with the sleeve of her black dress, and begins to talk of the murder. Now and then there is the sudden rustle of a hen as it flies in or out of the room through a hole above the door, but the predominant sound is the agony in the woman's voice.

"There were two men, one chasing the other and shooting at him. I was here in this very house with my son and mistook the shots for the noises of a truck. My son had just come back from Germany, where he had been working, and he was anxious to spend what little time he had with his mother. A little earlier he came in with a piece of meat and told me, 'I'd rather eat with my mother than with anyone else I know,' and he gave the meat to his sister to cook." The woman pauses, pained by the memory, and rocks her body back and forth murmuring: *"Sangu di miu cuore* [blood of my heart], it was with me that my son wanted to share his food.

"It was while the meat was on the fire that we heard the shots. I went to the door, expecting to see a truck, but instead there were these two men: one chasing the other, shooting as he ran after him. This grandchild of mine—" she pointed to a dark-haired girl of ten sitting on a box—"was playing in front of the door. She shouldn't be there, I said to myself, they might shoot her. I put her inside and was just starting to shut the door when the man who was being chased ran into me and almost knocked me over. I said to him, 'What are you up to? Who is chasing you?' Meanwhile, the man with the gun was coming toward us. Without saying a word, the man I was talking to entered the house and hid behind the door.

"While this was happening, my son was inside waiting for the meat to cook. 'I'm hungry,' he was saying to his sister, and he picked up a morsel of bread to munch on. The bread remained forever in his mouth. The man with the revolver came in and shot just once. He shot and killed my son in the stomach. My own son, my innocent blood. 'Mamma, I am dead,' he said, and he was. That was how my son died, my own son, *u sangu di miu cuore.*

"Paullido was like a father. He was! 'You are getting old,' he would say to me and my husband, 'I will work for you.' And how he worked. He dug the soil, he peddled what he grew. He did whatever he could that would earn him money to bring to us. Then he went to work in Germany, and from there he would send money every month, always with this message: 'Dear Mother, eat and drink, and use some of the money for my sister's trousseau.' "

The woman begins to cry and her body rocks back and forth as she sobs: *"sangu di miu cuore, sangu di miu cuore . . .*

"That, Signore, was the death of my son," she whispers after a while. "And we remained, his two old parents, desolate and with our hearts broken. Later my daughter got married. It was on her account that my son had come from Germany for a few days. He came to attend her wedding, and instead he went to his death. And here we are, our lives ruined, we who have never done anyone any harm.

"When the man with the revolver shot my son, I went after him. I ran and I tried to catch him. 'You've killed my son,' I kept saying to him while I ran. He was a young man of the same age as Paullido, twenty-two years old. He kept running, and then he disappeared into a garden. My *compare* happened to be on the street and when he heard what I was saying he said to me: 'Are you crazy? How could he have killed your son?' He wouldn't believe that that's what had happened. 'What kind of insanity is this?' my *compare* kept saying to me.

"I'm too old to try to catch a young man who is running. So I returned to the house, and found that they had placed him on the bed, *sangu di miu cuore*. They took him to the hospital, but he was already dead.

"We hired a lawyer. There was no need to do that because the law itself would have defended my son, but the neighbors began to say this and that and ask us why we weren't looking after our son's interests. And we, ignorant persons that we are, hired a lawyer when there was no need to. We hired a lawyer to defend my son, my innocent blood."

The woman weeps and moans, and is too lost in her sorrow to hear Franco or me trying to comfort her. When she regains enough control to speak again, I ask her a few questions.

Did they ever find the man who killed your son?

"The law got hold of the man who came here to hide, and they probably forced him to tell the truth. At first he wouldn't. They brought him to me and said to him: 'Tell the truth. Console this mother who doesn't know the name of the man who killed her son.' There was no doubt that he knew who the man was because as soon as he caught sight of him he jumped off his bicycle and began to run. This meant he must have recognized the man as an enemy. Otherwise, why would he have started to run? He didn't

210

tell the police the man's name in my presence. But he must have told them later because after three days they came to me and said, 'Signora, we have found a dog at his table.' They meant that they had arrested the man while he was eating. Then they said to me: 'But you must make sure you identify the right man. It would not be right for you to destroy the life of some innocent mother's son.'

"And so they placed six men in front of me and asked if my son's murderer was among them. He was. He was the one in the middle. The moment I saw him my heart began to beat hard. 'He's the one,' I told them.

" 'How can you be so certain?' they asked me.

" 'Because he came into my house, and I saw him and I am not blind.' That's what I told them. I could not have been more certain because he was still wearing a dark blue jacket that had been smeared by the whitewash my son had put on the door only the day before.

"They told me later that he was a man from Roccamena. At the trial the judge said to him: 'You went into that house and committed this stupid crime. If you wanted to kill Lombardi (that was the name of the man he was after) why didn't you drag him outdoors and kill him? How stupid to kill an innocent man.' "

Did anyone try to help you catch the murderer when you were chasing him?

"There was no one. No one at all. All the doors were shut tight. As soon as the sound of shooting was heard, everyone locked his door. Everyone. Who would want to get involved in anything like that? If they were outside, they went inside, and shut their doors. I was the only one who chased him."

What time of the day was it?

"It was almost noon. And now after five years I still feel as though it happened yesterday. Yes, five years have passed since they buried him, *u sangu di miu cuore*. And as if that calamity was not enough, a few months ago they shot at another son of mine . . ."

That is news to Franco. "Another son?" he asks.

"Another son, the father of three children." Her voice wails at the memory. "He was carrying his infant daughter in his arms

211

when they shot him in the leg. They took him to the hospital and the doctors stitched his leg with a machine, but he can never work again. And yet we are all innocent. Innocent, signore. In this family there is no one who is smart; in fact, we are more stupid than smart. Ours is a family that doesn't count in this world . . ."

She moans through her tears and presses her hands against her face as though to stop its quivering. Ashamed I have evoked so much anguish, I decide to cut the interview short, but as I try the woman suddenly dries her tears and urges me to continue.

Where was your son's murderer when this last shooting happened?

"In jail. At the trial they sentenced him to jail for life; yes, he is still alive while my son is dead. My other son was shot at night, about nine o'clock when there were people all around. No one would say they saw it, but people came to my house and told me: 'Go to the hospital. Your son is there.' *Si, Signore,* with three small children to feed, my son was shot while he carried his newborn daughter. He is employed but he cannot work. His employer feels pity for him and keeps him on so that he can feed his children. But he is a man who cannot work . . .

"All of my sons, all of us, are innocent. It was the Police Commissioner himself who said: 'This is a family that does not count in this world.' Yet look at what has happened to us."

Have you always lived in Partinico?

"I was born and raised in Partinico and I have never been anywhere else. And that is also true of my husband, except that as a young man he left Partinico while he was in military service. We have been nowhere and we know no one, and that is why the police have never had to question us about any trouble except our own."

How old are you, Signora?

"Sixty-seven, almost sixty-eight. My second son also went to Germany to look for work but he couldn't find any. And when he returned, they shot at him, just as they shot at Paullido. And now we no longer live with him. We live with our other children, but one of them has five children of her own, this one has seven, and there's another with eight. How can they possibly take care of me and my husband when they can't manage for themselves?

"I often look at the photograph of my dead son and say to him: *Sangu di miu cuore,* why did you die? Without you to protect us, fire and darkness have come into our lives.' And I cry. What else is there to do?"

She is crying when we leave.

APRIL 16

Today, Good Friday, was originally set aside for the journey to my relatives but we decide to postpone it by a day in order that I may attend an historical occasion, the opening session of the Center's Institute.

Danilo, who has just returned from Palermo, drives me to Trappeto. It is a perfect spring morning, and the fields are dazzling with a new crop of wildflowers. Danilo, in a cheerful mood, keeps exclaiming at their beauty. We have not seen one another since our contretemps earlier in the week, but neither one of us refers to it. I have no wish to mar his mood by telling him I am to meet with Jordan and the American General Consul early next week to determine what our next step should be. Danilo's attitude toward me, which is as friendly and relaxed as ever, strengthens my suspicion that, consciously or not, he has decided to disregard my own feelings about wishing to withdraw as a speaker and blame only the American officials for the situation.

Apropos of a letter Danilo has just received from Aldo Capitini, most of our conversation centers on his former mentor. When I ask why he broke with Capitini, Danilo replies that they are still good friends who agree on many basic issues, but that they have differences of opinion as to what methods should be used for achieving social reforms in Sicily and in other underdeveloped regions of the world. Danilo believes that the people in these regions need to be "stimulated and activated to take practical steps that will be to their ultimate benefit." Capitini's attitude is that people in need of help will readily respond to a useful philosophy and will apply its wisdom to their lives with little urging. Danilo is unable to believe in Capitini's optimism, which, he says, manifests itself further in his tendency to "complete his circles of thought too quickly." He adds: "Capitini is the kind of man who is sin-

213

cerely convinced that eventually the big fish will stop devouring the little fish."

He himself, Danilo makes it clear, has no fixed concepts. He has no idea what will ultimately happen to man. He views life as a drama, as a series of conflicts that are difficult to resolve. Yet he has a clear sense of man's potential both as an individual and as part of a group, and he considers it essential that this potential not go to waste.

As we approach Trappeto, Danilo urges me to make Capitini's acquaintance before leaving Italy. "Capitini is a great man; he was one of the few Italian university teachers, by the way, who gave up his post rather than sign up as a member of the Fascist party. In all of Italy there were only five Italian university teachers who were willing to take that stand. By the end of the war, Capitini had won so much respect as an anti-fascist that he could have had any government position he wished. Instead he chose to write a book on the theme of the human conscience in modern times, an important timely work for all intellectuals."

Conscience is the keynote of Danilo's opening remarks at the new school. "Conscience does not provide you with an infallible method of doing things," he tells the twenty students, "but it is a beginning. You develop your conscience by being faithful to your own sense of what is true. In that way, conscience becomes an instrument for constructive action. But little can be achieved through individual acts; you must work with others. Group conscience, another fundamental instrument, is far more potent than individual conscience. Conscientious nonviolent group action can rescue modern man from the economic and psychological morass that is burying him alive . . ."

Danilo's remarks are brief. He and Lorenzo, who presides over the seminar, are more interested in stimulating discussion than in offering the students ready-made observations. "What forms of waste have you observed in this zone of Sicily?" is one of the questions Lorenzo puts to them after explaining that if they can learn to recognize what needs to be done in the villages they know best, together they will learn what needs to be done throughout the entire zone.

In their responses, the students give major consideration to

214

human waste (unemployment) and the waste of water that is permitted to empty into the sea without being utilized for irrigation. Most of the students are in their twenties and thirties and have the equivalent of a high-school education. Among the less educated is a forty-year-old peasant who says: "In my opinion, the greatest waste is to be found among the people in power. They don't have the qualifications to do their job properly. They are the sort of people who sit on their fat asses and expect their box of figs to be brought to them. But they know nothing—and care nothing —about all the problems there are to growing figs."

Among the students are a half-dozen unemployed teachers. One of them answers Lorenzo's question by pointing out that there are thousands of unemployed teachers in Sicily and many more thousands of children with little or no education. "It is a waste of human potential to keep these two groups apart . . ."

During the lunch recess I become acquainted with two students from Corleone, one a designer of men's clothing by training, the other a land surveyor. The latter is a personable young man of twenty-six who had dominated the morning discussion with his eloquence and intelligence. It does not surprise me to learn that during his stint in the Italian army he was singled out as officer material. Soon after he became a first lieutenant he became infatuated with Fascist ideology and dreamed of helping to resurrect it; but as he became older, he realized how sterile it was, how unrelated to the reality of everyday existence. He also lost his enthusiasm for a military career, and quit the army. After receiving training as a land surveyor, he returned to his home town and found himself in competition with twenty other young men who had also decided to become land surveyors. "Gradually, I began to appreciate the necessity for socio-economic planning that would take into consideration both the physical and the spiritual needs of man. I yearned to see a better world come about and felt frustrated because I could do nothing about it. Then a few months ago I learned about Danilo Dolci and his Center and realized that it is trying to do some of the very things I hoped could be done. That's why I'm here."

His townsman, the designer, is not nearly so self-assured. The sorrowful brown eyes and pinched face bespeak a young man who

215

is more inclined to communicate with himself than with others. Not until we converse for a few minutes do I become aware of the root of his sadness: his right arm is made of wood. At the age of five, while he was playing in the fields, an American-made bomb exploded near him and shattered one arm. "From that moment my life which had seemed like a radiant morning became a gloomy night."

Although trained to design men's clothing, he had never been able to make his living as a designer. "Palermo was the only city in Sicily where I could have found work but the pay offered to me was so low I could not afford to live there. And now it is too late. For when I first learned the trade a designer did nothing else but design, but now a designer is expected to sew as well. And, of course, that is something I can't do."

He tried to become an accountant but after four years of studying he became seriously ill; after that, there was not enough money to return to school. Except for a few months of work as a designer's assistant, he has never had a job. At the age of twenty-seven he is still dependent on his parents for support.

"By now I've become convinced that our political system has very little relationship to the basic problems of its people. I suppose that is true in most countries. When I look at our sick world, I see it as a body in which some limbs have been overdeveloped while others have remained infantile in size. The world needs to be a normal body that can function properly for the benefit of all its people. I never used to have much use for sociology or economics. But now I realize that if planning is honest, thorough, and intelligent, people can have an existence that makes their life on this earth worthwhile.

Nearly all the students I speak with have been exposed to the vicissitudes of trying to earn a livelihood, but there is one who is more attuned to the world of books than to the world itself. His formidable vocabulary and his propensity for abstract thought mark Orazio as the only hothouse intellectual of the lot. With his closely cropped black beard and small trim figure, he seems to have emerged straight out of a Chekhov play. When Lorenzo asks each of the students to describe what he hopes to accomplish in his village after he has completed the course, Orazio replies:

216

"My hometown, which is Sambuca, is nearly dead and needs a major stimulus. The people who live there have slept in the arms of the past too long. I shall make it my task to waken them, to lead them into the twentieth century. In so doing, I shall also be awaking myself to a more modern concept of reality. I realize after this morning's discussion that I have been too vague, too theoretical, and too disorganized. I need to be more organized, more specific, and more active. To act is to make mistakes, but the worst mistake any of us can make is not to act."

The surveyor and the designer are more specific. Speaking for both of them, the surveyor says: "In Corleone we shall try to analyze the state of its underdevelopment and convey what we learn to all the agencies in the community that can utilize the information to its best advantage. One of the first things we shall try to determine is the amount of illiteracy in Corleone. We shall also make an inventory of persons in the community who might have something to contribute to its welfare. Once we have completed our researches, we will form a citizens' committee to assume leadership for what has to be done."

Speaking of his work and plans, Fiffidu Rubino, a member of the Partinico Center, says: "Lately, my chief concern has been to make sure that all goes well with the construction of the Jato dam. Thanks largely to Danilo's personal efforts, the dam is in its final stage of construction, but there are a number of difficulties that threaten its completion. One is the possible intervention of the Mafia, which after all this time is still trying to create obstacles that will bring the work to a dead stop. My job is to keep the workers at the dam alert to this danger and to do whatever we can at the Center and in the community to avert it."

Lorenzo Barbera says: "My immediate concern is this school, making it as effective as possible, so that each of you can create a kind of radar within yourself that will best direct your efforts. I am also interested in trying to establish a pilot activity in Roccamena that will clearly indicate to the other villages in the Belice valley how to cope with the various problems that will result from building a dam there. My long-range goal is to help establish machinery for the regional planning of this zone. As a first step, we are planning a meeting in Partanna soon that will be attended by

217

representatives of all the villages in the Belice valley. There we will begin to relate the concept of local planning to that of regional planning.

"With so much work to do, I need to gain more time and to develop better study habits. I can do this by going to bed earlier and rising earlier and, like Danilo, using the silence of the morning hours for thinking and studying. To have more time for myself, I must learn to insist on taking it. That means I must learn to be less polite. One of my failings is that I tend to be too polite."

When it comes to Danilo's turn, he says: "Every morning I rise early and spend three hours trying to work out some of the problems that confront the Center. The rest of the morning I devote to the daily work of the office, and I use the afternoons to develop contacts with persons outside the Center. But my first responsibility is always that of the Center . . .

"Presently I'm concerned with the task of trying to develop a closer rapport with the people of Palermo. The rapport has been lacking, probably because the publicity that has come our way has created barriers of envy and misunderstanding. I am trying to overcome those barriers because I realize that Palermo can be a primary source of collaboration and strength for everything we are trying to do."

Franco arrives toward the close of the afternoon session and suggests a trip into the village so that he can show me the room where Danilo conducted his first fast in 1952. The room is in a small abandoned building on a dirt road that is only a few yards away from the sea. The road was once part of what Franco describes as "a valley of open drains and filth." Thanks to the public works program that resulted from Danilo's fast, there are no more open drains. But the huge sewer pipe leading into the sea is not long enough and the stench of sewage is overpowering.

The tiny airless alcove where Danilo fasted has an opening in the ceiling, which its inhabitants used as an escape hatch whenever the room became filled with sewer water. Danilo selected this room for the fast because it was there that a baby had died from lack of food. "Danilo almost died of the same thing," Franco recalls. "One day I found he had no pulse and I became so alarmed that I got on a motorcycle and sped to Palermo where I talked to all the authorities that would see me. Everyone was very courteous but no promises were made, and when I rode back to Trappeto I cried all the way, thinking I had failed. But help did come . . ."

Although it is Good Friday, the atmosphere of the village is not of mourning. The big wooden cross in the main square has been adorned with bunches of wildflowers, and near the church a gang of young boys are gleefully banging together wooden clappers, in accordance with an ancient Good Friday local custom whose significance has been forgotten. Inside the church not a single statue is covered with crepe, and the altar is festively bedecked with daisies and poppies.

The people themselves exude cheerfulness. Many recognize Franco as we wander from one street to another, and greet him affectionately. The women seem far less timorous than those in Partinico; they smile at both of us. "The men and women are less inhibited here, possibly because they live so close to the sea," Franco says. "But by the same token they don't have the dignity of Partinicans. For example, the people here are never shy about asking you for a gift. A Partinican would never do that; should he accept a gift, he will usually find some way of repaying you twice over.

"People here were very unhappy when they learned that Danilo had decided to move to Partinico. They begged him to stay and told him it would be a terrible mistake to live in 'the city of the bad people,' which is the meaning they ascribe to the word 'Partinico.' They even offered to make him mayor if he remained."

On our way back to the school I marvel at the cleanliness of the paved streets, particularly at the sight of two sweepers working the same pavement. "There's no doubt about it," Franco tells me. "Danilo has left his stamp on this town."

Easter in
Agrigento

THE LARGE DELEGATION of relatives waiting to greet us as we arrived in Agrigento consisted of two factions, those related to me through my mother and those through my father. Even before we finished embracing and kissing, they were in fierce verbal combat, squabbling over the question of who was to entertain us first. I had assumed that Uncle Pitrinu, who was taller and worse-tempered than any of them, would win the battle, but at the age of eighty-six he had apparently lost some of his prowess as a despot; and while he was still sputtering with rage that anyone should dare challenge his prerogative to entertain us for as long as he wished, one of my first cousins and his wife, who had recently returned from a lengthy residence in the States, took firm possession of us for the rest of the day.

Before the delegation had dispersed, each faction was treating the other with icy disdain, and every hour of our weekend sojourn, except those allotted for sleeping, had been snatched by one relative or another. Except for my insistence on having Easter day dinner with my uncle, there was little attention paid to what our wishes might be. That both factions had a need to envelop and hold us fast in their clutches as long as possible was partly explained by the reverence they felt toward my mother or father, partly by their fondness for me, a fondness suddenly grown intense by eighteen years of separation; partly by their curiosity over Patricia (it was the first time I had come to Sicily as a married man), and partly by the deep ego satisfaction they derived from frustrating one another.

Under the funereal gaze of Uncle Pitrinu, my first cousins scooped us out of the railway station and, depositing us in their son's plush Fiat, took us to their home, a modest third-floor apartment which was almost the exact duplicate of the one they had occupied in Rochester, New York. There was one striking difference. The luxurious bathtub and the superspeed washing machine, transported all the way from Rochester, could only be used sparingly because of the general scarcity of water in Agrigento. The situation was no better than it had been eighteen years before: only for one hour every two days was water available. Yet engineering experts were unanimous in agreeing that there was a plentiful supply of it in the immediate area; the problem was simply that of piping more into the homes. My cousin could not tell me why this difficulty had not been overcome. When I quoted Danilo to the effect that the water problem in Agrigento would never be solved as long as the Mafia remained strongly entrenched there, my cousin curtly dismissed the subject by saying that "Danilo Dolci, everyone knows, is a Communist."

While we feasted on a supper of roast kid, a giant television set engulfed the apartment with the histrionics of soap opera. "Just like America," Ciccio said, and turned up the volume. Only because we were seated next to one another could I hear my spinster cousin Paulina, who had journeyed from Realmonte to dine with us. Recalling that she had acquired a reputation for performing miracles during the war by praying for the return of soldiers from the village who were reported missing in action (two or three of them actually turned up), I asked whether she still spent most of her time in church.

Paulina's blue eyes regarded me mischievously. "You remember how some people made fun of me because I was always in church?" she asked. I had not known this but it did not surprise me. "Well, I put one over on them. Don't misunderstand me. I did go to church to pray for the missing soldiers and for all of God's purposes but I also went for my own reasons. I worked so hard for that church that finally the priest felt duty-bound to make me an official member of his staff. And now I receive a pension from the

221

state for these past services. That's what helps to support me . . ."

After I had congratulated her on her foresight, she informed me that she still prays in church, though not as much as before. "For a few years after the war I prayed that a good man would come along to marry me and take me away from Realmonte. But now it's too late for that. I'm too old. Now I pray mainly for the good health of the people I love, people like your mother. And you," she added as an afterthought. "Do you remember how I pleaded with you to marry me and take me to America? That was when you first came to Sicily and we were both young."

I kissed her on the nose, as I had when she proposed to me, and reminded her again that as first cousins we were too closely related to marry.

"You were right in saying no. I am a woman with no education. The only real talent I have is that of prayer." She smiled at Patricia across the table. "Your wife is lovely. And I'm sure she has had more education than I."

Shortly after dark, Ciccio and his son Alfredo took us for a drive around Agrigento's famous Greek temples, which are now illuminated at night. The five temples rise on a plain between Agrigento and Porto Empedocle. Their ingenious lighting effects, arranged so artfully as to conceal the intervention of man, silhouette each golden temple against the Stygian darkness, endowing each one with a poetic radiance that expresses explicitly what the ancient Greek worshippers must have known implicitly.

At Ciccio's insistence, and over his son's protests, we left the car and scrambled up the short hill where the magnificent temple of Juno is situated. No sooner had we entered the temple than Ciccio tripped over a couple making love on the stone floor, and we were obliged to beat a hasty retreat. Alfredo laughed when Patricia recalled from history that among the ancients Juno was considered the patroness of female virtue and marriage.

"That may explain why the girl on the floor was allowing herself to be seduced in that particular temple," he said. "Of course, few girls in Sicily get seduced without hoping there will be a marriage. I'm surprised you saw only one couple. All the temples are filled with them at night. Girls are much freer than they were when you were here the last time. After a while they will all be like American girls . . ."

When I asked Alfredo whether or not he favored the traditional code of behavior, which allows Sicilian women no freedom, he said he was against it. "The code has to die, just as Sicily has to become more Americanized. Yet I myself could not bear the idea of any woman in our family breaking any part of the code."

His candor was the most appealing aspect of him. He was an ambitious young businessman whose main concern was making money and enhancing his social prestige by emulating the behavior pattern of those more prosperous than he. He drove us to San Leone, a nearby beach resort that has become fashionable among the wealthy families of Agrigento, and showed us a tract of land he owns where he plans to build a luxurious home as soon as the travelers' hotel he owns and operates shows more profit.

"My son is the most American Sicilian I know," Ciccio said proudly. "In Rochester he could become a millionaire in no time."

"I'd like to be a millionaire here, not in Rochester," Alfredo said. "A rich man commands more respect here because he is such a rare bird."

"Rich or poor, I would prefer to live in Rochester," his father said. "But with all my children living in Sicily I had no choice but to come back here, as soon as I qualified for social security . . ."

On the way back to Agrigento I noticed the new skyline of the city for the first time, and was appalled by its close resemblance to that of the Bronx. The old sandstone buildings that once lined the edge of the city above the valley of the temples have been replaced by high-rise apartment buildings, one adjoining the other to form a solid front of severely rectangular shapes. The sharpness of their lines make a mockery out of the soft lilting grace of the ancient temples.

Ciccio could not understand my indignation. "What is wrong with modern architecture? You see it in the richest American cities. Don't you want Sicily to become modern?"

"You may be right," Alfredo conceded. "The new skyline probably does mar the beauty of the temples. But you forget that one always has to pay for the price of progress. In Sicily we will have to pay with sacrifices of beauty because beauty is the only commodity we have in plentiful supply."

Alfredo woke us on Easter morning by telephoning to say that he had ordered breakfast sent to our room. "Since you won't find time to have a meal at my house, the least I can do is provide you with one at your hotel." After we ate, we went for a walk along the Via Atenea, the main street, chiefly to get away from the stench of sewage pervading our first-class hotel.

Despite the Bronx skyline, the town was crowded with earnest tourists intent on examining the ruins of what Pindar once described as "the fairest of all mortal cities." Before it was sacked by the Carthaginians and the Romans, it was one of the most prosperous cities of the ancient Greek world, with a population of 200,000 spread all over a lofty hill and an area that extended well beyond the valley of the temples. Now Agrigento has only 35,000 inhabitants and they are huddled together on only one sector of the hill. Nearly all the glory that was Greece has been reduced to a state of ruin; the predominant atmosphere is a dour residue of Arabic and Spanish influences.

Its name notwithstanding, the Via Atenea is the antithesis of the ancient Greek spirit that reveled in open sky and long vistas. A claustrophobic skinny canyon, it slithers darkly from one end of town to the other, its tall brown buildings and high-rise edifices almost completely obstructing the classic views of the temples and the sea. The gloom of the street is somewhat alleviated by its numerous elegant shops, but on this Easter morning their elegance was spoiled by the same aroma of sewage that had driven us out of our hotel, a redolent reminder of aged corruption.

Back at the hotel we were greeted by the next brace of relatives who were to take us in tow, my cousin Nardo and his son Mario. To my delight and surprise they were accompanied by an old friend, Dante Vittorini, whom I had known when he was a young bachelor and a secret writer of poetry. Now Dante was married, the father of two young children, and had become a leading authority on the history of Sicilian art as well as a chief administrator of Palermo's principal museum. He explained he had come to Agrigento to spend the holiday with his mother and, on learning I was in town, decided to offer us his services as a guide.

"Do you have my relatives' permission?" I asked him.

"I gave myself permission," he said. "Didn't you know that we have been related for several years?"

I did not understand what he meant.

"After an absence of eighteen years you must allow for a few extraordinary developments, even in Sicily . . ."

When I continued to look blank, he asked: "Hasn't your cousin Mario told you that we are now brothers-in-law? I had nothing to do with it. He went and married one of my sisters."

It was news to me.

"Of course," Dante went on, "if our being related, however distantly, is distasteful to you, I will disclaim the relationship here and now."

"You can't," Mario said. "Not while your sister is pregnant again."

"Again?" Dante exclaimed in mock horror. "And without my permission?"

Nardo, whose sense of humor was not his strongest asset, frowned at this levity. "Let's get going," he suggested.

To give Patricia some notion of what has made Agrigento a mecca for travelers, Dante led us on an extended tour that began with the Cathedral of St. Gerlando (the first bishop of Agrigento), located on the city's highest summit, and ended in the valley of the temples. At the doorway of the cathedral I renewed my acquaintance with the sacristan, who still remembered I had photographed him with a pet crow on his shoulder some thirty years before. "I trained nine crows but they all died or ran away. The last one disappeared in 1950. I believe he was kidnapped by one of the parishioners who kept saying that all crows are birds of evil because they are black. Mine weren't. Not when I got through with them. They were angels, every one of them. As for being black, they were angels in mourning, as I tried to explain to people."

In deference to our long acquaintance, the sacristan showed us a number of church treasures which were under lock and key, including vestments brocaded in silver and gold that had been worn by the bishops of Agrigento during a period of three hundred years. The treasure he still cherished most is one that is displayed to the public in a glass case: the preserved body of a twelfth-century Norman crusader who fell in battle on the island of Lampedusa. The sacristan directed our attention to a scroll of parchment next to the armored body which had recently been retrieved from

225

the archives. "No one has ever been able to read the writing on it," he said, "not even the most learned professors. For that reason perhaps they call it 'the letter from the Devil' but why would the Devil be writing a good Christian like this crusader?"

"It's very simple," Dante said when the sacristan was out of earshot. "The Devil was simply dunning this fellow, demanding why in hell he hadn't paid up as he had agreed to do . . ."

"It's best not to make fun of sacred things," Nardo said stiffly.

"But what's so sacred about a letter from the Devil?" Dante said.

In a more serious mood, he pointed to an exquisitely carved wooden ceiling of Spanish workmanship, and cited it as one of the few fine architectural features of the fifteenth-century building that had survived the "aggressively bad taste" of the cathedral's bishops. "The fact that a man becomes a bishop doesn't necessarily mean that he knows the difference between good and bad art. This ceiling almost became a casualty in the twenties when the reigning bishop claimed he had received a message from God ordering him to destroy it and replace it with one that would better reflect His glory. Had it not been for the intervention of some wealthy foreign connoisseurs of art, the bishop would have had his own way."

Nardo, who had been a member of the Fascist party, said: "It wasn't the foreigners so much as it was Mussolini who saved the ceiling. He appreciated beauty . . ."

His son objected. "All that Mussolini appreciated was his own importance."

Nardo ignored him. Outside, he indicated the piles of dirt and rubbish gathered around the cathedral walls and declared: "Under our present system of government nobody gives a damn what happens to this cathedral. In Mussolini's time the people charged with its care would have gone to jail if they didn't do their jobs properly. And that's the way it should be."

"The older he gets the more perfect Fascism seems to him," Mario whispered to me.

"Not all the bishops were bad judges of art," Dante said as we strolled through the valley of the temples. "Concordia, which is one of the best preserved Greek temples in the world, was saved from destruction by an Agrigento bishop, Gregory II. But Gregory was a rare exception. Most churchmen of power are like the bishop who permitted the columns from the temple of Zeus to be used in the construction of the Porto Empedocle harbor . . ."

The mention of Porto Empedocle reminded me it was high time we were delivered to my uncle. We arrived there a half hour past the appointed time, and found Uncle Pitrinu waiting at the door, furious that we were late. "By all rights," he fumed at Nardo, "my nephew and his wife should be spending all their time with me. After all, his father was my brother. There's no one else in this world who can say that."

Dante, in an apparent effort to change the subject, pointed to some dense clouds of smoke rising from the recently built Montecatini chemical plant. "Progress, I see, has come to Porto Empedocle."

Mario said that at first no one in the village objected to the smoke, so delighted were they with the employment prospects a chemical plant might offer. But now disillusion had set in. Only a few of the jobs had gone to villagers; the best jobs were filled by technicians imported from northern Italy. Moreover, the villagers began to discover that the chemical plant represented a health hazard; its chimneys were not tall enough to protect them from the poisonous fumes. "*Stratto* [tomato extract], which every housewife used to make," Mario added, "is no longer made in this town because the fumes give it a vile flavor. Now the people are beginning to wonder what the fumes are doing to their lungs; but there is nothing they can do about it except leave . . ."

"I am too old to care about such problems," my uncle said. "Besides my grandson is one of the few young men of Porto Empedocle to have a job at the plant and for that I am grateful." He turned to me. "Now tell me why in hell it has taken you and your wife all this time to visit your old uncle. You should have come here the same week you arrived in Sicily . . ."

The others got up to leave. "Don't forget that you're dining with my daughter and her husband this evening," Nardo said just before Mario was to drive off.

"What!" my uncle roared.

"Enjoy your relatives," Dante shouted in English.

After I had placated my uncle with a promise to return to Porto

227

Empedocle before we left Sicily, he took us on a tour of his house. One of his sons and his family lived with him until a few years ago but, unable to put up with his bad temper, they had moved to a place of their own. "I'm all alone now," he said gloomily as he showed us the main bedroom, where the photographs of his two dead wives hung side by side over an enormous bed. "I have nightmares about them when I use this bed, so I no longer sleep in it. I had a good life with each of them but the moment I fall asleep here I am plagued by memories of the worst times we had together. I've tried separating the photographs but that doesn't seem to help . . ."

I remember to give him the bottle of pills I had brought from the States for his arthritis; he kissed both of us for remembering the request. "What can I do to show my gratitude?" he moaned. "I had hoped that you would sleep on this bed—see, I had fresh clean sheets put on it—but I can see there is no likelihood of that."

He was proud of his garden, a strip of land some ten yards square that was cluttered with trees and animals. Between the lemon, orange and fig trees lived two dogs, ten hens, two roosters, four cats, five kittens, and a goat which Nardo's daughter, Mimi, had named Signor Dioda, after a government official in Agrigento with whom my uncle had been conducting a quixotic battle for more than a decade.

The hostilities began when the authorities informed my uncle that the plot of ground he had been assiduously cultivating for many years belonged to the State, not to him. After recovering from the shock of that news, my uncle began negotiations to buy the land. His rage at hearing the price set by the government appraiser resounded from one end of the province to the other, according to Mimi; he swore he would never pay such an outrageous sum for a piece of land that would be worthless except for the value he had given it with the sweat of his brow. But a year later, noticing how rapidly real estate values were rising in town, he announced his willingness to pay the price, only to be informed by a second appraiser that the value had quadrupled. There followed a long and stormy campaign to buy the land at the price set by the first appraiser. There were constant visits to officials in Agrigento and Palermo, and a vast correspondence with everybody who might provide him with free advice or influence. The high-points of the campaign were his rambunctious encounters with Signor Dioda, who on more than one occasion ordered him forcibly ejected from his office. After nearly ten years of this my uncle suddenly decided to drop the matter, proclaiming he would go on using the land without paying for it, and inviting all the authorities concerned to go to hell.

"We were immensely relieved," Mimi wrote. "It was as if a big war had come to an end." But it proved to be a false armistice. A few months ago Uncle Pitrinu began to hear rumors that the local authorities were planning to build a school that would encompass most of his garden, and he swung into action again.

"How is your battle with Signor Dioda coming along?" I asked him.

His eyes narrowed, then brightened. "Ah, so the news has spread to the United States!" he exclaimed. "Have they told you the whole story of how that pack of thieves has been trying to swindle me?"

As I listened to his saga on our way to his son's house, where we were to have our Easter dinner, it occurred to me that his battle is ideal therapy for someone of his age and temperament. As long as he can excite his blood cells, he will never suffer from boredom, the inevitable fate of most old men. As we climbed the long stairs up to his son's fifth-floor apartment, he stopped at one of the landings, not to catch his breath, but to ask: "If what you have told me about Danilo Dolci is true—that he is trying to help the poor—do you suppose he could help me buy my land at a decent price?"

In the apartment the target of his anger became his son Paolino, who had grown monstrously fat since I last saw him. "He's already had one heart attack and the doctor keeps telling him he must eat less," my uncle ranted, "but does he listen to the doctor? Just look at him putting it away." Actually, Paolino was not eating any more than anyone else but, accustomed to his father's bullying, he smiled gently and said nothing. All during the dinner my uncle fussed either at him for eating too much or at me and Patricia for not eating enough.

Paolino's two older brothers had escaped their father's domination by becoming police officers in Rome and Florence. As the youngest, he had been obliged to become his father's assistant in an enterprise that combined the manufacture of coffins with the burial of corpses. But the business failed to flourish and eventually it dwindled into a carpenter shop which Paolino operated with a partner. Now, a sick man at the age of sixty, he was worried about his ability to resume work. "The more I worry about it," he confided, "the more I need to eat."

His daughter Rosina, a pretty brunette of nineteen who had grown to twice the weight of her mother, was similarly afflicted. Her trouble began after she completed her schooling and, in accordance with Sicilian tradition, became confined to her home. Although permitted to leave the apartment with a chaperone, there was no one to fill that role. Her mother was too lame to venture the long stairway, and her brothers were occupied with school or work. Even the customary means of communicating with young men—conducting discreet flirtations from the balcony—was denied her by the fact that their balcony, five stories high, could barely be seen from the ground.

Gradually, Rosina had turned to food for comfort, and by now had become so fat that it embarrassed her to be seen in public. "I've even stopped going to church," she told me in private. "If I could put my secretarial training to use at some office job, there might be some hope for me. But neither my father nor my grandfather will let me work in Agrigento, and there is nothing available here."

Unlike most of my relatives in Agrigento, this family had not improved its situation during my absence. The two-room apartment was absurdly small for four adults and a child. And although there is an ample supply of water in Porto Empedocle, there was no plumbing in the apartment. The huge television set dominating the tiny dining room suggested that here, as among most Sicilian families, the problem is not always one of poverty but of ignorance and apathy.

"Why don't you allow Rosina to get a job in Agrigento?" I pleaded with my uncle and her father.

"Why?" my uncle exploded. "Because Porto Empedocle is a town of cursed gossips who would dishonor her with their talk. When they got through with her, we would all be dishonored, and no one would ever want to marry her."

230

Paolino dolefully agreed. "It is better to avoid gossip. I wish we could find her a job in Porto Empedocle but there is nothing here for a respectable girl."

Before returning to Agrigento, we called on Peppino Misca, who had once been married to my father's half-sister. She died more than thirty-five years ago and Misca remarried some ten years later, but he still worshiped her memory with a life-size photograph that dominated his living room. "Ah, Gerlando," he intoned, "hardly an hour ever passes that I don't think of her beauty and her nobility, *bon arma.*" In the next breath he asked, "Have you told your wife what a fine poet I am?"

Until his retirement, Misca had been the local train starter, who exasperated the townspeople with his indifference to time schedules. When Fascism was defeated, he began to claim that his lack of punctuality was nothing less than a calculated effort to undermine Mussolini's famous boast that he made the trains in Italy run on time. But Misca no longer thought of trains; poetry had become his consuming passion. There were none of the usual inquiries about my family in the States or my reasons for being in Sicily; all the amenities had been eaten away by his obsession to become a celebrated poet before he died. As if our last meeting had taken place the day before, rather than eighteen years ago, he immediately plunged into a recital of his poems, most of them long and sentimental odes addressed to the personages he most admired: Victor Hugo, Dante, Winston Churchill, Garibaldi, Pirandello, and John F. Kennedy.

"So where does that get you?" Uncle Pitrinu would ask in the middle of a poem. "You're going blind writing stuff that doesn't earn you a penny." With each such interruption, Misca would trot out some flattering letter of acceptance (or rejection) from some editor of an obscure magazine. Uncle Pitrinu had a sneer for each one. "All that means," he would say, "is that you are wasting good money on postage and subscriptions."

"Your uncle is an idiot," Misca kept on saying, but finally he gave full vent to his indignation and cried out: "How can an ex-undertaker who never reads possibly understand the sensibility of a born poet. Money is all he thinks of. Ignoble money. But what use is money if you don't have a soul? Not for a billion lire would I change places with him . . ."

Uncle Pitrinu's retort to this outburst was to rise and announce that the last bus to Agrigento was leaving in five minutes. Misca tried to continue his poem but as soon as he opened his mouth my uncle walked out of the room, bidding Patricia and me to follow. Misca read a few more lines as he accompanied us to the door. Uncle Pitrinu was hurrying down the street. "Do me a favor when you return to your country," Misca pleaded as we said goodbye. "Ask Mrs. Kennedy if she ever received the poem I sent her about her beloved husband. It is a masterpiece and she should have written me a letter praising it."

Actually, the bus was not scheduled to leave for another hour. "I had to lie about the bus because I couldn't stand another moment of him," my uncle grumbled. "We used to be close friends but that was before he became a full-time poet." He took us to the same café where my father as a young man had learned the art of making *cannoli*. While my uncle went on abusing Misca for his poetry, we munched on our *cannoli* and watched the ritual of the evening *passeggiata* in the twilight.

Mario and his sister Mimi were the only relatives I visited that weekend whose attitudes had changed markedly in the thirty years that had elasped since my first journey to Sicily. Originally, I had known them as noisy and mischievous brats who irritated me with their Fascist songs and slogans. In the forties, when I knew them as teen-agers, they were more subdued but they were still echoing the political sentiments of their father, speaking of the fallen Mussolini regime with the affection one might have for the memory of a beloved and distinguished ancestor. This was no longer true. While Nardo's attachment to the image of Fascist glory had grown even stronger, that of his children had completely disappeared.

The pudgy child of the thirties who had taken sadistic delight in screaming Mussolini quotations at me had become a vibrantly sensuous woman with a cupid face and a winsome voice. Now the mother of a young boy, Mimi was married to a haberdasher by the name of Pippo Battaglia and lived in an elegantly modern apartment overlooking the valley of the temples. "We have grown older and wiser," she said of herself and Mario when I teased her about their past enthusiasm for Fascism. "Not that democracy in Sicily is working very well but at least there is some hope that it will one day . . ."

232

"Fascism was a stupid dream that never offered the Italians anything but a make-believe future," her husband said. "But some Italians, like your father, will never understand that."

"Poor Papa," Mimi said. "He misses Fascism because he could feel important then. He had a good job and people respected him. Now he has no job and no wife and everything about the past seems better to him. Mention anybody in the past—Mussolini, Garibaldi, or even Verdi—and tears will start coming out of his eyes."

While Pippo left the apartment to drive their servant home, Mimi spoke fondly of their eight years of marriage. "He's no intellectual like Dante"—Dante Vittorini had been her first love—"but he is intelligent and he has taught me a good many things. I know now how stupid I must have seemed to you in the past. One of the nicest things about Pippo is that he is not like other Sicilian men. He allows me to work in an office—I would go mad if I had to be a housewife all day long—and believe it or not he's an advocate of birth control."

"I believe it," I said. "Otherwise you would have had at least five children by now."

"One is not enough, of course," she said. "We are planning to have our second next year."

I asked what her priest said to such family planning, and she laughed. "The priest and I are no longer on speaking terms. I haven't been to confession since I got married."

"Don't you believe in hell any longer?"

"My husband talked me out of it. I told you he's modern."

Patricia wanted to know if she planned to baptize her next child.

"Oh yes," Mimi answered quickly. "There are limits to how modern you can be in Sicily."

Unlike most of the Sicilians I have encountered, Mimi, Pippo and Mario accept change as a desirable factor of life and are definitely inclined to look to the future rather than to the past for their way of life. In that sense, they represent the new Sicilians—enlightened members of the middle class with social attitudes that were once the monopoly of intellectuals. Mario, at whose home we dined the next day before leaving for Palermo, was even more explicit in his views than his sister. In addition to legalized birth

233

control and abortion, he firmly believed in increasing women's rights and in secular divorce laws. And unlike most of my relatives, to whom Danilo Dolci was merely a name they occasionally saw in the newspapers, Mario was thoroughly familiar with his work and convinced of its usefulness.

"If Dolci can have his way, if his ideas can be more generally applied, Sicily will finally stop being the stepchild of Rome. He is the only man I know of who has a comprehensive view of what is wrong with Sicily and what can be done about it. I hope he lives for a long time because it is going to take many years to defeat the ignorance and inefficiency that keep Sicilians down . . ."

Yet Mario's own sense of efficiency in his position as station-master of Agrigento was not nearly as developed as it might be. "There will be plenty of seats," he assured us on the way to the late afternoon train. "Most of the visitors and tourists won't be leaving Agrigento until tomorrow." Yet the train was already jammed. Second class was so crowded we had to switch to first, and moments after Mario left us, there were no seats at all to be had and the aisles were closely packed with standing passengers, some with babes in their arms. Mario, no novice at this job, could have prevented the jam by adding two or three extra cars, but he had failed abysmally to foresee the heavy Easter Monday traffic.

The journey to Palermo, which normally takes two and a half hours, became a ten-hour happening, a classical enactment of the Sicilian mind reacting to the unknown forces of a punishing world.

At first there was nothing but the usual confusion one finds on crowded Italian trains: yowling infants, parents barking orders at children and at each other, passengers squabbling over spaces for their baggage. I surrendered my seat to a young mother with an infant in her arms and a husband and eight children in the aisle. The woman's voice rose above the pandemonium as she nagged her husband to keep track of the children. The infant, who had been sleeping, opened his eyes and began screaming. In an effort to quiet him, his mother unbuttoned her blouse and stuck a breast into his mouth, only to be interrupted by an officious conductor insisting she move to second class since her family had no tickets for first.

234

The woman argued passionately for a few minutes; then, becoming disgusted with him, yanked her breast from the baby's mouth, buttoned her blouse over it, and rising like a furious queen commanded her husband and eight children to follow her into second class. As we all watched the woman vainly struggling against the crush in the aisle, the conductor experienced a sudden change of heart, and roared out an edict to the effect that all distinctions between first and second class were henceforth abolished because of the unusually crowded conditions. "Signora," he yelled. "Come back to your seat." When the woman hesitated, he gallantly took the infant from her arms and led the way back, obviously delighted to prove that he was a man of compassion. His behavior nearly succeeded in impressing all of us, but just as he was ready to return the squawking infant to his mother, the baby urinated all over his sleeve.

In retrospect this became the only agreeable episode in the happening. Fifteen miles from Agrigento, in front of a village train station, the hubbub ceased as did all movement, and our long ordeal began. The first indication that anything was wrong came when we realized that all the conductors had disappeared. About an hour later four policemen ploughed their way through the aisles, looking neither right nor left, leaving in their wake the rumor that one passenger had stabbed another in the hand while quarreling over a seat. A half hour later the rumor returned in modified form: no one had been stabbed, a man had cut his hand on the train door. The presence of the policemen on the train remained unexplained. By now there was no one to ask; the policemen had also disappeared.

As darkness blotted out the scenery, none of the passengers appeared perturbed by the mysterious delay, nor did any of them show the slightest interest in its cause. Except for the complaints about the stifling heat, the general atmosphere was one of silent resignation. My main activity during this phase of the night was to open and shut a window for an elderly dictatorial woman who had alternate fears of catching pneumonia and dying by suffocation. Threatening to vomit if she did not have fresh air at once, she would demand I open the window; a few minutes later, she would grumble that the night air was dangerous and order me to shut it. Now and then a woman who was her daughter would rise from her seat at the other end of the train and ask her how she felt. The mother would shrug with the petulance of a spoiled matriarch and display a long-suffering expression of woe that promised nothing. Yet in another respect she was a tower of strength, an uncomplaining mattress for three small children who, tiring of standing in the aisles, had piled on top of her big peasant body and fallen fast asleep.

When more than two hours had passed and no one yet knew the reason for the standstill, I suggested to some of the young men standing near me that we form a delegation to request an explanation of the local stationmaster. "There is nothing to worry about," one of them said. "We paid for our tickets and sooner or later they will have to take us to Palermo." Another pointed out that it would be dangerous to leave the train; it might go off without us. A third ventured the theory that the conductors, policemen, and the stationmaster were probably all dining together. "As soon as they've finished their espresso, they will start the train again."

A little later a new report began to circulate which suggested an authentic explanation for the delay: the local stationmaster, alarmed at the crowded condition of the train, had refused to assume responsibility for letting it continue, and had insisted that empty passenger cars be sent to relieve the congestion. It was generally assumed that the empty cars would come from Agrigento which was close by, but an hour later word got around that the cars were being sent from Palermo.

In all the six hours of waiting the only complaints we heard were those that Patricia and I exchanged with one another. There was not a single burst of anger or rebellion; there were only sighs and groans of fatigue, interspersed with increasingly faint sallies of levity from the young men. At one point, when they saw me writing in a notebook, one of them asked: "Are you reminding yourself never to return to Sicily?"

The final (and most puzzling) act of the happening took place at one in the morning when a string of empty cars pulled up alongside our train. The conductors, who had been absent for six hours, suddenly reappeared and began announcing that there was no further need to stand in the aisles; passengers would find plenty of seats in the train that had arrived from Palermo. I had expected there would be a wild rush for the exits, but no one made any move to leave the train. Patricia and I considered leaving but were discouraged by the solid barrier of human bodies that stood between us and the door. The announcement was repeated three times but all of the passengers remained where they were, without even discussing the possibility of transferring to the empty cars. No one, except ourselves and the exasperated conductors, expressed any surprise that after their grueling ordeal the standing passengers would not jump at the chance to sit comfortably during the rest of the trip.

As we sped toward Palermo, I asked some of the young men around me why they had not availed themselves of the empty seats. "I've gotten accustomed to this train," one of them joked. "It's like a second home to me." Another replied: "I don't trust any of these conductors. How do we know they wouldn't try to charge us a second time for this trip?" A third one simply said: "I'm too tired to try anything new at this hour of the night." One of them, who was a college student, answered my question with two of his own: "How do we know what we would have found on the other train? Don't you think we've had enough uncertainty for one night?"

These answers from strong and young Sicilians underlined what I had already sensed: behind the passengers' refusal to improve their situation were apathy, suspicion, and resistance to any new experience—the dominating habits of mind that had been implanted in Sicilians by centuries of crushing oppression and vigilant self-preservation. But most Sicilians have a simpler excuse for their difficulties. It was identified in one word by the old matriarch for whom I had been opening and shutting the window a good part of the night. As we were stumbling out of the train at the Palermo station at four in the morning, the old woman was assuring her daughter that her father would not be angry with them for keeping him up all night. "He'll understand that it was *destinu.*"

Destinu, the most established of all Sicilian bogeymen.

A Visiting
Madonna

THE NEXT MORNING, still exhausted by the train experience, I met with the American Consul General and his staff to discuss Danilo's refusal to release me from my promise to speak in the Center's cultural series. His threat to issue a press statement that would blame the American government for my withdrawal from the series took them by surprise; no one imagined that a pacifist would take such a militant stand on so minor an issue.

"Well, how do you feel about your friend Dolci now?" asked Charles Stout, remembering, no doubt, my previous defense of him.

While I admitted being hurt by Danilo's refusal to consider my personal feelings in the matter, I made it clear that his stand did not change my basic opinion of him; if anything, it reaffirmed my impression that he is a man so completely dedicated to his mission that he will let nothing stand in his way. As I spoke, it occurred to me that Danilo's lack of personal consideration for his ex-collaborators may explain most of the defections that have taken place from his staff.

"Then you think he is pretty serious about his threat?" Robert Jordan asked.

When I said yes, the group agreed that, under the circumstances, I had no alternative but to participate in the series. As I left, the Consul General tried to cheer me. "The series may collapse by the time it gets around to you," he said. "Lecture series in Sicily seem to have a high mortality rate."

These words appeared prophetic as I returned to Partinico and found a worried Danilo on the telephone frantically trying to reach Renato Gattuso, the celebrated Sicilian painter who was to appear in the series that evening but of whom there had been no sign of life. "He must have forgotten all about it," Danilo groaned as he finished calling a friend of the painter in Venice who knew nothing of his whereabouts. "I've been telephoning all over Italy for the past three hours."

He finally gave up on Gattuso and concentrated on trying to find a substitute speaker. Eight times he tried to reach his old friend Carlo Levi in Rome, but each time the line was busy. He telephoned three or four other writers and artists, without any success, and grumbled, "I would be willing to fast for two days if I could get this thing settled."

In a burst of compassion, which I should have repressed as it was to my advantage to have the series collapse, I proposed the name of Bruno Caruso, the Sicilian artist I had met in Rome, and gave Danilo his telephone number. When he failed to get an answer, I suggested he try to trace him through Caruso's parents, who lived in Palermo. In a few seconds, to everyone's astonishment, Caruso himself was on the telephone. "Are you a mindreader?" Caruso asked. "I just arrived two minutes ago. Not even my parents knew I was coming."

Danilo described his predicament, mentioned the 10,000 invitations that had been mailed for the event, and soon convinced Caruso that no one was better qualified to take Gattuso's place. Joyous in his relief, Danilo pushed aside the telephone in a sweeping gesture and, grabbing my hand, kissed it and thanked me for my "great inspiration." Before I could take advantage of his gratitude to ask that he release me from my promise to participate in the series, he was out of his office and on his way home to lunch.

Dutifully, Patricia and I attended the Bruno Caruso meeting in Palermo that evening, along with the staff members of the Center. I found it even more disquieting than the Sciascia event. The polemics from the audience were more numerous and more blatant, and because the meeting was presided over by a science professor who lacked Danilo's firmness, the orators took advantage of the situation by monopolizing the microphone originally reserved for the speaker. Caruso satisfied the most extreme leftwing elements present by his repeated avowals that art should be the handmaiden of the people's revolution; but this did not diminish the oratory from the audience. The whole evening seemed like a dismal portent of what was in store for me.

While Danilo remained in Palermo to interview a newspaper publisher and an ex-assassin for his next book, Patricia and I returned to Partinico to attend a reception our landlord and his wife were giving for no less a personage than the Madonna del Ponte on the eve of her feast day, which is Partinico's chief religious event of the year. The reception took place in our landlord's living room, with a life-size wooden replica of the Madonna reclining on the dining room table for the guests to admire. Except for the total silence of the guest of honor, who had been rented from the nearby church for a few hours, the occasion was the closest thing to a cocktail party we had encountered on the Via Emma.

Dourness, the standard trait of Partinicans, gave way to conviviality as the guests drank toasts to the Madonna and enthusiastically briefed us on her history.

In the fifteenth century a Prince and his hunting party discovered the Madonna living in a cave. While the Prince was trying to persuade her to leave the cave and make her presence known to his people, she managed to escape him, leaving behind as the only evidence of the encounter a footprint on a bridge. To commemorate the episode, the Prince ordered a shrine built near the bridge and commanded his people to celebrate the Madonna del Ponte with an annual feast. After the Prince died, the shrine became the scene of an annual pitched battle between the men of Partinico and the men of Alcamo, who fought with knives to determine who would have the privilege of borrowing the statue of the Madonna for the celebration. Eventually, it was agreed that the Partinicans could have the Madonna provided they came for her before the stroke of noon; should they fail to do so, it was understood that the people of Alcamo would be entitled to borrow her from then on.

In order to make certain that the statue bearers arrive at the shrine on time, it has become the annual custom for hundreds of Partinican families to accompany them on the eight-mile trek.

With them they bring large quantities of wine and slaughtered sheep, which are roasted over open fires near the shrine and consumed before noon. "So far," the landlord told us, "the Partinicans have always arrived on time, despite the heavy drinking they do on the way. There is more punctuality among them on that day than there is the rest of the year."

The next afternoon Patricia and I joined the throngs moving toward the cemetery where the procession bearing the Madonna would make its entrance into Partinico. It was one of the few times when the women were permitted to show themselves without fear of censure, and they were taking full advantage of the opportunity. They were everywhere—in doorways, on balconies and even on rooftops. The married women were in the streets with their husbands and children, a rare sight in Sicily where men prefer to socialize with one another and leave their families at home. For once, the ponderous masculinity of the town was absent.

The mood became solemn when the Madonna entered the outskirts of the town, preceded by four hundred supplicants, men and women of all ages bearing lighted candles in an attitude of pious concentration. The Madonna rode on the shoulders of twenty-four men who, for some unknown reason, wore pirate costumes with blue kerchiefs tied around their heads. Behind them came a contingent of twenty cornet and trumpet players and a single drummer, whose huge instrument sat on the shoulders of two young boys. Last in the procession were the Partinicans who had gone to the shrine that morning to make certain the statue bearers got there on time; after all their marching, drinking, and consuming of roast sheep, they looked like groggy sleepwalkers.

Only the drummer was performing as we came on the scene, booming out a rhythm that had the dark overtones of an African dirge. Yet once the procession had passed the cemetery, its spirit suddenly became exultant, and the band burst into a brassy song of joy. While the crowd shouted in a frenzy of applause, the Madonna was transferred from the shoulders of the pirates into an oval frame of red and yellow electric lights that sat on a two-wheeled cart. As the Madonna was fixed into her gaudy niche, the band increased its volume and a bomb exploded to initiate the first of two consecutive fireworks displays.

241

The announcement that the first display had been awarded the prize money precipitated a bitter storm of protest from the losing pyrotechnician. Soon the loser, the winner, and the judges were engaged in a roaring argument that threatened to explode in physical violence. I was mystified to note that the crowd, including the policemen, seemed more amused than perturbed by the fighting until an elderly man near us explained that it was a mock battle, staged every year to provide the audience with some extra entertainment. "No matter who is announced as the winner, the two men always divide the prize money."

We fell in behind the procession with the old man and two of his friends and followed it as it moved toward the center of the town. Every few yards the men pushing the Madonna's cart would stop the march to solicit money from the townspeople lining the sides of the street in solid blocks. There was a long ceremonial stop in front of the town hall when the church bells pealed madly, while the mayor and his family appeared on the balcony of the municipal building, their faces dead white, their eyes squinting, in the glare of the spotlights. The lights were then turned on two new contingents of marchers joining the procession: the priests of Partinico robed in scarlet vestments and, after them, a group of the town's most devout Catholics, our landlord among them, who stole the show with the elaborate candelabra they carried high on long poles. In the enveloping twilight the procession became an Arabian Nights extravaganza, an exotic show of force against those who would sever Sicily's umbilical cord with the past.

Relieved to hear we were *Americani,* not *Tedeschi,* as he had supposed, the old man displayed a Department of Justice card identifying him as a bona fide resident alien of the United States. Two years before, when he became a widower, he went to Detroit to live with his son, a prosperous cabinetmaker who resides in the suburbs with his Polish wife and six children. After a year the old man got bored because he could not find a soul in the neighborhood with whom he could speak Italian or Sicilian, and returned to Partinico. "I am eighty-one years old," he said, "too old to travel or learn another language. If my son and his family ever want to see me again, they will have to come to Partinico."

One of his two companions, a well-to-do farmer, had never traveled anywhere but he could not imagine a more agreeable town in the world than Partinico. "What is the point of going anywhere else? We all like it here, and everyone is well off."

The other companion, a middle-aged bachelor, cited the large number of retired policemen who settled in Partinico, though they hailed from other parts of the country, as proof that there was no better town in Sicily. The old man could not agree with that. "The reason the policemen stay here after they retire is because they are married to local women who won't let them go anywhere else."

The bachelor regarded him with amazement. "You mean to say that a policeman would let himself be bossed by his wife?"

"It happens," the old man said dryly.

"It is God's way of getting even with policemen," the farmer said.

The three men were intrigued to learn my reason for being in Partinico; it was the first time they had spoken with anyone who knew Danilo in person.

"Frankly, Danilo Dolci has always been a mystery to us," the bachelor said. "Although he goes on fasts, just as devout Catholics do, you never see him in church or in the company of priests. No one is sure what he is up to. A cousin of mine who works at the postoffice says that a great deal of his money comes from foreign countries. Now why would foreign countries send him money unless they had their reasons? So we ask ourselves what those reasons might be . . ."

"There is far too much speculation about Danilo Dolci," the old man said impatiently. "The simple fact of the matter is that he is trying to start a Protestant religion in Sicily and that takes quite a bit of money. Since he can't get any money from the Italians, he gets it wherever he can."

The farmer, who had surreptitiously fallen behind the others, quietly signaled me to join him. "Danilo represents a secret," he whispered, "and I know what that secret is. The man is a spy. I don't know which country he is working for—I think it must be Russia or America—but there is no doubt in my mind that he is a spy."

By now the band had dropped out of the procession, leaving

only the drummer to beat out his brooding African rhythms. The old man informed us that the procession would continue all night until it had passed through every principal street. After that the Madonna would be carried into the town Cathedral where she would remain until August, when there would be a second festival for her.

"You must try to come to the second festival," the bachelor said when we announced our intention of going to bed. "You'll see fewer priests and much more gaiety. There will be horse races and group singing . . ."

"Also group drinking," the old man said.

They would not say goodnight until they had treated us to a candy that is prepared especially for the feast day, a green and pink nougat with an intensely sweet flavor. "If you eat it all, you will have the Madonna's blessing all year around," the farmer told Patricia. "Every wife in Partinico makes sure she eats at least one of these candies during the festivals."

When we inquired about his wife, he replied that she was home. "Later on I may take her for a walk. But this evening I wanted to be with my friends."

At three in the morning I was awakened by an exploding bomb that signaled the Madonna's entrance into the Cathedral. Patricia was already awake. "Thanks to the Madonna's blessing I haven't been able to sleep," she said. "Do you remember where you put the bicarbonate?"

The next day I kept an appointment my landlord had made for me with the priest in charge of the church near the Via Emma. While I waited for him in a gloomy reception alcove, I fell into conversation with a twitchy skeleton who, not to my surprise, turned out to be the culprit whose furious bell-ringing transformed the neighborhood into bedlam. As I watched his fingers convulsively torturing one another like wrestlers, I commented that his job must keep him occupied all day long.

"Not any longer," he replied morosely. "I used to ring the bells all day long when someone in the parish died, but they won't let me do that any more. No matter how many people of our parish die in a single day, I ring the bells only three times."

244

"Only three times?" I asked skeptically.

"Only three times," he repeated.

But I could not believe him, and I became even more convinced that bell-ringing was compulsive therapy that his nervous system required to retain any semblance to a system.

Father Alfano utilized the first few minutes of the interview to impress me with his earthy charm, then launched a tirade against Danilo which did not end until a telephone call summoned him to the bedside of a dying parishioner.

"As a priest I cannot speak badly of anyone, even of Danilo Dolci," he began, "but I can tell you this: he is a man who is interested only in himself. Millions of lire have poured into his pockets, but has he ever spent any of it to help the Sicilian people? Never. He spends most of it building up his personal fame . . ."

"What about his efforts to get the Jato dam built?" I interrupted, weary of hearing such cliché criticism.

The priest made a face. "He had nothing to do with it. The Jato dam has been planned and discussed since 1911. I can show you government documents to prove that."

"Isn't it possible that without Danilo Dolci the dam would still be in the discussion stage?"

"That is possible," he conceded. "But who needs the dam? It won't help anybody. We already have fine water. Have you tasted our Partinico vegetables and fruit? Aren't they wonderful? Why should these vegetables and fruit have more water when they do very well with what water there is? Moreover, we don't export our produce; we consume it right here. Ergo, there is no need to grow more vegetables and fruit, and there is no need for more water. Logical? In the distant future a dam may provide a means for cheaper electric power, but for the present it only creates problems . . .

"Another thing we don't like about Danilo Dolci is that he is vague about his religious attitude. Although we know he is not a Catholic, we don't know what he is. He attracts a great many Protestants in Sicily as well as some Catholics who don't know any better. He fools everyone, and he doesn't hesitate to use the Catholic Church as a cover for his deception. Do you see this magazine?" He held up a copy of *Orrozonti*. "It is supposed to be one of the most intelligent Catholic periodicals published in Italy. Yet when I wrote the editor to inform him that Dolci was really doing nothing for the Sicilians, do you know what happened? He published my letter with an editorial note saying that he disagreed with me because he was certain that Dolci was succeeding in 'moving the waters' in Sicily. Can you imagine?

"As a Sicilian what I resent most about him is his determination to have the world believe that nothing improves here. He never tells people that gradually things are getting better. Ten years ago, for example, there were no sewer pipes in Partinico. Now we have some . . ."

I reminded the priest that it was ten years ago that Danilo arrived in Partinico.

"Mere coincidence," he replied. "Things change in spite of Danilo Dolci, not because of him. He is not a man who will get very far with our people. He is not one of them and has no real connection with them. No one in Partinico treats him like a great social reformer or like the Gandhi of Sicily, as he likes to consider himself. People keep their distance and he is wise enough not to get too close to them. Actually, he is no more interested in the Sicilian people than an Eskimo would be. All he cares about is making a big impression on the foreigners who send him his money . . ."

He was interrupted by a telephone call from a woman who was afraid her father would die before the priest could get to him. As we parted, he said: "Tell your countrymen that we are not so badly off here as Danilo Dolci would have them believe. I visited St. Louis a few years ago and saw worse conditions there than those we have in Partinico. Yet America is considered a progressive country, is it not?"

I did not see the bell-ringer on my way out, but as I approached the Via Emma I heard his bells again, pummeling the neighborhood like demented demons.

Crisis at
the Dam

UNLIKE SOME of the other Communists I knew in Partinico, my landlord's son-in-law, the barber, had refused to attend the Feast of the Madonna and expressed disgust for those comrades who had. "The only feast day that should concern workers and their families is May Day."

As usual, his father-in-law disagreed with him. "The blessed Madonna with her long record of miracles gives people greater hope and comfort than all the May Day politicians and their promises put together."

"My father-in-law is a religious cretin," the barber said as soon as we were alone with him. He urged us to attend the May Day celebration that would take place on the site of the Jato dam. "You will find it far more impressive than any Feast of the Madonna."

But he was wrong. Despite free bus transportation to the dam and the promise of a modern jazz band, most of the townspeople stayed home. The few who came were chiefly dam workers and their families. They brought with them chunks of meat which they roasted over open fires near the shade of olive trees. While they picnicked, a sextet of young men in pink tuxedo jackets performed rock and roll numbers and a girl, who could not have been more than fourteen, sang at a microphone in a throaty, sexy voice that seemed grotesque coming out of a body so young. A few young teen-agers moved their bodies in a variation of the twist but

247

their movements were self-conscious and awkward; they were obviously imitating what they had watched on television.

Arriving after we had lunched in Partinico, Patricia and I wandered among the olive groves until we spotted Danilo and his family under a large tree. Vincenzina was bent over a fire roasting pieces of mutton. All five children were perched on the tree's lower branches, quiet while they munched. Danilo was sprawled on the ground with a book in one hand and a hunk of bread in another. Dressed in a white cap, white shirt and light gray trousers, he looked like one of Renoir's brawny picnickers. While he ate, I told him about two of the Partinicans I had met during the procession of the Madonna, the man who was convinced that Danilo was a spy and his friend who believed that his mission in Sicily was to start a new Protestant religion.

The townspeople's attitude toward him was a constant source of wonder, Danilo said. One day a neighbor in Spine Sante had taken him aside and said: "Danilo, I finally realize what your religion is. There has been a great deal of speculation on the subject but I am sure I have the correct answer. But you need not fear I will tell anyone; I will keep it a secret." Curious, Danilo had asked the neighbor what religion he had in mind. "You are a sun worshiper," the neighbor said, and explained he had arrived at this conclusion after observing how frequently and with what reverence Danilo and his family watched the sun set.

Danilo glanced at his wristwatch and rose. The May Day speeches were about to start and he said it was important that he be seen in the audience (that may have explained the white cap). However, he added, he would leave at once if a certain Fiorino showed up. He was the Socialist leader who was said to have persuaded his party to boycott the Roccamena demonstration in March. "I don't want people to become confused. I want to make it absolutely clear that there can be no collaboration between me and a man who works with *mafiosi* elements."

Fiorino did not appear and Danilo remained throughout the two speeches in the center of a small standing audience, in deep concentration. Hardly anyone else listened to the oratory. The first speaker was a leftwing Socialist party hack who spoke euphoniously about the glorious future in store for the Sicilian labor movement without giving any details. The second was a young Communist, a recent university graduate, who used long words to expound on the current generalizations of his party. He spoke at length about the need to resist the "obscene activities" of the imperialists in Vietnam and South America; he touched lightly on the progress of the Jato dam and even more lightly on "our good friend" Danilo, then wound up with an encomium on the working class's eventual triumph over the evils of capitalism.

Danilo applauded politely at the end of each speech, but on our way back to Partinico complained that both speakers were "stuffed with clichés" and had said nothing that was meaningful to the people of Partinico. "The arrangements committee selected them because of their skill with the Italian language. It would have been better if they had selected a couple of speakers who could talk specifically about local problems that Partinicans are concerned about, no matter how ungrammatically they spoke."

But it was unlike Danilo to be completely negative about any situation. "'What made the whole affair worthwhile was neither the speechmaking nor that miserable music but the sight of families enjoying each other's company in the olive grove. Don't you agree that was a beautiful sight?"

That evening Danilo, Patricia, and I dined in Palermo with Leslie Blackensee, a retired English businessman in his sixties who, through his participation in the Danilo Dolci committee in England, had become an ardent champion of Danilo and his cause. The two men had met in London the year before and, despite language barriers, had become good friends. Blackensee was tall and gangly, vigorously English; whenever he spoke his sharp nasal voice rose and fell, as though he were conducting deep-breathing exercises while verbalizing.

The Englishman took copious notes while I briefed him on the latest developments at the Center, which included the fact that only that morning Kenneth Bennett had written to say that Oxfam had voted a grant of 2,000 pounds toward the maintenance of the Center's new institute in its first year. The news that interested Blackensee most was that more than eighty members of the Swedish Parliament had recently nominated Danilo for the Nobel Peace Prize.

249

He pointed out that were Danilo to win the prize, the English committee and all the other Danilo Dolci committees would have an easier time raising funds for the Center.

"Certainly there would be advantages to winning it," Danilo agreed. "But there would also be certain disadvantages. For one thing, it might hinder my work. As Italy's first Nobel Peace Prize winner, I would become a national monument. At the age of forty-one I don't consider that an agreeable prospect. People would no longer feel free to speak with me naturally. There would be more respect and less frankness in their discussions."

Blackensee wanted to know what he would do with the prize money should he win the award.

"Franco and I have already discussed that," Danilo replied. "We would use the money to step up our campaign against the Mafia. Every year we would offer a prize of a half million lire for the best analysis of the Mafia activity in a particular community. Exposing the Mafia with documented information is one of the most effective techniques I know for wiping it out."

The general lack of efficiency in Sicily became a topic of discussion at the gourmet restaurant where we dined. Underlining its scarcity, Danilo quoted an executive officer of the Banco di Sicilia who had told him that "it is easier to find a billion lire in Sicily than it is to find a reliable employee for our staff." Danilo added that the same bank was a notable example of inefficiency. Some years earlier when he was trying to gather statistics on unemployment in Sicily, he had called on one of its directors and requested whatever data the bank had. The director, who had not caught his name, told him that the only person in Sicily who might have such information was Danilo Dolci.

As he bemoaned the inefficiency that also prevailed in the national Italian government, Danilo asked how the British felt about the present government in Rome.

"The British pay no attention to matters of that kind," Blackensee replied. "Those over eighteen think of nothing but sports. Those under eighteen think only of the Beatles. Both groups, however, are interested in anything that is said or printed about any sex scandal . . ."

Failing to appreciate Blackensee's humor, Danilo persisted with his question. This time Blackensee answered it by saying that the

British can't tell one foreign government from another. "They usually ignore foreigners. The only foreigners they paid any attention to were Hitler and Mussolini during the war, Eisenhower and Kennedy after the war. And now they pay attention to Danilo Dolci."

In a more sober vein he added that the average Englishman is interested mainly in those events that might have an influence on his life, "such as the war in Vietnam because it might lead to a bigger war that might involve England. Actually, only one percent of our population knows what is going on or cares . . ."

Danilo expressed surprise. "Each time I have visited England I have met men and women who are extremely well-informed and have a broad perspective on world affairs."

"We carefully see to it that you meet no one else," Blackensee said. "Seriously," he added, "you're apt to encounter only the cream of the crop—the Englishmen who are concerned with what is happening in Sicily and in other places where people need help. I wish there were more of them."

While we were exchanging goodnights at Blackensee's hotel (the same one that Patricia and I had used on our arrival in Sicily), I happened to use the word "Mafia" and was at once shushed by Danilo, who said it was unwise to use the word indiscriminately in Palermo, particularly at this hotel, which was renowned as a traditional meeting place for Mafia chiefs.

"What luck for me to be staying here." Blackensee laughed. "My dreams are bound to be more interesting tonight than they have been lately. So this is where the Mafia people meet!" His piercing voice carried through the lobby; everyone in it turned to look at us.

"A good thing the Mafia doesn't bother with foreigners," Danilo murmured as we hurriedly left.

The evening had been a success. Blackensee had arrived in Palermo at a time when the Center was in bad financial straits. Although no mention had been made of this fact, the Englishman seemed to sense it, and we both felt that he would use the information he had gathered about the Center's latest activities to try to prod the English committee into sending some extra funds as quickly as possible.

"It is gratifying to deal with a man like Blackensee who has such an intelligent understanding of our problems," Danilo said as he delivered us to our door on the Via Emma. "How could I possibly have managed this evening without you?"

"You would have found a way, Danilo," I replied. And I was certain that was so. I have never known a more resourceful man.

Danilo's resourcefulness, his talent for taking prompt and positive action in any situation, became indelibly impressed on me three days later when a major crisis developed at the Jato dam. Until then its construction, which was started in February 1963, had proceeded in fairly orderly fashion with no serious interruptions, despite earlier threats of the Mafia to sabotage it. Now, out of the blue, the company charged with the construction of the dam had issued orders for a mass layoff.

I was interviewing Danilo in his office when seven grim-faced dam workers, still in their overalls, barged in, drew up chairs around his desk, and informed him of the news. Some 180 men were to be released from their jobs on the following Monday, apparently because the Cassa di Mezzogiorno, which controlled the government financing of the project, and the construction company had not yet reached an agreement on a new wage scale. The gray-haired spokesman of the group asked Danilo what the workers should do to counter the layoff.

Although he had no official role in the construction of the dam, the workers recognized him as the prime mover in getting the dam built. In September 1962 when it became evident that the Mafia was succeeding in its efforts to have the project shelved indefinitely, Danilo had gone on a nine-day fast, his first in five years, which had the effect of pressuring the government into eliminating all the obstacles causing the delay. Danilo, like an anxious guardian angel, had kept a close eye on the construction ever since, never hesitating to demand action from the authorities in Rome whenever anything threatened its progress.

The attitude of the seven men was not that of a group asking for favors; they treated Danilo with no more deference than they might have for a union shop steward whose advice they trusted because of his superior experience in such matters. Danilo lost no time getting to the heart of the matter. It would be a serious

252

mistake in strategy, he told the men, to make an issue of the wage question; that was something for the government and the construction company to settle between themselves. Their chief aim must be to prevent the layoff. To accomplish this they must stage a demonstration that would dramatize their situation vividly enough to receive wide press coverage.

"You must occupy the tunnels because that is where you are doing most of your work just now," he said, "and you must refuse to budge until the layoff order has been rescinded. But before that happens you must acquaint the press with your problem; they must carry articles about the layoff as quickly as possible, so that when the tunnels are occupied both the public and the government authorities will understand the reason for the action. The occupation itself should be kept a close secret until it takes place. It will draw more attention if it comes as a surprise and also, of course, the police won't be at the tunnels to stop you from entering them. I will be with you when the tunnels are occupied . . ."

A small scrawny worker sitting next to me shouted in a shrill voice: "Danilo is right. We must create a scandal. Our slogan will be: 'Our babies and our families must eat.' "

"I don't agree, Danilo," the spokesman said, "that we should occupy the tunnels. The police will station themselves at the entrances and we'll be cooped up in there like chickens. It would be better if we occupied the barracks and the kitchens and in that way prevented the technicians and foremen, who are not being laid off, from staying at the dam. Why should the gang foremen continue collecting wages when there won't be any gangs to boss?"

"Yours should not be an action against any other workers," Danilo replied. "Your main objective should be to let the work continue for everyone. As for being at the mercy of the police, do you really think they would harm any of us? They wouldn't dare, especially with me among you." He smiled. "I don't say this because I consider myself in any way superior to you or any of your comrades; but the police would realize that if any harm came to any of us, my presence in the tunnel would create publicity in many parts of the world. The local authorities don't want to be responsible for trouble of that kind; they prefer to have Rome shoulder the responsibility for whatever goes wrong here . . ."

The spokesman offered no further objections and everyone appeared to agree with Danilo's point of view. The only voice heard was that of the scrawny man shouting: "We'll sit in those tunnels until they let us work again."

"The timing is important," Danilo said. "The occupation of the tunnels should take place while you are still officially on the payroll. I would suggest Saturday."

A short, blond man who had said nothing so far spoke up: "Saturday would be too late. It would not leave enough time for the government and the construction company to get together and resolve the situation. I think we should start the demonstration the day after tomorrow, on Thursday, or at the latest on Friday."

Danilo was the first to admit that the worker was right, and suggested that a general meeting of all the dam workers and their families be held just before the occupation of the tunnels to work out the final details. The conference ended with the little man shouting more sloganlike phrases. Then each of the men shook hands with us as they left.

Danilo sighed when they were all gone. "A crisis of this seriousness should be taken up with their unions, not with me, but there is no leadership in those unions, except the spurious kind represented by those May Day orators we heard. So they come here for help. . . . More and more as I gather material for my book I find a lack of organization on all levels of Sicilian society. I've been interviewing Communists lately on the subject of group action, and you know what they tell me? That there is little or no organization in their party. They tell me this in detail, knowing full well I will publish their observations . . ."

He interrupted himself and reached for the telephone. "I must make sure that the newspapers know about the layoff."

The dam workers asked Danilo to attend their general meeting but he refused to do so on the grounds that they must make their own final decisions. Without his presence to bolster their courage, the men succumbed to the fears of the majority and rejected the idea of sitting in the tunnels for an indefinite period; they voted instead to occupy some of the barracks and the area adjoining them. "The thought of sitting in those muddy tunnels and catch-

254

ing pneumonia or suffering from suffocation didn't appeal to many of us," one of the workers told me. "We decided our health was more important than any extra publicity we might get. Danilo may be a superman but we are not."

Nor did the workers accept the suggestion that the dam be occupied before the end of the work week. Afraid the construction company would withhold their salaries if they did so, they waited until they had been paid for the week. Thus it was not until Sunday, the day before the layoff order was to go into effect, that they converged at the dam and declared their intention of remaining there until the order was canceled. Only half of the 180 men affected by the layoff turned up. Danilo explained that some of the absent workers had families they could not leave alone and some had prison records and were afraid of being arrested. "There are also the cynics," Danilo said, "those who have no faith in group action. The encouraging thing is that there are this many who have that faith and the courage to act on it."

Minutes after the occupation the police arrived and took up quarters in a wooden structure on the grounds known as the administration building. All day long high-ranking officials came and went, observing the conduct of the men and holding whispered conferences. True to a prediction Danilo had made earlier, the police made no effort to eject anyone from the site of the dam nor was anyone threatened with arrest. By evening, it had become evident that the police would do nothing more than keep tabs on the dam workers. Whether this policy was determined in Rome, Palermo, or Partinico no one could say for certain, but Danilo was convinced it must have been influenced by the precedent established in March by the occupation of the public square in Roccamena.

From the outset of the occupation, the workers accepted Danilo's leadership unquestioningly. Although few of them may have understood his motives for involving himself so directly with their problems, they seemed to trust him much more than they trusted one another. He became the chairman of all their meetings, the organizer of their activities, and their chief spokesman in every encounter with the representatives of the construction company and the government. While performing these various roles, he con-

255

ducted a vigorous campaign to make the workers more aware of democratic procedure, constantly drumming at the importance of thinking as individuals and taking action as a group.

His most trying problem became maintaining the morale of the men, in face of the fear that their families might go without food. There was enough food for the men themselves, mostly bread and macaroni donated by the merchants of Partinico, but the problem of how their wives and children would fare once they had no more money worried them more than anything else. One worker, whose family had already spent its last lira, expressed the anguish of his comrades the first evening they sat down for supper. As he looked at a piece of bread in his hand his body began to tremble like that of a man with the ague and tears rolled down his face. Throwing the bread on the floor he walked away from the table crying: "How can I possibly eat when my wife and children have nothing to eat tonight?"

Some of the workers could not bear being separated from their families. Every night three or four of them would sneak away after the others had gone to bed and spend the night with their wives. In the early morning, before their comrades were awake, they would return and pretend they had spent the night at the dam. One of these was the small man who had shouted slogans in Danilo's office. He and his family of five children lived in a one-room hovel not far from me on the Via Emma.

"Why can't arrangements be made to have the families join the men here?" I asked Danilo.

"The men would never permit such a thing. They firmly believe that a wife's place is in her home with her children."

"They don't seem to be critical when your family comes here to visit you," I observed.

"That's because I am not a Sicilian."

After the fourth day several of the men became bored or discouraged and returned to Partinico. One of those who left was a young tough by the name of Calogero, who was said to have been planted at the dam by the Mafia. At first his job had been that of security guard but when the other workers learned that he was a *mafioso* they demanded, through their trade union, that he be deprived of his security job and be made to do manual labor like the rest of them. "Good riddance," one of the workers said of him after his departure. "He was nothing but a goddam spy."

Danilo, noting my interest in the young *mafioso*, obligingly showed me some notes he had taken during an interview he had with him. The point of view they expressed was curiously similar to that I had encountered among young Fascist toughs of the thirties:

"I'm not one for workers' organizations but after I got married I decided I would join a union in order to have the booklet that entitles me to extra money and other benefits for having children. I signed up with the CISL because that is a union run by the Church and it is easier getting things through them. Nowadays the priests have a lot to say. If you help them, they will help you; they will find bread for your children. If you do favors for them at election time, they are bound to feel an obligation to help you . . .

"I have a very good impression of the military life. I went off as a soldier at the age of nineteen like a colt without testicles, without knowing the meaning of danger. I had never been outside my village, and I had many important experiences for the first time. Being a soldier smartened me up. I became less timid in my dealings with other men, and I became an expert with women. I had three and a half years of it and enjoyed all the discipline. There was order and I like order. There was someone to tell you what to do and there were the others who had to obey. That's the way it should always be."

The main events of each day were two meetings presided over by Danilo. The first took place immediately after breakfast and dealt with immediate problems, such as trying to collect more food from the merchants, putting more pressure on the local authorities to provide a welfare fund for needy families, establishing more effective sanitation methods, fixing new dormitory schedules so that the men who had been sleeping outdoors could exchange places with those who had been enjoying the luxury of indoor accommodations.

The purpose of the afternoon meeting was educational. It usually took place outdoors, and included whatever visitors might be present. Danilo never missed an opportunity to make these sessions as lively as possible. One morning he announced to the men that the afternoon meeting would be attended by twenty *dopo-scuola* teachers who were attending a training seminar in Trappeto conducted by the Center. When the men learned that more than half of the teachers would be young women, there was an instant rise of morale, followed by an extraordinary amount of shaving and washing.

That first meeting with the schoolteachers may have been an historical event for that part of the world, the first time perhaps that men and women who had not known each other previously came together for purposes of discussion. We all sat on rough planks arranged in a big square, just a few yards away from the building where the police had established their quarters. One of Danilo's currently favorite questions furnished the theme for the initial discussion: "What are some of the difficulties you have encountered working within a group?"

At first both the workers and the teachers seemed reluctant to speak frankly, but with Danilo expertly prodding them the discussion soon gained momentum, the barriers between the two groups dissolved, and there remained only the insistence to be heard. At one point Danilo interrupted the meeting when he noticed that a group of policemen near the administration building were obviously straining to hear what was being said. He shouted to them: "This discussion concerns you as well as the rest of us. Come closer so that you can hear us more easily." The policemen conferred with one another but no one made a move. "What are you afraid of?" Danilo persisted. "Come closer. Who knows? You may learn something useful." This time the youngest of the policemen stepped forward and stood near some of the workers.

"Bravo," Danilo cried, and led the meeting in a round of applause. He repeated the discussion theme for the sake of the young policeman, then called on one of the men who was eager to be heard. As I listened to all the comments I was again impressed by the talent of the average Sicilian, educated or not, to articulate his thoughts with an easy and often poetic flow of rhetoric. With the exception of the policeman, everyone at the meeting contributed to the discussion. These were some of the more representative observations made in reply to Danilo's question:

"The trouble with every group I've worked with is that there has been too much suspicion. Sicilians are afraid to trust one another."

"Everyone thinks only of himself."

"People are too afraid of their employers and this prevents them from acting intelligently."

"Sicilians suffer from either too much superiority or too much inferiority. This is one reason why they find it hard to accept the point of view of others."

"There is a Sicilian proverb that says: 'He who plays alone never loses.' Unfortunately, too many Sicilians take that proverb too seriously."

"Something is fundamentally wrong with education in Sicily. Too many of our people are still the victims of superstition and tradition. Their ignorance prevents them from accepting the concept of group action."

"There is always too much talk but no action. There are many decisions reached, but they are not carried out."

"Sicilians are too secretive for their own good."

"Sicilians haven't had enough experience in democratic procedure. How can they be expected to understand the advantages of group action?"

The liveliest part of the discussion came when Danilo narrowed the question to a specific point: "What about the difficulties of working within that group known as the family?"

One of the first to comment was a pretty schoolteacher with red hair. "The Sicilian father represents a type of dictator who runs his family accordingly," she said. "He usually assumes that no one in the family can be trusted, particularly his wife and his daughters. He demands respect from every member of the family and will either frighten or punish them in order to get it. Worst of all, he thinks he is always right."

Several of the workers disagreed with her. One man, who had fought in the war against Albania, said: "It is always the duty of children and wives to be obedient to the father because he is the head of the family. In Albania I saw wives who were kept blindfolded by their husbands so that they wouldn't look at other men. This comes out of the love that a man has for what is his. While we don't blindfold our wives in Sicily, we do hold them on a leash.

259

And our wives know that is good for them. If the woman and the children do as the father says, there is plenty of liberty for everyone in the family."

"If it weren't for fathers," another worker added, "children would grow up with bad manners. It is the father who tells his children how to conduct themselves with other people and how to tell the difference between those who wish you well and those who wish you ill. The saddest children are orphans because they have no fathers to guide them through life."

"It isn't their advice we object to," another young woman said. "It's their tyrannical attitude. How can we ever have democracy in our society if we don't have it in the family?"

"Fathers don't always give their children good advice," a worker observed. "Some fathers I know praise their children when they rob. The only advice they give them is: 'Try not to be robbed.' "

The gray-haired spokesman I had met in Danilo's office commented: "To his sons a father gives advice as well as orders. To his daughters he gives orders without giving them advice. 'Don't stick your face outdoors; you'll catch cold.' What he means is 'Don't keep looking at the young men.' He doesn't explain what harm might come to her if she becomes involved with a young man because he thinks she will be shocked."

"If our daughters were so shockable, all of them would become nuns," one of his comrades joked.

"Unfortunately, too many of them do," another dam worker retorted.

Orazio, the young intellectual who resembled Chekhov, denounced "the great lack of community feeling between husband and wife, parents and children." "It comes from the average Sicilian's lack of faith in people, even in members of his own family. The same lack of faith is extended to relationships outside the family. But we children are as much to blame for all this as our parents. We who live in a new world and have experiences that are foreign to our parents don't lift a finger to educate them, to explain the value of working and thinking together . . ."

"That is easier said than done," snapped a recently widowed young schoolteacher who had a magnificent figure. "Parents should be open to new ideas but aren't. Parents should respect the

260

CRISIS AT THE DAM

personalities of their children but don't. Parents will get a great deal more obedience out of their daughters when they learn to trust them."

Danilo closed the discussion by summarizing the salient points made, then announced that the dam workers were extending an invitation to all visitors present to lunch with them. A few of the teachers, including the recently widowed one, accepted. The rest of us, suspecting that the workers could not afford to be generous with their limited food supply, made excuses and returned to Partinico.

Danilo's daily involvement with the workers provided me with my first opportunity to observe at close hand the effect of his personality on Sicilians of little education. It also provided me with a partial answer, at least, to the question that had long been on my mind: Could Danilo ever become a popular leader? I already knew how readily he could influence intellectuals, even those unaware of his heroic legend. But the same qualities that could impress intellectuals sometimes had little effect on non-intellectuals. I remembered how lukewarmly the workers at the Belice demonstration had received his talk, although it was the only substantial one of the lot. No silver-tongued orator, he is invariably precise, direct, and calm, without any of the rhetorical circumlocutions and histrionics that can win the hearts of mass audiences. Danilo has had his share of applause from large audiences, but it has usually been in foreign countries, when his interpreter has augmented his remarks with an emotionalism of his own.

During the occupation of the dam Danilo made no speeches. Whatever impression he made on the workers was chiefly through the language of action. They watched him constantly acting in their behalf as he conferred with officials who might be instrumental in restoring their jobs, stimulated publicity in the press, and enlisted the aid of a number of high-ranking politicians, including two senators who visited the dam and promised the workers their support.

The total absence of criticism of Danilo's leadership was perhaps the clearest indication of how the men felt toward him. That

261

and their willingness to follow his advice. Almost to a man they treated his suggestions as orders (sometimes to the distress of Danilo, who would have preferred more discussion) and showed him all the deference due to a respected leader, even to the extent of providing him with an honor guard to protect his privacy whenever he was resting or writing. Their general attitude toward him was not so much that of zealots fired by his teachings (despite the educational meetings) but that of willing soldiers anxious to obey a trusted field commander who might save them from disaster.

Whatever doubts some of the men may have had of Danilo's qualities as a leader were routed in the first days of the occupation by the zeal with which he applied himself to their varied problems, and by the naturalness with which he adapted himself to their primitive living conditions. He appropriated no special privileges for himself, and what was even more astonishing in an intellectual he was genuinely interested in what they had to say. Every day he would interview two or three workers and make careful notes of their statements for use in his next book. That a man of superior attainments would consider their opinions interesting enough to record augmented their awe of Danilo, without enhancing their understanding of him.

Occasionally Danilo would invite me to participate in his interviewing. One afternoon we talked with a man who was extremely well read (Dostoievsky was his favorite author) in spite of the fact that he had never spent a day in school. "I received most of my education in jail," he said. "As you know, there were many of us in this part of Sicily who were obliged to steal after the war in order to prevent our families from starving. I was one of those who got caught. Perhaps it was the best thing that could have happened to me, for if I hadn't gone to prison I would have remained an ignoramus and I would never have been able to read Dostoievsky . . ."

My question as to what first prompted him to learn to read produced an embarrassed reaction. Only after I had assured him that I would not use his name in my writings did he provide me with the answer.

"It all started with a letter my father wrote me shortly after I went to prison. Not being able to read it and having no idea it contained terrible news, I asked one of the prisoners to tell me what it said. What he told me was that my sister had become pregnant by a man who was nowhere to be found. I felt doubly dishonored—first because my sister had brought disgrace to our family; secondly because I had deliberately shared this scandalous information with a perfect stranger. Then and there I resolved I would learn to read any letter that came to me. . . . My sister died giving birth to her child, but by learning to read and write I became reborn."

A surprising number of the workers interviewed by Danilo had been to jail for stealing during the lean postwar years. None of them was ashamed of the fact; they had all robbed to feed their families. Giuseppe, a worker with a philosophical point of view, said: "Ever since the birth of the world men have worked and men have robbed. In bad times all kinds of men rob. When times are not so bad the timid ones work and the bold ones rob. The bold ones are usually the troublemakers; they not only rob but they also demand respect of those who don't rob. For example, one is obliged to say of a man who is the son of a *mafioso:* 'His father is a man with seven pairs of testicles because he has robbed and killed.' Too many Sicilians have a genuine admiration for such a father and that is unfortunate for everyone . . ."

Giuseppe continued: "People can be so damn ignorant. I once knew a man named Alongi who worked for a *padrone* called Russo. Alongi had worked for this man all of his life. When he became old and died, he left what little patrimony there was to his *padrone,* not to his grandchildren. He was so much under the thumb of his boss that he probably felt like a dog feels about his owner—a hunting dog that catches a rabbit and takes it straight back to the owner."

One of the dam workers was Sarridu, an old friend and former neighbor of Danilo, who had participated in a number of his demonstrations, including the famous strike in reverse. The job at the dam was the first regular work Sarridu had been able to find in sixteen years. He was more optimistic than Giuseppe: "Times are changing. The bosses are no longer the lords. Once the common people remained passive like pieces of salami. Now they are beginning to see the value of acting together. Things are different. Ruthless strength, the kind the *mafiosi* brag about, is not enough. What is beginning to matter is justice ..."

But his brown eyes became mournful as he spoke of his own situation. "If my work at the dam stops, where will I go? Back to my usual life, I suppose; back to hunting for snails. I will start reliving the old dirty life and feeling suffocated again."

At Danilo's suggestion the workers who were able to write prepared letters describing their plight and mailed them to the president of the Cassa di Mezzogiorno and other government officials. The letters, written after five days had passed with little or no indication that their jobs would be restored, reflected the fears and sorrows of all the men.

"You have no idea how happy I was when I was able to quit my job in Germany and find work at the dam close to my wife and babies," wrote a man named Carmelo Marullo. "But my happiness came to an end when we were laid off. For five days we have slept on the ground in the cool and damp of the night. If this goes on much longer, we'll all wind up being sick. But we are determined to defend our work and, if necessary, will remain here until we die."

A worker named Antonio Cinquemane, who was a reformed ex-*mafioso*, wrote: "There is a question I keep asking myself for which I can never find the right answer. Why is it that we southern Italians are tortured day and night by lack of work, that indispensable instrument of love and justice? It is as if the government were saying to all of us: 'Get the hell out of Italy. You are a stranger and for that you must be punished.' "

Giuseppe Lo Biondo, another neighbor of mine on the Via Emma, wrote: "I am a ditchdigger with seven children. Until last week I managed to feed my family with the miserable pay I received. Now, without work, you can imagine what darkness has descended on me and my family's future ..."

The man who had learned to read and write in jail wrote: "We must win this campaign; otherwise we shall all be ruined, for there is no other opportunity to work in these parts. In our hearts we all feel like workers, and we need to work. If we can't work, there will be all sorts of terrible consequences; for if a man can't provide for his family, he will have to turn to crime. But we are workers, not criminals, and we want to remain workers."

Danilo combined these excerpts from the letters into a statement for the press. The final excerpt, written by Domenico Campisi, summarized the situation of the workers as well as any: "I am the father of four children who in a few days will be crying for bread. No father can bear the tears of his hungry children without being driven to desperate straits. But apart from this problem, you must know that work is as essential to a man's soul as food is to his stomach. Please relieve our physical and spiritual anguish by giving us back our jobs as quickly as possible."

"For or Against
the Mafia?"

As THE DAYS AND NIGHTS of the occupation dragged on, Danilo by
his persistent efforts succeeded in bringing together various elements concerned with the construction of the dam that had long
been at each other's throats. Among these were the representatives
of the left- and rightwing trade unions, the CISL and the Camera
di Lavoro, the union to which the majority of the dam workers
belonged. At their meeting the two unions were able to agree on
common goals but only after the Camera di Lavoro had accepted
the CISL demand that Danilo's name be omitted from any publicity issued jointly by the unions. This ironical development
neither surprised nor disturbed Danilo, but Franco was furious
that the Camera di Lavoro, which for many years had leaned heavily on Danilo for help and guidance, should agree to anything of
the kind.

The other meeting which Danilo was instrumental in organizing brought together trade union representatives with government officials and engineers. The two groups placed the blame for
the layoff on the group not represented at the meeting, the construction company. The layoff, they declared, was nothing less
than a brazen method of putting pressure on the Cassa di Mezzogiorno for more construction funds. Danilo, who came to the
meeting armed with facts and figures, stole the show by counter-
ing the claim that the construction company had been employing
too many men. Presenting his analysis of the dam projects that still
needed to be completed (the carefulness of his analysis attested to

his architectural training), he was able to prove that at least one hundred more men would be needed to complete the construction of the dam on schedule.

I had been going to the dam every day but during the second week I was obliged to visit Palermo for several days to make final arrangements for Patricia's art exhibit at the headquarters of the United States Information Service. The opening of the show was a convivial and crowded affair that included nearly all the staff members of the Center, the employees of the U.S.I.S. and the American Consulate, as well as a wide variety of Sicilians, among them Rosita Lanza, who had just arrived from Rome to check on her birth control project.

Robert Jordan, who was the official host of the occasion, introduced me to an arrestingly beautiful woman who had come alone. She was a young English-speaking matron who lived nearby. On learning that I was gathering material for a book about modern Sicily, she asked if I intended to deal with the subject of the Mafia. It was not my main interest, I explained, but the subject was unavoidable in any discussion of western Sicily.

"I do hope you will write about the Mafia with more understanding than other writers have shown," she said. Then, before I could comment on that, she asked: "Tell me, are you for or against the Mafia?"

The question astonished me. "Are there people other than *mafiosi* who are *for* the Mafia?" I asked.

"Of course there are." It was clear that she was one of them. Before I could find out why anyone should be sympathetic to the Mafia, we were interrupted by some relatives of mine who had just arrived from Agrigento. She had gone when I looked for her again. Afterwards I learned that her husband was a successful Sicilian engineer busily involved in constructing Palermo apartment houses, a fact which shed considerable light on our brief conversation. Also busily involved in the Palermo construction business was the Mafia.

As we stepped off the bus in Partinico, we were greeted by the local detective who reminded us that our sojourn permits had expired and needed to be renewed. Apparently fearful that we might misconstrue his request as an act of unfriendliness, he then insisted on treating us to an espresso.

"How did the Signora's art exhibition go?" he asked when we got to the café.

Patricia expressed surprise that he should know about it.

"Knowing what is going on is my business, Signora," he said. "Moreover, I am a serious devotee of art . . ."

"Since you are so well informed," I said, "how are things at the dam progressing?"

"Very well it seems, thanks to Danilo Dolci. The workers are fortunate to have him working for them. Without him, they would long have become forgotten men. With him, they may succeed in getting their jobs back. And that would be good for everyone, including the police department. The more jobs there are the easier our work becomes. Believe me, it is no pleasure arresting poor bastards who steal out of necessity . . ."

When I brought up the subject of the Mafia, he said that its power invariably increased during hard times because a larger number of "honest men" turned to crime then. But he added that the Mafia was changing rapidly, leaving the small towns, where it had long been entrenched, and going into the cities, where there were greater possibilities for acquiring power and wealth. "The strongest members of the Mafia are now in Rome serving in the Government."

That afternoon I visited Danilo at the dam. After ten days of outdoor living, his fair skin had finally tanned. But although he looked healthy, he complained of exhaustion. "All the tension we've had at the dam has acted as a powerful stimulant, but now that I see some hope of having this affair come to an end I'm beginning to feel the full extent of my fatigue."

He and Franco were busy preparing job statistics for a series of conferences that were about to take place with representatives of the construction company and the government. "The prospects look encouraging," Danilo said. "I expect that ninety percent of the workers' demands will be met." He had decided not to participate in the conferences. "I don't want to be put in the position of arguing about details because that would detract from the general solutions I am proposing."

268

He yawned and grinned. "It will be good to be sleeping in my own bed for a change . . ."

At present his bed at home was being occupied by a middle-aged Swedish couple that had recently arrived for their annual visit to Partinico. The wife was the energetic executive secretary of the Friends of Dolci Committee in Stockholm. An unabashedly fervent disciple of Danilo, she and her husband had been coming to Partinico ever since 1958, when the Swedish committee was founded.

I met them that same evening. The husband was a benign bear of a man who, unable to speak any other language but Swedish, smiled at everything that was said. His wife spoke Italian and English brokenly but fluently; her only problem of communication stemmed from a tendency to do more talking than listening. A small blonde with a strong will, her devotion to Danilo over the years must have been nurtured by her awareness that in terms of will power she had met her match in him.

"Danilo keeps having trouble with his collaborators because he is a man who must have his own way," she said apropos of Eyvind Hytten, who was once her friend. "His collaborators have not always understood that his way is usually the wisest way; so they get angry with him and leave. But I don't worry about them. Danilo's most valuable collaborators, people like Lorenzo and Franco, will not desert him because they appreciate his true worth. What worries me sometimes is that not enough people realize how important Danilo is, not only to Sicily but to the whole world. His philosophy is good for everyone. He is truly a great man." She smiled. "Did you know that my husband and I are sleeping in his bed just now?"

Danilo and the charms of the Sicilian spring drew another foreign visitor the next day, this one the secretary of the Dolci committee in London. At Danilo's request, I met her at the bus station and escorted her to the hotel. As I took in the conventionality of her appearance and manner, I hoped that the bordello traffic at the hotel would be at a low ebb during her week's stay. She told me it was her first time in Sicily; her connection with the British committee was a recent one, made with the understanding that she

269

would have a free trip to Partinico in order that she could famil-
iarize herself with Danilo's projects.

In the afternoon the new visitor and the Swedish couple met in
our living room for cocktails before going out to dinner. At first
the Englishwoman seemed even more diffident than she had at the
bus station; she impressed me as a shy middle-aged lady who had
spent a lifetime imprisoning herself within a fortress of gentility.
But as she imbibed more vodka martinis an astonishing personality change took place. With each drink, her opinions became
stronger, her jawline firmer. Toward the end of the party, her diffi-
dence had vanished and the fortress had fallen. There emerged a
woman as resolute and aggressive as her Swedish counterpart.

Fascinated by the transformation, the Swedish woman openly
courted her, declaring at one point that she felt an affinity toward
her such as she had never felt toward any other English person.
"The English are too cold and too conservative. But you, my dear,
are different." As we were about to leave for the restaurant, she
went even further: "I feel, my dear, that you are an adventuress at
heart, just like myself."

The Englishwoman nodded gravely. "I am a tramp," she said
proudly. "It makes me unhappy to be in one place or at one job
for more than three years. My late husband was like me. When he
passed away after we had been married for twenty years, I was
afraid I would want to stay put." She paused to drain her drink.
"But I haven't and I won't," she said, her eyes flashing.

"You are my sister," the Swedish woman murmured, and helped
her on with her coat.

Ordinarily, the presence of foreigners at the dam, particularly
women, would have delighted the workers. But by now they had
become too discouraged to respond to such distractions. Few of
them shared Danilo's belief that they would win most of their
demands; they had little faith left in their union leadership, and
they were disgusted with the authorities in Partinico for not supporting their cause more energetically. How much their morale
had sagged soon became evident at one of Danilo's educational
meetings which included I. Vilfan, a high official in the Jugoslav

government, who had come to Sicily to be the next speaker in the Palermo cultural series.

The first question asked of Vilfan was how socialism was faring in his country. He replied that although Jugoslavia was too besieged with problems of unemployment and illiteracy to be considered a worker's Utopia, the country was better off than it had been twenty years before. The per capita income had risen from $120 a year to $500 and workers were participating in self-government to an increasing degree, even to the extent of deciding how their factories are to be run. "If the situation you have here at the dam were to exist in Jugoslavia," he added, "the director of the project, together with all the engineers, would be thrown out by a vote of the workers and replaced by more competent persons . . ."

"In this country, particularly in Sicily," one of the workers interjected, "the people who made the biggest mistakes get the biggest statues erected in their honor."

"In Jugoslavia we have confidence in the judgment of our workers," Vilfan continued. "We know that they make mistakes but they are honest mistakes and they are their own mistakes."

"The only time a worker has anything to say around here is at election time," another worker said. "But what happens? Some *mafioso* comes along with a few lire and buys his vote. It happens in Partinico during every election . . ."

"So what is wrong with that?" one of the men shouted without waiting to be recognized by Danilo.

"There's nothing wrong with that," the worker sitting next to him said. "We who want to get our jobs back have our special techniques for trying to get what we want. Senator Messeri has his own techniques. What if he does have friends who are willing to pay money for votes? It costs money to get anything you want. This strike would have ended long ago if we had been able to pour some money into the right pockets . . ."

There were shouts of disapproval, but one strong voice rose above the others with the ancient Sicilian slogan: "Everyone should mind his own business."

Danilo waited until the uproar had subsided, then asked in a tense voice: "Isn't it the business of everyone that we in Partinico are represented in Rome by a senator who utilizes the services

271

of a gangster to win his elections? Isn't it the business of everyone that the Mafia has repeatedly tried to prevent the building of the dam?"

The worker he was addressing replied: "Why talk about such matters? The subject cannot possibly interest our foreign guests." He gestured toward Vilfan, then toward the Swedes and the Englishwoman sitting near me.

"I for one am greatly interested in the subject," Vilfan said, "since my purpose in coming here was mainly to learn."

"Let's not be afraid to name names," a worker urged, "even though they are Mafia names. Coppola was the gangster who helped Messeri. And Centinnaio, may he rot in jail, was the *mafioso* who did his best to stop the dam project."

"Centinnaio," Danilo added, "received a sentence of four years for illegal manipulations of the lands which the government was trying to acquire for the construction of the dam. He is the man who objected to my efforts to get the dam built and who once told me I would be sorry if I continued with them."

"He is also the man who let it be known that bombs would be placed on the site of the dam if it ever got under way," Franco said.

"But we've never seen any bombs around here," a worker said.

"Wait until Centinnaio gets out of jail," another worker jeered. "Then you'll see them and hear them."

"Senator Messeri should also be in jail," my Via Emma neighbor said. "I am a Christian Democrat and I don't like the idea of a Christian Democrat senator depending on the friendship of a gangster to get himself elected."

"It's none of your business how he gets elected," snapped a worker who was my neighbor's brother-in-law.

"It's everybody's business," Franco said vehemently. "How can you ever hope to have a democratic kind of government working for your interests when you let a gangster determine how people shall vote?"

"I have never set eyes on Coppola the gangster or Messeri the senator," Danilo said, "but I am against these persons, not out of any personal animosity but because they hinder the development of this zone. We can't ask people to support projects like the dam

272

when we are represented in Rome by a man who works hand in glove with a criminal."

Franco, fixing his eyes on my neighbor's brother-in-law, added: "Our shame in Sicily is not so much that we have serious problems but that we do nothing to eliminate the evils that nourish those problems. That is our true and our horrible shame."

The meeting ended on this note.

The occupation of the dam suddenly came to an end two days later. I first heard the news from my Christian Democrat neighbor on the Via Emma, whose voice kept breaking as he told it to me. He had not been among those rehired. "They are calling it a victory for the workers but what kind of a victory is it when forty-seven of us are back on the street? They have agreed to give us some severance pay but how am I going to feed my seven children when that is gone?"

The construction company, with the consent of the unions, had agreed to retain only the men who had been employed on the dam for a year or more. My neighbor's term of employment had been for only three months. "I gave up my job in Switzerland when I heard there was work available at the dam, so that I could be with my family. Now I'll have to leave them again and see what I can find. God help me."

At the Center I found Franco putting the finishing touches on a news bulletin he was about to telephone the Palermo newspapers. It said nothing about the men who had lost their jobs. The first paragraph read: "On the streets of Partinico automobile and motorcycle horns blare as the workers of the Jato dam parade to demonstrate their joy for having won back their jobs. For twelve days and thirteen nights the dam workers valiantly resisted the layoff orders of the Vianini Construction Company. This morning union representatives meeting with the Commissioner of Labor and agents of the construction company were finally able to reach an agreement that will enable the construction of the dam to continue without any further loss of time."

Chapter

14

The Killers
of Carnevale

THE SWEDISH COUPLE relinquished their bed at the Dolci home for one at the hotel, but Danilo had little time to use it. No sooner had he come home from the dam than he plunged into the onerous task of trying to assemble local and regional officials to discuss ways and means of increasing employment in the area.

Watching him hard at work on a Sunday morning, Franco and I offered to cancel the automobile trip we had planned for that day in order to give him a hand, but Danilo would not hear of it. Inasmuch as my sojourn in Partinico was drawing to a close, he argued, I owed it to my project to have further discussions with Franco. "Besides," he added, "after spending more than twelve days and nights with nearly one hundred men, I need to be alone for at least one full day."

Accompanied by Franco's wife and children, we first journeyed to the outskirts of Bagheria, east of Palermo, where we inspected the palace and grounds of the Prince of Palagonia, an eighteenth-century madman who had succeeded in imposing the dictates of his insanity on the world around him, chiefly in the form of sculpture. The palpable evidence of the Prince's monstrous vision leers at mankind from the rooftops. Arranged in tidy rows are sixty-two statues of hunchbacks, dwarfs, and cripples, each one a vivid rendition of human ugliness. The Prince himself was no sculptor but whenever a friend or relative incited his ire he would give vent to his hatred by drawing his concept of that person, and commissioning a sculptor to translate the drawing into stone.

274

Our guide was an old woman with a gargoyle face and buck teeth who, in petrified form, would have easily fitted into the macabre lineup on the rooftops. The reason she knew the Prince's history intimately, she explained, was that she was the direct descendant of one of his most trusted servants, "the same one who discovered the Princess cuckolding her husband in the bathroom, with two men at the same time." She showed us a long single-story building containing rows of rooms where the Prince's three hundred servants once lived. "The Prince knew the servants by number, never by name. When people try to tell me there has been no progress in Sicily, I remind them that the only Sicilians who are now known by number are those in jail."

From Bagheria we drove up the coast to Cefalu and ate our lunch on a hill overlooking the sea and the city. Franco's wife, whose classical loveliness reminded me of a dancing girl on an Etruscan vase, entertained us with an amusing account of her experiences as a dress designer for the wealthy but stingy ladies of Palermo. "Fortunately, they pay enough to keep us out of debt," Franco said. "I don't know how we would manage without this extra income." He expressed concern about the current financial crisis at the Center; there was not enough money to meet the next payroll. "I'm lucky to have a wife who can earn extra money but I worry about the others who have families with children . . ."

Franco informed me that a man who had often pulled the Center out of the red was Edoardo Watjen, a staunch German disciple of Danilo, who was expected to arrive for his annual visit the following week. "If the British committee can't send any extra funds, perhaps Edoardo will have some suggestions for raising money quickly."

I looked forward to meeting Watjen. He was a lawyer and a philosopher, the Center's chief advisor and its self-appointed international missionary. As a firm believer in Danilo's ideology of nonviolent revolution, he had been instrumental in establishing groups similar to the Center in such underdeveloped regions as Algeria and Turkey. During the war he had played an important role in the German underground and figured in the plot of the German generals to assassinate Hitler. His association with Danilo began in 1958 when, lured by Danilo's exploits and writings, he came to Partinico with his car and served as a volunteer chauffeur

for the Center until his more intellectual capabilities became recognized.

"You will enjoy Edoardo," Franco said. "He speaks English
fluently because his mother was an American. Through her he is
related to some very wealthy capitalists, a fact which he seems to
find embarrassing, probably because he is a Marxist. But he is not
a Marxist in the usual sense of the word. You could almost say that
he is a Marxist mystic, except that none of the mystics I've known
love to talk as much as Edoardo does . . ."

After the picnic we went east for a few miles to the village of
Santo Stefano di Camastra, which is filled with ceramists. Franco
and his wife led us to their favorite shop where they haggled in our
behalf as we bought a half dozen hand-painted giant butterflies
and an assortment of tiles. It was now time to head back to
Palermo, but after traveling a few miles Franco impulsively
turned into a road leading to Sciara, the village where Salvatore
Carnevale had been murdered. Of the thirty-five Mafia murders of
trade-union leaders in the postwar period no other murder caused
as many repercussions and received as much attention in both the
press and the courts of law. At the age of thirty-two Carnevale was
killed in broad daylight on May 16, 1955, while on his way to the
quarry where he was employed. In true Mafia style, there were
wounds inflicted on the corpse's face to indicate contempt, and the
day after the murder there was the customary Mafia theft of forty
hens for the banquet celebrating the deed.

Carnevale had aroused the ire of the local Mafia by two trade-
union actions: first by leading the peasants of the area in a movement to claim lands to which they were legally entitled under the
government's land reform program; then by organizing a strike of
quarry workers who demanded payment of back wages and the
reduction of an eleven-hour day to eight hours. Both actions
struck deeply at the interests and prestige of the Sciara Mafia,
which had close alliances with the Princess Notarbartolo, who
owned the local quarry as well as the lands claimed by the peasants. Several mafiosi, who were employed by the Princess as over-
seers, tried to bribe Carnevale into discontinuing his union activities. When this failed, they threatened his life. According to
Carnevale's mother, his reply to the threat was: "If you kill me,

276

you kill Jesus Christ." A few mornings later his corpse was found near the quarry.

The murder was so obviously the work of the Mafia that no one, except the mother, dared come to the funeral. From past experience with such matters, the villagers expected that the police would conduct a routine investigation of the crime, ascribe it to motives of honor or personal vengeance, and eventually ignore it. The Mafia had literally gotten away with murder with every one of its thirty-five assassinations of trade-union leaders; there was no reason to think that the same thing would not happen again. But then came a startling development that transformed the saga of Salvatore Carnevale into a national legend. Defying the traditional code of *omerta,* which imposes silence on all matters pertaining to the Mafia, Carnevale's mother not only loudly protested the killing of her son but also denounced his murderers in the courts of Palermo.

After many years of litigation the four men charged with the murder were sentenced to life imprisonment. In a triumphant statement the lawyer who had acted for the mother at the trail said: "The quasi sovereignty of the Mafia, which asks for and obtains the silence and the *omerta* of the lower classes as protection for their crimes, as well as the silence and *omerta* of people in high stations, has come to an end." But in his euphoria he failed to take into account the Mafia's tenacity for asserting its power. Appealing the case, the Mafia intimidated key witnesses into changing their stories, employed the best legal minds in Italy, and succeeded in getting the four condemned men released after they had been in jail for eight years. One of the men died shortly after his release; the other three had resumed their residence in the village where the crime was committed.

Sciara is a small place, brown and dilapidated and as homely as a bale of hay. The homes are low dark hovels that seem to crouch under the weight of the poverty-stricken atmosphere. Until we reached the piazza we saw no people, only goats, chickens, mules, and their manure. As we pulled up to the piazza, we noticed a group of ten men in black suits carrying funeral wreaths. The men had just started walking down a small dirt road, followed by four armed policemen. A village guard confirmed my hunch that the procession was headed for Salvatore Carnevale's tomb. By a stroke of luck, we had arrived at the very moment when the tenth anniversary of Carnivale's death was about to be observed.

Franco quickly parked the car and we all scurried down the road leading to the cemetery, a half-mile obstacle course of filth, mud, and stones, especially treacherous for our wives in their flimsy shoes. At one point the road suddenly became impassable when a huge black bull planted himself squarely in the center of it and showed no intention of moving. Franco, who was leading the way, finally dispatched the beast with a well-aimed stone. By the time we caught up with the procession it had reached the cemetery and the men were arranging their wreaths around Carnevale's tomb, an oblong box stuck into a cement vault along with scores of other boxes, like a drawer in a mammoth filing case. The only identification on Carnevale's box was a small photograph bearing a notation of the dates of his birth and death.

One of the men, an old acquaintance of Franco, informed him that eight of the ten men honoring Carnevale were members of a minority Socialist faction; the other two were Communists. "The regular Socialist party members should have been here in large numbers," he said bitterly, "but for political reasons they decided to boycott this ceremony. The bastards. In ten short years they have forgotten that this man gave his life for all of us." Tears gathered in his eyes. "Salvatore and I were close friends," he said, and dried his eyes with his fingers.

An old man lingered behind after the others had left, anxious to speak to us. His jacket was torn and his trousers patched; I realized he must be extremely poor to be dressed this way on a Sunday and at such an occasion. Identifying himself as Salvatore Carnevale's uncle, he said: "As strangers to Sciara you must have wondered why Salvatore's mother was not with us today. I feel I should explain that she has always taken part in this ceremony but this year she is sick and in the hospital."

As we trudged back to the piazza, I asked the old man whether there was still any Mafia activity in Sciara. Assuming that by "activities" I meant killings, he replied: "Murders are committed in this village all the time. They never stop. The last ones were committed three months ago. A peasant and his wife, both of them very good persons, were clubbed to death in their bed one night. Nobody knows why. After they killed the couple, the murderers tried to set their bed on fire but the fire didn't take."

When he learned I was a writer, he said: "A great deal has been written about Salvatore, and they even sing ballads about his deeds. But the poor boy is dead and his assassins are alive and free, and now the people of his own village are forgetting about him. Every year fewer and fewer villagers pay respects to his memory. It was just as well that Salvatore's mother wasn't here today . . ."

Near the edge of the village the old man expressed the hope that we would listen to the speeches that would be made about his nephew in the piazza "as soon as the loudspeaker is connected." But Franco had other plans for us. "Where can I find Mangia-fridda, Panzica, or Di Bella?" he asked, naming the three surviving men who had been tried for the murder.

The old man shrugged and scowled. "We don't talk about them," he said coldly, and without another word turned his back on us and went toward the piazza.

Franco thought he might be able to find Panzica because his house had been pointed out to him on a previous visit to Sciara when he interviewed Carnevale's mother. "If we find him, I'll introduce you as an American writer," he said. "But be sure to play the part. Don't use any Sicilian; he's liable to clam up if you do."

As we followed Franco through a series of roughly cobblestoned streets, I could feel eyes peering at us through windows and shutters. Now and then I would catch a glimpse of a face that was either hostile or curious. Franco finally stopped before a closed wooden door and banged on it until a young woman with dark sullen eyes opened it. Introducing himself, Franco said he was with an American writer who was eager to make her father's acquaintance. The woman, steeped in doubt, started to say that he wasn't feeling well and couldn't be disturbed but then her eyes lighted on Patricia, the only one among us who did not look like an Italian, and her attitude changed. She invited us in.

She led us through a short dark hallway, then turned abruptly into a small dreary room that was unlighted except for a few thin streaks of daylight. The only furnishings were some straightback

279

chairs and a table. We had barely seated ourselves when a tall lanky figure entered and shook hands with each of us. It was Giuseppe Panzica. He looked about sixty years old, with gray hair, intensely blue eyes, and a fairer skin than most Sicilians have. His hand was hard but his handshake limp. He wore a black cap, which he kept on throughout the interview. I had difficulty thinking of him as a killer, mainly because he resembled one of my favorite uncles; yet I knew that until the third trial, when a key witness changed his testimony, Panzica had been identified as one of the men leaving the scene of the crime.

Panzica said he was a widower; his wife had died "two years before this other misfortune befell me." His manner of speaking was that of a typical Sicilian peasant, with the same frequent evocation of God to witness the truth of whatever he was asserting. Never at a loss for words, he ejected them in small hard bunches, while his hands and arms gestured in almost constant motion. He must have told his story frequently in and out of the courtroom but one would never have guessed that from the spontaneity of his delivery.

"As you know, there were three trials for us. At the last one they dropped all the charges against us because we were innocent. But they continue to bother us. I don't know what they want from us any more. Isn't it enough that we served eight years in jail? Eight years. It is terrible to be in jail when you are innocent and, as God is my witness, I am innocent. When you're innocent you suffer a great deal more in jail than you do when you're guilty. If you're guilty, you more or less become resigned to your fate. But when you're innocent you never become resigned. You suffer . . .

"Your health suffers too. I lost my health in jail. I can't eat as much as I once could and I have constant pains all over the body. I'm not the only one who became sick. One of us got so sick he died a few months ago. The other two are better off because they are younger and were more able to take the hard life of prison. Yet I still manage to do a little work in the fields. I have a little property—not much, about two acres; with what I grow on that land and my pension I get along somehow. But God should not abandon me. He should have pity on those who were really guilty of murdering Salvatore Carnevale but he shouldn't abandon those of us who were sent to jail by mistake.

"I blame the whole misfortune on politics. If politics hadn't entered into it, we wouldn't have been arrested and suffered the terrible things we have. Because Carnevale was a Socialist and we are Christian Democrats they decided that we wanted to kill him. But I hardly knew Carnevale and I certainly had no ill feeling toward him. I didn't care that he was a Socialist and a union leader. My job was to do what the administrator of the Princess Notarbartolo told me to do. Every morning I was told exactly what I should do on that day. That was my job and that is what I did. Sometimes I would tell a peasant what to plant, or where to plough, or what to pick. That's the kind of job I had—doing what the administrator told me to do. There were four of us who did that kind of work . . .

"On the morning when all the trouble took place the administrator had asked us to check on the production at the quarry. The company that operated the quarry claimed that it produced a certain amount; the administrator wanted to find out whether or not what they claimed was true. Our assignment was simply to determine how much stuff the workers were turning out. It wasn't that we had a personal interest in the quarry, as they claimed at the trial. I swear by Jesus Christ and all the blessed saints that I didn't have an iota of interest in anything connected with that quarry. It was just our bad luck that we were sent to the quarry on the very day when Carnevale was killed . . .

"They said at the trial that we were *mafiosi* but the company that ran the quarry was from Bologna. So it must mean that the Mafia is everywhere in Italy, not only in Sicily but also in the north. Such nonsense! Everybody talks about the Mafia but what is it? Maybe there was such a group in the old days, many years ago, but now when they say "Mafia" what do they mean? They called us *mafiosi* but they never told us what it meant.

"The only person I took orders from was the administrator who worked for the Princess Notarbartolo. The administrator's name is Marsala; he is a lawyer who lives in Termini. I'll explain how I met him. My wife, *bon arma,* owned a house on which we owed some money. The bank was in financial difficulties and was putting pressure on all of its creditors. We owed the bank 16,000 lire, which in those days was a good sum of money. The bank claimed that with the interest that had piled up our debt was close

281

to 30,000 lire, which was far more money than we could pay. My wife suggested we talk to a lawyer. We went to Marsala because my wife had known his family and felt that he would do his best to help us. She was right. Marsala managed to convince the bank that it should accept 16,000 lire and close the account.

"A few months later I received word that Marsala wanted to talk with me. I thought to myself: has the bank changed its mind and decided to make us pay more money? But it wasn't that at all. Marsala told me that he was handling the estate of the Princess and wanted me to work for him. I told him that since I had a little land from which I could make a living I saw no reason why I should change my way of life. But he talked to me for a long time and argued that it would be to my advantage to have a fixed salary rather than depend on the whims of nature for a good crop, as we peasants are obliged to do. Finally, he convinced me that it would be wise for me to go to work for him . . .

"The job lasted for three years, until the terrible misfortune that you know about befell me. I think there was one other reason why I was blamed for the crime. Jealousy. Politics and jealousy—those were the only reasons. You would think they would let me alone now after spending eight years in jail and losing my health. But they don't. They are constantly bothering me."

At this point his daughter appeared in a coat and hat and announced that she had to leave. She shook hands with each of us, nodded briefly at her father, and made her exit.

Fixing his gaze on me, as he had during most of his talking, Panzica said: "Everyone in my family has suffered a great deal because of my misfortune. As you can imagine, it took a pile of money to pay for all those lawyers. There were three of them. I don't know how much the others paid but my brother paid out about a million and a half lire . . ."

I interrupted him to ask whether Giovanni Leone, the Christian Democrat senator who had barely missed becoming president of Italy a few years before, was one of the lawyers.

"Giovanni Leone, did you say?" His eyes flickered and he hesitated for a moment. "Yes, I believe Leone was one of the lawyers."

Franco and I began to question him closely about Leone, being certain that a man of his political prominence and stature would not have associated himself with a case that had been so widely identified with the Mafia unless powerful pressures had been brought to bear on him. When we asked Panzica to tell us how Leone's services had been acquired, he looked embarrassed and for the first time he was unable to look me in the eye. Suddenly his whole being seemed to sag, and he said no more.

Franco made an effort to revive the conversation by recalling that a recent newspaper article reported that Mangiafridda, one of the accused men, had been seen going about Sciara with a shotgun, the same type of weapon that had been used to kill Carnevale.

"I don't know anything about that," Panzica said slowly. "We hardly ever see one another. Sometimes I run into him because this is a small village but we don't see much of each other."

There was a long pause. Then Panzica rose from his chair and, holding the palms of his hands in front of him, he said: "These are hard hands. You have only to look at these hands to know what I am: a peasant who works the land."

As we filed out of the gloom into the glaring sunshine, there were faces at neighboring doorways and windows staring at us with hatred. We walked rapidly toward the piazza, hoping to hear one of the speeches about Carnevale, but it was too late. Except for a couple of men dismantling the public speaker system, the piazza was empty.

Chapter

15

Edoardo,
the Peacemaker

EDOARDO WATJEN arrived in Partinico on a Saturday morning, in time to attend a Center staff conference, the last one in which I was to participate. A rangy Nordic with graying features, he sat at the conference table with his eyes shut most of the time in tight concentration. The knitted skull cap covering his baldness gave him the aspect of an aging handsome actor cast in the role of a cardinal.

A brief conversation with him before the meeting on the subject of Danilo had overwhelmed me with its candor. "I can never be Danilo's friend," he had said, "but I will always love him. Danilo is a man who is willing to sacrifice his life to make Sicily and other underdeveloped countries better places for their people. I don't believe that many of his collaborators have ever understood this essential fact about him. Certainly, Danilo has many defects; there are a hundred things wrong with him. He would probably be the last person on earth one would deliberately pick out to run the Center. But Danilo has a genius for doing the right thing at the right time, and he doesn't mind stepping on toes to get what he wants accomplished. But how can you explain him to those collaborators who have left him? How can you make them understand that they are all better people, changed people, for having known him, no matter how badly they believe he has treated them?

"Of course, Danilo will never admit treating anyone badly. He

284

will find all sorts of reasons to give for people leaving the Center. He will not face up to the fact that he interferes with their work sometimes, that he will get angry with them for no particularly good reason. Yet he will never come out and tell people that they must leave. He will wait until they go. He certainly should have fired that German nurse, particularly after her public blast against him, but as you know she is still working for the Center.

"I was and still am the friend of Eyvind Hytten. I had a difficult time when he was having his big fight with Danilo, but I finally had to let him know that he was wrong and Danilo was right. Eyvind told me that his hatred for Danilo started when Danilo was conducting his 'conversations' with the people of Partinico. It made Eyvind furious that Danilo gave up the discussions as soon as he had collected enough material for his next book. I asked him why, if the conversations meant so much to him, he didn't conduct them himself. He couldn't answer me. None of them is a Danilo; none of the people who have left the Center have been able to carry on its work on their own initiative. They can't because they don't have his determination, his genius, and his willingness to die for principles. Whatever success I've had with the redevelopment centers I've started in foreign countries is because of Danilo. Without him I would be nothing . . ."

Danilo opened the meeting with a report on the conference he had recently called in Partinico to discuss methods for increasing employment in the area. At his request Carlo Levi had come from Rome and delivered a stirring plea that Sicilians be given a chance to lift themselves from their economic morass. But only a few of the government agencies that had promised to send delegates kept their word. The only achievement of the conference had been to present data on unemployment and on employment possibilities which had been prepared by the Center. But Danilo refused to be discouraged. Although he wryly observed that the Mayor of Partinico, who had been among the absent, had scolded him roundly for revealing at the conference the unemployment figures provided by his office, he regarded the event as "a firm step in the right direction, in the direction of grassroots planning."

Edoardo Watjen opened his eyes to ask what the Center had done about the reforestation phase of the Jato dam project. From the silence that followed it was obvious that nothing had been done about it. "If we talk of grassroots planning," he said, "we should be deeply concerned about this problem. How could we have forgotten about it?"

"I don't believe we have forgotten about it," Danilo answered. "The problem is to determine who is capable of doing that work . . ."

"Our staff should include at least one person who concerns himself with reforestation," Watjen insisted. "It takes three years to reforest an area. Now is the time when we should be providing the leadership to achieve reforestation." He studied each face around the table like a trial lawyer impressing himself on a jury. "Danilo can't do everything," he added.

"We don't have any funds for that kind of work," Michele said.

"That should not be our answer," retorted Watjen. "We should assume that the government can provide funds for reforestation experts who will decide what the program is to be and educate the farmers to carry it out. If necessary, we should go on a hunger strike for reforestation. If we don't provide leadership of this kind, who will?"

No one seemed willing to argue the point. "Shall we proceed?" Danilo asked blandly, and called on Lorenzo to report on a regional conference he had been organizing for several months in behalf of the twenty-two villages in the Belice valley that stood to profit from the construction of a dam. The first meeting of the conference was to take place in Partanna the following day, with delegates of all twenty-two villages and of every political affiliation, except the blatantly fascist. It was the most ambitious effort toward grassroots planning that the Center had ever undertaken. The Center's only official delegate was to be Lorenzo. Danilo, Franco, Watjen and I were to attend the first meeting as observers.

As frequently happened at staff meetings Dr. Borruso became the focal point of a controversial discussion, this one more bad-tempered than any of the others I had heard. It began when Danilo called on him to present a prospectus for a three-year study of hospital needs in western Sicily which Dr. Borruso planned to conduct with a young Swiss sociologist who had recently come to

Partinico for that purpose. Although the sociologist looked like a young and jolly Santa Claus with his golden beard and flashing blue eyes, there was nothing jolly about the opinion he had developed of Danilo and his program. Soon after his arrival, he had openly allied himself with the German nurse, even to the extent of using some of her phraseology; and he was now filled with painful doubts as to the advisability of continuing his association with Danilo. "Apart from the character of the man, which I find most disturbing," he had told me a few days earlier, "there is too much serious disagreement between us on fundamental points of social planning."

Their basic disagreement, as it became evident after Dr. Borruso had presented their prospectus, was on the concept of grassroots planning. The Swiss sociologist held that while grassroots planning could be applied to community *development*, it was not feasible in community *planning*, which he considered the sole province of experts like himself. "It does little good to ask people what their hospital needs are because they will think only of their own personal wants and not of those of the community at large," he argued. "I found this so when working on a hospital plan in Switzerland, even with persons as well educated as doctors. The doctors knew what they wanted for themselves but they were incapable of taking into consideration the general picture . . ."

Danilo, Watjen, and Lorenzo disagreed. They saw no need to make a distinction between community development and community planning; and although they acknowledged the need to have experts formulate final recommendations, they believed the recommendations would be useless unless they were based on data obtained directly from the very people who were to benefit from the planning. Danilo said that the files of government agencies were jammed with plans for Sicily prepared by experts, which were valueless because they were too abstract.

After considerable debate, the Swiss sociologist and Dr. Borruso reluctantly accepted Danilo's suggestion that they discuss the subject further with Watjen and then present the group with a revised prospectus.

In retrospect the acrimonious tone of the discussion seemed mild in view of what developed next. Without warning, Lorenzo erupted with a blast against Dr. Borruso, accusing him of "behaving more as an enemy of the Center than a collaborator," of disparaging its work in Palermo and wherever else he could find an audience. It was a stinging five-minute attack which the doctor vainly tried to interrupt with protests that he had been expressing "not disparagement but criticism." Danilo, to my surprise, in an angry voice elaborated on the attack with further observations of the doctor's "destructive attitude." Franco, barely able to control his rage as he listened to Lorenzo and Danilo, climaxed the onslaught by openly losing his temper and declaring that he for one would no longer tolerate the doctor's "vicious actions."

These thunderclaps of fury, astonishing to all of us, particularly to Watjen, who kept his eyes wide open during the whole storm, were followed by an embarrassed lull during which the doctor appeared too stunned to retaliate. Danilo finally broke the silence with the phrase, "Shall we proceed?", then in a drastic change of mood reminded the group that they were to go to Palermo on the following Tuesday to hear Jerre Mangione speak. Turning to me with his most benign smile, he said: "You are all set for this important event, I assume."

I was in no mood to provide him with any false assurances. "I am not set for it, nor can I ever be," I declared. "I've had nothing but nightmares these past months just thinking of what will happen when the Communists in the audience start identifying me with American foreign policy. The whole thing is bound to be a fiasco . . ."

Danilo refused to take me seriously. "Nobody will attack you," he said placidly. "You'll charm them. The moment you open your mouth and the audience hears how delightfully you mix Sicilian with Italian, they will all be on your side."

After the meeting Watjen, who had fully sensed my anxiety, asked me why I had agreed to do something which I obviously preferred to avoid. I told him the whole story, including the American Consulate's concern about the propaganda repercussions the event might produce. "It is very wrong of Danilo to push you into this," Watjen said after I had finished. "As your friend, he should take into consideration your feelings in the matter, and release you from your promise . . ."

When I expressed the opinion that Danilo tended to place his work above friendship, he agreed with me. "Danilo is incapable of the kind of relationship that you and I consider friendship," he said. "Although he is intensely friendly, he has no real friends. He is a man in love with his ideas on how to help people; it is a blind love that often excludes the feelings of individuals. He literally stops listening if someone is saying something that is contrary to what he is thinking. He probably never did hear your explanation of why you don't want to participate in this Palermo affair . . ."

That evening we met again, with Patricia this time, at a new restaurant in a Partinico alley where we were the only customers. Watjen continued to talk about the Center, with little or no prompting. "We used to get all kinds of weird people at the Center. We still do now and then. They come here with all kinds of crackpot schemes for saving the Sicilians from their misery and are disappointed when no one will take them seriously. Or they come with the idea of working with a saint and, of course, they soon realize that Danilo is not the kind of saint they had in mind and they go home disenchanted. Danilo is very patient about all this."

He laughed, recalling a conversation he had had with Danilo the morning before he began working for the Center. "I wanted to tell him what my daily work schedule would be like, so he would know what to expect from me. I began by saying that every morning right after I got out of bed I would start the day with an hour and a half of *ridendo*. My Italian was much worse than it is now. I really thought that *ridendo* was the Italian word for *reading*. I had no idea, of course, that it means *laughing*. I remember that Danilo looked at me long and hard but didn't say anything. About a year later, when I had got to know him and Italian better, I asked him what he thought when he heard me make the statement. 'So many strange people come to the Center,' Danilo said, 'that I really thought you started each morning by spending an hour and a half laughing.' "

Patricia asked Edoardo (as he preferred to be called) why he had not brought his wife with him. "My wife, alas, is among those who have become disenchanted with Danilo," he replied. "She lost her faith in Danilo's abilities as a community developer when she saw how he and Vincenzina were bringing up their children. It shocked her that the children were allowed to do as they pleased. Then, of course, there is the business of their having so many children in a country where there already are too many . . . I must say I get very nervous every time I return to Sicily, thinking that Vincenzina might be pregnant again."

Yet, when I mentioned Rosita Lanza's birth control crusade in Palermo, Edoardo declared himself against it. "Birth control never succeeds among people who live in a state of economic misery," he said. "That is proved by the experience in India and especially in Japan, where the people in the eastern part of the country— the more highly developed area—practice birth control but those in the western sector, which is economically underdeveloped, do not. In the psychology of misery, neither a husband nor wife pays much attention to the future. How can they when they have the problem of existing from day to day? They make love and have children because that gives their life an immediate objective. They can't believe in the future, so they make the most of the present . . .

"In the most terrible slums of Palermo you will sometimes see the children of the very poor wearing extremely pretty dresses, for example. A father, whose daughter begs him for the price of a new dress, is apt to give her whatever money he has on him, even though he doesn't know where more is coming from. Desperate people do extravagant things, and have an extravagant number of children. But let these same people acquire a certain amount of security, let the father of a family feel, for example, that he doesn't have to worry about paying his bills for a whole year, then the daughter is less likely to get her dress.

"People like Rosita Lanza should study the experience of the Sicilians who migrated to Milan and began to enjoy a certain amount of economic security for the first time. As soon as that happened, without any urging from anyone, they began to practice birth control. Those families seldom have more than two children. They act more intelligently because they can afford to.

"Instead of giving poor people birth control advice and propaganda we ought to give them free television sets. Television is excellent for people who live in misery. I didn't use to think so but Danilo pointed out to me that only by looking at television will people begin to understand the opportunities that exist outside of their own world; their horizons will broaden. Just now their lives are like those of certain birds that live and die within a confined area, without ever learning that they can escape the narrowness of their particular world. Television will help make poor people unhappy with their own situation, and when they become sufficiently unhappy, less resigned to their misery, they will be more open to the prospect of social revolution . . ."

Inevitably, we returned to the subject of Danilo's difficulties with collaborators. "Trying to maintain peace at the Center has become one of my principal occupations," he complained. "I try to maintain an objective point of view by living in Borgetto; it means cleaning out rat nests and excrement whenever I return in the spring but those few miles between Borgetto and Partinico provide me with a perspective that I must have to function as peacemaker. It is not an easy role because Danilo is not a simple man; he has all the complications of the charismatic personality . . ."

I asked Edoardo one of the questions which Danilo's critics had been putting to me: How can Danilo hope to stimulate group activity among Sicilians when he has difficulty keeping his own group together?

"A leader of his charisma," he replied, "attracts his followers not by kindness, sound reasoning, or impressive experience but by the genius of his personality. And here we come to the kernel of the matter: the work which Danilo earnestly believes he is doing and consciously wants to do *cannot* be done by him but has to be done by others—by people like Lorenzo, who are steady and intelligent and have a love of people that nurtures their faith in democratic growth. But it is Danilo who provides the leadership for the non-violent revolution we are trying to create in Sicily. Not one of his collaborators, past or present, would be capable of assuming that leadership."

A little later Edoardo added: "The sadness is that sooner or later Danilo's most talented disciples find themselves at loggerheads with him. They come out of the trance imposed on them by his personality and begin to attack him for his lack of democracy and for his other faults. Because they do this in the most undemocratic way—slyly and mostly behind his back—they develop self-hatred for what they are doing and this increases their desire to revenge themselves on Danilo to a point where he is obliged to attack them in order to save the work of the Center from destruction.

"Several things must be done for the protection of Danilo and the collaborators. We have to safeguard the work of the talented collaborators from being frustrated by Danilo's interference. At the same time we must save Danilo from the destructive tendencies of his collaborators. This can be done by emphasizing the beauty, courage, and unselfishness of his genius and the profound importance of his work, a work that is small in quantity but enormous in quality . . ."

We talked until midnight, then met again the next morning with Danilo, Franco, and Danilo's son Cielo for our trip to the regional conference in Partanna. Edoardo, seated next to Danilo, who was driving, went on talking. It was a lyrical May morning, and his words complemented the Sunday aura of peace and contentment that hovered over the green countryside like a joyous promise. He was speaking of his successes as the Center's roving missionary and also of his high hopes for the regional organization that was about to be born at Partanna. Danilo seemed to be glowing in the warmth of his commentary; it was evident that he respected Edoardo's opinions. Then, when there could be no doubt about the mellowness of Danilo's mood, Edoardo suddenly pounced on him with two rasping questions: "What the hell are you doing to our friend Jerre? Why do you insist on subjecting him to a situation that might cause him a great deal of anguish?"

There was a stunned moment of silence. Then Danilo turned his head toward me, ignoring the road, and with wide-eyed innocence asked: "Don't you really want to take part in Tuesday's program?"

"Of course I don't," I replied vigorously.

Danilo blinked. "I guess I misjudged you. I thought you would enjoy all the publicity that goes with the program, and I thought, too, that it would enhance your prestige as an American writer in Sicily. But I'm beginning to realize that personal publicity is of no interest to you. Your main concern is your work . . ."

I did not know what he was driving at with this somewhat exag-

gerated statement but I did not disagree with it. Instead, I evoked
a fresh argument for not speaking on Tuesday—my Sicilian temper
—and reminded him that as chairman at one of his Philadelphia
talks some hecklers in the audience had caused me to lose control
of my temper.

"Ah yes," Danilo said. "I remember. It was quite a Sicilian outburst . . ."

"I'm liable to lose my temper again on Tuesday," I said.

"That would be terrible." Danilo stared at the road for a few
moments without saying anything more, and I thought that was
the end of the discussion, but suddenly his eyes met mine in the
mirror, and he asked: "Tell me, Jerre, would you be offended if
we got someone else to speak in your place—someone like Yevgeny
Yevtushenko, who is in Palermo just now? I met him at a reception
last night. If you have no objection . . ."

"None whatsoever," I shouted. "A brilliant idea, Danilo," and I
went on to say that Yevtushenko would undoubtedly draw a much
larger audience than I ever could.

Edoardo leaped in with a reinforcing argument: "The series
needs a famous poet to give it the kind of excitement it should
have."

"With your permission then," Danilo said to me, "I will ask
Yevtushenko to take your place."

I heaved a deep sigh of relief, and with my eyes tried to thank
Edoardo.

Edoardo was not finished with Danilo. A few miles away from
Partanna he began to scold both Danilo and Franco for their in-
temperate attack on Dr. Borruso. "As long as Vincenzo Borruso is
a member of the Center, he should not be treated as though he
were a devil . . ."

Danilo replied that he could readily understand the sense of
opportunism that motivated the doctor's association with the Center—"after all, there is some opportunism in all of us"—but as long
as Borruso remained at the Center and continued to use it to
further his personal ambitions, he had no business criticizing its
activities to outsiders. Franco, as usual, upheld Danilo's point of
view, yet neither one could justify abusing Borruso at the meeting
with much conviction.

"You are much too hard on people," Edoardo told them, and went on to another subject.

The meeting in Partanna was successful beyond all expectations. Lorenzo, its chief engineer, had done his work well. More than five hundred Sicilians (not a woman among them) jammed into the local movie house to hear representatives of the twenty-two towns in the Belice valley express their need for economic progress and their willingness to integrate their local community planning with an overall organic plan for the region. The star performer of the occasion was the energetic Christian Democrat mayor of Partanna, a tall, handsome gym teacher in his forties, who had participated in the demonstration at Roccamena. In a country where the word politician is generally considered synonymous with graft Enzo Culicchia had won the hearts of his constituents after his mayoralty election by refusing to accept the stipend of his office.

His opening remarks generated an excitement that set the tone for the rest of the meeting. In simple and forceful language he described in detail a proposed program of action that was obviously inspired by the goals and the philosophy of the Center. Lorenzo, who had been Culicchia's mentor for several months, spoke next. Although he was not as impressive a personality as the mayor, he held the attention of his audience by his careful delineation of the problems that confronted the villages.

The twelve mayors present at the conference, the trade-union leaders, and all the other delegates had their say. They were each allotted ten minutes but nearly all of them spoke much longer. One delegate spent thirty-five minutes discoursing on the tendency of the average Sicilian to be infatuated with his own rhetoric. Another took a longer time speaking on the Sicilian's proclivity for self-deprecation and pessimism but wound up his remarks by asserting that "our faults as Sicilians are rapidly receding as the clock of progress begins to move in our beloved land."

Despite the tiresome barrage of oratory and despite a painfully prolonged sour note from one of the speakers, who insisted on recalling that a past conference of a similar nature had proved to be a miserable failure, the delegates succeeded in electing a regional board that would function for the economic welfare of all the towns in the Belice valley. The Mayor of Partanna became its president; Lorenzo, its executive secretary.

On our way back we ate prosciutto sandwiches and bananas in the car, and talked at great length about the encouraging aspects of the conference, which Danilo considered an historic event. Edoardo, dwelling on its "revolutionary significance," declared that "the meeting demonstrated what Karl Marx said, what Rosa Luxembourg believed, and what Lenin forgot." As I listened to him exulting in his claim that the conference represented "theory translated into action, a revolutionary dividend of the Center's increasing contacts with the common people," I thought of the millions of Sicilians who had never heard of Danilo Dolci and of the long centuries of Sicilian apathy that confronted Danilo and his small band at every turn, and I marveled at Edoardo's staunch faith in the Center's ability to propagate a social revolution.

Yet even as I engaged in this reflection, my skepticism was challenged by the historical fact that nineteen centuries earlier another small band of nonviolent men, inspired by another leader willing to die for his cause, had succeeded in spreading and establishing their gospel throughout the world, against far grimmer odds than those confronting Danilo and the Center.

Journey
Around Sicily

TOWARD THE END of our stay in Partinico the editor of *Sicilia,* a posh magazine in five languages published under government auspices, offered us a car and chauffeur for a ten-day swing around the island, in exchange for my writing an article for the publication. The offer was made with the understanding that we would be free to go wherever we wished.

With the flies and heat becoming increasingly oppressive, I jumped at the chance to leave Partinico for a while and get a comprehensive view of the Sicily that is outside Danilo's territory. I was particularly eager to visit Riesi, where Tullio Vinay, a Waldensian pastor, is conducting a valiant social reform program; and Palma di Montechiaro, reputed to be the most miserable town in Sicily, where a Dutch priest-sociologist had tried to establish a social reform program for three years, until the Cardinal of Sicily found out what he was up to and had him transferred out of the island.

On a hot June morning a large black Fiat driven by a young Palermitano named Giovanni picked us up on the Via Emma and drove toward the northwest corner of Sicily, two hours away. Our destination was Erice, a town perched on a promontory 2,465 feet above sea level, where the Venus cult of love and fertility enjoyed centuries of popularity until routed by Norman conquerors and their Christian puritanism. Without giving any reason for his judgment, Danilo had declared Erice to be his favorite Sicilian town. "You will know why I say this when you see it," he told us.

There is nothing typically Sicilian about Erice or its immediate surroundings. In a land where trees are rare, the mountain on which the village sits is covered by a dense pine forest that encircles it like a perfumed girdle. As we drove up the mountain, we had the definite impression that we were entering a foreign country, an impression that was further confirmed when we reached the village by the consistently medieval character of its architecture and by its pervasive and uncanny silence.

After the pandemonium of Partinico and of other Sicilian villages, the drastic change of atmosphere is disquieting at first. You think that something must be seriously wrong, that possibly a fierce epidemic has suddenly stricken the population. There are no chickens and dogs in sight scavenging for scraps. In fact, there are no scraps. The glossy pavement stones are spotlessly clean, as though each one had been individually scrubbed; and, wonder of wonders, there is not a single clothesline in sight.

Everything about Erice—its tangle of skinny and empty streets, the fairytale vistas of castles and medieval façades embellished by trees, sky, and sea; and, above all, the holy silence—makes it a seductive retreat far removed from the traumas of modern times, and explains Danilo's attachment to the place. For him Erice must represent a dream of tranquillity and the end of strife, an oasis so suspended in time that history becomes a joy instead of a hindrance. But where, we asked one another, were the people of Erice?

One of the first villagers we encountered was the caretaker of the fabled Rock of Venus, who was watering some tomato plants growing in what had once been the floor of the Temple of Venus. Built by Erice on the edge of the sea to honor his mother, this was the temple that became an altar of love for three civilizations—for the Greeks, who knew their love goddess as Aphrodite; for the Phoenicians, who called her Ashtoreth, and for the Romans, who celebrated her as Venus. At one time two hundred Roman soldiers were stationed in Erice to guard the temple's treasure trove of gifts received from grateful visitors who had enjoyed the amorous rites of the sacred prostitutes. Only fragments of the temple survive but

297

surrounding the site are the magnificent ruins of an Arab-Norman castle that once served the town as a mighty fortress.

"Where do the people of Erice live?" I asked the caretaker. "In Erice," he replied and went on watering his tomato plants. Although he would not be more explicit, he embarked on a ten-minute monologue on the evolution of the temple-fortress, in which dates and facts were scrambled in a surrealistic mishmash. One of his choicest statements was that after Venus had been born in the sea below the rock, she ascended the mountain with a force of cupids and put them to work building a temple in honor of San Giuliano. "But didn't Venus belong to the pagan religion and wasn't San Giuliano a Catholic?" I couldn't resist asking. "In those days," the caretaker replied without any hestitation, "everybody was all the same."

We wandered through a wooded park nearby, below which we could see the city of Trapani, and talked with a ninety-three-year-old patriarch who suggested that we make the acquaintance of the town historian at the local museum. So it was that Professor Vincenzo Adragna, a young widower, became our mentor for the rest of the day. Adragna showed us some exquisite Greek and Phoenician miniature heads and statuary of the goddess of love, then rambled through the streets with us, spouting historical lore, including the information that during a sojourn in Erice in the late nineteenth century Samuel Butler, the British novelist, had gathered "evidence" to show that the writer of the *Odyssey* was not Homer but a woman of Trapani, his chief argument being that the author showed a dismal ignorance of such subjects as farming and seafaring but was remarkably well-informed on household matters.

"What about the present?" I asked the young professor. "Where are the people of Erice? Here it is past the siesta hour but it still looks like a ghost town."

Adragna's eyes saddened. "You have touched on the tragedy of Erice," he said, "the reluctant flight of our population. In the twenties the population was 13,000 and nobody had any intention of leaving, but it became increasingly difficult to make a living and now there are only 1,200 of us left. No one ever wants to leave, for to be an Ericino is to be a member of a select nobility which has had a remarkably close marriage with history. This fierce sense of

298

local pride is quite old. In the fifteenth century, for example, when the townspeople heard that King Carl of Spain was planning to sell their city because he was in need of money, they imposed an extra tax on themselves in order that the king could have his money and they could retain their identity as Ericini."

"But what about today's Ericini?" I persisted. "Where do they live?"

"We will go to my home and you will see." On our way he apologized for talking of the past so much. "Yet it really can't be helped because the past is always with us in Erice. In some ways it is good for the soul because it prevents us from falling prey to that twentieth-century malady known as alienation, but unfortunately it does not feed the belly . . ."

Adragna pushed open a gate on the street and we followed him through it, past a crooked lane until we came upon a courtyard filled with flowers. The mystery of the empty streets vanished as I saw that the courtyard was surrounded by houses. Unlike other Sicilians, the families of Erice have retained the housing habits of their Spanish ancestors, living in secluded courtyards, away from prying eyes. Adragna explained that a few wealthy families have their own private courtyard but usually the courtyards accommodate from two to six houses. There the children play, the women embroider, weave, wash clothes, and peel vegetables; and the old men sit in the sun.

"This semi-secret way of life makes it easier for Ericini to preserve their old traditions," Adragna said. "The tradition of trying to keep women virtuous, for example." He nodded at a young mother in the courtyard whose face bore a striking resemblance to one of the heads of Ashtoreth he had shown us. "There is a great deal of concern about protecting our women," he added, "because they are without a doubt the most beautiful in Sicily. Of course there is no reason why they shouldn't be since most of them, whether they realize it or not, are descendants of the goddess of love."

We remained in Erice until sunset. As we were bidding Adragna goodbye, I admired the tranquillity of the town and remarked that it must be one of the few places in that part of Sicily which had not known the Mafia.

He grimaced. "During the war Erice became a Mafia stronghold. It was here that all of its bigwigs gathered with the American bigwigs to direct the military operations of this area. As a result, not a single bomb was dropped on Erice. It was quite a different story in Trapani . . ."

When I asked if there were any *mafiosi* in Erice at present, he said that two or three of them were living in retirement there but were too decrepit to be active. "Actually, Erice is a poor place for the Mafia. There isn't enough here to exploit; furthermore, Ericini aren't easily intimidated. I suppose our history gives us a genuine sense of superiority."

We spent the night at a Jolly Hotel in Castelvetrano, where the food was ordinary, the prices high, and the management's skullduggery infuriating. We were charged for air-conditioning, though there was none, and the cost of our room exceeded that shown on the rate card hanging over our door. The clerk's blasé explanation for the discrepancy: "Our company is such a big one that we cannot keep up with all such minor details."

Our next destination was Palma di Montechiaro; on the way we stopped in Menfi to talk with Michele Mandiello, who was jubilant over the news he had just received that the wine cooperative he had been organizing had been officially approved by the Regional Government. It meant that the cooperative could probably start functioning within a few months.

Some three hours later, after driving steadily through intense heat, we approached Palma, the town where in April 1960 Danilo had presided over a congress of sociologists and government authorities that heard Dr. Pampiglione's shocking report on local sanitary and hygienic conditions. "An impalpable veil of chalky dust, loaded in summer with fecal residues and in winter with mud, hangs over the entire town" was one of the observations in the report. The veil was still present, along with its overpowering stench that assailed us even while we were on the outskirts. As long ago as 1930 a Baedeker guide described Palma as "the most dilapidated town in Sicily." It still remains so, despite the Pampiglione report, despite funds appropriated by the Regional Government for improving conditions, and despite the noble efforts of Father Salvinus Duynstee, the Dutch sociologist who came to Palma in 1960 to attend the congress and remained behind when he found that the group had no plans to help the villagers. With the assistance of some young sociologists from the University of Catania, he founded the Center for Community Development, but the project ended three years later in frustration when he was ousted from Palma by the hierarchy of the Catholic Church, despite his declaration that he had come to Palma "as a sociologist, not as a priest."

Symbolically enough, one of the first signs of human activity we witnessed on reaching the center of the village was that of a squatting little girl having a bowel movement. She and a gang of ragamuffins were playing in a grimy square, oblivious of the excrement about them. Near the square a once imposing stone stairway, at least twenty yards wide, led up the side of a hill to the eighteenth-century Cathedral that had been presented to the townspeople in honor of God by the Lampedusa family in its heyday. The stairway had become a travesty of grandeur; harsh weeds grew in profusion between each stair, and garbage and trash were scattered over most of the steps.

The exterior of the Cathedral has been degraded by wanton neglect. The walls are in bad repair, the finely carved wooden doors encrusted with grime. Only the edifice's baroque towers with their elegant cupolas suggest its original splendor. Some children were throwing a ball against the doors but stopped long enough to let us enter. Surprisingly, the interior was wonderfully clean and fresh. The predominating sky-blue of the decor suffused everything with a brightness that made the wretchedness of the town seem remote. The church was almost empty. Before an altar with a bleeding Christ two black-shawled women prayed with their heads bowed, as though the brightness was too much for them. There were also two young boys who were playing tag up and down the aisles, and a sacristan with a moronic mouth who was chasing them. As we were leaving, he had caught one of the boys by the scruff of the neck and was slapping him across the face.

The stench and squalor of Palma have not prevented readers of *The Leopard* from coming there to visit the thirty-room eighteenth-century mansion which was once occupied by the Lampedusa family. The crumbling mansion has fared even worse than the church. Part of the lower floor has been appropriated as a community latrine, despite its total lack of toilet equipment. Twenty-eight of the rooms are completely empty and serve no

301

purpose whatsoever; the other two rooms are utilized as the offices of the local police department. Except for a few elaborately painted ceilings, one containing the Lampedusa family crest with its snarling *gattopardo,* there is little to see. When we asked the policeman guiding us through the mansion where the hero of Lampedusa's novel had studied the stars, he pulled open a rickety shutter and pointed to a distant tower near the sea.

After an hour we had seen enough of Palma but could not leave until I had delivered a message from Danilo to the secretary of the local Camera di Lavoro. The message was in reply to a letter written in March.

Dear Danilo Dolci:

We have noted with great satisfaction the successful demonstration you led at Roccamena for the construction of the dam. Once again you achieved world-wide attention for placing your services at the disposition of peoples in depressed areas who need help.

You will recall that at Palma di Montechiaro in April 1960 you conducted a great convention that became a subject of discussion throughout the world, except among the rulers of Sicily and Rome who shut their ears to the subject.

After a long campaign the workers of this area managed to get the Regional Assembly to pass a special law for the relief of Palma and of Licata, a law that provides for a series of public works which must be initiated within a three-year period. Two years and a month have passed since the law was approved and not a single work project has been started. The administrative bodies of these two towns, harassed by a series of internal crises, seem to be paralyzed. The Regional Government, for reasons of its own, has not lifted a finger to intercede in the situation and evidently would like to see the special law expire before it can be applied. As a result, the unemployment situation here gets worse and our people continue to leave Sicily in search of work.

We ask you to please do something for Palma di Montechiaro, so that the special law will be put into effect before the expiration date. Today we turn to you and ask you to come to our assistance again, possibly with another congress or perhaps with a demonstration similar to the one held in Roccamena.

Hoping for an early reply, we salute you cordially.

Camera di Lavoro
Secretariat

The man who had written the letter was working in another town, but I was able to find one of his colleagues at the headquarters of the Camera di Lavoro, where he was engaged in a game of *briscola*. He left the card game as soon as he heard I was from the Center and talked with me in an adjoining room that served as the union's office, explaining first that he was one of its chief officers. The man's eyes were the color of freshly picked olives; he had a grizzly gray beard of two or three days' growth which he kept rubbing while I broke the news that Danilo was unable to comply with the request in the letter.

"But he should help us because he is partly responsible for that special law," the man argued. "If it hadn't been for the congress he held here, we could never have gotten the special law passed. As a result of the congress, everybody got to know how terrible the conditions are in Palma. But unless something is done about the special law soon, the conditions will continue to be terrible."

Danilo's staff was a third of what it had been in 1960, I explained. He did not have enough personnel to extend his activities to a town that was beyond the area where he and his collaborators were now working.

"Then let him come alone," the man said. "Surely he could spare us a few days of his time for so urgent a matter."

I repeated what Danilo had told me: his work is done with the help of his staff; he does not work alone.

The man stopped arguing and told me that a public meeting would be held in Licata soon to determine what could be done to put the special law into effect in time. "Maybe Danilo could come to the meeting. His mere presence would help us. Please try to persuade him to come."

I promised to do my best.

"Danilo must know that nothing in Palma has changed since the days of the congress," he continued. "The Dutch priest did some excellent things of an educational nature but he couldn't stay long enough to be effective. The main trouble was that the only support he could get was from us Socialists and Communists. The priests in town took advantage of this fact and began to say that he was too far to the left to be a priest; they finally saw to it that he got booted out of Palma. I'm not fond of priests as a rule but I got to like and respect Father Duynstee. At first it was hard for some of us to understand why a foreigner, and a priest at that, would want to help us but then we got used to the idea and tried to help him as much as we could. That was our mistake, I suppose. If we hadn't given him our support, he might still be here."

I asked whether he had ever heard of Tullio Vinay, who was doing work similar to that of Father Duynstee in the town of Riesi.

The name was new to him. "Is he also a priest?" he asked.

I explained he was a Waldensian pastor from the north of Italy who had been working in Riesi for five years.

"Wait until he does something the Church doesn't like. The Cardinal will have him thrown out of Sicily."

"But the man is a Protestant. The Cardinal has no jurisdiction over him."

"That doesn't make any difference to the Cardinal," he said, rubbing his beard.

He invited me to have an espresso with him. When I declined because Patricia was waiting for me in the car, he held out his hand and said that in that event he would go back to his card game.

Four miles away we stopped in Licata long enough to note that it is as miserable as Palma but somewhat less malodorous. Afterwards we drove through the mountains to Riesi for three hours, without passing through another village. There were many desolate stretches on the way but a half-hour before Riesi we began to look down on a long and enticing valley of densely cultivated parcels of land, a green and gold collage of changing tones and shapes that continued to the edge of the town. There the misery began again.

Founded more than three hundred years ago by Spanish land barons who worked the fields with imported criminals, Riesi is still enmeshed in its unsavory past. The descendants of the Spanish barons continue to own most of the surrounding land; the rents and taxes they impose are still exorbitant. Eventually most of the descendants of the original settlers learned to be law-abiding, but until the recent anti-Mafia drive the town was in the grip of a small but powerful band of *mafiosi*.

Yet Riesi is no worse off than scores of other villages in western Sicily. Here, as elsewhere, the illiteracy and infant mortality rates are appallingly high; housing conditions are indecent—frequently eight to ten persons live in a single room along with their livestock; streets are filthy and generally without sewers; and, despite the exodus of workers to foreign countries, the unemployment situation remains desperate. What sets Riesi apart from the other slum villages of Sicily is its geographical remoteness. To get to Gela, the nearest town, it takes two hours by car.

Riesi's isolation, which accentuates the town's predicament, was one of the considerations that led Tullio Vinay to establish his Servizio Cristiano there. That and the remarkable fact that the town already had a Waldensian congregation with its own church building. Waldensians are a rare religious breed in Italy; although they form the largest group of Italian Protestants, they represent less than two percent of the total population. Few Italians and even fewer Sicilians know that their Protestant history antedates Luther by some three hundred years.

Tullio Vinay has been an outstanding Waldensian figure for more than a quarter of a century. As pastor of the Waldensian church in Florence during the latter years of the Fascist regime, he played an important role in helping Italian Jews escape persecution. After the war he became the principal founder and influencing force of AGAPE, a highly successful international youth center in the Italian Alps that espouses liberal Christian thought.

From my first moments with Vinay, I could not help comparing him with Danilo. Physically they are quite different. Vinay, who is fifteen years older and silver-haired, is of average height and has Mediterranean features; he can easily be mistaken for a Sicilian. Danilo is several inches taller; his blue eyes and blond hair make him look more Teutonic than Latin. Intellectually, however, they are brothers under the skin. Both men are profoundly concerned with the fate of modern man and are devoting their lives to that concern. Both have spiritual and economic goals for the Sicilian poor which they believe can be achieved through nonviolent and democratic means. Both men regard Sicily as a testing ground for principles which, in their opinion, have universal application.

Vinay is a more relaxed and less reserved personality than Danilo. He exudes warmth, Danilo brilliance. Their personality differences are easily noted in their writings. Danilo's style has a classical purity about it; it is consistently objective and informative. Although much of it springs from a deep well of indignation, it tells us little about his emotions as an individual. Vinay, on the other hand, whether he is writing or talking reveals whatever frustration, anguish, or elation he may be experiencing from his work. His frequent contributions to the Servizio Cristiano's bulletin, *Days in Riesi* (published in English, Italian, and German), which are remarkably vivid evocations of the town's life and atmosphere, have the intimate sound of letters written to close friends.

Some of their most important differences emerge in the way they operate. Vinay and his associates conduct their work in the name of Christianity, referring to themselves as "witnesses of Christ." Danilo and his collaborators, who avoid all references to "God" or "Christ," pursue their goals in the name of humanity. The avowed purpose of Vinay's Servizio Cristiano is to bring about a rebirth of Riesi. Danilo and his collaborators have more ambitious aims: to change the social structures of western Sicily. Both groups work with the hope that they will be emulated in other needy regions of the world.

"Danilo spreads himself too thinly," Vinay said in his only criticism of the man he supported as early as 1952. "His program has no firm skeleton on which to grow. Here our program is carefully defined; we know exactly what we want to accomplish each step of the way. And that is useful because it creates a dialogue with the people. Step by step we can show them how to achieve a rebirth in which the basis of life will not be competition but love . . .

"Nowadays the general attitude in the world seems to be 'death to everyone.' People have been conditioned to think: 'Your death —my life.' They have forgotten that Christ's attitude was the reversal of that: 'My death—your life.' They have forgotten that we live because Christ died for us. Christianity, or whatever other name we want to give it, is the only hope for survival. Not Christianity as a theological truth but Christianity as a social and economic force. In that sense, Christianity has still to realize the full implications of its teachings. In our work there is no religious or political proselytizing. We simply try to show what Christ showed us by his resurrection—that it is possible to be reborn through love and a sense of service. It is the only basis on which the world can continue to exist."

Vinay and his group have made an impressive start in the rebirth of Riesi. On a forty-acre tract of high land near the edge of the town, called the Hill of Olives because of its 175 olive trees, they can point to tangible evidence that a new Riesi is rising. Four stunningly modern community buildings, designed by the Florentine architect Leonardo Ricci, have already been constructed under the auspices of the Servizio Cristiano. At least three more are in the planning stage. The completed buildings include a grade school, a school for the training of mechanics, and living quarters for members of the staff. On the grounds there are also two large poultry houses with 6,000 chickens, a large vegetable garden, and various fruit trees.

The long-range plan, Vinay told us, is to make the Hill of Olives a self-supporting settlement inhabited by as many families of Riesi as will join it. With this in mind, the Servizio Cristiano is planning to offer the villagers, at cost, lots on which low-cost homes, also designed by Ricci, can be constructed. "In the meantime," Vinay said, "while we are trying to raise money for constructing the buildings that will serve the whole community, the people of Riesi are using the Hill of Olives as a park. They often come here on Sundays and on feast days, whole families of them, to sit in the shade and enjoy the view."

A gang of men were working at great speed to finish the building that was to house the staff. I observed that they were by far the most cheerful workers I had ever seen in action. "They are cheerful when they have work," Vinay said. "It is only when they are without work that they become morose. Unfortunately, they won't have much more work from us until we can raise more money for our building program."

Vinay added that Sicilians were the best workers he had ever encountered anywhere, a judgment which I had also heard from Danilo. He also praised their courage, and told me what had happened when one of them had been seriously injured while unload-

307

ing stone and required a series of blood transfusions. None of the workers had ever given blood before. They believed, as many uneducated Sicilians do, that death will soon come to anyone who gives his blood. Yet of the twenty-five men on the job, twenty of them were willing to give their "life," as they called their blood.

The desperate need for work in Riesi was the subject of an article in one of the recent issues of *Days in Riesi*, with which Vinay supplied me before we left to spend the night in Gela. Written by Vinay's son, Gio, the report said: "Even on Sundays we cannot walk a hundred steps without being stopped by someone asking for work. We cannot say yes to everyone. This troubles us, for some of those who beg are fathers of families in great need. These are some of the things they say to us:

" 'I have five children. I don't know how to feed them. Give me a job or else I shall have to go and steal.'

" 'There are eleven of us, all depending on me. I'm only asking for work.'

" 'I have two sick children but can't call the doctor because I have no money. And not having worked for a year, I have no health insurance. Give me only a week's work, so that I can have a right to health insurance and help my sick children.' "

Gio Vinay's comment was: "There are not three or thirty or three hundred, but three thousand who are in this situation in Riesi, and we don't know how many millions there are in Sicily."

Not all of the reports in the bulletins were grim. One told of a diverting episode that took place in the Servizio Cristiano's medical dispensary while a long line of villagers were waiting their turn to be inoculated. A woman who appeared to be quite old had taken her place at the head of the line, insisting that she had to get home as quickly as possible to nurse her infant son. The men in the line listened to her explanation with great merriment; some began to address her as "grandmother" and josh her for trying to pretend she was capable of having an infant son at her age. After putting up with their jeers for a while, she suddenly became angry and, baring her breast, squirted a stream of milk into the face of the nearest heckler.

The next morning, at Vinay's suggestion, we visited the embroidery workshop that the Servizio Cristiano established in the

308

village. Supervised by Mrs. Vinay, the workshop, with its dozen young women, represents a revolutionary hope for the future—liberating the women of Riesi from the prison of their households. Embroidering in the home has long been a customary activity among Sicilian women. But for women to embroider within a group outside their homes represents a drastic break with tradition. The girls are paid by the hour; their work, which is superb, is sold in various European countries. All proceeds go toward maintaining the workshop. "More important than the money the girls earn," said Mrs. Vinay, "is the fact that for the first time they move in a world outside the family."

On being asked whether it was difficult to persuade the girls to join the workshop, Mrs. Vinay replied that it was the parents who required persuasion, not the girls. "They were quite reluctant at first but our argument that the girls would bring home money gradually changed their attitude."

At the midday meal, to which we were invited, I counted twenty-five persons around the communal table; among them were five members of the Vinay family, including Gio's Danish wife and her mother. The diners included teachers, social workers, agricultural experts, nurses, office workers, an engineer, an electrician, and a cook with a degree in music. Vinay and I conversed in Italian but also spoken at the table were French, German, English, and Danish.

Despite differences of nationality, age, and education, there was close harmony within the group. Unlike Danilo, Vinay has not had to contend with mutinous elements. One reason for this is that the ideology of his staff members is more or less the same—they are all of the same or similar religious persuasion. Another reason is that the course set by Vinay, being more limited and easier to define, is less susceptible to divergent opinions. There is also the fact that Vinay's actual image does not differ from his public one; unlike Danilo, whose image has been exaggerated and distorted by eager publicists, Vinay is less likely to disenchant those who hitch their ploughs to his stars.

When I asked whether he would accept volunteers who are of the Catholic or Jewish faith or who have no religious affiliation, Vinay replied that any volunteer who believes in the goals of his

309

group and who can make a needed contribution to its work would be welcome to join his staff. He cited Father Duynstee as a person with whom he would have happily collaborated. The Dutch priest came to Palma only a year before Vinay arrived in Riesi. The two men quickly became good friends. "It was our hope to work together. There were a number of things we could have accomplished as collaborators that would have benefited both Riesi and Palma, for Father Duynstee was an excellent sociologist. But, unfortunately for all of us, he was obliged to leave Palma before we could join forces."

Vinay makes no secret of his discouragement with many of the daily problems that badger him, including the omnipresent one of raising enough money to meet the payroll and continue his building program. Yet there is never any doubt about his determination to continue with the work, no matter how thorny and hopeless it may seem at times. The strength of his determination has rubbed off on many of his collaborators, who plan to devote the rest of their lives to the rebirth of Riesi.

Our final topic of conversation was the Riesi Mafia, which was one of the greatest stumbling blocks Vinay and his group first encountered. "The Mafia was very powerful here but during the past few years, while the Anti-Mafia Commission has been doing its work, the *mafiosi* have either left town or gone into hiding. What will happen when the commission expires nobody knows . . ."

He smiled wryly. "They tell me that if the Mafia returns to power, my life will be in danger. I am also told that the best way I can protect myself against the Mafia is to become so well publicized that they will not dare harm me. That sounds logical, but where is there time for that sort of thing?"

The farther away we traveled from western Sicily the less abject the poverty became. Yet only in such large centers as Siracusa and Catania was there any notable evidence of postwar economic growth. Gela, the city where the discovery of oil after the war led to the expectation that there would be enough jobs to create prosperity, is still in the throes of poverty. Two modern oil refineries, one at either end of the city, sandwich the population between them like ogres from another planet, spewing their putrid fumes night and day. The refineries employ some 2,000 men but nearly all are technicians imported from the north of Italy.

Yet we encountered surprisingly little resentment of this industry which has polluted the atmosphere without relieving the city's unemployment problem. The more sanguine citizens pointed out that the wages spent by the technicians have bolstered the local economy; they also believed that having attained one new industry, Gela will eventually be able to attract others. The eagerness with which the residents embraced this dream was reflected in their walking, which struck me as jauntier than any I had observed in Sicily since our arrival.

The jauntiest of all the citizens we met was the cane-bearing seventy-five-year-old discoverer and custodian of the Great Wall, a mammoth expanse of stone built by the ancient Greeks to defend themselves against invading Carthaginians. The old man was garrulously proud of having found it while tilling his vineyard in 1948. Much to the annoyance of the Italian Tourist Office official who was trying to lecture us on the archaeological aspects of the wall, the old man kept talking about his discovery and at one point, using his cane as a sword, he demonstrated how a Greek guard, with his back to the wall, fought off the enemy single-handedly until he was able to slip through a secret door.

The old man was delighted with my observation that he looked like a twin brother of the late King Victor Emmanuel. "The King himself was struck by the resemblance," he told us. "Three times we saw one another and three times we stared at one another, too amazed to say anything. It was like looking into a mirror. But there was one important difference in our bodies. The King's legs were crooked. Mine, as you can see, are perfectly straight."

In an effort to shake off the old man the disgusted official marched us to the edge of the archaeological area and pointed to the bay where the Americans, following the example of the ancient Carthaginians, amassed their landing forces for the Sicilian invasion of July 1943. He was in the midst of describing the scene, which he had witnessed as a boy, when the Discoverer of the Great Wall joined us. Interrupting the official again, he informed us that the invasion had cost him thirty barrels of wine owed to him by

311

Sicilians who, afraid of the American invasion, had taken to the hill and never returned. "Do you think I could get my money back if I sued your government?" he asked me. "After all, if it hadn't been for your country's invasion I could have collected the money due to me . . ."

Heading inland again, we visited the spectacular Roman mosaics at Piazza Amerina and then proceeded to the nearby village of Aidone where, since 1953, a team of Princeton University archaeologists has been unearthing the ancient Greek city of Morgantina, which at the time of its destruction had 30,000 inhabitants. For all of his experience with tourists our driver Giovanni had never heard of the place. As we drove over a precarious country road leading to the plateau that contains the city, it became clear that nothing had been done to encourage sightseeing at Morgantina, despite its proximity to Piazza Amerina, one of the most popular tourist attractions in Sicily.

There were no other visitors. We wandered among the excavated foundations and walls until a man with two suitcases suddenly appeared from nowhere and with suspicious eyes asked us what we wanted. I was equally suspicious, for I thought the suitcases contained artifacts he had stolen from the ruins. But he turned out to be the guardian of the diggings and the foreman of the seventy men who are employed by the Princeton archaeologists when they come there in the summer. The man became the soul of congeniality as soon as he learned we were Americans. He showed us various sections of the ruined city that had escaped our attention: a villa with the Greek word meaning "welcome" at the entrance, elaborate floor mosaics which were more finely designed than anything we had seen at Piazza Amerina, and part of the altar of Demetrius, a slab of stone on which the rite of human sacrifice was performed.

On our way to the next village, where our guide lived, he told us that he had worked on the diggings at Piazza Amerina for twelve years but preferred the work at Morgantina. "Being Greek, Morgantina is older and far more fascinating. Yet hardly anyone comes there. The ruins could become the salvation of Aidone because the town is dying from unemployment and emigration but not a thing is done to promote Morgantina as a tourist place. The previous mayor was too much of a drunkard to bother about it—a true Christian Democrat. The present mayor, who is a Socialist, is trying to stir up the authorities. At least, that's what he claims. In the meantime, Aidone is sick and dying. When will our stupid government officials wake up to the fact that Morgantina could be as much of a gold mine as Piazza Amerina?"

After a day of reveling in the dazzling baroque art of Noto and Comiso, where the tourists were noticeably few, we drove to Siracusa, and for the first time saw a Sicilian city that has been drastically transformed by postwar economic developments. What was once a drowsy and charming small town with the atmosphere of an outdoor museum has changed into a booming modern city. The old town has been pushed into the background by a new business and shopping area. In less than two decades Siracusa has more than doubled in size. Oil is the ingredient that has powered its growth. Twenty miles away, enveloped in dark clouds of chemical fumes, is the city of Augusta where the giant Esso Raisom (Raffinerie Siciliane Oilii Minerali), which sprawls on 400 acres, has grown into one of the largest plants of its kind in Europe and made Augusta Italy's second largest port. In the wake of this success the coast between Augusta and Siracusa has become dotted with industries which supply the 350,000 inhabitants of the province of Siracusa with enough jobs to give them their first taste of affluence.

As happened in Gela and Porto Empedocle, the choicest jobs went to technicians from the north of Italy. They came to Siracusa by the thousands with their families. Along with them came a higher standard of living and a set of mores that are sharply at variance with those of Sicily. At the same time a high percentage of peasants in the Siracusa area, lured by the security of a fixed income, abandoned their struggle with the land to fill the lesser jobs created by the new industries. The influx of these two groups into Siracusa has generated a local social revolution, the like of which had never been known in Sicily.

How deeply the revolution has penetrated the Sicilian psyche became apparent to me that first evening in the city when, strolling down its broadened esplanade, which is now lighted by gay neon lights bunched together like multicolored parasols, I saw for the first time young Sicilian couples necking in public. Occupying dozens of benches, they clung to one another busily amorous, while Siracusans promenaded before them without raising any hue or cry, as blasé as the sophisticated residents of any metropolis.

In an apartment from which we could see both the new and the old sections of the city a friend of Danilo, who is of English and Sicilian parentage, told us that Siracusans are better prepared to shed their old traditions than their compatriots in western Sicily. "These people are less afraid of change, more willing to try something new if they think it will improve their situation. There is no Mafia here because people have the capacity to trust one another. In Siracusa you can leave your valuables in an unlocked car without any fear they will be gone on your return. You wouldn't dare do that in Palermo. Yet the situation here is not a happy one. To use one of Edoardo's favorite terms the people here are rapidly succumbing to the sickness of 'alienation.' Capitalism came too suddenly; it bombed their sense of values and battered their psyches. That's what happens, of course, when there is no grassroots planning. Things get messed up. The Sicilians have had centuries of experience coping with poverty—they've become experts at that—but they have no idea of how to cope with so-called progress."

Another friend of Danilo, an economist, was not so much concerned with the Sicilian psyche as he was with the instability of the local economic situation. "The technicians from the north, who earn as much as 400,000 lire a month, want things of quality and are willing to pay for them. Their spending power has raised prices to a point that is disastrous for people with little earning power. But the fault isn't entirely that of the technicians. As more and more peasants keep abandoning the land in the hope of finding work in the city, food prices keep going up. We may soon have to follow the example of the American government and subsidize farmers to stay on the land, in order to make food available at prices that poor people can afford to pay."

The women of Siracusa are already emulating the Americans, the head of the local tourist bureau informed us when we mentioned the necking couples. "The coming of industry has liberated our women to the point that they do nearly everything American women do. They take jobs outside their homes, they walk the streets alone day and night without worrying that they might be mistaken for prostitutes, and they date and make love without being at all secretive about it. For their elders, myself included, this is a painful period of transition. My niece, who was a shy ugly duckling ten years ago, now smokes, dates, drives her own car, and when she sees me, her middle-aged uncle whom she was trained to respect, she offers to race her car with mine. The girl has a job; she is independent. She is the new Sicilian woman, God help us."

The social revolution has not spread to Catania, which still retains its place as the leading commercial city of Sicily with a population second only to Palermo. Despite new industries and the proximity of another large petrochemical plant known as Sincat (Societa Industriale Catanese), the city remains a stronghold of tradition; apparently the technicians from the north who have come there have not been sufficiently numerous to impress their mores on the population. The city is more socially advanced than the communities in western Sicily in that many of the Catanese women work in factories and offices and are seen walking the streets alone on their way to and from work. But there are no couples necking in public, and at night few women are seen, even with escorts. At all hours clusters of darkly dressed men dominate the scene, adding their dourness to that of the lava-dark city.

We were guided around the city by a chubby sociologist of the University of Catania who had worked with Father Duynstee in Palma for two years. Professor Giuseppe Benvenuto spoke of the Dutch priest with an admiration that amounted to hero worship. It was the priest, he told us, who was chiefly responsible for the special law enacted by the Sicilian Regional Government for the welfare of Palma and Licata. "If Father Duynstee were in Sicily now, he would never permit that law to expire." The professor recalled that, thanks to the priest, one of its clauses provided funds for a staff of social workers and teachers who would make certain the villagers learned how to profit from the improvements ordained by the law.

"Poor and ignorant people have to be educated," the professor said. "Otherwise the help they receive will be wasted." He showed us a newly developed commercial area in the center of the city,

315

which he said had been the former site of Catania's worst slum. As part of the city's slum clearance program, the 40,000 residents in the area had been moved to public houses built especially for them. "But those people are really no better off now than they were then. They haven't been taught to adjust to their new quarters. Nor has anything been done to solve their basic problem—unemployment. In a few years their new housing will degenerate into another terrible slum area."

On our way out of Catania we saw printed on a stone wall in huge letters: "USA Assassini." Our driver Giovanni became embarrassed and tried to make excuses for the Catanese. "They don't like the fact that most Americans go to Taormina and bypass their city. Moreover, they are a people with a bad disposition because they live too close to a volcano. It makes them a nervous people." After a few moments he added: "Mt. Etna makes me nervous too. Frankly, I don't know why people want to go there."

We had planned to spend most of the day on Mt. Etna but once we reached the region of the upper plateaus and became imbued with the desolation of the landscape around us, we began to share Giovanni's feelings. All about us, like a vast burnt-out inferno, stretched a chilling expanse of lava-encrusted terrain that dipped in and out of the earth to form various-sized craters. In the sunlight the terrain was the color of old blood. We explored some of the smaller craters, then, to Giovanni's relief, decided we had seen enough. A few miles away, with Giovanni driving faster than he usually did, the mountain became less ominous and by the time we reached Taormina it had fully regained its postcard snow-capped prettiness.

If Etna expressed the total alienation of the human spirit, Taormina epitomized its gregariousness. No longer the cherished resort of the international elite it had been for nearly a half century, the town has become Sicily's Atlantic City, the most popular haven for middle-class Sicilians on vacation. During the two days we spent there, the main street was constantly thronged with visitors parading up and down, their eyes fastened on one another and on the scores of shops along the thoroughfare. Almost no one visited the golden ruins of the town's Roman-Greek amphitheater overlooking the Ionian Sea, which is one of the world's most glorious spectacles.

"The tranquillity for which Taormina was once famous is gone," our hotel manager complained. "The Philistines have driven away the poets by force of numbers; the place is now theirs. There is more business, of course, but at such a terrible price on the nerves." Some of the shopkeepers had similar complaints. An old man, who had operated the same gift shop when I first visited Taormina in 1936, said: "There is quantity of people now but not quality. The wealthy celebrities don't come here as often as they once did, nor do they stay as long. Now we get large numbers of nonentities who come here looking for bargains."

A few miles beyond Taormina we climbed a tall mountain on a treacherous road to reach the Norman-built village of Forza d'Agro, which is higher than Taormina but has none of its opulence. The top of the mountain is crowned by a fourteenth-century castle built by Count Roger. Immediately below it, commanding breathtaking views of the straits of Messina and of Calabria, are stone shells of small houses that were originally built for the Count's servants and are now abandoned. One of the shells could have been ours for a few hundred dollars. "Buy it," urged the young surveyor acting as agent for the owner. "In a few years Forza d'Agro will become another Taormina and everyone who owns property here will be rich. We're especially anxious to have foreigners live here because they are the ones who bring prosperity with them."

As tempting as the idea was, we said "no" to the young man, and talked with some of the old women sitting in front of their one-room hovels, sewing and peeling vegetables. "We like it up here," an octogenarian great-grandmother said. "There is plenty of water and the air is as good as anything you can breathe outside of paradise. Once I had to go to Catania to see a doctor about my pains and he recommended that I move to a village where the air would be perfect. 'Where would that be?' I asked him. 'Forza d'Agro,' he replied. 'But I already live there,' I told him. 'In that case,' the doctor said, 'I would advise you to stay there.' "

Overhearing this, another old woman told us: "She can talk that way because she has a son who supports her. But what good is fine air if there isn't enough to eat? All it does is make you hungrier."

Acting on a recommendation made by Edoardo Watjen, we abandoned the coastline a few miles above Forza d'Agro and trav-

eled northwest through a seldom visited zone which, with its heavily forested mountainous terrain, suggests what much of Sicily
must have looked like when it was colonized by the Greeks, before
exploiters denuded it of its trees. One reason perhaps why this area
escaped that fate is that many of its mountains are too precipitous
to be cultivated. Yet we passed several villages which subsist entirely on agriculture. Near one of them we saw, for the first time,
groups of Sicilian women working in the fields. We also saw one of
those monuments of futility which we had supposed existed only
in the wastelands of western Sicily: an entire village constructed
by the Fascist regime, which has never been occupied.

When we came out of the interior we were on the north coast of
the island, a few miles west of Messina, at the ancient settlement of
Tindari, which is the last of the Greek cities established in Sicily.
The Greek ruins sit on a hill next to the sea, above a long stretch
of sandy beach that parallels the Mediterranean like a golden carpet. Not a soul was on the beach. We spent the night at the only
hotel in Tindari, where we were the only tourists. The hotel is a
gloomy, ramshackle building but from our window we had a fine
view of Mt. Etna, and in the night we could smell the flower
gardens that bordered the hotel on all sides.

The next morning we inspected the ruins of the old city, and
then strolled to the next settlement, Rocca di Femmina, where a
few peasants try to eke out a living. We were more than one
hundred fifty miles from the impoverished zone where Danilo
operates, but their problems were the same. When one of them
heard me admire the view from his house, he became annoyed.
"Maybe the view means something to you because you come from
the city," he said. "But it doesn't mean a damn thing to me. All I
know is that this place is little more than a rock with no water
and no hope of getting any soon."

He was a powerfully built man in his late thirties with red hair
and blue eyes. He said there was plenty of water available but the
town authorities wanted to charge him one hundred dollars to
have it conducted to his land, even though he had agreed to provide whatever manual labor was necessary. "Who can afford that
kind of money?" he growled. "Those bastards must think I have
an American father."

318

His wife, a woman in her early twenties who was dressed in black, held a naked baby in her arms and looked worried. When the child demanded her father, he took her from his wife and smiled for the first time. "The trouble is that nobody cares whether we starve or not," he said less angrily. "Every time I complain to the authorities about my situation they either shrug their shoulders or suggest we go somewhere else."

Patricia asked whether he ever found any Greek artifacts during his ploughing. "There is no hope of that," he replied. "Too many other people have dug this same land before me—the Saracens, the Normans, the French and the Spanish. They took everything that was to be had. And now there is nothing left but rock."

I asked whether he had considered the possibility of finding work in another country.

"That doesn't interest me. It takes too much money to travel anywhere. Besides, why should I leave my children behind? They are the only joy I have in life." He smiled again, and kissed the baby in his arms so hard that she began to cry.

On the final day of the journey Giovanni, who for nine days had struck us as a young man of few words, suddenly became eloquently autobiographical. It began in Tindari, when he asked if he could take his meals with us as his employer had failed to supply him with enough expense money, and it continued until he delivered us to our door in Partinico. We learned a great deal about his wife, who supplemented the family income with the embroidery she produced at home; about his two children (he loved them dearly, he said, but was determined there would be no more), and about his immediate ambition: to purchase a car like the one we were riding in so that he could quit his present employer and make more money working directly for the Hertz organization in Palermo.

He was still talking of his ambition as we entered Palermo, but the sight of motorcycle policemen clearing the way for Cardinal Ruffini's black limousine caused him to switch to the subject of Salvatore Giuliano, who was his hero. "All the important church people and bigshot politicians respected and helped Giuliano because they knew that he stole from the rich to help the poor."

Giovanni had known Giuliano in person through his uncle,

319

who had been a close friend of the bandit. When Giovanni was five years old, Giuliano had attended a party given by his parents and danced all evening. "I saw him several times after that in Montelepre with my uncle. I have never understood why Giuliano was so fond of a man like my uncle, who is neither honest nor good. Unlike Giuliano, he is a man who steals from everyone and gives to no one. He owns twenty-two houses but I have never asked him for a lira, except what he owed me. I worked for him once as a mason's helper but he wouldn't pay me the wages I had earned. After many months, he offered me a few lire to try to keep me quiet, but I wouldn't give him the satisfaction of taking them. I want all that is owed to me or nothing, I told him . . .

"Can you imagine a man of such dishonesty being a close friend of Giuliano? He was such a close friend that when the police were trying to catch Giuliano they also looked for my uncle. They finally found him but he managed to wiggle out of being arrested by pretending his legs were paralyzed. Nowadays he walks the streets of Palermo and is respected by everyone. But not by me."

My attempt to convince Giovanni that Salvatore Giuliano had been more of a villain than a hero proved futile.

"Many terrible crimes were committed by persons who pretended to be Giuliano," he said firmly. "Giuliano was an excellent man. If he were still alive the terrible poverty we saw on this trip would be wiped out. He would have seen to that."

"Do you think that the work Danilo Dolci is doing will help wipe out poverty?" I asked.

He took a long time answering. "I've heard you and the Signora mention his name a number of times," he said, "but I'm not sure I know what his profession is."

After I had described some of Danilo's activities, Giovanni said: "I think that Giuliano's methods for helping the poor were better —more direct and more efficient."

Peppina was sweeping her doorfront as we arrived on the Via Emma. "Welcome back," she shouted. "Who is that young man driving—your son?"

Giovanni beamed. "I wish I were," he said to me. "What a wonderful thing it would be to be an American and live in a country where there is no poverty."

320

Encounters
in Palermo

DURING MY ABSENCE from Partinico, Danilo, always a man of surprises, requested and obtained an hour's interview with his old adversary Cardinal Ruffini. It was Franco who broke the news to me (Danilo was in Palermo interviewing a princess about her group experiences) and who showed me a transcript of the conversation.

Danilo's ostensible reason for seeking the interview was to question the Cardinal about his group experience as the head of the Catholic Church in Sicily. But beneath this public motive I detected Danilo's fondness for doing the unexpected, as well as an assertion of his turn-the-other-cheek attitude, an element in his philosophy of nonviolence which he is sometimes able to use with finesse. As was to be expected, the interview was a fiasco. The Cardinal took the offensive from the start, monopolizing the conversation to such a degree that Danilo never got a chance to ask his questions.

Yet the encounter had all the elements of a fine historical drama that is expertly cast. Neither of the protagonists was a Sicilian, yet more than any other two men, they symbolized the Sicilian conflict between the old and the new. Cardinal Ruffini had long been an ardent champion of the status quo, a staunch authoritarian who once declared that Spain under the reign of Generalissimo Franco represented the ideal state. Danilo, on the other hand, was irrevocably committed to the proposition that basic changes in the

Sicilian social structure were long overdue. Although the Cardinal was in his late seventies and Danilo was young enough to be his son, both men were dynamically engaged in activating their principles. Both knew Sicily well, the Cardinal from the heights of his papal authority, Danilo from the bottom-dog level of the poor. And both had been there for many years. The Cardinal arrived in Palermo in 1946; Danilo came to Trappeto six years later.

From the outset the Cardinal did most of the talking; yet in their first few minutes together there was enough of an exchange to suggest some of the fundamental differences between them.

DANILO: I thank you for having granted me this appointment. With so much misunderstanding between us, I thought it best to have a personal meeting with you.

CARDINAL: I'm glad to know you personally. I know many things about you. Not all of them good. I have had information about your activities which hasn't always been pleasant, and I have attacked you publicly. But now I am glad to know you directly. . . . You were with Don Zeno, were you not? At Nomadelfia? Yes, yes I know a good deal about you. As a student you were president of FUCI . . .*

DANILO: How much you know! It's a shame that your information about me hasn't always been accurate.

CARDINAL: There, there. You will see that I am well-informed. You were with Don Zeno, whom I know. I had to deal with him when I was in Rome. He too is a strange type. Are you a Christian?

DANILO: My parents had me baptized.

CARDINAL: Ah yes, you were a Christian, then you strayed away. You wanted to do good, good for the people, but you strayed away and then you couldn't find the right road and you wound up being ensnared by the Communists . . .

DANILO: I don't believe I'm the sort of person who permits himself to be ensnared . . .

CARDINAL: You have played the game of the Communists. The Communists have exploited your name. That is so. Yet I've been thinking that there must be some good in you because when I attacked you, you did not say anything. Something good must be in you. You might be a man of good faith searching for a way of helping people and you might be successful, but you have taken the wrong road. You have searched, you have done a certain amount of

* A Catholic youth organization.

good, but it is obvious that you need a tutor. You should
have first come to me. I could have helped you avoid certain
errors. You are young—you are forty or forty-five years old,
a youth. If you had come to me in time you would not have
lost your faith. You are a Christian who left Christianity
and grew up alone. You grew up badly and made serious
errors. I have kept informed.

DANILO: But has the information you received always been accurate?
The information from the police, for example . . .

CARDINAL: Yes, I've had information from the police. But I have also
seen your book. What you say about Palermo is not true. It
was in Germany that I saw your book. And with what photographs! As though Palermo were really like that. Yes, there
is poverty here but to misrepresent Palermo . . .

DANILO: May I point out that in the preface I stated specifically that
my analysis was limited to the phenomenon of poverty and
misery . . .

CARDINAL: Palermo is a city where a great deal of building is going on.
There are whole new sections . . .

DANILO: I did not say in my book that Palermo is all misery. In the
preface I defined the limits of my research. I don't like to
generalize needlessly. My procedure is to document each
situation, each problem. For example, as your secretary
may have informed you, I am now trying to understand the
extent of group activity in the province of Palermo, to find
out what are the difficulties that impede it. People often
ask me, even in foreign countries: What does the Cardinal
think of this or that problem? Not wishing to say anything
that is inaccurate, I have come to you to ask what your
thinking on this subject is . . .

CARDINAL: I am considered a reactionary yet I have been responsible
for the building of two new towns. I have established in
Palermo social service centers, new schools and shelters for
the old. I have assisted more than 10,000 sick persons.
Through our facilities we feed many of the poor. The
Commune owes me eighty million lire for my projects. They
officially acknowledge they owe me this money but claim
they haven't got it. You see I speak frankly. Even with you I
say what I think. I am a simple man. Yes, a simple man but
not a stupid one. I believe in having faith in one another,
but also in being prudent. In Rome when anyone did
anything against me I did not want to know who it was. I
have received you. I didn't have to. Through these chambers
pass ambassadors but I am ready to receive the most humble
citizen. In that chair where you are recently sat the director

of *L'Ora*, a Communist. I speak with everyone. I listen. But it isn't necessary to play ball with the Communists. I was in Church and they told me you were at the head of their peace parade . . .

DANILO (trying to interrupt): If you will permit me . . .

CARDINAL: They speak of peace but if it weren't for the Americans we would all be under the domination of the Communists . . .

DANILO: I am against all wars. At the age of eighteen I was arrested as a conscientious objector . . .

CARDINAL: The idea of being a conscientious objector is nonsense.

DANILO: You really believe that?

CARDINAL: Yes.

DANILO: Don't you believe that fundamentally Christ was a conscientious objector?

CARDINAL: The individual cannot oppose public opinion. The individual must know that those who have power over him know more than he does. Your objections serve no purpose. He who is in charge knows what to do . . .

The Cardinal continued to control the direction of the interview with filibuster and nonsequiturs. At one point, apropos of nothing, he flatly stated that he had no use for Danilo's fasting; it accomplished nothing. He was certain that the dams in Sicily would be built without any of his fasts, but when Danilo asked what dams he had in mind, he was unable to name any. In another nonsequitur, toward the close of the interview, the Cardinal attacked the Communists for their love of luxury and expressed pride in "personally owning nothing in this world." He added: "I should show you where I sleep. A worker would want something better than the bedroom I use. And my dining room has only two mirrors."

"Only two mirrors," Franco sighed. *"Povero Cardinale*. And he is such a handsome old boy." More seriously, he said: "I've been trying to decide whether the man is senile or shrewd, and I've finally concluded that if he is senile, there is method in his senility."

At our conference the next morning Danilo was more eager to hear of my journey than he was to discuss his interview with the Cardinal. He was particularly interested in my reactions to Erice, Siracusa, Palma di Montechiaro, and Riesi. Although he was already aware of the pressing predicament in which Palma and Li-

324

cata found themselves, he promised that he would discuss it with Edoardo to determine whether or not the Center could be of any assistance. When the name of Father Duynstee entered the conversation, I asked him point-blank why he had not made any effort to communicate with the Dutch priest during his three years at Palma, adding that this was one of the frequent criticisms aimed at him by some of his ex-collaborators.

"The man is a first-rate sociologist," Danilo said, "and I was always fully in sympathy with what he was trying to accomplish. But I deliberately had nothing to do with him. I knew that any communication between us would have further jeopardized his situation in Palma. The Church was constantly looking for some excuse to get him out of there, and I didn't want to be the one to provide it."

He was far more reserved on the subject of Tullio Vinay. "There are various ways of accomplishing the same thing," he commented on Vinay's criticism of him. "Vinay is an excellent person."

The final point in our discussion dealt with my impending move to Palermo, where we would live for a month before leaving Sicily. Danilo was pleased to hear that despite the move, I would continue to attend the Center meetings and be available for any interpreting chores that might come up.

"You may want a final conference with me after you have talked with some of my critics in Palermo," Danilo said with a smile, and proposed that we arrange to meet away from his office so that there would be no interruptions. I agreed, of course, and he encircled a Sunday on his calendar that was close to the date Patricia and I were to leave Sicily. Before we parted, I invited him to a party which Robert Jordan planned to give in my honor at his Mondello home (Jordan had suggested I invite some of my own friends), and he accepted with enthusiasm. "I want to meet the American officials. It would be to our mutual benefit to become friends and clear away any misunderstandings there may be between us."

The eve of our departure from the Via Emma was a melancholy one with the neighbors clustering around to say their goodbyes and beg us to return for a visit before leaving Sicily. For them final farewells are as anguishing as death. The language barrier had prevented any real rapport with Patricia, but the women all took turns kissing and embracing her. Then each of them presented us with tokens of their affection. Donna Vincenzina was apologetic that she had no other memento for us but a bottle of wine. Peppina gave Patricia a bottle of perfume called *Paradiso Perduto* (Lost Paradise) and Maria pressed upon us a litre of three-year-old Marsala, which turned out to be the finest I had ever tasted. The landlord and all of his family, including Teresa, who looked more wistful than ever, threw a lavish dinner party for us, with a great deal of champagne and a noticeable lack of argument between our host and his belligerently Communist son-in-law.

A mammoth Dodge station wagon, provided by Robert Jordan's office, transported us and our belongings to Palermo. On the way, at the suggestion of our driver, whose name was Seminario, we visited the shrine of Santa Rosalia, Palermo's patron saint, which is in a cave high on Monte Pellegrino. "You will fare better in Palermo if you pay your respects to Santa Rosalia first," Seminario promised.

We found the saint reclining on a dais robed in a golden costume. Her face has the conventionally pretty features of most religious statuary. One elbow is propped up and delicate fingers are cupped around an ear, as though the saint were listening to a voice from heaven. A crown adorns her head, jewels festoon her chest, and all around her is a gaudy sea of trinkets, gifts from grateful visitors for whom she has done favors. A font of Sicilian lore, Seminario told us that Santa Rosalia had been performing miracles for the past eight hundred years. Her major miracle was her first; it saved the people of Palermo from the devastation of a cholera epidemic, at the cost of her life.

Before she became a saint, Rosalia was the daughter of a wealthy aristocratic family of Palermo who ran away from home when she was denied permission to become a nun, and took up residence on Monte Pellegrino in the cave where she is now enshrined. "Thanks to her, the epidemic ended within twenty-four hours," Seminario said. "Afterwards her body was returned to the cave, and ever since then the people of Palermo have celebrated her

326

memory with a big annual feast which goes on for a week and doesn't cost anyone a penny. It is financed by money which Santa Rosalia herself left to the church in her will. She thought of everything."

Actually, our patron saint in Palermo was Rosita Lanza, who, on learning of our difficulties in finding housing for a month, offered us the use of a small apartment which she maintained in the city as a *pied à terre* for her occasional visits and also as the headquarters of her birth control activities. There was only one stipulation made: on Fridays, which was the day when the women of Palermo could visit the apartment for advice on family planning, we would have to clear out early to make room for them.

This slight inconvenience was nothing compared to the worry we had at first that the police might, at any time, choose to overlook the prestige of Rosita Lanza's aristocratic family and raid the apartment while we were in it. It was all too easy to imagine the kind of headlines that would result.

AMERICAN PROFESSOR AND WIFE ARE ARRESTED
AS POLICE RAID ILLEGAL BIRTH CONTROL CLINIC
SPONSORED BY CRUSADING SICILIAN PRINCESS

But we were soon able to dispense with such fears for, as readily became apparent, the birth control campaign in Palermo had made so little headway that it was not likely to provoke any police action; nearly all the women of Palermo ignored the clinic or knew nothing about it. "The few women who come to us for help," complained Rosita Lanza's assistant, "are mostly fairly well-to-do women. We are not reaching the women we should be helping, those from the slums. They have been frightened off, either by their own fears, or by their husbands' orders, or by the threats and propaganda of the priests."

We were seldom in the apartment, except during the night and at siesta time. There was too much to do and too many persons to interview. Only during the siesta, when life in Palermo came to a standstill, could I find time for the two activities that seemed essential: recording my impressions of what I had just seen and heard, and perusing Palermo's two daily newspapers, the leftwing *L'Ora* and the Christian Democrat *Giornale di Sicilia*.

Although the political views of these two newspapers differed, they were surprisingly alike in their vigorous anti-Mafia stand and in their persistent exposure of local government inefficiency and scandal. They were also similarly obsessed with Sicilian "crimes of honor," a subject which in both newspapers took up more space than any other. There was never any lack of variety in the crimes. One man disposed of his love rival with dynamite; another chopped his wife to death because he suspected her of infidelity (his final accusation was that she had been sleeping with her step-son) and then hanged himself; a young man returned from his job in Germany to murder the lover of his twelve-year-old sister; a woman shot and killed her brother's sweetheart because she did not consider her worthy of him; a wife stabbed her husband's suspected paramour with a knife she had concealed in the bouquet of red carnations she offered her victim.

To many newspaper readers "crimes of honor" must have seemed like a routine part of daily life, no more surprising or reprehensible than the latest government scandal or tomorrow's unfavorable weather forecast. As for their effect on the reader whose "honor" had recently been violated, the heavy daily doses of such crimes must have acted as a potent stimulus for fresh mayhem.

Only anti-American bulletins on the Vietnam war and the juiciest reports on government corruption and inefficiency could relegate "crimes of honor" to inside pages. The sudden lack of drinking water in half of Palermo for a two-week period in July was one of the government scandals that dominated the news. Another front page scandal that month, one which titillated Palermitani, concerned two government agencies at war with one another over an outstanding debt. The Palermo office of ERAS had obtained a short-term loan of seventy-eight million lire from a government financing agency the year before, and had not yet paid. To get its money back the financing agency decided to resort to drastic measures. One morning, before any of the two thousand ERAS employees arrived for work, a group of finance officials and policemen, equipped with two trucks, invaded the ERAS offices. Over the shrieking protests of a watchman, they stripped the offices of every typewriter and calculating machine, and spirited the booty

328

away to a secret hiding place. There it remained until ERAS paid its debt.

At first the violence recorded daily in the newspapers seemed to be at variance with the serene and sensuous face of the city. The heavy postwar increase in automobile traffic had destroyed the quiet of Palermo and the leisurely *passeggiatta* that used to take place on the Via Liberta, but the sidewalk cafés were as crowded as ever with men and women unhurriedly partaking of their *espressi* and *gelati,* and there were still a surprisingly large number of horse-drawn carriages in the streets. And although the many high-rise apartment buildings that the government had constructed for its employees were in jolting contrast to the city's nineteenth-century architecture, the old elegance still prevailed. The city still represented a hypnotic synthesis of Arabic, Norman, and Spanish sensibility.

But for anyone who looks at the city closely the hypnosis cannot last for long. Under the ingratiating façade are century-old layers of corruption and cynicism. In Palermo, as nowhere else on the island, the essense of their evil permeates the atmosphere like the sweet smell of death, a seductive perfume which the casual visitor tends to ascribe to the opulence of the city's natural beauty. Nowhere else in Sicily does the character of a community suggest the immense obstacles that block the actions and hopes of a Danilo Dolci. For unlike most corruption, which eventually destroys itself, Palermo's corruption has become a bastion of strength for those in power, an integral part of the social structure firmly kept in place by attitudes and habits so ancient that they have become second nature to most Palermitani of all classes.

As I became better acquainted with the mentality of Palermitani, the seemingly absurd question once put to me as to whether I was for or against the Mafia lost its absurdity. For it became increasingly evident that whether the subject under discussion was the Mafia, crimes of honor, government corruption or any other self-defeating factor of Sicilian life, the primary consideration was not so much one of morality as of tradition. In all strata of society, the people seemed to be willingly entrapped by the past and its values. There were, of course, many Sicilians who appreciated the need for a more progressive set of values but there were not enough of them and, as often as not, they disagreed with one another as to their aims. The most eloquent members of this group were the frustrated idealists who spoke the language of cynicism.

Among the latter was the highly articulate director of the Mormino Foundation, an educational philanthropic agency established as a memorial to the founder of the Banco di Sicilia. He saw no hope for Sicily as long as its present educational structure remained the same. "The educators need to be more educated, and the entire school curriculum needs to be drastically revised. Did you know that it doesn't include a single course that deals with the subject of civic responsibility? No wonder there are so many villages in Sicily that haven't changed since the days of Homer. We also need many more schools. The law requires all children between the ages of five and fourteen to attend school, but it is a silly law because in many towns there aren't any schools for children beyond the fifth grade. And those that do exist are often little more than stables."

Like most Sicilians, the director blamed the politicians for Sicily's backwardness. "With a population of more than four and a half million people Sicily deserves better representatives than it gets. Our politicians aren't qualified to be in government service; for one thing, they have less civic responsibility than anyone else. As soon as they get elected, their main preoccupation becomes to line their pockets as fast as they can. The Communists are the only ones whose hands are clean but the reason for that is that they have not been in any real position of power in Sicily. As soon as they are, they will begin to do the same thing."

Corruption, he added, seldom disturbs the voting public. "Take the case of the present mayor of Palermo. He came into office a poor man but became a millionaire in a very short time. Everyone knew by what dirty methods he had become rich; yet in the next election he was voted back into office. There is a great deal of vote-buying. A mere kilo of pasta can buy a vote but politicians sometimes spend as much as five and ten thousand lire for a single vote. Recently my maid received five thousand lire *in the mail* for her vote. It is absurd to hope for democracy in Sicily as long as this kind of thing continues."

When I asked why his foundation did not work with Danilo Dolci's educational program, the director replied that it could not associate itself with anyone who depends on Communists for support. "Why does he do that?" he asked. "He should be able to work without them." I tried to explain that Danilo used the Communist press as another means of bringing public opinion to bear on the actions of the government in Rome. "The government in Rome doesn't give a damn about public opinion," he said. "It is completely indifferent to everything."

As a final expression of his cynicism, he loaded me down with weighty and elaborately printed tomes published by his foundation which dealt with the history, culture and economic promise of Sicily; then, looking me straight in the eye, declared: "The only solution to all the Sicilian problems is to let a tidal wave submerge Sicily long enough to wipe out everything, then start anew."

Robert Jordan, through whom I had met the director, also introduced me to Father Noto, a Jesuit priest who had studied Business Management for four years at Marquette University in Milwaukee. Known as a liberal churchman, he was the head of an educational project called "The Center for Social Studies," which sometimes collaborated with the United States Information Service in offering courses and seminars to leaders of *la classe dirigente*—the Establishment. "It is too frustrating and difficult to work with the masses," he told me, "so we begin from the top level of society and work downwards. In that way our leadership learns more about its responsibility and becomes more aware of the problems of Sicily, and everyone benefits. Our main job is to influence people who are in a position to be influential. We want to bring about changes but without revolution, without destroying the social structure. We do not want to make any enemies."

The Jesuit's chief objection to Danilo Dolci was based on Danilo's associations with the Communists. "They are people of bad faith who do everything for political motives. They are against people, not for them. We don't work with them because we don't want to be used by them."

His thin bespectacled face puckered in disdain when I asked how closely the leaders of the Catholic Church in Sicily work with the Christian Democrats. "Our bitterness about the Christian

Democrats is that they don't listen to our desires. They do as they please and we are in no position to influence them, for they know we have to go along with them. We are obliged to support them because they are, after all, the only force large and powerful enough to oppose the Communists."

As might be expected, nearly all the Sicilians I met through the offices of the American officials in Palermo were members of the Establishment who had no wish to change the social structure. A number of them attended the party that Robert Jordan gave for me in the garden of his charming home in Mondello. Danilo was conspicuously an outsider. He wore a natty black business suit but no necktie; the collar of his shirt was unbuttoned this time, with the ends of it neatly tucked inwards to form a triangle at his neck.

"He looks like an unfrocked priest who forgot to buy a necktie," remarked Dante Vittorini, who was one of the guests invited at my request. For Dante and for most of the other guests it was the first time they had laid eyes on Danilo. At first his presence prompted considerable wariness but after a couple of drinks their curiosity got the best of them and they clustered around him to ask questions or listen. Danilo, dodging chitchat as always, made the most of the opportunity by talking about the Center.

Among the guests who engaged Danilo's attention, as well as my own, was a prominent Sicilian baron named Agnello, whose name and title had been a household term to me since childhood. On being introduced, I could not help exclaiming over this fact and explaining to the Baron that my parents had grown up near his hometown of Siculiana, where the name Baron Agnello symbol- ized wealth and power to such an extent that it became, among my relatives, a favorite metaphor for extravagant living. Whenever any of the children in our family asked for the purchase of any- thing which my father considered beyond his means, he would shout at us: "Who do you think I am—the Baron Agnello?"

Amused by the story, the Baron suggested we meet again to swap reminiscences about our relatives, and gave me a telephone number and address in Palermo. After the party Danilo explained that the Baron had more or less given up living in Siculiana. A few years before some men had kidnapped him and held him for ransom at the bottom of a well for twelve days. It took the police that many days to find the kidnappers and the Baron.

There was no time to meet with the Baron again, so crowded was our schedule of social engagements. At one dinner party our host was Charles Stout, who had recently returned from a trip to Rome and missed the Jordan party. By now Stout was eager to make Danilo's acquaintance and discuss Sicilian problems with him; he had made an independent study of his activities and had a far clearer view of them than he had when he first arrived in Sicily. More than most other American officials I had encountered in my various trips to Sicily, Stout impressed me with his willingness to learn from Sicilians on every class level and with the thoroughness of his researches.

By and large American officials, like other foreign officials, tended to adhere to the law of gravitation and socialize with one another and with members of the Establishment. The higher the rank of the official the higher was apt to be the social standing of his guests, but the more trivial the content of the conversation. At a more or less typically elite dinner party given by an important American official and his wife the twittering of his guests filled the atmosphere like the evening sound of starlings gathered on a public building.

"My dears, I have discovered miniature avocados and have fallen in love with them," exclaimed a middle-aged dowager with the gushing passion of a young girl. "I don't know how I shall ever get along without them when we return to the States . . ."

The most animated discussion of the evening was on the problem that American women abroad have when being greeted by European men. "How can one tell whether an Italian is a hand-kisser or not?" one woman asked plaintively. "It's so awkward not knowing what to do," another woman commiserated, "whether to put out your hand so that he can kiss it or whether to extend it in such a way that he can shake it."

Among the guests that evening was my friend Corrado Niscemi, looking more bored than usual. I presented him with a print of San Corrado which I had picked up at the Church of San Corrado in Noto. He thanked me, saying that it would undoubtedly bring him good luck. Then, becoming weary of the general chatter, he drew me to a corner of the room and resumed his lifelong monologue on the history and character of the Sicilians, a theme that invariably engaged his deepest feelings of love and rage.

It was the last time I was to hear the monologue. The San Corrado print did not bring him enough luck. A few months later he fell in his bedroom at the Villa Niscemi and died of internal injuries.

Accidentally, through an American television director at Robert Jordan's party, I learned about the existence of a Waldensian pastor in Palermo who heads a task force of teachers and social workers that are trying to help the city's slum dwellers. Although neither Vinay nor Danilo had ever mentioned Pietro Panascia to me, he is like them in the intensity of his dedication and in his keen awareness of the factors that keep Sicilian misery in its virulent state. Like Vinay, Panascia regards religion as a necessary instrument for social justice. Unlike Danilo, he believes in the efficacy of individual acts of charity. While he has neither the scope nor the breadth of vision of Danilo or Vinay, he is endowed with a valuable asset which the other two men lack. Being of Sicilian origin, he can talk with Sicilians in their own tongue without being considered an outsider.

As a clergyman who puts the spirit of Christianity above religious dogma, Panascia is one of the few churchmen in Palermo who can circulate among the slum dwellers without any fear of rejection. Often it is he, rather than a Catholic priest, who is summoned to the bedside of a dying slum dweller. "It makes no difference to these families that I am not a Catholic, just as it makes no difference to me that they are. They call on me because they feel antagonistic toward priests and also because I don't charge them anything. These are people who trust almost no one but I think that some of them are beginning to trust us . . ."

With a staff of twenty helpers, Panascia operates two schools, one attached to his parish church, which is in the heart of Palermo, the other in a slum. The one hundred and fifty children who attend the slum school are fed and clothed because, as Panascia, put it, "no one else will do that for them if we don't." This act of charity is not without its problems. "Sometimes children come to school only long enough to get some shoes or a coat and then disappear. Some are without homes and we can never find them again. One of the most complicated problems is that of personal cleanliness. Some have nits and a surprising number of the children don't know anything about soap. 'I still have that piece of soap you gave me last Christmas,' one boy said to me the other day.

"But what can you expect?" Panascia sighed. "Their families live in a state of primitive degradation among the dirt and the rats. How can the children be any better than their elders unless they are lifted out of the mud with love and education? Unfortunately, we don't have the facilities to help many children. It is awful to realize how many are without any care whatsoever. Education is compulsory by law but the authorities don't bother making it compulsory for slum children. The less the authorities have to do with the slums the better they like it."

One weekday morning, at the pastor's invitation, we accompanied him on his rounds of Cortile Cascino, one of the slums in the center of the city which we had visited briefly with Franco. This time we were able to see, hear, and smell more closely. The settlement consisted of some fifty families living in dark, dilapidated hovels that were grouped around a rectangular courtyard. The place was deafening. Swarms of naked, screaming children chased each other through the deep mud. In their doorways or around the water fountain in the center of the courtyard the women, unkempt and of all ages, chattered and shouted. The men were the only quiet ones. Most of them were lined up with their backs against a brick wall at the entrance of the courtyard. Panascia greeted them as we passed but the men glared at him without saying anything.

Once we were in the courtyard, the pastor was surrounded by a gang of women noisily demanding to know when the next free distribution of clothes would take place at his church and when their children would be admitted to his school. A slight, middle-aged gentle man with a soft voice, Panascia could not make himself heard above the din. Trying to explain he had calls to make, he managed to push his way through the crowd and enter one of the hovels. We followed him into a foul-smelling room less than eight feet square which had no windows; the only light came from the open doorway. The room held two beds, one for the parents and the other for their six children. There was no kitchen and no toilet. The mother stood at the entrance as there was not enough space in the room for all of us, and kept shouting: "Is this any way for *Cristiani* to be living?" She quieted down when the pastor told her that one of her children could be admitted to his school the following week.

The pastor had visited this settlement at least once a week for more than two years, yet his rage over its condition was as fresh as though he were seeing it for the first time. "These people live worse than pigs, but they don't eat as well," he fumed.

The gang of women in the courtyard, which had grown larger, mobbed the pastor as soon as he came out of the hovel, voicing their demands in a frenzied hullabaloo. Two of the women began to fight, one accusing the other of getting more than her share of the free clothes distributed by the pastor's church. As they clawed and scratched one another, another woman turned on the pastor and, charging him with favoritism, tongue-lashed him with obscenities. Seconding the assault, another woman screeched at him over and over: "Either you give to everybody or you give to nobody."

Panascia seemed to be indifferent to their fury but when one of the men began to curse him, he drew him to one side and, quietly addressing the sullen and ugly face of the man, asked him what the trouble was. It took a great deal of prodding before he finally expressed his grievance: at the last distribution of clothes the women had grabbed everything and he, the only male present, had come away with nothing. After describing how the women had pushed him, jabbed him with their elbows and even spat on him, he asked: "Why should I have to compete with women, I who have been a bachelor all of my life?" He suddenly became angry again. "Why shouldn't you hand me whatever clothes I need? I'm a man, not a woman, and if you're any kind of a goddam minister of God you'll bear that in mind."

A scrawny boy with paralyzed legs dragged himself along the ground until he reached the pastor. His pallid face broke into a smile as the pastor greeted him. The smile vanished when Panascia asked him what he had done with his wheelchair. "That's what I wanted to talk to you about," the boy mumbled. "I need another wheelchair. The other one is broken and someone stole the tires."

The boy's father joined us and confirmed the information, adding that the wheelchair was beyond repair. The pastor admonished the boy for not taking better care of it, then the father for permitting his son to go begging around the city in the wheelchair. The father tried to deny this but the pastor himself had seen the boy begging in the streets several times. "Why don't you try to get a job?" the pastor asked him.

The hard lips tried to pout. "Who would have me, *padre?* Have you forgotten I have a criminal record?" He grinned at me reassuringly and nodded toward the men against the brick wall. "I'm not the only one. There isn't a man here who hasn't."

On our way to call on the boy's mother the pastor told us that Toto could have been cured had his parents permitted him to attend an institute in Switzerland where he would have been treated and taught a trade. The parents had consented to the pastor's arrangements but when the day for his departure came they changed their minds. "We love Toto," they told him. "We can't bear to part with him."

Toto's home was no better than the first one we had visited. We found the mother sitting on a bed breastfeeding a thirteen-month-old child. The pastor asked why the child had not been weaned. The woman clutched the child closer to her and smiled. "My baby enjoys feeding off me." Her gaunt face looked serious again. *"Padre,* how about getting Toto another wheelchair? He really needs it . . ."

"It would be better to send him to Switzerland," the pastor said. "It can still be arranged."

"No, *padre,* never. God gave us children to enjoy, not to send them away."

Afterwards we learned the woman had had eight children; three of them died before the age of five. "Children easily get sick here," the pastor said, "because their parents know nothing about food values. A baby will get a few crusts of bread but never milk from a cow or goat. So they die. Sending them to a hospital can save them sometimes, but to most of these families letting a child go to a hospital means sending it to its death. They are terribly afraid of hospitals."

On our way to another hovel the pastor pointed to a scrawny

337

child playing in the mud and said that when the boy had become desperately ill the year before he had been obliged to wrest him from his mother to get him to a hospital in time. "The doctor saved his life but a week before he was well enough to be discharged the mother came and took him away. She hid the boy and wouldn't tell me where. It is a miracle he is still alive."

Our last call was in a home where, as we entered, a frail woman in black was anguishing over the death of a teen-age son recently killed in an automobile accident. The weeping woman was surrounded by her five children, three of whom were tots. The oldest son, a young man in military uniform home on leave, was trying to comfort her in his boy-awkward fashion. The father was in jail serving a long sentence.

Through her tears the woman begged the pastor to get her son released from the army so that he might try to find a job and support the family. Panascia promised to do what he could but even while he was speaking she gave vent to her agony. Snatching a photograph from a bureau, she thrust it close to my eyes and wailed the story of her son's death. As we each examined the cockily handsome boy in the photograph, she churned herself into a state of frenzy until she began to pull at the roots of her hair.

Panascia grabbed her wrists and finally managed to quiet her with the suggestion that they pray together. "Oh Lord," he began, "console this poor mother in her hour of darkness and grief, and relieve the suffering and misery of this family and all the other families in this neighborhood who live in such destructive poverty. And please, Lord, please open the hearts of those who can help these poor people but don't. Let us all pray . . ."

The last ten days of our Sicilian sojourn were spent in a series of farewell encounters with Dante Vittorini and his family, Marco Pasquale and his girl Erica (whom he was about to marry), Lorenzo and Paola Barbera, Rosita Lanza, and, of course, my relatives. I also had an audience with Cardinal Ruffini, at Charles Stout's suggestion; and met with Danilo for our final conference.

We began our farewells with a weekend in Agrigento and Porto Empedocle. Uncle Pitrinu wept as he embraced us, and promised to stay alive three years longer if we would promise to return to

ENCOUNTERS IN PALERMO

Porto Empedocle within that time.* We promised. On our return
we picnicked with Rosita Lanza on the island of Mozia, the ancestral home of the Whitaker family, which was now presided over by
an octogenarian spinster. The island houses a private museum
filled with archaeological treasures, which is available to friends of
the Whitakers and to tourists who obtain special permission. Rosita showed us some of her favorite museum pieces but birth control, not archaeology, was uppermost in her thoughts.

She was indignant to hear that Edoardo Watjen did not believe
in the efficacy of birth control for the poor. "He is like a certain
demographer in Rome who seriously maintains that the more pro-
teins people eat the more inclined they are to practice birth control. Both men are dodging the real issue, which is that we can't
afford to wait for poor families to become prosperous. We have to
educate them on the subject of birth control now."

I told her about Pietro Panascia, of whom she had never heard,
and she eagerly noted his name and address.

We also picnicked with Lorenzo Barbera and his family, among
the ruins of Solunto, a rarely visited Phoenician settlement near
Palermo that commands idyllic views of the sea and the mountains. For dessert we ate wild strawberries, which a peasant had
thrust on Paola that morning when he noticed that she was pregnant. "A pregnant woman need never go hungry in Sicily," Paola
said. "The peasants will take bread out of their own mouths to
feed her. They believe that God favors this kind of charity above
all others."

"Nearly every peasant superstition can be traced to some practical purpose," Lorenzo commented. "During feudal times giving
food to pregnant women was probably an act of group self-
preservation. But inevitably, a religious connotation was attached
to it so that those who gave food would feel they would be rewarded in heaven."

The picnic gave me the opportunity to talk with Lorenzo about
the early chapters of an autobiographical novel he had shown me
at my request. I found that he is extraordinarily talented, with a
style that is both poetic and vigorous. The chapters had impressed
me deeply with their honest portrayal of Sicilian peasant life. I

* He died of a cerebral hemorrhage the following year.

339

urged him to continue with the manuscript, but he said that his conscience obliged him to put the work of the Center ahead of everything else. "With all the problems we face in Sicily, how can I take time to indulge in the pleasure of literary creation? The chapters you've read were written before I became so seriously involved with the Center."

Lorenzo was amused to hear that I was to have an audience with the Cardinal the next morning. "I hope you fare better than Danilo did," he said; then suggested that if the opportunity arose I ask the Cardinal about his dealings with an illiterate *mafioso* who was a former associate of Giuliano. "Giuseppe G—— is one of the *mafiosi* who has been able to use the influence of the Church to his financial advantage. In exchange for his pledge to pay for the construction of a new church, the Church authorities made it possible for him to buy very cheaply a large tract of land in Palermo which he was able to parlay into a considerable fortune."

Lorenzo knew Giuseppe G—— well. "He is one of the reasons why the building of the dam at Roccamena keeps being postponed. By intimidating small landowners into selling their holdings, he has accumulated some 400,000 hectares of the site that is proposed for the dam. Each hectare cost him less than a half million lire; he'll hold out until he can get three or four million. For a man whose only means of livelihood used to be transporting grain with a cart and a mule, he's become quite an impresario . . .

"The other day he offered me some money if I would write a letter for him to *L'Ora* refuting an article which had attacked him as a *mafioso*. He couldn't understand why I refused. 'I'm not a *mafioso*,' he kept saying. 'I wouldn't harm a fly.' Then he told me that a few months ago the Anti-Mafia Commission made the 'mistake' of taking his gun from him. He telephoned his friend the Bishop of Monreale and within hours a police agent came to his house with his gun and an apology. 'You don't do such things against good people like me' was the way he summarized the incident."

My audience with Cardinal Ruffini took place in his chambers at the Cathedral. For forty minutes I waited in a huge reception hall of black and scarlet décor which was furnished with ponderous chairs and tables. On arriving I was cross-examined by the

Cardinal's secretary, a monsignor who, with a fixed smile, wanted to know who I was, what I wanted, and whether I was a Catholic. When I answered that I had not been a Catholic since I was sixteen, his eyebrows went up but he maintained his smile. "But you were baptized a Catholic," he said pointedly. His eyebrows went down when I acknowledged the fact.

The reception room kept filling up with priests. I talked with one of them, who told me he was on his way to visit Chicago where he would find more than five thousand men and women who had migrated from the village where he had his parish. He had come, like the others, to receive the Cardinal's blessings. Everyone froze as the prelate made his entrance. The Cardinal nodded at me, as though to indicate he had not forgotten I was waiting, then slowly made his way around the room, holding out his ring to be kissed by the priests and blessing each one as he knelt. Although the Cardinal was seventy-seven, he had the robust body of a much younger man. His features were strikingly handsome, almost pretty. The eyes were disconcertingly shrewd but his smile was the essence of geniality. When he was through with the priests and it was my turn to be greeted, he held out his ring to me to be kissed. He smiled as I ignored the ring and shook his hand instead, and led the way into a small and elegantly furnished antechamber. Curling himself into a red satin chair, he bade me sit near him on a sofa, and began to ask the same questions put to me by the monsignor.

In reply to his question as to what I was doing in Sicily, I described my project briefly; then, pointing out that the last time I had been in Sicily was the year after he had assumed command of the Sicilian church, asked him what in his opinion were the most important changes he had observed in Sicily in the intervening years. He replied that three changes struck him as significant: the establishment of the Sicilian Regional Government, the growth of Palermo—"we now have many new and beautiful apartment houses which are perhaps are attractive as those in your country"—and the Church's activity in the field of social work, for which he took major credit. "Have you seen my charities?" When I confessed ignorance of them, he said he would be pleased to show them to me, and arranged an appointment for the next day.

Before I could continue with my questions, he asked me point-blank why I was no longer a Catholic. I began my reply by describing a scene I had witnessed in church as a child: the Irish-American priest passing the collection basket became infuriated with an impoverished widow because she had donated only a nickel; he took the coin from the basket and threw it in the old woman's face. The incident, which took place in the pew in front of me, made a deep impression.

"Ah yes, that must have been a disturbing thing to a child," the Cardinal sympathized. "But surely one such episode could have been overlooked."

I agreed, but added that as I grew older and read more, I lost my faith in the Catholic doctrine, and the childhood episode became symbolic of the Church's failure to concern itself sufficiently with the problems of the poor.

"And what is your present religion?" he asked.

I belong to no church, I answered, but were I to join any organized religion it would probably be that of the Quakers.

"What do they do?" the Cardinal asked, and I could not tell whether he had misunderstood my pronunciation of the word or did not know of the Quakers.

In the middle of my trying to describe what they did, the Cardinal began to expound on the "absurdity" of Protestantism. His chief argument was based on the principle of seniority: Catholicism had been established as the first and only true Christan religion for fifteen hundred years before Martin Luther came along. "If Catholicism was the only true religion for so many centuries, how could it suddenly be in the wrong?" Luther, "an eccentric and weird individual," he insisted, was entirely to blame for the advent of Protestantism. My comment that there were several humanist philosophers who had paved the way for Luther's revolt was rebutted with the nonsequitur that the Catholic Church also had its brilliant philosophers, St. Augustine and St. Thomas among them.

The Cardinal's view of the Catholic Church in the United States was a pessimistic one: he believed that the number of American Catholics was sharply decreasing and that many of the churches were being abandoned. That was not my impression, I told him; as far as I could tell, the majority of children born of

Catholic parents remained Catholic. Black sheep like myself were a small minority; this, I pointed out, was certainly true of my Sicilian relatives and their American progeny.

The Cardinal was amused by my reference to myself as a "black sheep" and, a little later, even more amused when, on exclaiming how young I looked for my age, I attributed it all to a bad memory. Whatever hopes I had entertained for asking some of my prepared questions were dashed by the Cardinal's sudden informality. Either because he found it refreshing to deal with someone of Sicilian extraction who was not overawed by the authority of his office or because he felt challenged by the possibility of retrieving a lost black sheep, he declared his fondness for me, adding that I was "not a bad person but a good person with a feeling for truth."

It was at this moment that his secretary appeared at the doorway, probably to remind the Cardinal of his other appointments. I rose to leave. Waving the secretary away, the Cardinal exclaimed, "I love the truth," and with that threw his arms around me in a bear hug. Too astonished to say or do anything, I remained in his embrace while he proclaimed: "If you were to stay in Palermo just a little longer, I could persuade you to become a Catholic again. Yes, I could. Why, you're not a black sheep. You're a white sheep with the *tiniest* streak of black." He gave me another bear hug, then released me.

Before we left his chamber he offered me his hand again, apparently confident that this time I would kiss the ring. But I could not; once again I grasped the hand and shook it. Out in the reception room, which had refilled with priests, dozens of eyes stared at us as the Cardinal shook my hand and, with an impish grin, said "goodbye" to me in English.

Disappointed that, like some inexperienced reporter, I had fallen into the trap of being interviewed instead of doing the interviewing, I consoled myself with the thought that the next day I would have another chance to ask the Cardinal my questions. But on my return the next morning, a young monsignor informed me that he was to take me on the tour of the charities. Urgent business made it impossible for the Cardinal to join me; he would see me briefly at the end of the tour.

In the company of a Sicilian priest stationed in Brazil, who was

343

home on leave, we visited an infirmary whose facilities were sadly antiquated, a small housing complex for elderly persons without means, a spacious and well-equipped trade school nearing completion, and a stunning modern grade school on the outskirts of the city, where children of the poor boarded for periods of two and three months. Except for the clinic, these were impressive charities but, in terms of the vast Sicilian misery, too few in number to do much more than assuage the Cardinal's conscience.

On our way back to the Cathedral, the young monsignor unexpectedly stopped his Fiat before an unmarked building in the center of the city and, obtaining a key from the janitor, proudly ushered me into an overwhelmingly opulent auditorium, a seductive fantasy of lavish baroque resplendent with chandeliers and gilded furniture. "Another charity?" I inquired. The young monsignor, who was without humor, gravely explained that here His Eminence and his friends convened in the winter months to enjoy string ensemble concerts.

The sight of this luxurious oasis, so close to some of Palermo's worst slum districts, strengthened my resolve to ask the Cardinal as quickly as possible what the Church was doing about the problem of slum clearance. But he was still in a meeting when I arrived at his chambers. And when he finally emerged it was only to ask me to send him my book about Sicilian Americans and to wish me a *buon viaggio.*

Chapter

18

The Passion
of Danilo Dolci

ON OUR LAST SUNDAY in Sicily we picnicked with Danilo and his
family on the wooded slopes of a mountain near Palermo. Vincenzina fed us whole tomatoes, tuna, and hunks of fresh bread; for
dessert Patricia and I contributed some fine *pasticiotti* we had
purchased on the way.

As soon as the meal was over, Danilo, in his most efficient mood,
asked me to help him carry a small folding table and two chairs
from the trunk of his car to a narrow ledge on the mountainside
which he had selected for our conference. There, like figures and
furniture surrealistically imposed on a primeval setting, we sat
opposite one another and talked, while our wives and children, as
directed by Danilo, roamed the slippery and precipitous slopes
hunting for "the joys of nature," which he had assured them were
there for the looking. Sometimes the children, preferring the company of their father to anything in nature, approached our table,
eager for any crumbs of conversation, but Danilo would shoo them
away, once with an admonition that suggested the seriousness with
which he regarded this final conversation: "Go away, please. Can't
you see your father is working?"

Danilo began our talk by saying that he and Franco had been
working intensively lately on a project that would be certain to
create a "shock" when it was made public in two or three months.
He apologized for not being able to tell me more, but assured me I

345

would understand the reason for secrecy when I learned what it was.

As he spoke, I consulted my notebook to determine what to ask him and saw the word "enigma" followed by a question mark. This is the word that has long been the favorite of magazine and newspaper reporters who write about Danilo. "Enigma." I had never asked Danilo what he thought of it; I suddenly decided I would not do so now, for the word struck me as nothing more than an evasion, an empty and cheaply journalistic term intended to wrap the man in mystery while absolving the writer of the need to interpret him. Taking him at his face value, there is nothing "enigmatic" about Danilo. Granting him the sense of dedication to work for principles in which he has utmost faith, his career clearly follows a series of natural developments.

The mystery about a Danilo Dolci does not lie so much within the man as in the fact that the world seems to be incapable of producing more men like him. Unlike most idealists, he has managed to avoid those behavior patterns which might induce some form of compromise, and lives by his principles. Yet even among men of principles, he is a rare phenomenon in that he projects his thoughts and actions into a day-by-day revolutionary effort, leaving the role of oracle to those who cannot step outside the protected confines of conventional society.

Listening to Danilo now in this final conference, I saw him as a prophet who works in the field rather than from the pulpit, as a man of intelligence and imagination with a unique genius for translating his metaphorical view of life into direct action. In a land where hunger, violence, and mourning are dominant factors, he dramatizes hunger by fasting, violence by acts of nonviolence, and mourning by renditions of sorrow for the valleys dying of thirst and neglect. Like Moses, he is a revolutionary prophet who is trying to lead his people out of the wilderness, at the same time providing them with a new set of values that will liberate their minds from the fetters of feudalism. Like many prophets, he suffers from the fate of not being always understood for what he is.

"I know there has been a great deal of criticism against me," Danilo was saying. "There is considerable truth to the allegation that I have much to learn. There is also a great deal of misunderstanding as to what I am willing to do and what I will not do." He was speaking of the men and the women who had once worked with him and then left the Center disenchanted. "They find fault with me because I am not a Saint Ignazio di Loyola. And sometimes because I don't pay enough attention to them. It is true that if people don't have enough quality, I tend to have little direct communication with them; time is too valuable.

"Some get annoyed with me because they would like to have my personal appraisal of them and don't get it. But I cannot always give them one. In general, however, I try to find a common ground with all persons who work with me, and try to bring into our discussions their experience as well as mine. That, in effect, is how the Consiglio Tecnico functions." His eyes brightened. "By the way, have I told you that the Consiglio has not missed a single meeting since it became established in 1957?"

When Eyvind Hytten's name occurred, I told Danilo that in Palermo I had recently dined with his chief lieutenant, Mary Taylor, who was executive secretary of the Center when she, Hytten, and six other collaborators left it in 1964. She and Hytten were now trying to organize an institute in Palermo similar to the one founded recently by the Center.

"Eyvind Hytten is a man I can respect as an adversary," Danilo said pleasantly. "He has his faults but he is an extremely intelligent man. He is one of those who have never quite understood that I find it impossible to compromise on important matters. If I think that some proposed action is wrong, then I cannot go along with it, no matter what the other members of the group think. When Milazzo was soliciting the support of our Center, the staff voted twenty-five to one to give it to him. I was the only dissenter, but I insisted on having my way because I thought it was wrong for the Center to become enmeshed in politics. I may be wrong about insisting on my point of view in arriving at significant policy decisions, but after all the years of experience I have had in Sicily I feel that my opinions may have validity. Of course, if God would take me by the ear and tell me when I am wrong or right, that would make me happy . . ."

The sun had gone down and a stiff mountain breeze blew on us. I was chilled and willing to end our talk but Danilo, roused by his memories, showed no inclination to stop.

"You probably don't know that some years ago Andrelino Oli-vetti, the philanthropist industrialist, tried to form a liberal polit-ical party called *Communita*. The Center was invited to become part of it. I declined the invitation, saying that it was not for us. When I reported this fact to the Consiglio, there were all kinds of disgruntled questions from the collaborators. 'How could you have done such a thing?' 'Have you forgotten that we have families to support?' 'Why did you take it upon yourself to say no? Where is our democratic procedure?' I was even accused of being imperialis-tic . . ."

In declining Olivetti's invitation without consulting the Con-siglio first, Danilo added, it had never occurred to him that it would seriously consider forgoing the Center's policy of political abstinence.

It is this blindness to the foibles of individuals that is both his strength and his weakness, I thought. Principles usually come be-fore individuals; yet he is wise enough about people to know how to shape his principles to their capacity and aspirations. Because he is a practical thinker, the principles are lean, easily digested, with-out the fat of excessive idealism.

"No, I don't believe in compromise on basic questions," he re-peated. "If members of the Center want to leave and live accord-ing to their own ideas, that is important and salutary. Sometimes people discover themselves while they are members of the group. Many come to us because they are in disagreement with the world; some are in disagreement with themselves. They come, they grow, and they go away. That is fine with me. If I respect their qualities, I want them to lead their own lives . . ."

It crossed my mind that this liberal attitude was not always the one he expressed when there was mutiny in his ranks.

"I sometimes explode and lose my patience and say things that I regret later," he said, reading my thoughts. "I am not a saint. Aldous Huxley, though he meant well, did me a disservice when he described me as a saint. I may not have thought so at first but I do now. It has caused a great deal of misunderstanding and, of course, disappointment. A sick woman once threw herself at my feet, demanding that I exercise my powers as a saint to cure her. . . . Are you cold?"

He had finally noticed I was shivering, but I asked him to continue.

"People should get it out of their heads that we are a religious group or that I am trying to form an army for Jesus or Gandhi. The teachings of these two men are part of our ideology, of course, but there are significant differences created by the conditions of our times. People often suggest that we resort to primitive methods of production in order to make for more work. Lorenzo del Vasto, for example, wanted the Center to sponsor a work project consisting of people hand-weaving cloth. But we should not go backwards . . ."

"What about birth control?" I asked. "That is a modern technique that could benefit the poor. Why haven't you supported Rosita Lanza in her crusade?"

"I think we have more fundamental problems to cope with first, at least as far as our own work is concerned. Let Rosita continue her crusade. It has considerable merit, but it is not one that we can support at this stage of our efforts." He peered at me through his rimless glasses for a moment. "Besides, with five children of my own, how can I be a public champion of birth control?"

The last traces of the sunset were gone and a giant shadow had settled over our ledge and the rest of the mountain side. I looked around and saw our wives and the children nervously hovering on the edge of the clearing where we had picnicked, as though waiting for permission to approach. "They must be getting cold," I said, shivering in my own deep chill.

"The mountain air is good for all of us," Danilo said. He removed his elbows from the table, as though to end our talk. But he was not quite finished. "I believe in what I do and the way I do it. Money is of no interest to me; long ago I gave up the idea of becoming a financial success, in order to do what I believe in. That doesn't mean I feel like a hero. I am doing what I cannot help doing. I realize that some day I might be murdered. But in the meantime, I am alive, leading my own life."

Two days later, at Danilo's request, I returned to Partinico to act as interpreter for four visiting Englishmen, part-time fund solicitors for Oxfam. One was an accountant, another an engineer, the third a drygoods salesman and the fourth, a fat elderly giant in a pith helmet, a retired bookkeeper. As one of them put it, raising money for Oxfam causes in their spare time was their contribution to the improvement of humanity. The men were utilizing their summer holiday to get a firsthand look at some of the projects in Italy which had Oxfam support. None of them had been out of England before. Without exception, they were eager and jolly companions of admirable intention, and poignantly ignorant. "Would you be good enough to point out the local office of the Mafia?" one of them asked in all seriousness.

Although they knew enough of Danilo's reputation to enable them to solicit funds for the Center, they were unaware of its activities. It is doubtful that their three days in Sicily did little more than provide them with scores of photographs, taken with their families and friends in mind, and deepen their nostalgia for their favorite dish of "fish and chips" which, they were astounded to discover, was unknown in Sicily. Yet though they talked and behaved like Englishmen in slapstick comedies, their benevolence shone through all their deficiencies.

"Aren't they kind! Aren't they good!" Danilo repeatedly exclaimed, judging them by their faces. Inevitably, he decided that they must accompany him to inspect the progress of the Jato dam.

The fat man in the pith helmet was obliged to retire to his hotel room, the victim of a fickle sacroiliac. The rest of us drove to the dam with Danilo, and trudged after him through the heavy mud as he strode from one construction point to another, explaining how the dam would eventually function to vitalize the life of eighteen villages. This final view of the nearly completed dam, so charged with energy and optimism—Danilo's as well as that of the workers—reminded me of the closing scene of some grandiosely clichéd movie in which the good citizens of a community, having finally overcome the machinations of their evil brethren, are enthusiastically applying the finishing touches to a community project dear to them all.

A score of trucks roared back and forth gathering and dumping dirt; steam-shovels chewed away at the slopes of hills with grinding greed; workers under the scorching sun were drilling through rock, shoveling dirt, and dynamiting. "What a beautiful rhythm!"

Danilo kept chanting as he greeted gangs of workers or, more often, was greeted by them. From hillsides, tunnels, and ditches they yelled out his name and held out their hands to be shaken. And they took time off from their work to talk about the strike that had won back their jobs. They blinked as they recognized me, and pumped my hand and called me professor.

Through the mud Danilo kept charging ahead of us at a murderous pace, inspecting, explaining, and asking questions of the foremen in charge. "When will this part of the job be finished? Why should it take that long?" Encountering a group of executive engineers who were also inspecting the dam, Danilo asked similar questions of them. Some of the engineers were employees of the construction company and had been his adversaries in the recent strike negotiations between labor and management. I could sense their hostility toward Danilo through their exaggerated politeness. One of the government engineers, who was associated with ERAS, seemed to enjoy the expression of shock that came over Danilo's face as he told him that although the dam would be completed within the next year or two, it would take several years before its waters could be utilized for irrigation purposes. Danilo questioned each man closely, but all of the engineers agreed that the extra time was necessary for determining the proper level of the dam's water basin.

Danilo recovered his poise as he listened. When the engineers left us, he expressed the belief that the men may have exaggerated the time factor to protect themselves from being blamed for any delays. "I'm going to check their time schedules very carefully," he said. "If what I suspect is true, I'll let the workers know so that their unions can see to it that the irrigation system is finished within the period agreed upon."

Cheerful once more, he turned his attention to the Englishmen, who in their muddied new pants had been photographing everything in sight, including a dynamite explosion which narrowly missed burying one of them alive. Raising his voice above the din of the trucks and the pneumatic drills, Danilo made a single closing statement: "Undoubtedly you have seen dams that are far more impressive than this one. The reason for showing you this dam in such detail is not to impress you with its engineering techniques but to acquaint you with a project that has begun to mean hope to a people who had no hope."

On our way out of Italy there were two noteworthy interviews, first a brief one in Rome with the former senator Donato Pafundi, Chairman of the Anti-Mafia Commission. Despite the old senator's penchant for vapid generalizations—"The *mafiosi* we have succeeded in jailing should benefit from that punishment"—his remarks were quite illuminating; one of them, more so than he intended.

The Parliamentary act which created the Commission, he informed me, was the first piece of Italian legislation ever to use the word *Mafia.* "This, of course, imposed a serious obligation on the Commission." Speaking of its work, he said: "Our activity has been necessarily repressive yet we recognize that positive measures are required as well. A sociological investigation, for example, that would analyze the genesis and development of the Mafia phenomenon would constitute an important step toward its eradication. Another step would be to make certain that Sicilian justice operates as it should. Unfortunately, Sicilian judges are not always strong enough to withstand the various local pressures put on them." Ideally, he added, Mafia cases should be handled by non-Sicilian judges, but since there was little possibility of that happening, he and his Commission planned to recommend that Sicilian judges be moved from one district to another as frequently as possible.

The senator indicated that Mafia violence had been drastically reduced since the Commission began to function, but did not point out that a major reason for this development was the passage of special laws by the Italian Parliament that provided law-enforcement agencies with extraordinary powers. The laws circumvent customary legal procedure by eliminating formal courtroom trials; they subject suspected Mafia criminals to police surveillance and confine known Mafia criminals to areas away from their home territory.*

* Writing of the "special laws" in a *New York Times* dispatch (April 25, 1967) the Rome correspondent Robert Doty commented: "These measures, of doubtful legality by conventional standards in the absence of trial and conviction, were approved by Parliament because of the difficulty of breaking through the wall of *omerta*—the traditional compound of fear and pride that keeps witnesses to crimes silent, making convictions difficult."

"What happens to the Mafia problem when the tenure of the Commission expires?" I asked.

The senator looked disconsolate, and paused before he spoke. "It is our hope that the Parliament will continue to extend the Commission's tenure . . ."

Toward the end of our talk, Pafundi, in a more relaxed mood, let slip what turned out to be his most illuminating statement. Confiding that it was with considerable reluctance that he had come out of retirement to accept the appointment of Chairman of the Commission, he added: "As a retired senator, I was enjoying a life of tranquillity but then my good friend Giovanni Leone began to plead with me to accept the post and I could not say no to him."

Giovanni Leone. I tried not to register the shock I felt hearing the name, and asked the senator to repeat it to make certain I had heard right. I had. The senator's "good friend" who had persuaded him to head the Commission was none other than the Leone who had successfully defended the *mafiosi* of Sciara accused of murdering Salvatore Carnevale.

The last interview was with Aldo Capitini in his native town, where he had recently been appointed professor of education and moral philosophy at the University of Perugia. It was the second time he had come back to Perugia to live. The first time, in 1933, he had returned secretly after having been dismissed as a teaching assistant at the University of Pisa for refusing to join the Fascist party. For the next twelve years he earned his living as a custodian of the town's bell tower, a post he inherited from his father. The job served as an effective cover-up for his anti-fascist efforts, the most significant of which was the publication of a book entitled *Elements of a Religious Experience.*

"The book was totally anti-fascist in its point of view," Capitini told me, "but the police neglected to read it. They assumed, I suppose, that a book with the word 'religious' in the title could not be dangerous . . ."

I could easily understand Danilo's affection for this man; he was candid, warm, and pithy. For a man in his late sixties he moved with surprising alacrity, and he talked rapidly and concisely, like someone afraid of losing time. Yet he was a conscientious listener.

353

In many respects, he was like another anti-fascist intellectual I had known in my youth, the historian Gaetano Salvemini.

Speaking of Danilo's early days in Sicily, Capitini said he came down on Trappeto "like a parachutist." At first he was "a simple and religious humanitarian" but gradually, as he saw the necessity for a systematic organic plan of action, he adopted a sociological approach. "All this was to the good. The difficulty came when Danilo became famous, for then he ceased to function as an individual and began to function as an 'office' with a staff of assistants. As an 'office' he tends to be somewhat authoritarian—a fact which leads to periodic departures from his staff. Danilo, of course, is not the first humanitarian accused of not being as democratic as he should. St. Francis, among others, had problems of this sort.

"But people will have to accept Danilo on his own terms, for his contribution is fundamental and valuable and must be continued. After all, he is one of the few social reformers we have ever seen who knows how to apply basic principles in a practical manner. He is unique: a pragmatic man of action who is also an idealist. I have sometmes heard it said that Danilo is chiefly interested in maintaining his fame. But that it not true. To a certain degree, of course, he must maintain his fame in order to financially maintain his staff. But if fame were his chief consideration, he could have achieved it in some other easier, less dangerous way.

"No one should forget that Danilo risks his life every day. He is an extremely courageous man who will never give up his goals. Sometimes he is too astute for his own good—a fault which may be traced to his Jugoslav peasant ancestry—and sometimes he becomes too ambitious; that is, he spreads himself too thin with too many projects. For some time I have been urging him to stress quality above quantity in all of his efforts, and I am glad to observe that he has been coming around to that point of view . . ."

Two months after leaving Italy, the "secret" that Danilo had mentioned in our last conversation became public information. Appearing with Franco before the Anti-Mafia Commission (at its request), he accused fourteen members of the Christian Democrat party of having close associations with *mafiosi* and with the bandit Salvatore Giuliano. The charges were documented by a series of depositions gathered from Sicilians who were willing to testify in court. Among the most prominent Christian Democrats were Bernardo Mattarella, a senator from Sicily for more than twenty years who was then Foreign Trade Minister, and Dr. Calogero Volpe, undersecretary in the Ministry of Health.

The accused Sicilians, led by Mattarella and Volpe, promptly retaliated by filing charges of criminal libel against Danilo and Franco. There ensued in Rome a long series of trials in which the two defendants, ably represented by a team of volunteer lawyers, took the offensive by introducing more and more evidence and witnesses to indicate the close connections between the plaintiffs and the Sicilian and American underworld.

Professor Ross Waller, the chairman of the Dolci Trust in London, who visited Partinico during the early sessions of the trial, reported in his committee's bulletin some of the difficulties that Danilo and Franco were experiencing. "The collection of information, the persuasion of witnesses, are difficult and often saddening," he wrote. "I met a number of witnesses and I shall not easily forget one of them, who lives in Montelepre. Last year his house was burned down, and his wife died. Since he went to Rome to give evidence he has lost his job and is unlikely to get any other in the locality."

Commenting on the poor coverage the trials were receiving in the press, Waller observed: "Only the leftwing newspaper, *L'Ora* of Palermo, reports the trial sessions fully. Coverage in the national press has improved a little but Danilo complains that the real issues at stake are not widely understood: reports of the case render it too much in terms of Dolci versus Mattarella, whereas it should be understood as social order versus the Mafia. But I am inclined to think that in places where it matters the issue is understood pretty well. For instance, one eminent person I know, who has always been skeptical or even severely critical of Danilo's doings and writings, recently said to me: 'For the first time I am entirely with him.' "

Waller emphasized that one of the most significant aspects of the trial was the breakdown of *omerta*, the wall of silence that has permitted the Mafia to conduct its illegal activities without interference. "Dolci's witnesses are very courageous people, well aware of the dangers they are running. The first witness to be interrogated, standing up bravely and calmly to the furious attack of Mattarella's lawyer, began by saying: "I am a humble employee, living in a town dominated by *omerta* and fear, so I know what I am up against testifying here. But I am going to do so all the same because I am among those who believe in a better world."

In the year that followed, a succession of witnesses, ranging from simple peasants to university professors, testified to their knowledge of the political influence of the Mafia in their areas. But at the hearing on December 9, 1966, the presiding judge refused to let the defense introduce new documents or call further witnesses. This astonishing development stimulated an even more astonishing reaction in Danilo. He decided to boycott his own trial. When the court convened again on January 18, 1967, he and Franco and their lawyers were absent. Danilo was represented only by a letter addressed to the judge which declared his intention of not attending any further sessions of the trial on the grounds that the court was frustrating the trial's aims by denying him the opportunity to present further evidence and witnesses.*

In the only American news story of the trial published during its eighteen-month course, a *New York Times* dispatch by Robert Doty, dated January 18 and headlined "Dolci Boycotting His Trial in Italy," quoted Danilo as saying: "My trial is far more important than a quarrel among a few individuals. It should be the trial of a whole society against the politico-Mafia domination of Sicily. I will not participate if the court frustrates that aim."

In his letter to the judge, quoted in the same news story, he wrote: "Since I hold that a trial should be a digging out of the truth, I do not, in conscience, feel able to share the responsibility for an inadequate investigation of a matter on which depended and depends the lives and deaths of so many people."

Danilo concluded his letter with this statement: "Those who have begun to break the fear-filled silence—and as long as I live I will be among them—will find other ways. I have full confidence that the truth will make its way."

* One of the witnesses Danilo had planned to produce was a Sicilian priest, the Rev. Giacomo Caiozzo, who was willing to testify that Mattarella had attended a luncheon in New York arranged by American *mafiosi,* all of whom came from families originating in Castellammare, Mattarella's home town.

Danilo, as usual, meant what he said. In March 1967, he led a six-day eighty-mile march from Partanna to Palermo to protest Mafia corruption in western Sicily and to demand "a new Sicily for a new world." At times as many as 4,000 persons joined the march to affirm their belief in the manifesto prepared for the occasion. "The old systems can be broken down by dynamic new enterprises that are integrated in a development plan for the whole area," the manifesto read in part, and listed such objectives as the construction of more irrigation facilities, the reforestation of mountainsides to prevent further land erosion, the establishment of agricultural industries for processing local produce; the improvement of roads, drinking water facilities, educational and health services; the proper functioning of official agricultural development agencies; and the exclusion of *mafiosi* and their associates from public office.

The manifesto concluded with this exhortation: "A century ago Garibaldi said: 'Here we must create Italy or die.' Today we must set ourselves a new task: Here we must create a new Sicily, a new world, or we shall die."

"With this march we enter a new phase of our activity," Danilo said on the eve of the march. "Until now we have been obliged to adopt extreme measures, such as fasting, in order to awaken people on all levels of society to a sense of responsibility about an intolerable and static situation. Now life here is beginning to burgeon. More and more people want to take their destiny in their own hands. This march is not to be an expression of sadness but one of joy and self-confidence . . ."

The march received extensive European coverage and was even included in the news program of an American television network. It also became the subject of a British-made documentary entitled *Mafia, No,* which won first prize at the Venice film festival. A young Italian film student by the name of Filippo Ottoni, who was in Sicily for the first time, was especially impressed by the number of foreign countries represented in the march. "Their presence," he wrote, "reminded me that the evils these men are fighting are not only Sicilian evils. Sicily is nothing but a microcosm of today's world; the sufferings of its people and the violence perpetrated there are mere echoes from a world ruled and torn apart by self-interest and intolerance."

In his report, published in the bulletin of the Danilo Dolci Trust, Ottoni confessed that he had looked forward to meeting Dolci with mixed feelings, not being sure whether he was "a demagogue or a saint, a mystic or a frustrated politician." After observing him for two weeks he concluded that "he is a man who best combines and possesses the best qualities of these four archetypes: the vision of the mystic, the pragmatism of the politician, the capacity to inspire of the demagogue, and the humility of a saint. As for his methods, I saw how they could transcend mere ideologies and bring out the best sentiments in politicians who are traditionally wary of them."

Thanks to bulletins and letters from Partinico, Robert Doty's dispatches in *The New York Times,* and an unexpected visit to New York by Danilo in June of 1967, I was able to keep closely informed on the latest developments at the Center and in Sicily. The following were among the most notable:

·The building of the Jato dam was in its final stage of completion but, as predicted earlier by its engineers, it would take another three years before it could operate as an irrigation system.

·Government engineers finally determined that the Belice River will have two dams—one on each of its banks. The plans for both dams were officially approved by the Italian government, but the actual construction continued to be delayed.

·As a result of its pressures, the Center reported that the Carboi's irrigation system was gradually being extended beyond Menfi to a half-dozen other nearby towns. The Center was also pressing the authorities to bring more drinking water to more villages. "In no village in western Sicily is drinking water constantly available," its bulletin reported. "The more fortunate get it during certain hours of the day. In other villages the water is available only for a few hours every other day. And yet in nearly all these villages there are many unused wells."

·The Center's newly founded Institute, which continued to be partially supported by Oxfam funds, was beginning to show tangible results. Nineteen of the twenty-two villages that had become associated with the Belice Valley Intercommunal Planning Committee were now employing graduates of the Institute to assist with local and regional community development.

· Increasingly, Trappeto was being used for the Center's educational activities. In addition to courses for community developers and for teachers, it had established seminars to train Sicilians as leaders of cooperatives. While reporting on this development, Franco wrote that the institute which Eyvind Hytten and other ex-collaborators of the Center hoped to establish in Palermo had not materialized.

· The Partinico health clinic, which was founded by Danilo and his group, ceased its connection with the Center, and began to operate as an autonomous agency supported largely by funds from Germany. The announcement stressed the amicability of the divorce; it also repeated Dr. Borruso's hope that the clinic will one day be sponsored by the Italian government.

· Lorenzo and Paola Barbera moved from Roccamena to Partanna to work more closely with the Belice Valley Intercommunal Planning Committee. One of their enterprises was founding and editing a magazine entitled *Pianificazione Siciliana*. Each spring Lorenzo returned to Trappeto to head the school for community developers.

· Palma di Montechiaro and Licata remained in the same desperate straits they were in in 1965. "What we feared has happened," Franco wrote. "The special law passed for the relief of these towns was allowed to expire before it could be applied. The allocated funds no longer exist."

· In the same letter Franco announced the extermination of Cortile Cascino. "As long ago as 1955 we were trying to arouse the public conscience about the conditions of that festering sore. It has taken the Palermo authorities all this time to remove it. The 1,500 former inhabitants of Cortile Cascino now live in the new and clean quarters of a public housing complex at Viale Michelangelo, toward Monte Pellegrino."

· In July of 1966 nearly 10,000 persons were made homeless in Agrigento when the earth subsided and buildings crumbled. On April 24, 1967, Robert Doty in *The New York Times* reported that "forty persons in Agrigento, including the last three Christian

Democrat mayors and dozens of employees of the regional, provincial, and municipal governments, have been indicted for violations of building and zoning laws. They are accused of having permitted politically favored speculators to build housing on land known to be subject to slippage."

·The same news story pointed out that Sicily's experiment in regional autonomy after twenty years of existence is generally regarded as a failure. "No one, not even official defenders of the autonomous regime, pretends that it has done a good job in coping with Sicily's profound social and economic problems. There is general agreement, instead, that a large part of more than a billion dollars in development aid poured into the island in twenty years has been dissipated in political patronage."

In an earlier dispatch from Sicily that week Mr. Doty reported a sizable increase in the Sicilian per capita income—from $294 in 1951 to $560 in 1965. In the same period the national average per capita income rose from $477 to $896. In Sicily, Mr. Doty pointed out, the increase was accomplished by the investment of one and a half billion dollars since 1954, seventy percent of which consisted of public loans and grants. "In physical and human terms," he added, "even this progress has been uneven and the Sicilian scene is full of shocking contrasts."

·While Sicily was celebrating twenty years of regional autonomy, there erupted a financial scandal involving the former president of the powerful Banco di Sicilia, Carlo Bazan, who was charged with the misappropriation of more than one million dollars. Bazan was accused of making illegal loans in that amount to the Christian Democrat party; also of loaning many more millions of dollars to failing business enterprises with rightwing political connections. Among the Sicilians summoned by the Court of Rome to answer questions on the scandal was Guido Anca Martinez, one of the fourteen men whom Danilo had accused of having links with the Mafia.

Commenting on the Banco di Sicilia scandal the *Financial Times* of London said: "After twenty years of regional autonomy, Sicily is facing nothing less than bankruptcy, even though millions of pounds from public funds have been poured into the region for its development. Practically all the initiatives taken by the Sicilian regional authorities have been catastrophic failures, through which, however, a small number of prominent local politicians have accumulated large fortunes."

·Through a friend who had recently visited Partinico, I learned of an ominous incident in a café which involved Vittorio, the Center's mimeograph operator, and two Partinicans who are considered *mafiosi*. Overhearing one of the men say that Danilo had gone too far in denouncing Mattarella before the Anti-Mafia Commission and was liable to be killed, Vittorio told the two men that "nothing will ever happen to Danilo because he is too well known." One of the men smirked at this and replied: "John F. Kennedy was far better known than Danilo and look what happened to him."

·Late in April 1967 Danilo informed me that he planned to stop over in the United States for a few days in June, while on his way to several South American countries, where he had been invited to conduct, for the second time, a series of seminars dealing with the training of community developers. He wished to visit several American cities "to renew friendships" and also to appraise for himself the moral climate of the Americans during the Vietnamese war. Would I join him in New York and act as his interpreter during his four-day stay there?

Two weeks before Danilo's arrival, on June 11, *The New York Times* carried the news that his oldest and most influential adversary, Cardinal Ruffini, was dead at the age of seventy-nine. He had been stricken by a heart attack shortly after casting his vote in the Sicilian regional elections. The lengthy obituary, which discussed in detail the prelate's archconservatism, made no mention of his public attack on Danilo.

Danilo arrived by plane from London, slimmer and more relaxed than I had last seen him, bearing gifts: for Patricia a handsome portfolio of drawings by the Sicilian artist Cagli which commemorated the twentieth anniversary of the massacre at Portella della Ginestra; for me a recording of the march that was sung during the previous spring's "March of Hope," as it became called, with Sicilian lyrics written especially for the occasion by the island's leading folk poet, Ignazio Buttita. "It was the first time that Sicilians sang against the Mafia in public," Danilo said. "And they are still singing it."

I had seldom seen Danilo so cheerful. Yet, as I discovered moments after meeting him at the airport, he was burdened by a serious concern: the final session of his long trial, which he had been boycotting for six months, was in progress in Rome even as we talked. The judge was to pronounce sentence on him and Franco within the next four days. His cheerfulness, I learned, was largely caused by the news he had just received that more than one hundred Italian senators and deputies, professors, and writers had signed a petition urging the Norwegian Parliament to award him the Nobel Peace Prize. It was the first time in many years that so many distinguished Italian intellectuals had banded together to proclaim their faith in him. "With courage and perseverance Danilo Dolci conducts from Partinico a slow and difficult battle for the liberation of the people of western Sicily from its adversaries: ignorance, hunger, Mafia tyranny, and distrust of every form of group life," the petition read. It added that his peaceful methods and activities constitute "an effective contribution to the promotion of a democratic conscience toward the problems of peace."

Danilo appreciated the endorsement not so much for any possible effect it might have on the Nobel Prize Committee but because, having been issued just before the closing session of his trial, it might affect the nature of his sentence. "Because of the petition the judge will not dare impose too severe a sentence, for fear of repercussions," he said. "On the other hand, the sentence is not likely to be a light one. After all, Mattarella has been in the government for more than twenty years. The Christian Democrats can't afford to admit that they have been supporting a senator with *mafiosi* friends during all that time . . ."

He was delighted with the hotel I had chosen for him, mainly because it was close to the big newsstands near Times Square, where he could purchase the Italian newspapers carrying the news of his trial. When I commented on the failure of the American press to cover the trials, Danilo blamed neither the influence of the Catholic Church nor the negligence of foreign correspondents, as I had thought he would. Instead he placed the blame on those who were responsible for the scheduling of the trials. "Their strategy was to dilute the effect of the trials on public opinion by stringing them out over a long period of time, so that nothing of importance seemed to happen, as far as the press was concerned. In

362

the course of fourteen sessions only twenty witnesses were heard. For once it was not *omerta* that prevented Sicilians from testifying against the Mafia but the law courts themselves.

"Some of the most important witnesses were never called. Franco, for example, who has studied and worked with the Mafia problem for many years and become an expert on the subject, was never questioned. Neither was Lorenzo Barbera, who was born in Partinico, and whose firsthand experiences with *mafiosi* have made him extremely knowledgeable on the subject."

In our meetings with writers and editors Danilo often spoke of the "Mafia-client system," which he had long observed in Sicily— "a social study laboratory for the rest of the world"—but which he was convinced existed in similar form in most countries. "The system of reciprocal benefits—'you scratch my back, I'll scratch yours'—usually involves the politician and the vote-controlling 'client.' It thrives particularly in countries like Sicily, where the low economic level of the masses forces them to concentrate on the search for bread and work, so that everything else becomes of secondary interest. When it comes to voting, these are the people who are most often misled into supporting political efforts which are opposed to their own interests. . . . What makes the client or the Mafia-client system flourish is that people, becoming isolated by their economic condition, don't know how to use their political power, and resign themselves to the little they have." Pointing out that such situations create fertile ground for authoritarianism and monopoly of every conceivable sort, Danilo stressed the necessity to form and interrelate "new and open democratic groups" and do away with "the old paralyzing groups at every level of society."*

To an editor who asked him to appraise the strength of the Mafia in Italy, Danilo replied: "It isn't that the Mafia is so potent so much as it is that the people have been weak." His trial, he added, had decreased the power of the Mafia because it had given witnesses the strength to voice their convictions in public. In translating these statements, I added the information that in January 1966 Danilo, as a means of encouraging witnesses who were ready to testify against Mattarella, had fasted for one week in the senator's home town, Castellammare.

* Danilo Dolci discussed these points in greater detail in an article "Tools for a New World," published in the *Saturday Review*, July 22, 1967.

The subject of his fasts was of particular interest to a group of young pacifists who had requested a meeting with Danilo. The young men described some of the long fasts they had conducted as a protest against the Vietnamese war, and told how little publicity the fasting had generated. Danilo commented that every fast should be strategically planned around a specific purpose and should be carefully timed. He himself, he said, had never fasted with any sense of martyrdom and had no intention of doing so. "The attitude of the person who fasts should never be a suicidal one. It should, at all times, be aggressive and constructive."

When Danilo was asked his opinion about a biography of him by James McNeish titled *Fire Under the Ashes,* which first appeared in England in 1965, he replied that while he appreciated the author as a man of good intentions, he was disturbed by the "hagiographic tone of the writing" and the presentation of a hero whom he could not recognize as himself. "McNeish is an honest journalist," he said, "but he was in our area a short time and was never part of our staff. Frankly, I must say that I find his concept of Danilo Dolci pathetically romantic and old-fashioned. In focusing on his hero, the author misleads the reader and prevents him from understanding the fundamental role of the Center which, as it works within the population, is contributing to the growth of new democratic groups and to the destruction of Mafia-client groups . . ."

On his last day in New York, just before we were to leave the hotel for a television interview (his only public appearance that week), Danilo received the cable from Franco announcing the court's sentences: two years for Danilo, one year and seven months for Franco; also fines and damages amounting to approximately fifteen million lire. Both jail sentences were suspended. Danilo looked faintly amused as he handed me the cable. "The sentence does not surprise me," he said in a quiet voice. "We shall, of course, appeal."

After the television interview, we wished one another *buon viaggio* and parted. Danilo was traveling to Chicago for the weekend, where he was to meet with a group of admiring lawyers; after that he would go to Boston for three days, where some Cambridge professors were hoping to establish a new Danilo Dolci committee.

I returned to Philadelphia and, on the train, finally found time to translate the Sicilian words of the song that had been sung during Danilo's six-day "March of Hope."

The theme of the verses is the resurrection of Sicily; they describe how Sicily once lost her voice but has now become a great singer; how Sicily once lost her feet but now moves as though she had wings; how Sicily was once a blind woman but can now see even in the dark; how Sicily was once an "old hag but now has the vitality of a twenty-year-old girl." The final verse says:

Sicily was in a coffin
Having given her soul to God
But Sicily came to life
And took one look at death
And said no.

The chorus of the song reads:

To the Mafia she says no
To the reforms she says yes
To the schools she says yes
To employment she says yes
To the dams she says yes
To the Mafia she says no
To all war she says no, no, no!

The bulletins that arrived from Partinico in the months that followed were filled with news of fresh demonstrations (including a peace march led by Danilo from Milan to Rome), fresh achievements, and fresh frustrations. One of the items was particularly engaging. Originating from the Sicilian town of Castelvetrano and ominously entitled "A moment of silence for Danilo Dolci," it told how a semiliterate peasant had understood a radio announcer to say that the famous social reformer and writer Dolci was dead. The peasant had immediately communicated the news to a friend on the Community Council. The friend, bursting into tears, had repeated it to others, and soon all the leading community groups had gathered with the Community Council to commemorate the memory of Danilo Dolci. (Only much later was it ascertained that

365

the peasant had been mistaken; the writer who had died was a man named Deutscher).

An excerpt from the minutes of the Common Council of Castelvetrano, dated August 21, 1967, reads:

"At this point the Councilman Prof. Diecidue, in an anguished voice, related that he had just received news of the sudden and premature death of Danilo Dolci, a dear and constant friend, whose passionate and faithful efforts directed to the development of a new Sicily will become immortal in the memories of all good men and will be an effective influence in raising the social and moral level of our people . . .

"Councilman Prof. Porrato suggested a moment of contemplation. The President and the Council rose, and there transpired one minute of absorbed silence."

Afterword:
"Murder by Neglect"

ON JANUARY 15, 1968, an earthquake struck the very heart of the sector in western Sicily where Danilo and his group operate. Besides killing 280 persons and seriously injuring more than 500 others, it wrecked or damaged 51 communities. 50,000 persons were left homeless; many thousands more, afraid of being buried alive, abandoned their homes in freezing temperatures and fled into the countryside.

The earthquake totally demolished three farm villages—Gibellina, Montevago, and Salaparuta—and also destroyed Santa Margherita di Belice, Poggioreale, Santa Ninfa, and Salemi. The disaster was a prolonged one; tremors continued at frequent intervals until early March, a six-week period of terror during which entire towns were deserted. All the way from Palermo to Agrigento, the roads were jammed with refugees escaping the menace of crumbling buildings.

While fear kept most of the refugees in the open countryside, an estimated 15,000 of them, encouraged by the Italian government, quit the disaster area for other parts of the nation. "Jackal-like, sub-Mafia bands" were quick to exploit the situation, reported George Black in the January twenty-eighth issue of the *English Observer*. "They are driving about in cars, making offers for land, for beasts, corralling stray cattle, bullying their owners. They pay

367

a tenth of normal prices to refugees who are desperate to join in the great trek north."

The same reporter witnessed a deserted Palermo, and many other bizarre sights, including one hundred polished coffins with brass plates reading *"Gesu salvatore"* piled high in what was once the main square of Montevago, and "crumbled cemeteries, where florid angels lie alongside new-found corpses in plastic bags awaiting burial . . ."

Tullio Vinay, telling how the people of Riesi, even the poorest, had contributed several truckloads of food and blankets (many of them purchased on credit) to the homeless, described his visit to one of the devastated villages. "There was a strong smell of corpses. 'My house used to stand there,' a poor woman said to us as she wept. 'They have found my dead cows and the goat, but they have not yet found my husband and my son-in-law.' Some soldiers drew a goat and her kid out of the ruins. They were still alive. As soon as it was out, the kid started sucking at its mother's empty teats."

"It is not surprising that only the homes of the poor and only those old buildings which were in disrepair have fallen," Danilo wrote. "Had the earthquake struck a little further to the northeast the ruins of the slum sections in Palermo would have buried more than 100,000 lives." Shortly after the disaster he issued a statement which placed the responsibility for the earthquake's destruction on the authorities' continued indifference to the misery of western Sicily.

Danilo disagreed with those who viewed the tragedy solely as an act of God; he attributed it almost completely to the extreme poverty in the area. Speaking as a trained architect, he said: "Had the houses been constructed with the necessary reinforced concrete and steel required to make them solid and resistant; in fact, had the houses that were struck been truly habitable, *in all probability there would have been no victims.* Therefore, it is not a question of inevitable misfortune, but rather—this is a painful and truthful thing to say—a case of murder by neglect."

One month after the earthquake first struck, a *New York Times* correspondent observed that the homeless families in the destroyed villages were still waiting for barracks to be completed that would provide them with shelter. Every day corpses were still being pulled out of the wreckage, and there were strong fears of epidemics. The weather, the *Times* man reported, was the only bright spot in the situation. The bitter cold had finally given way to the warmth of spring and now "the fields around the ruins are filled with daisies and mimosa in bloom."

Conclusion to the
Transaction Edition:
Twenty Years Later

TWENTY YEARS HAVE PASSED since I lived and worked in Sicily with Danilo Dolci, gathering material to write this book. His frequent trips to the United States, where he has become increasingly popular as a speaker, along with my several interim trips to Sicily have enabled us to keep in fairly close touch. Now, as we face each other in my Philadelphia apartment, I try to compare the 60-year-old Danilo before me with the 40-year-old social activist I had observed in Sicily.

On the outside, at least, there has been little change. With his giant body and his mesmerizing flow of ideas, he is still a magnetic presence. He still combines two traits seldom found in the same personality: calm and vitality. His face remains unlined; he does not seem older than he did twenty years ago, but he is visibly heavier. Perhaps the most noticeable change is that, finally, he has been able to master some English, though hardly enough to dispense with interpreters when addressing American audiences.

Despite the obstacle of speaking through an intermediary, Danilo by now has become marvelously adept at establishing genuine rapport with this audiences. His English, however scant, makes him more aware of what is being said by his interpreters and discussants. Morever, he has become a master at involving audiences in a Socratic kind of dialogue. During one of his most successful speaking tours in 1983 he used the technique almost everywhere he went. "Through his Socratic method," reported one observer in Brooklyn, "he drew out of those in the audience gems of wisdom and aesthetic reponses which they themselves scarcely knew they possessed.'' The same observer noted that Danilo was able to apply this method even when faced with a large audience, "simply by treating the last row of the audience as the conversationalists, so that everyone between them and him felt involved.''

Perhaps the best description of Danilo facing an audience with an interpreter came that same year from a professor at Brown University:

From the moment Danilo sat down at a plain table on the platform of the large auditorium which was nearly filled, something more than the casualness of his dress and the combination of his calm and openness he projected bridged any gap between him and his listeners. When he began to speak, the clear Italian words, free of any platform manner, ascended and dropped back in graspable parabolas exactly suited to the modern-day parables they carried. The students listened so keenly that one half-felt the pauses for English versions unnecessary. The audience appeared transfixed. The utter quiet in the hall was broken only once—by laughter. The translator, repeating a bit of multiplication that Danilo had tossed off, found the quotient suddenly beyond him. Danilo leaned over and calmly supplied the figure in English.

Before I begin questioning Danilo about his work in Sicily during the past twenty years, I ask about the state of his health, not out of politeness but because I have been concerned about it ever since a letter from him last summer casually mentioned that he had not been feeling well, a complaint he had never made to me in the past. Now as I try to pry from him some specific information about his ailment, I learn that he had spent some time in a Sicilian hospital not long ago. Instead of describing his illness he informs me that during his stay he conducted a dialogue with himself on the question of whether or not he could face the prospect of death with serenity. "I discovered that I could," he says. "Yes," he repeats, "I would be serene." He beams, pleased for having arrived at so felicitous a prognosis while being objective about such a subjective matter. Then, pointing to my notebook, where I had jotted down some questions to ask, he suggests that we proceed with our own dialogue. When I persist in trying to learn the nature of the illness that had brought him to the hospital, I only succeed in discovering that the doctors wanted him to prolong his hospital stay and he refused, explaining that he had "too much to do" at his office.

Yet Danilo is not a careless person; he is imbued with a strict sense of order. I am certain that before leaving the hospital he carefully considered all the known facts about his physical condition and concluded he could return to his work without unduly jeopardizing his health. At the same time I am aware of his strong sense of urgency. "Given our situation today, we don't have much time," he told a Philadelphia audience a few years ago. In the same talk he stressed a recurrent theme that is more universal than the sociologically oriented themes he had been emphasizing in the 1950s and 1960s. "We need to invent new experiences, new methods, to create new kinds of strengths, to find real leverage to break out of our vicious circles. It's essential on all levels (personal, social, political, global) to develop structures that are nonviolent. . . . Perhaps you might think these are dreams. But without dreams we die."

More directly than ever, Danilo nowadays is speaking across national boundaries, to peoples of all nationalities, on all social levels. To reach them more effectively his vocabulary has become more personalized, more poetic. He was a poet even before he ever came to Sicily, and as he has grown older he has permitted that aspect of him greater leeway—without, however, abandoning his pragmatic approach to social conflicts and nonviolent solutions. Increasingly, he has become more metaphorical, more inclined to speak and write in parables. "If people explore their own shadows and lights," he recently wrote, "they explore the daylight of others." More than ever before he now emphasizes the importance of the individual, and the need to communicate with one's own self and with others as a means of achieving the wholeness of creativity and love. In a single paragraph he makes the point of communication unforgettable:

The father and the little boy are driving on the way to school. The little boy turns to him and says, "Daddy, when I talk with you my self goes away. But when you answer me, it comes back again." The father pulls over to the side of the road, turns off the motor, and with tears in his eyes, asks the boy to repeat what he has said. After a moment, the father says, "I love you too."

Danilo is anxious to proceed with our "business" and I turn to my notebook to ask him what, in his opinion, are the major changes that have taken place in the social structure of western Sicily in the past twenty years. He replies that there have been two basic changes. One relates to the concept of power, the other to that of communication. Both have resulted from the building of the Jato dam, which began functioning in the late 1960s. The dam, which stores 75 million cubic meters of water annually and irrigates 25,000 acres of previously unproductive land, has had a significant influence on the economic welfare of the people in eighteen villages of the surrounding area. But the dam's significance extends beyond its capacity to triple the zone's agricultural productivity. Gradually, it has provided the leverage for establishing a new power base for its farmers, one that has completely replaced mafia manipulation and intimidation of predam times. The power base, in turn, has created for the first time an avenue of direct communication among the people benefitting from the dam that is both anti-Mafia and democratic.

"These changes," explains Danilo, "began happening because the farmers needed irrigation water at a low price. At the instigation of our Centro they were willing to find out if they could achieve such an aim by working together democratically, without shooting. Making decisions together was a new experience for them, one fraught with difficulties, not the least of which derived from the fact that this was the first time they had acted communally on a matter that affected their personal welfare. Slowly but steadily they have learned and continue to learn, not by listening to our preachings, but through the exercise of their own interests, resolving their conflicts through discussion without the use or threat of violence.

"There are now 5,000 farmers who are organized to benefit from the democratic operation of the Jato dam. In a zone where the summer soil was always too dry to cultivate, everything is green now throughout all the summer months. There are other benefits. Instead of high unemployment, which in the 1960s sent most of the men in the zone to other countries in search of jobs, farmers and truckers work on home grounds, sometimes night and day in three shifts; and men who have been working abroad have been returning. That is not all. Now that there is no room in the zone for a mafia structure, delinquency of every kind has declined sharply. At one time homicides were almost a daily occurrence. In the past five years there has been only one. The psychological value of the Jato dam cannot, of course, be overestimated. Its very presence provides people with hope. In a culture where people have often felt they are the victims of destiny, the dam suggests to them that just as nature can be changed by building a dam, so can their own lives.

"The success of the Jato dam has inspired the construction of nine other dams in western Sicily which are either completed or nearing completion. The largest of them, at Roccamena, will start functioning shortly. The democratic power base that emerged out of building the Jato dam will, we believe, provide a model for the farmers living in the vicinity of the new dams."

I asked Danilo if he and his Centro plan to help those farmers organize into cooperatives. "Not unless they ask us to help," he replies. "We do not want to substitute ourselves for local initiative. Wherever possible, we want the people themselves to assume responsibilities and become self-reliant. The role of the Centro is that of catalyst but only when local initiative is absent. By the way, did you know that Michele Mandiello died this past year? Michele was one of our most effective catalyists."

I had first encountered Michele in 1965, when he had just begun the difficult task of trying to establish a cooperative for the manufacture of wine in a district where he was beset with a barrage of negative attitudes. Danilo says that the same Sicilians who would eventually become enthusiastic members of the cooperative were positive that Michele was wasting his time. " 'It just isn't possible,' they told him. 'It will never work because we Sicilians are all thieves.' " Michele, who was a Neapolitan, refused to believe them. "It took years of work that were often discouraging but the end results were gratifying." Through Michele's initiative nine more cooperatives were established and all ten formed a consortium to promote cooperation between them. Two of them, one in Menfi and one in Sciacca, were under Michele's supervision until his death.

"Now the idea of cooperatives has spread to other parts of Sicily through local initiative, without any assistance from the Centro. They function splendidly in a variety of fields: housing, irrigation, the marketing of agricultural products. Wherever they prosper they become significant steps in the development of democratic structures that can shut out Mafia intervention."

Danilo's mention of the Mafia prompts me to show him a recent *New York Times* article that speaks of Sicily as a Mafia-operated international drug traffic center. "It is inaccurate to say that Sicily is the chief center of the drug traffic. One has only to look at the statistics—they are frightening—to know that there is a large drug traffic in Switzerland, Ireland, France, and Colombia. The general public is more aware of the drug traffic in Sicily because of the aggressive anti-Mafia campaign currently being waged by the Italian government. There have been numerous arrests, some of judges who have been too lenient in sentencing Mafiosi. This is a fairly recent and radical development in Italy, one that is encouraging to honest judges and, of course, to most Sicilians."

Danilo recalls that "fifteen years ago, when we conducted our own anti-Mafia campaign, justice was not functioning as well as it is now. When Franco Alasia and I were arrested on charges of criminal libel for having accused fourteen members of the Christian Democrat party of having close associations with Mafiosi and with the bandit Giuliano, we scored an enormous victory on the level of public opinion, but the judges of that period had too many ties with politicians to act on their own. Ours was not a real sentence, however. We were fined but not jailed. The gratifying upshot of our trials was that the three high government officials who had charged us with criminal libel lost their posts soon afterwards. The public understood that this happened directly as a result of the accusations we had made against them.

"The situation of the magistrates is quite different nowadays; they are able to act more autonomously and courageously than ever before, regardless of their political party affiliation. The reason is that the present generation of judges have at their disposition legal prerogatives for investigating mafia crimes which their predecessors lacked."

I asked Danilo why the Centro did not continue its anti-Mafia activity.

He replies: "We *have* continued it, but our activity has taken other forms. In life it is important not to repeat oneself; to repeat is easy, to create development is difficult. The midwifery work we have been doing in developing a democratic structure, using the Jato dam as a lever, is one example. Another, which we can discuss later in this conversation, is our establishment in the mid-1970s of an experimental educational center for the area. At this center both children and adults learn how to make decisions together. This, too, is anti-Mafia work.''

"Your public image in the 1950s and 1960s was that of a militant pacifist. Your fasts, the march you led against the Mafia, the acts of civil disobedience put Sicily in the spotlight and made you internationally famous as 'The Gandhi of Sicily.' How would you describe your role in the seventies and eighties?''

Danilo replies: "In those early years we had to shock the establishment in order to call attention to the intolerable conditions in western Sicily and also to pressure it into building a dam that could help alleviate those conditions. Our motive was not entirely economic, for we knew that a dam that could improve the physical welfare of the people could also be used as leverage for developing social and psychological change. As soon as the dam began functioning we asked the people in our zone what change they wanted most of all. The answer we got, especially from women and children, was 'education.' From the information they gave us we understood that there was a need for an educational center where students could learn without being bored or intimidated, as is often the case in the schools of southern Italy.''

"There is nothing authoritarian about our education center," says Danilo. "It operates on the fundamental assumption that young children and children generally, have their own vital interests which they must discover for themselves, and develop them with educators who are willing and able to discover, to create and to stimulate interest." At the same time, Danilo points out that he does not accept certain antiauthoritarian methods of education that lead to the kind of permissiveness sanctioned by some progressive schools. He regards them as "confused and unproductive," and is quick to explain that the center's course curriculum includes traditional subjects as well as courses dealing with the arts, though they are not taught with traditional methods.

A paramount feature of the center's learning process is the Socratic kind of discussion Danilo likes to use with audiences. Danilo prefers to describe the process as "maieutic," an intellectual midwifery which through group discussion brings out latent ideas into clear consciousness. "Our aim is to find out and develop together with the children their deepest interests, transforming their

377

natural curiosity into a method of inquiry and discovery. The ultimate goal is to develop a wholly maieutic environment where everyone can be a midwife to everyone else while experiencing, experimenting, and verifying with clarity and precision how we can act creatively. Essentially, the center is a laboratory where we try to understand creativity, development, and relationships.''

"Relationships?"

"Very important," says Danilo, and I remember his writing that "the lack of attention paid to conflicts that occur in human relationships invariably sets the pattern for large scale social violence. Rage, doubt, and insecurity must be dealt with since they are born within the same human being, before they become dangerous projectiles threatening the stability of the relationships within a group or community." He asks, "How is it possible to resolve disagreements between nations if we don't know how to resolve conflicts between individuals?" And he blames schools, institutions, and governments for "perpetuating an atmosphere of dependence, hostility, and mistrust."

Danilo's recognition of the violence inherent in most educational systems for the young was one of the factors that led to the birth of the education center. He recalls visiting a kindergarten during a visit to Malta and being horrified to see a mother come in with a 3-year-old child under her arm. The child was struggling and crying and the mother was also crying. But then, to his surprise, she deposited the child and left. "I asked the teacher, 'Why don't you do this differently?' She said, 'But the children become *resigned* to it fairly quickly!' "

In the planning of the education center Danilo and his staff augmented the ideas they got from the children and adults in the community with those from a half-dozen eminent educators and psychologists, among them Otto Klineberg, John Galtung, Leonardo Covello, and Edwin H. Alton. Early in the development of the center Alton published an excellent pamphlet* about the center which describes it as "a necessary weapon" in combatting the authoritarian schools prevalent in southern Italy, and quotes Danilo

---

*Edwin H. Alton, *Experiment in Education: An Account of Danilo Dolci's New Education Centre in Sicily* (London, 1975).

as saying that research into the problems of schooling today in every part of the world is as important as the study of cancer.

Alton points out that in a general sense all of Dolci's efforts in Sicily have been educational. Using western Sicily as a social laboratory where problems of underemployment, ignorance, and illteracy might be analyzed and cured "in microcosm," Dolci has spent the last thirty years setting up models for all the world to observe. I sense that Danilo regards the education center as the most significant of his models. "If the world is to survive," he wrote recently, "its people must learn to live creatively. Without creativity there is emptiness and despair. We must learn to discover ourselves, so that we can discover others in the world. In a sense grass has a high culture more civilized than ours. It is nourished on things that have completed their life cycle. In our schools do we teach about the reciprocity that exists between the bee and the flower? Or do we give the model of the lion trainer and his whip?"

The education center, launched in 1975 after six years of preparation, began with children of 5 years old and under and now includes 6-year-olds; eventually, children up to the age of 14 will be admitted. "Generally," says Danilo, "the students come from poor families or from families with whom we have previously worked on certain ideas about education. We make it a point of encouraging parents to involve themselves with what goes on at the center as fully as possible. If the parents are unable to come to us—there are instances where a mother cannot leave her home because there are too many children to look after—our educators go to them. Parent participation is essential to the success of the enterprise."

Danilo, as always, attaches much signficance to terminology. He and his collaborators have chosen a series of terms for the center which is in keeping with its manieutic function.

Old Term	New Term
schoolmaster, teacher	educator
pupil (originally the word meant "ward")	student

class (the Latin word from which it is derived, *classis,* means "army" or "fleet")	group
headmaster	coordinator
discipline	responsibility
lecture room	council (a place for discussion)
grading, tests, examinations	collective assessment, objective and subjective

The education center is located in the outskirts of Partinico on a 20-acre tract of land known as Mirto, a place name that has been adopted as the name of the center. Adjacent to the mountain of Partinico, the site affords a vista of the entire valley and the Gulf of Castellamare. During most seasons Mirto offers children direct contact with flowers, plants, animals, earth, sand, as well as the waters of a stream that flows across the property. The new buildings are modern and functional in style and are constructed to withstand earthquakes. The workrooms dispense with the traditional rows of desks and have movable chairs and tables instead, some circular for group discussions.

To strengthen the links between the education center and the community, an amphitheater with a seating capacity of 600 was hewn out of Mirto's mountainside to provide Partinico and the surrounding towns with their first center for public performances. As if nature wanted to express her approval of the enterprise, a dazzling surprise awaited the volunteer workers when they began cutting into the mountain: the stone was white marble! Seen from a distance, as I had in 1978, the amphitheater conjures up the image of a giant jewel.

When funds permit, Mirto will have a small cabin on its mountaintop, where students can study the stars or go to be alone. There will also be a museum with exhibits representing different parts of the world, some prepared by the children. One of the main exhibits will consist of objects which survived the bombing of Hiroshima. For

Danilo it is important that the memory of all modern holocausts be perpetuated.

Danilo has been to Hiroshima. "For seven years," he says, "it was forbidden for anyone in Hiroshima to talk about the atom bomb. An architect was hired to reconstruct everything in such a way that the burnt city would not continue to scream through the centuries. I asked the mayor: 'Why not leave one square acre to remind us of the devestation?' He said, 'Land costs too much.' I said, 'But so does life.' He answered, 'We didn't think of that.' "

From the start, the problem of financing the education center has been a formidable one. The problem began in 1971, when money had to be raised for a deposit toward the purchase of the land. Part of the deposit came from Danilo's staff collaborators who, though poorly paid, agreed to forego their salaries for a time. The balance of the money, which arrived in the nick of time, was donated by the German Evangelical Church movement *Bort für die Welt* (Bread for the World). The final purchase payment came from Danilo's Sonning Prize money and from donations sent by Friends of Danilo Dolci committees in Europe and the United States. The same committees, along with other supportive groups, have tried to meet Mirto's financial obligations but there have been times when the weight of its debts threatened its very existence.

For nearly a decade Danilo and his staff have been expecting to ease Mirto's financial problems by taking advantage of an Italian law which authorizes the subsidizing of teacher salaries for experimental schools that have been officially recognized by the state. In his effort to obtain recognition for Mirto, Danilo, with bulldog tenacity, has been grappling with government bureaucrats almost single-handedly. Several times he was assured that recognition was forthcoming, only to be thwarted by still another bureaucratic obstacle.

Now, Danilo happily informs me, the final obstacle has been surmounted. Shortly, the state will not only pay all the salaries of the teachers but will also allow the center considerable input in their selection. But Danilo sighs: "We still have a long distance to cover. The work is slow and difficult. It will take at least another ten years to judge the results of our experiment."

"Would it have been easier to have conducted the educational experiment outside of Sicily?" I ask and explain my reason for the question: twenty years ago he had told me that there might come a time when he would leave Sicily and do his work in some under-developed South American area.

"Did I say such a thing?" He has obviously forgotten. "I certainly have no such intention, although I have traveled in South America in connection with my work. There is still much work to be done in Sicily."

"By this time you probably know the Sicilians better than any other non-Sicilian in the world. What do you say to those who either claim or imply that the Sicilians have a mafia mentality?"

For the first time in our conversation Danilo loses his calm, and speaks with an intensity that I seldom hear in his voice. "That is an utterly false charge. I have been working closely among Sicilians for more than thirty years and can say unequivocally that they do *not* have a mafia mentality. They have a loathing for violence. Over the years there have been small groups of Mafiosi who, in the absence of democratic structures, have been able to exert power for criminal ends, but they are a tiny minority of the population. In my years of knowing Sicilians I have fallen in love with them for their generosity, their intelligence, and their great capacity for self-sacrifice and serious dedication. Even among the least educated of them I find a profound sense of civility. Their love for family and for the aged is extraordinary, and they have a deep respect for nature. As a northerner, I have been able to observe them objectively and am able to say things about them which they cannot say about themselves without being considered self-serving."

"What about their concept of *omerta* (the code of silence which precludes giving information to the police)? Do Sicilians still adhere to it?"

"That depends on whether or not they feel strong enough. When they feel isolated, they become fearful. When they are together, *omerta* does not work. The people who are organized, who have acquired a sense of unity from pursuing mutual interests together, have no problem with *omerta*. Essentially, the Sicilians are a sound people."

Bearing in mind that Danilo has a train to catch, I ask my final question, which concerns the installation of 112 U.S. cruise missiles in the Sicilian town of Comiso. "Inasmuch as you are one of the world's foremost pacifists, some of your admirers as well as some of your critics have asked why it is that you and your collaborators have not responded to the placement of the American missiles in Comiso?''

"That is a good point; you are a fine midwife. Let me begin by saying that any form of atomic warfare is a disaster from any point of view. The situation at Comiso is not clear enough. That is one difficulty. I do not want to be the only one against the United States and I do not want to be against only one type of missile. With the Communists leading the demonstrations against the Comiso missiles and the Socialists sounding ambiguous and sometimes hypocritical about their position, the politics of the situation become quite confusing. Few Sicilians are joining the demonstrations because most of them don't trust the politics of those organizing them. There is another difficulty. There is the geographic reality that Comiso is on the other side of Sicily. One cannot do everything. I have chosen the education center as my major activity because it has a more profound potential than my involvement with demonstrations at Comiso. Between saying no to the missiles there or collaborating on the discovery of a potentially revolutionary approach to education, I have no difficulty making a choice.''

"Do you intend to continue working with pacifist groups?" I ask.

"Yes, of course, whenever I think I can be useful. This week, for example, I will be going to Hawaii for a few days to meet with a pacifist group there." He reaches into his briefcase and hands me a copy of a factual report (in Italian), based on his previous visit to Hawaii, which cites the adverse effects of the American military presence there on its lands and people. Nowhere else in the United States, he informs me, is there as heavy a concentration of armaments and military personnel. Since two of the pacifist activists working in Hawaii have mysteriously disappeared, we agree that it would not be prudent to mention his impending visit to the press, at least not until he has safely returned to Sicily.

There was a time, I reflect, when Danilo welcomed all the publicity that he and the Centro's activities could stimulate. This has become a thing of the past. Publicity then was a necessary tool for drawing public attention to conditions in western Sicily. The publicity Danilo received during the 1950s and 1960s when he was trying to "shock" the establishment into ameliorating the situation, made him internationally famous and won him the admiration of thousands of

Europeans and Americans, many of whom continue to support him to this day. His fame also served as a protective shield against the Mafia. Now that the Jato dam is a *fait accompli* and the education center has become his highest priority, publicity as a tool has far less importance.

Before he bids my wife and me good bye, Danilo asks if he may use our telephone to call his wife in Trappeto. She is Ellen Norman, a young Swedish woman on the staff of the Centro whom he married in the mid-1970s after parting with Vincenzina, his first wife. When I hand him our cordless telephone, he studies it carefully before dialing, obviously fascinated. After he has spoken with his wife, he talks with one of their sons. His opening words are spoken with the rising inflection of an affectionate father trying to convey a sense of amazement to his child. "Do you know what is so remarkable about my speaking with you this moment? I am speaking on a telephone that has no wires attached to it. Not one. *Veramente!* Imagine a telephone that can function without wires!"

When Danilo returns to Partinico he will, I suspect, take up the subject of a cordless telephone with the children at the education center, and they will discuss it maieutically.

Philadelphia
1985   J.M.

About the Author

Jerre Mangione was born in Rochester, New York, of Sicilian parents who came to the United States shortly after the turn of the century. He grew up among scores of relatives from Sicily and in a household where only Sicilian was spoken. *Mount Allegro,* which is regarded as a classic of American ethnic literature, is the story of that experience.

After receiving a B.A. degree from Syracuse University, Mangione became a staff writer on *Time Magazine* and a free-lance book reviewer for the *New Republic* and the *New York Herald-Tribune;* later, he was an editor for a New York book publishing firm. In 1937 he joined the New Deal in Washington as the National Coordinating Editor of the Federal Writers' Project. During World War II he was Special Assistant to the U.S. Commissioner of Immigration and Naturalization, a post he held for six years. After a second career in the field of advertising and public relations, he entered the academic world in 1961 in the English Department of the University of Pennsylvania, where he headed its writing program for twelve years. Following his retirement with the title of Professor Emeritus of American Literature, he became the founder and acting director of the university's Italian Studies Center. In 1980 the university awarded him the honorary degree of Doctor of Letters.

A Passion for Sicilians, Mangione's third book about southern Italy's island people (the second was *Reunion in Sicily*), was made possible by a Fulbright Research Fellowship. He has also received fellowships and grants from the Guggenhiem and the Rockefeller foundations and, from 1980 through 1984, from the National Endowment for the Humanities. Mangione's numerous literary awards include two Italian ones: the decoration of *Commendatore* (Knight Commander) from the Republic of Italy, and the *Premio Nazionale Empedocole* in 1984 for his books about Sicilians.

Among the best known of Mangione's ten books are *The Dream and the Deal,* which received front-page attention in the *New York Times Book Review* and was nominated in 1972 for the National Book Award in History; and *An Ethnic at Large,* the author's memoir of the 1930s and 1940s.